Agents of God

Agents of God

Boundaries and Authority in Muslim and Christian Schools

Jeffrey Guhin

OXFORD
UNIVERSITY PRESS

OXFORD
UNIVERSITY PRESS

Oxford University Press is a department of the University of Oxford. It furthers
the University's objective of excellence in research, scholarship, and education
by publishing worldwide. Oxford is a registered trade mark of Oxford University
Press in the UK and certain other countries.

Published in the United States of America by Oxford University Press
198 Madison Avenue, New York, NY 10016, United States of America.

Library of Congress Cataloging-in-Publication Data
Names: Guhin, Jeffrey, author.
Title: Agents of God : boundaries and authority in Muslim and Christian
schools / by Jeffrey Guhin.
Description: New York, NY, United States of America. :
Oxford University Press, 2021. | Includes bibliographical references and index.
Identifiers: LCCN 2020020551 (print) | LCCN 2020020552 (ebook) |
ISBN 9780190244743 (hb) | ISBN 9780197542996 (epub)
Subjects: LCSH: Religious education—Social aspects. |
Religious education—New York (State)—New York. |
Islamic religious education—New York (State)—New York. |
Christian education—New York (State)—New York.
Classification: LCC LC331 .G84 2020 (print) |
LCC LC331 (ebook) | DDC 371.0709747—dc23
LC record available at https://lccn.loc.gov/2020020551
LC ebook record available at https://lccn.loc.gov/2020020552

1 3 5 7 9 8 6 4 2

Printed by Integrated Books International, United States of America

CONTENTS

ACKNOWLEDGMENTS

Certain authors, speaking of their works, say: "My book," "My commentary," "My history," etc.... They would do better to say: "Our book," "Our commentary," "Our history," etc., because there is in them usually more of other people's than their own."

—Pascal, *Pensees* 43

This project would not have been possible without the kindness, decency, and patience of the four school communities described in this book. I hope my treatment of them in these pages is as graceful, big-hearted, and generous as their treatment of me. I am particularly grateful to the principals and teachers who allowed me to enter their schools, classrooms, and lives.

This book began as a dissertation, and so I am first indebted to the place where I completed it, Yale University. I benefited tremendously from Julia Adams, Elijah Anderson, Jeffrey Alexander, Hannah Brückner, Emily Erikson, Ron Eyerman, Zareena Grewal, Frank Griffel, Phi Smith, and Fred Wherry. I'm grateful to many of my fellow graduate students for help on this project, especially Sorcha Brophy, Mira Debs, Shai Dromi, Joseph Klett, and Gülay Türkmen. Obviously none of this book would have happened without my dissertation committee, chaired by Philip Gorski. I am indebted in countless ways to Phil and to Mitchell Stevens and Jonathan Wyrtzen. Thanks as well to Marcia Inhorn, who was part of the committee at an earlier phase.

Louis Cristillo was very helpful at an early stage in my research. Ruth Braunstein, Elaine Ecklund, Salman Hameed, Todd Fuist, Neil Gross, Shamus Khan, Paul Lichterman, Penny Edgell, Gerardo Martí, Besheer Mohamed, Terry McDonnell, Ann Morning, Isaac Reed, Micah Roos, Nick Wilson, and Grace Yukich have all been generous and wise in ongoing conversations about this project, especially in its earliest stages. I'm indebted to a wonderful group of faculty and students at the SSRC Religion and International Affairs Dissertation Workshop. Courtney Irby was generous with advice and guidance for the book's sections on gender, sex, and sexuality. I gave talks about the book at Notre Dame, Northwestern, Hampshire College, and the

University of California Riverside and the University of Nebraska Lincoln, all of which provided helpful questions and comments.

My three years in between grad school and my first tenure-track job were spent quite pleasantly at the Institute for Advanced Studies in Culture (IASC) at the University of Virginia. It's hard to express how grateful I am to James Davison Hunter for his mentorship and for believing in me, and to everyone else at the Institute, especially Christina Simko, whose comments and encouragement were life-giving, and Tony Lin, who's a hero. I am also extremely grateful for the opportunity to present my gender chapter at an ethnography workshop run by Allison Pugh at the UVA Sociology Department. The current form of this book would not be possible without a workshop on my book manuscript at the IASC, organized by the intrepid Joe Davis, featuring Mucahit Bilici, Molly Worthen, Dan Winchester, Iddo Tavory, and Charles Mathewes, at which I received wonderful feedback.

I finished this book in my first four years at UCLA, and it's been a wonderful place. I am grateful to the many faculty who helped me to think about the manuscript, especially Jacob Foster, Stefan Timmermans, Rogers Brubaker, Aliza Luft, and Gail Kligman, all of whom, along with LA-area professors Rebecca Sager and Amir Hussain, read an earlier version and gave me helpful comments at a lovely salon that Gail organized. They enabled and encouraged me to revise the manuscript into its current form. I am so lucky to be in a department that prefers good work over quick, and I am grateful for advice from Jessica Collett, Karida Brown, and Lauren Duquette-Rury for shepherding the book toward its end. I also taught an earlier version of this book in an honors seminar attached to a sociology of religion class, and I grateful to those students for instructive comments and conversation. James Bielo, Kelsy Burke, Sumita Pahwa, Allison Cruz, John Evans, Dan Hirschman, Marion Katz, Omar Lizardo, David Long, John O'Brien, Allison Pugh, Victoria Reyes, Brandon Vaidyanathan, and Luke Yarbrough all gave necessary feedback on one or more chapters. I am indebted to André Spicer, Fabio Rojas, and Timothy Hallett for thoughtful tutorials on institutionalism. I am also grateful for help in the very final moments before my proofs were due from Aaron Panofsky on science studies, Kelsy Burke on language about gender, and Isaac Reed on the nature of reality.

Thanks to my friends and family, especially Benjamin Krause and Brian and Allison Cruz. Thanks also to my three brothers and one sister, none of whom think I'm smart, and to my parents, who do.

This book's movement from dissertation to book would not have happened without my insightful and infinitely patient editor at Oxford, Theo Calderara, as well as the helpful comments of two reviewers for the manuscript. I am also grateful for other staff at Oxford, Brent Matheny for editorial assistance, Carol Neimann for proofreading, and Suganya Elango for production.

After Oxford sent me the proofs, someone I had only met over e-mail asked if she could help proofread and index the book. I am so grateful I said yes. I can never thank Amber Herrle enough for her brilliant and life-saving assistance. And thanks to Sam Perry for both encouraging me to do my own index and showing me how it's done, as he does about most things.

I also want to say that any book like this—especially a first book that comes out of a dissertation—is necessarily the result of countless conversations, friendships, conferences, coffees, drinks, meals, walks, classes, presentations, office meetings, phone calls, e-mails, lectures, songs, books, articles, chapters, shows, text messages, blog posts, tweets, facebook posts, DMs, and a thousand other things. I am sorry I cannot thank each person involved individually, but please know how grateful I am to be part of so many vibrant communities. This book only exists because of you. Even if our interaction did not produce an idea in this book, our relationships sustained me then, and they continue to sustain me now.

This book is about schools, and so it seems appropriate that I thank two final groups. First, all of my students at Yale, Fairfield, UCLA, and especially St. Joseph High School, whose students taught me how to be an adult. Second, all of my teachers, those mentioned above and Millie Brezinski, Jeannie Brayman, Ted Cotton, Tim Cox, Si Hendry SJ, Laurie Joyner, Ed McCaughan, and Marcus Smith. Most of all I thank the high school teacher who teaches me every day, my wife, Mary Katherine Sheena, to whom this book is dedicated.

What's good in this book might well be my doing, but, as any sociologist knows, it's hard to sort out what causes what. However, two things are certain about the causal relationship between the people I've just listed and this book: I couldn't have done what works without them, and they are not to blame for what fails.

CHAPTER 1

∽

Authority and Essence

Adam Morgan[1] is a tall man with dark hair and a debater's confidence. He teaches religion and Worldview at Good Tree High School, one of the four religious high schools where I did research in 2011 and 2012.

Mr. Morgan's courses prepared seniors for the spiritual dangers they might encounter once they graduate, entering a world less friendly to the Bible-believing Christianity they had, until then, largely taken for granted. The theory of evolution was one such worry, and teachers directly confronted the problem of evolution at both Evangelical schools, reminding students about the danger of doubting God's word. In a class I observed, Mr. Morgan was talking to his students about the Cambrian explosion, a sudden change in the fossil record in which various life forms emerged, seemingly out of nowhere. "Young Earth" creationists use this line from the fossil record as evidence of God's spontaneous creation. One piece of paleontology is thereby used to prove a literal reading of the Bible, despite the protestations of paleontologists.

Yet, using science to disprove science is not so easy to accomplish. One of the students, Sara, asked if the Cambrian explosion is a problem for short-day creationism or the belief, as some claim Genesis[2] teaches, that the universe was constructed in six literal days.

Mr. Morgan sat on a stool behind a podium. He leaned forward. "A lot of people defend a Biblical model of creation with the fossil record, and they are very pleased with the Cambrian explosion. There are no gradual changes from simple to complex forms going on, and also the fossils appear so suddenly."

Sara nodded.

Agents of God. Jeffrey Guhin, Oxford University Press (2021). © Oxford University Press.
DOI: 10.1093/oso/9780190244743.001.0001

Brian, a popular student leader shouted out without raising his hand. "You know about long-day creationism?" Long-day creationism is the theory, less popular today among conservative Christians than it was a hundred years ago, that the "days" of Genesis should be interpreted metaphorically and can be understood to contain many billions of years each. Some go further to then suggest that such "long days" make space for Christians to accept evolution, sometimes even the evolution of humans.

Mr. Morgan shrugged. "Long day, short day, theistic evolutionism. There's a lot of them," he said looking around, listing the various ways Christians have sought to reconcile the Genesis account with the scientific evidence. Mr. Morgan, like virtually all teachers at both Christian schools, is a short-day creationist, believing the days described in Genesis are literal 24-hour days.

He paused and made eye contact with Brian. "Yes. I'm familiar with long day."

Brian said, "Because there's a passage in the Bible, I can't remember it, it's like about how time is different for God, so like, a day is—"

The teacher cut him off. "A day is like a thousand years and a thousand years is like a day," he said citing 2 Peter 3:8, the same passage Good Tree's biology teacher had used to teach long-day theory in her class. "Here's the problem with that. . . . Here's a passage from another book and you take it out and apply it to this other passage from a different time period with a different author and a different context. That is *terrible*. You would never do that with any manuscript science or study of a document. It's just unwise. So that's the first problem. And the second problem is you read this text, and there's no evidence anywhere in scripture it's meant to be used as a primer or code for reading other parts of scripture, and the parts of Genesis it's used to read, there's no evidence those passages were meant to be understood symbolically. There are certainly parts of the Bible that are symbolic, but that's usually clear in the text. If it's meant to be symbolic, that's fine, but there's no indication the creation story is. And third, if you can use that passage to reinterpret other passages, then you can do it with anything, so what's to stop me from using it with Jesus and to say that actually Jesus wasn't dead for three days, he was dead for 3,000 *years*. And that means He hasn't even risen yet! Who are you to stop me from doing that?" He paused. "Do you understand the three responses? It's very dangerous."

Brian seemed a bit abashed. "I was just curious what you thought. I wasn't saying that I believe that stuff."

"No, I understand," replied Mr. Morgan. "You weren't saying you believe these things. You were just asking." And then class moved on.

I'll describe each of the schools I studied in more detail later in this introduction, but for now I'd like to explore how a central paradox unites each of them, a paradox revealed in this story about Brian and Adam Morgan. Mr. Morgan's class often encouraged free thought; I imagine that's part of why Brian felt free to ask his question. In our many conversations outside of class, Mr. Morgan regularly told me how important it was for students to think critically and really examine their beliefs. On the first day of school, he told his students,

> This is not a Bible class, this is not a propagandizing class . . . we're asking human questions that anyone anywhere would have asked. You were born in [this state] but you would ask the same questions if you were born in ancient Rome. We're talking about questions Christians try to answer, but so does every other philosopher . . . . But you might say, you're kind of leading us Mr. Morgan, the answer's sin and the solution is Christianity, but no, lots of people have seen these same problems and have identified very different solutions. It's not a Christian class, not a Bible class. We look at all the questions humans have always asked. Now I'm a Biblical Christian and your parents—at least one of them—are Biblical Christians who want you to be exposed to Biblical Christian perspectives and you will have those, but you will have many other perspectives as well . . . . [the class is] a chance to think about what's really real . . . it's a chance for you to say what you really think.

Yet if Mr. Morgan is so committed to free thinking, why did he respond so abruptly to Brian? Part of the answer, as is revealed in his lengthy response, might be that it wasn't only Mr. Morgan who was making this demand. It was Mr. Morgan's understanding of the bible's authority: how it must be read, understood, and carried out. The teacher's authority had been externalized to something else, so even though he awed a student into a denial of even considering another option, he was able to do so while making his practice of authority appear simply the carrying out of something bigger and more important than himself, the crossing of which constitutes something "very dangerous." External authorities helped all four of the schools I studied accomplish a central paradox at any religious school: compelling students into certain religious commitments while simultaneously insisting these commitments are freely chosen, rooted in an appreciation of the commitments' almost self-evident correctness. In this sense, certain "external authorities" became agents of God, compelling and requiring particular actions in the world.

These external authorities are not only agents of God. They could be agents of all sorts of things. While this book will focus on religious schools, it would be wrong to assume that these "external authorities" are simply religious phenomena, leftovers from the superstitious days before rational, scientific modernity. Especially in the United States, a society at least notionally focused on democratic equality, directly demanding something of someone else can feel too coercive: it is instead better to insist that it is not one person that demands something of another but rather "medicine" or "the law" or even "the Constitution" that makes certain demands.[3] These external authorities are then narrated and experienced as relatively autonomous entities that have an authority all their own. They are felt and described as agents, as entities that say and do and make demands. And the reason they are able to do so is because they exist within certain bounded communities in which such an understanding makes sense. Those communities might well be religious, but they could just as well be marked by any other social distinction. This book is a study of external authorities in religious schools, as well as the boundaries that help to constitute those authorities, yet its theoretical ambition is not limited to religion.[4]

SCHOOLS, ORGANIZATIONS, AND INSTITUTIONS

Why do religious schools work? Why do children who graduate from them more or less agree with the parents who put them there and the teachers who instructed them? Recent research shows that children and youth are quite capable of creatively adapting what their elders have given them; young people are not nearly as beholden to ironclad rules as previous theories of socialization might have claimed.[5] Nonetheless, youths' options for cultural expression are not infinite, and their limitations are often formed by the adults in their lives and the organizations in which those adults have placed them. Schools—like the ones I studied—are perhaps the most important of these organizations.

But what about peers? After all, many scholars consider peer groups as important or even more important than parents and schools in forming young people's identities. Indeed, parents who send children to private schools are deeply aware of that sociological insight: choosing children's neighborhoods, schools, and after-school activities helps to situate this influence as well, ensuring that young people's peers are more likely to be the peers that parents have chosen for them.[6]

Sociologists often call schools "organizations," and while I will rarely use the term, I draw upon a literature that examines schools as locations in which adults *organize* students' lives and moral commitments with better or worse success.[7] The organizational study of schooling in sociology has a tradition extending all the way back to one of sociology's founders, Émile Durkheim, especially in his study of *Moral Education*. Building off of Durkheim, John Meyer and his various coauthors showed how schools' organizational forms interacted with *institutions*, a term with about as many definitions as uses.[8] Yet for the sake of simplicity, an organization can be understood as a formalized group of people, and an institution as a set of rules regarding particular social things. For example, the high school I attended, Creighton Prep (the Jesuit high school of Omaha, Nebraska) is an organization. At the same time, Creighton Prep must contend with certain institutions, perhaps most important among them the institution of *schooling*, that is, the often-unwritten though sometimes legally formalized rules of what a school is supposed to be, what it's supposed to look like, and how it's supposed to be experienced. In other words, schools are organizations that conform themselves to various institutions, not least among them the institution of schooling itself.

Institution is such a capacious term that I will not be using it often, mostly to avoid confusion about what an institution actually is. (For example, isn't Creighton Prep also an institution?) Instead, I'll focus on two concepts that are kind of like institutions, but which have a bit more analytical purchase: *boundaries*, a term already quite used in the sociological literature,[9] and *external authorities*, a term I am developing here.

There are other terms I'll be introducing as I go, but one that is especially important to this book is *practices*, as I'll be arguing that both boundaries and external authorities are ultimately rooted in the practices that people do. The word *practices* is notoriously vague, and here I define the term more narrowly than is sometimes done. For example, the philosopher Alasdair MacIntyre provides medicine as an example of a practice; the kinds of practices I am interested in are more like a physical exam for a general practitioner or the examination of X-rays for a radiologist. They are specific, habituated, and bodily. Thus, I am not interested in religion as a practice but rather very specific sorts of religious practices—not just prayer or reading, but specific kinds of prayer and reading.[10]

EXTERNAL AUTHORITIES

The definition of external authority is a bit more complicated. By external authority, I refer to an old tradition in sociology that extends back to one of our other founders, Max Weber. Weber's use of terms could be somewhat complicated, but Weberians tend to distinguish between outright domination and agreed-upon authority by looking for legitimacy: in other words, if I ask you to do something and you do it without physical coercion, then I have *authority* over you. If I force you to do something against your will, then I might have *domination* over you, but that domination is not legitimate. Weber divides "legitimate domination" into three types of authority: legal authority (seen most clearly in bureaucracies), traditional authority (seen most clearly in patrimonial rulers), and charismatic authority (seen most clearly in religious prophets).[11]

The pages in which Weber developed these concepts have been debated for nearly a century with Talmudic intensity. One useful conversation has developed Weber's study of charismatic authority to explain how people understand and experience institutions. For Weber, charisma is a revolutionary and somewhat chaotic force: it is opposed to all rules and economic considerations, gaining its legitimacy, somewhat tautologically, from "as long as it receives recognition."[12] Yet what happens when a prophet—whether St. Francis or Steve Jobs—dies? Weber argues that a charismatic figure's administrative staff, driven by their own material or ideological interests, shift their community into one of the other forms of authority, whether legal or traditional, all while maintaining the veneer of that original charisma in another individual, or a role, or even the community itself.

Building on Weber, John Meyer and his colleagues have shown how such charismatic succession can apply to institutions as well as individuals. In a long string of studies within the framework of what they call "sociological institutionalism," Meyer and his coauthors show how institutions like education and science function with a kind of charismatic authority within organizations and around the world.[13] In his classic 1977 article on the effects of education as an institution, Meyer argues that regardless of what we might believe about schooling individually, its "myths" are so powerful that we "carry out our parts in a drama in which education is authority."[14]

In a similar way, Meyer and his coauthor Brian Rowan show how organizations can use "myths" of rationalized order to structure their operating rules and best practices. In certain kinds of organizations, especially schools, these rules can become separated (or "decoupled") from what actually happens in the organization: for example, what a teacher and students do in a classroom all day might not have all that much in common with what a school claims to be doing or what a society says about schools. That decoupling leads to a focus on "ceremonial" assumptions of good faith without real inspections or evaluations of whether certain myths are actually carried out. Meyer and his coauthors argue that a myth about schools' "rational purpose" contains a kind of charismatic authority more powerful than what actually occurs in schools, an insight that has proven quite fruitful for scholars of organizations and education.[15]

I build on these "neo-institutionalist" insights by shifting the focus of analysis from the broad and organizational to the individual and interactional, paralleling sociologist Timothy Hallett and his coauthors' efforts to "'inhabit' contemporary institutionalism with social interactions."[16] Meyer and his colleagues are especially interested in the diffusion of certain institutions across "world society" and the effects these institutions have on organizational practices and other institutional spheres around the world. While Meyer and his coauthors are implicitly concerned about how such institutions have an agentic capacity to affect social life, they do not usually show how the institutions are themselves narrated and experienced as agentic authorities in communities.[17] For example, what does it mean when someone says that the Constitution has authority, or that the psychiatrists' manual of mental disorders (the DSM) actually "says" something?[18]

The second half of this book is about these external authorities, a term I am using in place of "institutions." I am interested in how scripture, prayer, and science function as semi-autonomous sources of authority, allowing people in the communities I studied to solve problems, make decisions, and develop meaningful, coherent lives. Each of these terms— scripture, prayer, and science—is often described as the subject of its own sentence, as when people in the schools told me that prayer changes things, that science shows something, or that scripture gives us wisdom. Prayer, scripture, and science are *external* because they are not contained within any one individual or even any one organization, and also because that externality is to some degree the source of their authority, in the same way that a lever gains strength when its fulcrum is farther from the effort applied. While there are some social theorists who insist on the agency of non-human objects and ideas, I am not making such a provocative claim. In other words, I am not claiming that prayer, scripture, or science actually *do* things, at least not in a sense that's parallel to the way humans do things. However, I am claiming that scripture, prayer, and science (among other things) are *felt* to do certain things, and the experience of and belief in that authority gives people tools to solve problems and interpret their lives.

This argument builds on Meyer and his coauthors' study of the mythic power of institutions in daily life, though it is much more rooted in the interpersonal and interactional experience of people's narration and understanding of how external authorities like prayer, science, and scripture solve problems, pose challenges, and accomplish tasks. In an article published in 2000, Meyer and Ronald Jeppeson wrote about how agency itself is an institution that has diffused across society. However, while Meyer and his coauthors have examined agency as an institution, they have not looked, at least not explicitly and interactionally, at how institutions are narrated and experienced as agentic, even if this is an implicit assumption of their work all the way back to the 1970s.[19]

Nonetheless, even if Meyer and Jepperson's article does not analyze how institutions function as agents in their study of the "cultural construction of social agency," they do show how *individuals'* agency has come to be understood as free from others' coercion and as thereby making each individual capable of making free, conscious choices. I found this emphasis on autonomous agency in all four schools, with both teachers and students alike insisting on the importance of not *forcing* religious ideas or practices.

Such an insistence has old roots. Evangelical Protestantism, many historians argue, comes out of the same time period in European history as modern liberalism and what we now think of as individualism, or a commitment to individual autonomy and self-expression. The famous Lutheran idea of every man being his own priest is an early (patriarchal) expression of this commitment, later influencing Enlightenment ideas about the integrity of the (male) self.[20] Contemporary American Evangelical Protestants have taken that commitment to the individual even further than Luther would have intended, with much less of a focus on trained ministers and a growing insistence first, that communal sacraments are not required for salvation (thereby decreasing the necessity of attending church), and second, that the Bible can be easily approached by anyone with a sincere desire to know God (thereby diminishing the training often required to understand scripture).[21]

Similarly, in both Muslim schools, students and teachers quoted a famous passage from the Qur'an, verse 256 of al-Baqara, containing the phrase, "let there be no compulsion in religion." The phrase has a complicated history in Islam, given how certain Muslims (like certain Christians) have been punished, sometimes by execution, for leaving the faith. Yet many contemporary scholars believe the line is a lodestone toward religious equality and tolerance, both for Muslims in the West and for religious minorities in Muslim-majority nations.[22] Relatedly, and in parallel with the Evangelical democratization of Protestantism, Muslims around the world are increasingly suspicious of religious leaders, arguing for each individual's capacity to read holy texts all on their own.[23]

While not usually as individualistic as it can be for Evangelicals, there is nonetheless a commitment to an individual's relationship with God within Sunni Islam that Protestants might recognize as similar to their own, one that goes all the way back to the Qur'an itself, even if that relationship to God is much more than simply the content and experience of texts. Unlike Catholicism (and in different ways, Shia Islam), Sunnis and certain kinds of

Protestants do not need anyone else to mediate or navigate their salvation. As one of the science teachers at Al Haqq told me, "There is a certain guardianship up to a certain age . . . you instill within your kid certain morals, certain ethics, certain ideologies. And then when they get to a certain age it's on them whether they're going to follow through with that."

In a related way, Tomas Lopez, a Bible teacher at Apostles, was discussing cults with his students, contrasting his way of teaching the Bible with theirs: "Imagine if I only taught you half of what's in here," he said, picking up the Bible and patting it, returning to his typical sermon-like perambulation at the front of the classroom. "I just taught you what I wanted you to hear, not what Jesus wants you to hear. I'd be leading you astray. Ultimately where would I be leading you?"

"Hell!" called out a student.

Mr. Lopez nodded, smartly pointing his finger at the student as if to say, *exactly*. "Where's Jesus Christ in all of this?" he asked. "Imagine these young kids, young girls, young boys, and all these older men, in cults like this. How many of you work well being forced?"

A boy raised his hand, and the teacher seemed surprised. "You work well being forced?" he asked the student.

"I work well under pressure."

"Pressure and force aren't the same thing," Mr. Lopez responded. "I could give you lots of deadlines but I'm not saying do this or else."

The student nodded, and the class moved on.

The ironies here are rich and important. Mr. Lopez is threatening hellfire but then insisting he is not coercing. He is necessarily only giving the students part of the story (he cannot possibly read the whole Bible each class), yet he castigates those who tell the story they want, not what Jesus wants. This is not to claim that Mr. Lopez was never challenged by his students. He told me in a private conversation that many of Apostles' students are preachers' kids, bringing certain previous commitments to the classroom. He said he generally responded to such disagreements by telling students, "Well, I'm not going against your father. I'd ask you just to keep reading the word [the Bible] and let it act on you."

Contained within this story are many of the questions I'm interested in exploring in this book, especially the problem of force, the containment of boundaries, and the strength of external authorities. These are not, however, entirely separate questions, and how they link together forms much of my overall argument. In brief, boundaries provide the setting in which communities and individuals can establish their identity. That identity is then experienced as real through certain practices, and those practices and boundaries are maintained via certain "external authorities."

These external authorities are critically important, in that they are at once practices themselves and the institutionalization (what some might call reification) of these practices, things that people do (read the Bible, pray, invoke science) but *at the same time,* things that seem to exist above and beyond any individual person and seemingly with the ability to act on people themselves. As I will describe more in the conclusion, this focus on practices and boundaries as helping with the "reality maintenance" of certain social communities builds upon the phenomenological insights of Peter Berger and Thomas Luckmann, especially their focus on institutions and reification. However, unlike Berger and Luckmann, I am much more explicitly focus on habituation and embodied practices as they are revealed within boundaries and what I'm calling external authorities.

These external authorities are important for any community, but especially for those with a strong commitment to individual autonomy. If, like Mr. Lopez, I can believe it is the Bible (rather than me) which acts on you, then I can institute a situation in which authority compels certain actions and beliefs without me being the one who does the compelling. As Mr. Lopez insisted, "I'm not saying do this or else." In Mr. Lopez's framing, the Bible does the heavy lifting here, not the people. Yet this is not simply a religious story. One can imagine a similar way of describing the Constitution, or even a category as amorphous as "medicine" that shows, does, and demands quite a lot.

Such external authorities are numerous and varied in the life of any school or any individual. Think of a mother who asks her young girl to take a certain pill. That mother is not arbitrarily imposing her power on the child but is instead acting on the behalf of someone else, someone the sociological theorist Isaac Reed would call a *rector*.[24] In this case, that rector is the child's doctor, who asked the mother to get the child to take the pill. Building on the work of Julia Adams, Reed shows how such interactions form "chains of power" through which various people or groups function as rectors sending people to do certain actions in their name, at which point those actors might themselves become rectors, sending others to act, and on and on. Schools are easy enough places to see such chains, with a school board sending a principal to, for example, encourage greater school spirit, at which point the principal sends a teacher, the teacher sends a student, and the student might well send another student, and so on.

One of this book's theoretical contributions builds upon Reed's argument by suggesting that external authorities enable and legitimize rectors' ability to get actors do what they want, and they do so through externalizing the authority that makes such demands intelligible.[25] Such externalization is especially helpful in democratic or quasi-democratic contexts, in which few have the *right* to force someone to insist someone do something else simply because of who they are.[26] As such, to return to the example, it is not a doctor sending a mother to get a child to take certain pills, but rather *medicine* that tells the doctor and then the mother and then the child what they ought to do—just as a cop pulling over a driver can argue the action was not his own capricious exercise of power but rather the mandate of the *law*. And, to return to both Mr. Morgan and Mr. Lopez above, they can insist that their demands on their students are simply what the Bible demands from them. In this sense, these external authorities are actors in the world functioning as agents of God.

Yet, what is key about each of these examples is that the external authorities I am describing—medicine, law, the Bible—are all, in fact, human constructions, containing within them certain practices, beliefs, symbols, and emotional expectations, all of which are historically contingent and subject to change. The doctor could have prescribed a different medicine, the cop did not actually have to pull anyone over, and Mr. Lopez might well have read the Bible in a different way. What makes external authorities so powerful is that they are understood within certain bounded communities as being relatively fixed entities with a legitimate power all their own. Of course, people within those communities can still disagree about what such authority actually means and what carrying out its commands might entail, but one of the key boundaries of the community itself is a common agreement about the importance of this or that authority. In other words, to the extent we share a commitment to a certain external authority, then we are bounded together into a commitment to that authority's relative coherence and stability. We can then understand and narrate both our individual lives and our communities as maintained and moved forward through time via certain practices—practices that are both contained within and commanded by authorities seemingly entirely external to us, even if, in sociological reality, it is our continual commitment to these authorities that both maintains them and gives them their legitimating power.[27]

In this book I focus exclusively on the pragmatic pay-off of external authorities, that is, how they help people solve or avoid problems for themselves and their communities.[28] It doesn't actually matter whether *I* argue that scripture, prayer, and science (the respective subjects of Chapters 5, 6, and 7) are really real entities with their own autonomous authority. What is instead important is that my respondents argue they are, and they understand, practice, and feel these authorities as meaningful actors within their lives.

Each of those three words is important. First, people *understand* external authorities as actors with real authority in their lives. That understanding occurs through a process of habituation that necessarily requires regular *practice*, which is the second key word. In contrast to earlier understandings of socialization, especially those often attributed to sociologist Talcott Parsons,[29] I am not arguing that cultural understandings are "downloaded" into community members, with those internalized ideas and values then motivating action. Following the pragmatism of John Dewey,[30] I suggest the process is much more dialectical: people develop certain practices and then those practices habituate them to certain understandings, and also certain emotions and values—values often felt within oneself through a certain affective response.[31] Feelings are the third key piece of this account: people can become aware that a certain practice is effective and that a certain external authority is powerful not only because of what they *understand* about it but because of certain *feelings* they experience. While social psychologists have developed a complicated set of defining characteristics that separate emotions, feelings, values, and identities from each other, for the purposes of simplicity I will primarily focus on the act of feeling itself and its role in establishing a sense of the real. Finally, while I am indebted to Isaac Reed's and his interlocutors' subtle analysis of the meanings of "power," for my purposes here I use the word *power* simply to mean any kind of capacity to impose a will (or a perceived will) upon a person or the world. In contrast, and in the Weberian tradition, I refer to *authority* as the socially legitimate form of that power.

A brief example might be helpful here. While I will discuss this more in the chapter on prayer, my respondents often identified their feelings as the method through which they could adjudicate prayer's success and effectiveness. In a discussion with Shane McNulty, a Bible teacher at Good Tree, I asked him how a Christian would understand the answer to a prayer, using the example of a student choosing which college to attend. "Certainly even some kids here will be like, 'Yeah, I feel like God told me to do this,'" he told me. He went on:

> Most kids, by the way, don't say that. Most kids would say, "I was reading scripture, and the passage spoke to me." . . . And I've certainly had that experience. And I don't know if these are people misspeaking or if they truly think that God has told them something. Again, are we now putting too much into words and semantics of what is said? You know, God spoke to me. I don't know if God does speak. I've never heard him speak directly; I've never heard the Word of God. But I've felt it. . . . Are you attuned to it? Or, are you thinking and processing and

doing logical formulations of pros and cons and coming to your own determination of what's right?

There are three things worth pointing out here. First, Mr. McNulty explicitly contrasts feeling to thinking, with feeling winning out. One senses the effectiveness of a practice, as well as the power of an external authority, through feelings as much as (if not more than) through understanding. Second, he speaks to an "attunement" achieved through practice and careful work, something quite similar to Dewey's model of habituation. Finally, he describes God acting through prayer and scripture, yet there is something interesting in the sentences themselves. Note how both scripture (a Bible passage) and the phrase "Word of God"—which can be understood as either scripture or an answer to prayer—are described as themselves capable of action, the first of which is capable of "speaking" and the second of which is capable of being heard and felt.

It is important to remember that both Evangelical Christians and Sunni Muslims believe that prayer and scripture are ultimately from God. However, it is nonetheless the case that prayer and scripture come to have a certain power understood and felt as relatively autonomous from God, even if God is always the originator and most important element. Such distinctions are not unique to religious experience. Think about how often people discuss the Internet or Twitter as things in themselves even though Twitter and the Internet are seemingly only vessels for separate individuals to post content, add comments, and reply to tweets, not to mention the many other possibilities for hope and despair the Internet provides. Yet, through the repeated use of these practices, people develop certain understandings and emotions of relatively autonomous entities that are felt and experienced as separate from the various people tweeting, commenting, and posting. Of course, Twitter is itself a part of the Internet, and this gets to another important point: external authorities can be subcategories of even larger external authorities, just as organizations and institutions can be parts of larger organizations or larger institutions. The important question, though, is not whether the external authority is larger or smaller but a much more pragmatic one: is it experienced as an authoritative entity in itself whose agency has real effects?

Of course, "real effects" does not mean "total effects." As I will show throughout this book, schools are generally not as effective as they intend to be. Students complain, teachers don't buy into the mission, principals disagree with parents, school board meetings erupt into chaos. Yet such disagreement is not necessarily evidence that external authorities lack power, especially if the disagreements are *about the authorities themselves*. In his effort to develop an anthropology of Islam, Talal Asad helpfully shows that any tradition is often marked by disagreement, yet what holds the tradition together is that people agree with each other about the content of their disagreement.[32] A similar distinction can be made about Bourdieu's concept of a field: what links those on the field is not their total agreement but rather the agreed basis of their contestations. In the communities I studied, people often disagreed about scripture, prayer, science, gender, sexuality, and politics. Yet very few disagreed that these were things with a power in their lives, whether as an authority that drives particular actions (science, prayer, scripture) or as a boundary that separates them from the rest of the world (politics, gender, evolution, and also prayer and scripture). Levels of commitment unsurprisingly varied, as I will discuss in the chapters that follow, and there was an occasional student who admitted to me in a private interview that they didn't believe any of it. Yet, perhaps because these are private schools with parents who select their students into conservative religious environments, these disagreements were generally regarding questions of degree and implementation rather than salience and relevance. Almost everyone agreed about the stakes, and that common agreement is part of what bounded them from the rest of the world.

BOUNDARIES

When I say boundaries, I mean the ways these communities differentiate themselves from the rest of America as well as from others. As with my study of external authorities, these boundaries are practiced and made real and relevant through both conscious and subconscious habituation. In this sense, both boundaries and external authorities are practiced and gain much of their power, as Dewey describes, through the power of ongoing habit.[33]

Boundaries become important because they distinguish us from those to whom we are in some sense near, whether physically or in some other sense. Boundaries are therefore not quite the same as differences. For example, there is a near infinity of possible physical differences between France and Spain, but there is only one physical boundary. Similarly, symbolic boundaries develop not because of a need for difference but rather because of a need for *distinction*.[34] Just as physical boundaries firmly establish whose property ends where, so symbolic boundaries establish the nature and extent of a particular social group. It is proximity and similarity that create a need for boundaries rather than difference and variety. The difference between a pen and a pencil is usually more important than the difference been a pen and an eggplant. Like external authorities, boundaries gain their strength via repeated practices that develop an implicit habituation, although toward a different end. While external authorities come to be felt and understood as relatively autonomous means of *maintaining* a particular identity, boundaries come to be felt and understood as a means of *differentiating* that identity. Boundaries and external authorities thereby have a mutually constitutive relationship, with boundaries identifying and distinguishing a community and external authorities driving that community's identity forward through time. The external authorities help to legitimatize the boundaries, just as the boundaries help to demarcate the external authorities.

I build upon some of my previous work in these chapters to describe the content of these boundary contestations, looking at what I'm calling "sites of boundary contestation." For example, if *gender* is the boundary that separates us from the outside world, then what is it about gender? As I will describe below, I find that the Muslim and the Evangelical schools I studied distinguished themselves from the rest of the world through their practice of gender but in quite distinct ways. The Evangelicals I worked with tended to emphasize ideological distinctions from the concept of feminism, and the Muslims I worked with tended to emphasize more specific practices such as gender separation and clothing. Looking at the sites of boundary contestation helps us to recognize with greater specificity how and toward what ends communities distinguish themselves from others.

In three chapters on, respectively, politics, gender, and sexuality and the Internet, I will show how these boundaries help to constitute and distinguish these communities. However, such distinctions are never complete: they are, as Christian Smith has described in his study of American Evangelicals, examples of "distinction with engagement."[35] That commitment—to be in America but not entirely of it—is especially clear in the first chapter on politics, in which I show how both the Christian schools and the Muslim schools are deeply committed to a certain kind of American project. These schools distinguished themselves from what they thought of as unholy and unwholesome, yet they had no desire for complete separation from America, a nation they thought of very much as their own. The difference is as much temporal as religious: conservative Christians believe they have lost an America that was once theirs, while Muslims (conservative or not) believe they could gain an America that holds promise if only it would cease its Islamophobia.

I conducted this research in 2011 and 2012, during the Arab Spring and Obama's reelection campaign. It was well before Trump as a presidential candidate, let alone as a president. Times were different than when

I completed this book in 2020, especially for Muslims, but not altogether different: as many scholars of American religion have argued, what we see under Trump is a difference of degree rather than kind. White American Evangelicals were already deeply invested in the Republican party and Christian nationalism. Muslims were already targets of fearmongering and bigoted attacks.[36]

Nonetheless, despite these political polarizations, the people I worked with thought of themselves as distinctly and unquestionably American. Indeed, this was a source of some generational tension in the Muslim schools, with immigrant parents sometimes describing customs or practices as "American" rather than "Muslim" and their children insisting that, because *they* are Muslim and American, then whatever they do must be both as well. These tensions within the American Muslim community are already well established, and I will discuss them further in Chapter 2. I noted a similar generational shift in Evangelical students' disagreements with their parents, although more about sexuality and gender than about national identity, something I will discuss in Chapters 3 and 4.

In all of these cases, my respondents insisted that their distinctions from the rest of America were only partial critiques rather than wholesale condemnations. While they did not use this Aristotelian language, they would have identified their disagreements with the rest of America as "accidental" rather than "essential." For example, it might be the case that most American women do not wear hijab, yet for my Muslim American respondents, a covered head is still *essentially* American, just as, say, a blue house would essentially be a house, even if its color were to change. To use Aristotle's terms, the house's blueness is accidental, and the house's *houseness* is its essence, just as, for the Muslims I talked to, not wearing a hijab is accidental to American identity, while something like being committed to democracy is considered much more essential.[37] As I will discuss more in the next chapter, I am most assuredly not making the claim that anything in social life is actually essential or accidental: I am instead building upon work in the psychology of social cognition[38] to understand how people think about their own social worlds, with some parts essential and others accidental.[39]

For my purposes, what matters is the sociological construction of these categories, that is, how social groups decide together what is accidental and what is essential to a particular identity, both in the broad sense of national identities and in the more specific sense of religious and communal identities. Boundaries—and especially sites of boundary contestation—help communities to establish what is essential and what is accidental.

These boundaries are both dualistic and multifaceted, sometimes emphasizing an "us" as distinct from the rest of the world and other times emphasizing smaller distinctions from similar groups, as when all four schools, each of them religiously conservative in its own way, separated themselves from more liberal co-religionists. That "boundary work" is never entirely self-directed: each of the four schools was worried about how the rest of the world felt about them. In conversations—both those I overheard and those in which I took part—I heard about how "they" think about "us," with that *they* often assumed to be a generically secular United States public, one suspicious of religion, sexually liberal, and altogether too permissive. Yet they also understood America as a place full of economic opportunity and freedom for self-expression. These opportunities had their limits, and the Evangelical schools felt their freedom to express their beliefs was fading, just as the Muslim communities felt like their chances to be themselves had not yet fully appeared. As such, all the schools were interested in correcting stereotypes and often saw me and my eventual book as a way to set the record straight.

CONTRIBUTIONS OF THIS BOOK AND
A GENERAL OUTLINE

This book contributes to a few different conversations in sociology and related disciplines, especially religious studies and cultural anthropology. The primary contributions are to the sociologies of religion and culture, though with additional contributions to the sociologies of education, science, emotions, gender, and morality, as well as an ongoing dialogue with sociological theory throughout the text.

The Basis of Comparison and the Question of Orthodoxy

This book adds to growing conversations in religious studies, cultural anthropology, and the sociology of religion about American Islam and American Evangelicalism,[40] two important areas of study that are rarely explicitly compared, particularly not in qualitative work.[41] Additionally, there are few studies of these communities' private religious schools, and none (that I am aware of) that compares them.[42] Of course, simply because something has not been studied is not a reason to study it. This comparison is useful not simply because it exists but because the study of these two different groups provides analytical leverage to better understand boundaries, authority, and differing forms of religious practice.

The categories of American Evangelical Christians and Sunni Muslims provide a tenable comparison because, in the United States context, both are coherent religious subcultures.[43] One potential problem with this comparison is that American Evangelicals—especially white American Evangelicals—tend to be much more politically conservative than their fellow Christians and much more conservative than their fellow Americans. Only 28 percent of Evangelicals identify with the Democratic Party while 56 percent identify with the GOP; when considering white Evangelical Protestants, a full 90 percent support Donald Trump's presidency, indicating an even deeper conservatism. In contrast, two-thirds of American Muslims identify with the Democratic Party, even if, like Evangelical Democrats, they tend to be slightly more conservative on social issues like the acceptance of gays and lesbians.[44] In this case as well, Muslims as a whole are less conservative than Evangelical Protestants: in 2014, 36 percent of Evangelicals believed "homosexuality should be accepted by society" as compared to 45 percent of Muslims.[45] While the Muslims with whom I worked in these schools revealed a wide range of politics—as Chapters 2 through 4 should make clear—they were nonetheless generally more conservative than most American Muslims. Ethnographic work on other Muslim American communities—especially Justine Howe's study of "suburban Islam" and Muna Ali's analysis of "young Muslim America"—reveal the much greater political diversity within American Islam.[46] Nonetheless, even if the people at the Muslim schools where I worked were more conservative than most American Muslims, their theological conservativism was complicated and sometimes hard to classify, and their political conservatism was rarely if ever expressed by voting Republican. At all four schools, one way they were more conservative than most other (middle-class) Muslim and Evangelical Americans was in their decision to *conserve* their identities through private schooling. While private schooling is a choice only possible for those with the necessary financial and social capital, it is nonetheless a choice most middle-class Muslim and Evangelical parents could make but choose not to. Additionally, the point of the comparison is not looking at two *conservative* religious subcultures but rather simply two religious subcultures.

A political problem with this comparison might be that I am recapitulating an old Western scholarly habit of comparing every other religion to Protestantism. The fact that I am personally a Catholic, a religion whose focus on practice and ritual seems to have more in common with Islam, might mitigate this a little bit. Yet I am still a Christian (even if one conservative Christians might not recognize as such), and there is therefore a real risk I will only view Muslim experiences through a Christian lens and hold them to a Christian standard. As someone who has written an article about why sociologists should engage Edward Said, I take such concerns about the politics of scholarship very seriously. I can only hope that I have not reproduced any misrecognitions or forms of empistemic violence in this book.[47]

If anything, I have tried to underscore the degree to which Protestantism is more like Sunni Islam than many Protestants might be comfortable admitting. I take from Islam (and Catholicism) an emphasis on practices, arguing throughout this book that even Evangelicals' ongoing commitment to *right belief* (or orthodoxy) is itself a form of practice, or orthopraxy; to make it a maxim, *orthodoxy is a form of orthopraxy*. As I hope to show in this book, Evangelical Protestants are much more orthoprax than they might normally describe themselves.[48] As such, while there are more specific contributions to the social-scientific study of religion in each individual chapter, one of my broader goals in this book is to show how orthoprax religions (such as Islam) can help give us a much better way of understanding *all religions*, including and especially the ostensibly orthodox ones.

This distinction is complicated by the degree to which recent scholars of Islam—most famously Talal Asad and his interlocutors—have emphasized the "orthodoxy" of Islam, yet by this phrase they often mean something somewhat different from the focus on *right belief* alongside a suspicion of practices that I will describe later. In Asad's words,

> It is therefore somewhat misleading to suggest, as some sociologists have done, that it is *orthopraxy* and not *orthodoxy*, ritual and not doctrine, that matters in Islam. It is misleading because such a contention ignores the centrality of the notion of the "correct model" to which an instituted practice—including ritual—ought to conform, a model conveyed in authoritative formulas, in Islamic traditions as in others.

He goes on to distinguish his understanding of orthodoxy from those who claim Islam is best characterized by a focus on correct doctrines: "orthodoxy is not a mere body of opinion but a distinctive relationship—a relationship of power to truth. Wherever Muslims have the power to regulate, uphold, require, or adjust *correct* practices, and to condemn, exclude, undermine, or replace *incorrect* ones, there is the domain of orthodoxy."[49] Asad's theory of orthodoxy here is an intriguing one, though it is much more all-encompassing than I intend here. Indeed, as Wilson writes in his critique of the over-use of the term *orthodoxy* in Islamic Studies, Asad's use of *orthodoxy* appears "to be a purely sociological concept which simply means 'conventional,' 'established,' or 'correct' for a particular context, its configuration of power, and its current understanding of the discursive tradition."[50]

The concept of orthodoxy for Asad, therefore, bleeds into his broader concept of a discursive tradition, with orthodoxy appearing to indicate the current power configuration which establishes the "correct" way that this discursive tradition is to be put into practice. As such, I have no problem acknowledging that Islam is orthodox in the sense that Asad articulates (as is any religion lived in communities). Yet, more important for my argument, this orthodoxy is lived out via *practices*. Indeed, even the establishing of *what to read and how* is itself a series of habituated practices. As a result, the question of which precedes which, orthodoxy or orthopraxy, teachings or practices, can become entirely perspectival, a problem of chicken and egg.

Yet my perspective, drawing from sociologists Michael Strand and Omar Lizardo's insistence that beliefs are themselves a form of practice, shows how even the most orthodox of actions is nonetheless *an action*. For example, in contrast to classic introductions of Islam that characterize Muslims as more orthoprax than orthodox, Islamic Studies scholar Norman Calder argues that it is ultimately belief rather than actions that will keep a Muslim from hell: "The Muslim jurists are careful to distinguish between those who fail . . . to pray five times a day—they do not cease to be Muslim—and those who deny the incumbency to pray five times a day who might be apostates."[51] Yet note how both of these theological outcomes are still rooted in the act of saying or believing. This focus on practices is not therefore a denial that beliefs or teachings matter or have real theological weight; it is simply an insistence that we as sociologists look at how those beliefs are declared, denied, enacted, or habituated via actions in the world that can become habituated practices.

Culture and the Problem of Power

Throughout this book I will gradually develop what I hope can be described as an advancement of various conversations in cultural sociology. As described briefly above, this book is about how boundaries and external authorities work together to maintain a community's identity while simultaneously managing the problem of power. By "the problem of power" I refer to an ongoing debate well outlined in Isaac Reed's recent work on the rector-actor-other triad and Amy Allen's powerful synthesis of German critical theory and French poststructuralism. Yet there are many important voices in this conversation, not least Julia Adams, Steven Lukes, Judith

Butler, Pierre Bourdieu, and Michel Foucault.[52] What I take from each of these often quite different thinkers is a concern about what Bourdieu might call "symbolic violence," that is, a social group's ability to make a certain way of experiencing the world feel obviously and self-evidently correct, or at least generally so.

Some of the most important works in the sociology of culture—among them Durkheim's *Elementary Forms of Religious Life* and Berger and Luckmann's *Social Construction of Reality*—have generally downplayed the importance of power in explaining how and why the world comes to be experienced as it does. In contrast, scholars like Foucault and Bourdieu are accused of thinking too much about power, reducing much of what is valuable about culture into, in the final instance, just another "hermeneutic of suspicion."[53] I try to chart a middle way here, showing how social life is necessarily infused with power, but that such power cannot be its ultimate explanation. Indeed, as I (and others) argue, power can sometimes be a *problem* in that in certain contexts, there is a normative commitment not to impose commitments upon others but to help them to come to those positions on their own.

Far from a hermeneutic of suspicion, Foucault and two of his most careful readers, Talal Asad and Saba Mahmood, are excellent at showing how power in these contexts is just as much *constitutive* as it is constraining, in that certain kinds of impositions form the possibilities for further kinds of action.[54] I build upon these insights in poststructural theory and the anthropology of religion to show how boundaries and what I am calling external authorities are integral elements of communal socialization. I use the word *socialization* with some trepidation in that the term has been generally avoided in cultural sociology due to its alleged Parsonian baggage. I hope this book helps to reinterpret the concept in the Deweyan sense of ongoing, active habituation which I use here.[55]

Finally, it is worth pointing out that my use of the term *external authority* bears certain important similarities to other cultural sociologists' use of the word *institution*. Because *institution* is such a capacious term, it might well be the case that external authority, as I understand it here, is also an institution. However, when I say external authority, I mean something subtly different from how the "institution" is often used by sociologists, especially cultural sociologists. I refer specifically to a social entity that is felt and understood to have a certain kind of agency and authority in the community itself, an agency and authority that is maintained through practices, experienced through emotions and identities, and understood through beliefs. What matters for me is how these communities experience the world, and I bracket the questions about these external authorities' *real* agency for philosophical debates which largely depend upon certain priors. What is important for my argument is that they are *understood, felt,* and *narrated* as agents, and that these understandings, feelings, and narrations help actors both to maintain their traditions and to shift the problem of explicit coercion into an experience of external authorities above and beyond them.

Sociology of Morality

In many ways, this book is centrally about the sociology of morality, albeit in a more broadly Aristotelian sense of the way a life ought to be lived. However, despite a recent and burgeoning interest in an explicitly self-described sociology of morality, both the sociology of culture and the sociology of religion have been interested in these questions virtually since their beginning, and so this book is also quite squarely within already existing traditions in the sociologies of culture and religion.[56]

By *moral* I do not necessarily mean the explicit study of what is right and wrong, and neither do I mean my own description of the best action at an any given moment. Instead, I refer to a much broader and more diffuse sensibility, a vague and hard-to-articulate sense that someone is living life the way it ought to be lived. This sense of morality is rooted not in explicit rules and careful deliberations but in subconscious habits and the maintenance of everyday emotional expectations, similar to what Gabriel Abend calls "the moral background" and what Charles Taylor calls a "moral imaginary." Morality, for my purposes, is therefore less important as a series of discrete questions about particular actions and more relevant as a way to frame what a good life resembles, generally through a series of habituated practices.[57]

If morality is lived out in practices, then those practices are often supported by and adjudicated through emotions. There is debate among moral philosophers about how much emotions *should* matter in morality,[58] yet it seems clear as a social-scientific claim that people's moral sense is deeply guided by their emotions, an insight within sociology at least as old as Durkheim's study of the elementary forms of religious life.[59] This is not to deny that morality has a rational element: arguments can and often do change people's minds about the right and the good. Yet even if arguments can and do matter in moral experience, they often matter less than the resonant experiences through which unconscious moral expectations align with everyday interactions with people, objects, and events, or else the dissonant experiences in which someone feels an emotional struggle, generally through a sense of disgust, fear, annoyance, or regret—similar to what Lukes, borrowing from Galen Strawson, calls "reactive attitudes."[60]

People might not be able to articulate precisely why they feel these emotions or attitudes, or their explanations might be inconsistent with some of their other commitments or claims. Yet this inarticulacy does not necessarily mean that people are basically immoral or that their morals totally change in each new context. It can simply mean that their moral life is complex, with a variety of often competing commitments, some of which people want to achieve even if they are not always able to do so. More importantly for my purposes, it shows how moral life is *situated* via certain boundaries and external authorities, and that people are often able to check on the relative power of these boundaries and external authorities not only through their ongoing understandings of them but also through their feelings regarding them, as well as potential threats to them.

Indeed, threats form a key part of this story, both actual dangers and, much more often, their potential occurrence. Following Dewey's focus on interrupted habits, it is exactly such dissonant interactions that force people to reflect on their moral experience, sometimes adapting to new contexts and sometimes digging in to pre-existing boundaries and authorities. This book builds on work that connects the sociology of morality to the sociology of emotions and the sociology of culture,[61] arguing that we come to our moral identities through boundaries and external authorities, and we often come to recognize the relevance of those boundaries and authorities through our feelings.

Sociology of Education

While this is a book about religious schools, its overarching themes—external authorities, boundaries, and the diffusion of power—could easily be found in other contexts, including public schools. Studies of religious education provide excellent cases for broader studies of subcultural communities that seek simultaneously to construct and contest boundaries with the outside world.[62] Also, while schools are often noted for their "loose coupling" of what administrators or districts might want and what actually happens in the classroom, religious schools are noteworthy for tightly coupling commitments to certain moral commitments and the day-to-day practice of instruction. This book is therefore one attempt among others at a sociology of education not squarely focused on socioeconomic inequality,[63] one with roots all the way back to Durkheim's study of moral education and Du Bois's concern about African American students' development as citizens.[64]

Politics and the Internet

Chapters 2, 3, and 4 examine how these schools distinguished themselves from the rest of America. There is a thriving literature on religion and politics in the United States, with a good amount of it about Evangelicals and Muslims. Chapter 2 builds on these conversations and generally supports a common finding: all four schools I studied are suspicious of America, partially for its secular values and hedonistic dangers, but also because of what Evangelicals feel they have lost and what Muslims feel they have yet to be given. I leverage the book's comparative angle to fine tune these distinctions, also using the schools' identities *as schools* to study two key sources of distinction: in Chapter 2, public schools provide a sense of who the schools are not, and in Chapter 4, the Internet provides a constant source of danger requiring a continual need to reaffirm what is actually essential about the schools' identities. While much has changed about online life since 2010 and 2011, many of today's concerns already existed at that time.

Sociology of Gender and Sociology of Sexuality

Chapters 3 and 4 examine gender and sexuality as boundaries in the schools I studied. I build on important works in the sociology of religion, especially those examining Muslims and Evangelicals.[65] Yet I also develop some of the ideas in these works through the comparison itself, showing how a site of boundary contestation can vary between religious communities. In some ways, Chapter 3 is the most challenging to my argument about orthodoxy and orthopraxy in that the stereotypes appear to be true. I found that the Evangelical schools are more troubled by feminism, a challenge to their orthodoxy, while the Muslim schools were more concerned about students not wearing the hijab, a challenge to their orthopraxy. While there is truth to this simple summary, I use this chapter to show how orthodoxy and orthopraxy—and by sociological extension, beliefs and practices—are much more interpenetrated than they may at first appear. It is the Evangelical *practice* of rejecting feminism that matters in these communities, and it is the relative flexibility of *beliefs* about the hijab that allow some latitude about gender in the Muslim schools. In each of these three chapters on boundaries, I also emphasize the concepts of "essence and accident" as helpful tools that sociologists could adapt from psychology and philosophy. Describing distinctions as essential and accidental can help sociologists not only to describe how people distinguish themselves but also how some of those distinctions become much more important than others.

Scripture and Prayer as External Authorities

Chapters 5 and 6 are about scripture and prayer, both relatively understudied topics in the sociology of religion, despite their importance to religious communities.[66] My study of how scripture and prayer function as external authorities and, more specifically, how certain ways of praying or reading scripture work as sites of boundary contestation build upon my study of gender to challenge easy distinctions between the orthoprax and the orthodox. These chapters also stand on their own as broader analyses of how scriptures and prayers help religious actors to distinguish themselves from both co-religionists and the rest of the world. Once those boundaries are established, I am better able to show how scripture (Chapter 5) and prayer (Chapter 6) are understood as having an agency and authority all their own. That "external authority" exists because it is maintained through practices and boundaries, working together to make people both feel and believe in the authority of scripture and prayer.

Science as an External Authority

The book's seventh chapter is about science, and its analysis of science differs from most contemporary sociological studies of science in two ways. First, and perhaps most relevantly, it builds on a growing set of conversations about the relationship between science and religion.[67] Yet the chapter is also an engagement with an older tradition in the sociology of science, one that is less interested in the work of scientists in the lab (sometimes called the sociology of scientific knowledge) and instead focuses on how non-scientists engage and understand science as an external authority with real power in their lives. Working scientists and those who study them might well be skeptical of a coherent thing called science, yet whether or not such a thing exists in the lab, it very much existed in the schools I studied. This chapter is therefore more along the lines of ongoing work in the public understanding of science, albeit with a more explicit focus on how religious people and organizations consume, understand, and experience scientific knowledge and expertise.[68] Most importantly, I argue that the authority of science is networked among a variety of nodes, especially teachers, tests, and textbooks, and so its external authority is felt less intensely than that of scripture or prayer. The one exception to this distinction is when my respondents, nearly all of whom were creationists, took it upon themselves to engage science with science, proving evolution wrong and creationism right. It was in these moments of practical activity that science also functioned as an external authority in the ways I have been describing it.

THE SCHOOLS AND THEIR CONTEXT

Private religious education is quite old in the United States, although Muslim and conservative Protestant schools are generally much younger. According to the National Center for Education Statistics, there were 49,522,000 students enrolled in public elementary and secondary schools in the United States in 2011, while 5,268,000 were enrolled in private schools of some form.[69] In a 2011–2012 survey of the "private school universe,"[70] the Department of Education found that 607,130 students were in unspecified Christian schools (much like Good Tree) with another 309,558 in schools run by theologically conservative denominations (Assemblies of God, Baptists, Calvinists, Church of Christ, Church of God in Christ, and Church of the Nazarene). That total of a little more than 900,000 students is still not even two-tenths of a percent of the total number of American students, and it is a number much lower than conservative Protestants' share of the population, usually estimated at around 25 percent, though that number is subject to some debate.[71] In that same 2011–2012 study, the Private School Universe Survey identified 229 Islamic schools with 32,478 students, an even smaller fraction of one percent of the total student population. There are far fewer Muslim schools, and most Muslims do not attend them. In 2009, Islamic educator Karen Keyworth argued that around 4 percent of Muslim school-age children attend Muslim schools, based on 2007 Pew data. Muslims make up around one percent of the United States population, according to Pew.[72]

There is some debate about the origins of conservative Protestant education in the United States, which became much more common in the 1950s through the 1970s. Conservative Protestants themselves identify their origin as related to an increased focus on secular science and a decreased tolerance for religious practices like school prayer. While these changes are certainly real, it is also hard to ignore the marked correlation between school integration and the development of largely white conservative Protestant private schools, especially in areas with forced integration, whether via legally mandated busing programs or through the dismantling of Jim Crow segregation.[73] However, despite the racially exclusionary origins of conservative Protestant schools, many, especially in the North, are nonetheless often marked by a relative diversity in their student body and the maintenance of a color-blind ideology, that is, the belief that racial inequality can be explained by individual and cultural differences rather than structural inequalities.[74]

Muslim education in the United States, like the experience of Muslim Americans in general, is bifurcated between a much older tradition of Black Islam and a much more recent tradition of immigrant Islam, with those immigrants usually (but by no means exclusively) from the Middle East, North Africa, and South Asia. As far back as the 1930s, Black Muslims developed separate institutions for primary and secondary schools, and, as the Nation of Islam coalesced under the leadership of Elijah Muhammad, a broad network of "University of Islam" schools developed in cities across the country, called "universities" because of the universalism of their intention. In the 1970s, after the death of Elijah Muhammad, his son Warith Deen Muhammad shifted from his father's more heterodox teachings, renaming the Nation of Islam the American Muslim Mission to reflect their more orthodox Muslim theology. Warith Deen Muhammad changed the names of the schools as well, honoring his mother, an important teacher and leader in the movement, by calling them Sister Clara Muhammad schools.[75] Sister Clara Muhammad schools remain important educational institutions for Black Muslims across the country, sometimes educating immigrant Muslims as well.

Immigrant Muslim schools are often much more recent stories. Most, like the schools in my study, are no more than 30 years old. The 1965 Immigration and Nationality Act radically changed the sources of immigration in the United States, ushering in a new era of American diversity. The initial post-1965 Muslim immigrants tended to view America as a largely foreign country, a place of conflict and chaos as described by Mucahit Bilici, a sociologist of American Islam.[76] Yet over time the Muslims themselves came to change their mind about America, and new immigrants shared their optimism. So did the immigrants' children, both those born in the United States and those who came here young enough to consider themselves more American than anything else. As Bilici describes it, immigrant American Islam has shifted from visitor to citizen in the past 50 years, and developing schools was a key part of that process, even if it can also be understood as a rearguard maneuver to protect children from the potentially pernicious influences of public schools.

To be clear, the vast majority of American Muslims (like the vast majority of American Evangelicals) send their children to public schools. These Muslim young people might well find no tension among their many non-Muslim fellow students: after all, not all Muslims wear hijab, just as not all Muslims take time out of the day to pray. Yet for those Muslims who do take these practices seriously, many find effective strategies to maintain their identity, even if others feel afraid public school is forcing them to lose key elements of their religious life.[77] However, certain parents—and students—worry that these strategies will not be sufficient, making a separate Muslim school, at least in their eyes, a religious necessity.

Choosing the Schools

I began my dissertation planning to compare one Muslim and one Evangelical high school in New York City area to one Muslim and one Evangelical high school in Amman, Jordan. For my first two (New York City) schools, I wanted to find a school within commuting distance of central Manhattan for reasons both methodological and personal. Methodologically, I considered the "New York City area" to end at the outer limits of its commuter line, an effective even if somewhat arbitrary means of establishing a border in the Eastern megalopolis that extends from metropolitan Washington DC to metropolitan Boston. This limit was also effective for personal reasons, as I lived in Manhattan and did not have a car, requiring me to find a way to commute to the schools each day via public transportation.

In November of 2010, I sent letters with Yale letterhead to eight Evangelical schools in commuter range of New York City and, within a month, I had heard back from only one school, The Good Tree Christian Academy, whose secretary put me in touch with the school's principal (I later got a voicemail from another school saying they were too busy). I was invited to campus to discuss my project. Meanwhile, a contact familiar with New York City Muslim schools gave me the names of some schools I could contact and recommended that, rather than sending a letter, I should phone ahead and then set up a conversation over the phone. I called 24 different schools, and after a few tries with each, I finally got someone who was willing to see me. When I called Al Amal, I was put in touch with the school's guidance counselor who, upon finding out I was from Yale, invited me to come to the school's college fair to represent Yale, at which I could talk further about my project with the school's principal.

While doing my fieldwork, I decided the original goal of an international comparison would have too many moving pieces. I was also asked to leave Al Amal early, and so I decided that I needed to study another Muslim school, at least for a semester. For purposes of symmetry, I decided to look for another Christian school as well. In consultation with my advisors, I realized that this would actually make the study much more thorough in that I could check that what I had discovered in the first two schools was also the case in similar schools that differed in certain key ways. Because the first Christian school did not take state exams for biology and was in a suburban area, I sent letters to Christian schools that did take state exams for biology, focusing particularly on schools in urban areas (though, because there were not that many conservative Christian schools, I cast my net fairly wide). Because *Al Amal* did take state exams for biology, I sent letters to Muslim schools that did not, hoping that I would find a school that was in a suburban area.

I sent ten letters each to Muslim and Protestant schools on Yale letterhead, making regular phone calls to administrators at each of the schools. I eventually received interest from one of the Protestant schools and one of the Muslim schools. After talking with the Protestant school principal, he decided he would not have time for me to work there and that it would be too much of a burden on the faculty and staff (though I could not shake the suspicion he was also uncomfortable with the fact that the study involved Muslim schools). The Muslim school, *Al Haqq*, invited me to come over to talk with them in December and agreed to begin letting me do research there. I found *Apostles* by simply going to the attached church and asking the pastor after worship was over if I could do research at the school.

The Good Tree

In early November of 2010 I rented a car and drove to The Good Tree, a complex of former army barracks surrounded by government buildings on the right and left and, across the street, a neighborhood of modest homes. The train station I would eventually use each day was about two miles away, connected to the school by a state highway with strip malls of diners, convenience stores, and the ubiquitous Dunkin' Donuts. There are buses available to the students, but many get a ride or drive. The school is on a side road from a state highway.

The school's eight buildings are all U-shaped, with a courtyard in each center. There were two buildings with their centers filled in: one for a chapel and the other for a cafeteria. The school also built an impressive gym with male and female locker rooms, a stage, and offices for athletic staff. The chapel—which doubles as a grade-school gym—is sparse in the Calvinist fashion. I asked the principal, Brenda Forrest, about this, and she told me "it wasn't intentional," and this lack of consciousness about the Calvinist roots of the school's theology showed up regularly in my fieldwork. Ms. Forrest is a former student whose name graces the gym wall for scoring over 1,000 points as a high school basketball star.

The school was founded in the mid-twentieth century, and many of its parents and teachers are former students. There are approximately 350 students in the school, with around 200 students in the high school. Students in the high school have to sign a statement of faith. In a survey I gave to all but three of the approximately 200 students in the high school, a little less than half the students identified as white, 10 percent as Black or West Indian, 7 percent as Latino, 25 percent as Asian, Asian-American, or Arab, and 10 percent as mixed race. In that same survey, I learned that there was a tremendous diversity among the students' religious views, though the overwhelming majority are Protestants. The varied Protestant denominations within the school might reflect the fact that the school is neither affiliated with a denomination nor a specific religious community. Around 5 students in each class were Asian students (usually Chinese) who were not necessarily Christian but were primarily there to learn English (and pay full tuition). These were the only students who were not Christian. Leaders of local congregations were involved in various leadership roles in the school, but its principals and its superintendent are laypeople.

I started doing fieldwork a month and a half after my first visit, in early January of 2011. I was given a desk in the high school office right next to Ms. Forrest's administrative assistant, Marie Shumacher, to whom I became very close over the year and a half I spent at the school from January of 2011 until graduation in the spring of 2012.

Al Amal

Also in early November of 2010, I got on a series of trains to get to the middle of an urban section of greater New York to represent Yale at Al Amal's college fair. As I walked the few blocks from the train to the school, I passed posters for a drag show, a bus of Orthodox Jews, and various twenty-somethings with tight pants and fashionable facial hair. The school's front face is a large building, boxy and architecturally plain, with Arabic and English text written on its outside wall. There is a set of temporary one-story buildings in the back lot, and between them the students play basketball during their breaks. Right away I noticed the girls wearing hijabs and *abayas*, the separation of students into boys and girls, and the subtle looks and nods the students used to circumvent their segregation.

After waiting a few minutes, I met with the principal. It appeared almost a moot point that he would have me work at the school. He was much less defensive than any other high school principal I've approached. Through talking to the teachers at the college fair going on that day, I learned that the school was about 20 years old and that it had been only a grade school but had gradually become a high school as well. The school had about 300 total students, with around 200 in the high school. All classes are gender segregated except the advanced placement courses, though most teachers teach both genders. While I did not give a survey to students at any school except Good Tree, my sense of Al Amal was that about two-thirds of its students had Middle Eastern or North African ethnicity, and about a third was ethnically South Asian, a figure I checked with teachers.

When I came back to the school to start my fieldwork in January, I walked into the school office, and the principal, Brother Naguib, was walking out of the office when he saw me and welcomed me. I sat down in his office and changed out of my snow boots. The books on his back shelf were a combination of Arabic-language reference texts and many white binders of what appeared to be forms. We went over the letter he would eventually send to the parents at the school. I agreed with everything he said, trying to be amenable. And then he took me to class. I did not realize that Brother Naguib would be abruptly fired shortly before the start of the following school year, and that my relationship with the new principal would be much more tenuous. That more difficult relationship—along with concerns that I spent too much time with female students—led the board to ask me to leave the school, a topic I discuss briefly in Chapter 3 and in the methodological appendix, and more extensively in a separate piece.[78] I was at Al Amal from January to October of 2011.

Al Haqq

Al Haqq School is in a suburban neighborhood full of religious diversity: the place feels a bit like Jerusalem, as the women in hijabs and men in yarmulkes wander among those wearing more secular clothing. I rented a car to be sure I would make the appointment in time (though I would ride a combination of trains and buses during my fieldwork) and was pleasantly surprised at the ample parking. Like Good Tree, Al Haqq is in a quiet area surrounded by residential homes and local shops. Unlike Good Tree, though, the shops around Al Haqq feel a bit more "towny," slightly more upscale with fewer homogenously suburban chain stores (even if, as with all three other schools, Dunkin' Donuts coffee appeared to be the primary form of currency). The school has around 180 students in its high school (it also has a junior high). Its student population, like Al Amal's, has a majority of students from the Middle East and North Africa, with a substantial South Asian minority and a few students of African and Southeast Asian ethnicity.

I was welcomed into the principal's office, which looked cleaner and more organized than any of the others I had seen. A Palestinian woman who had worked in Jordan, Sister Saida had something of an accent as she told me about her position at the school and her passion for her work. She appeared to be in her mid-50s with a serious demeanor and a kind smile. I noticed later that she was the only adult at the school who went by her last name, although, like almost everyone else at both Muslim schools, her title was "Sister" (the men go by "Brother"; in both schools, I was always "Brother Jeff" or just Jeff).

The principal looked up from all the forms she had printed from my e-mail and said, "I could have gone two ways with this [request to do research] because there are all kinds of things people are saying about Muslims, and I didn't want to add to that—media are always calling me for interviews, and I never call them back. But then I thought, we are American, and we should try to fight these stereotypes." I thanked her and said I would do my best. I was at Al Haqq for the spring semester of 2012.

Apostles

In early December of 2011, I went to a large church in an urban part of the New York City area. There were taxi lots, mechanic shops, and bodegas as I walked from the train to the church/school complex. The church had a warm reception area and a massive altar that stretched maybe 200 feet across with about a 50-foot ceiling. There were huge projection screens on the right and left side of the altar, with a podium and altar-piece in the center. As with many contemporary Christian churches, an impressive array of sound equipment, musical instruments, and, later, actual musicians stood at the altar performing praise and worship songs. In front of the altar were two floors of chairs that I estimated could seat around

2,000. Like a lot of Protestant churches, there was not much ornamentation, though there was an altar and a communion celebration the day I attended (grape juice and unleavened bread were distributed by ushers).

At the end of the service, I walked up to the church's main pastor, a man in his 70s with remarkable energy and bright white hair. I waited patiently for him to finish his line of conferees and then told him I had sent him a letter asking if I could work at the school. He said, "We'll do whatever we can to help you." He told me he'd have to talk to his daughter and then get back to me, and I said that would be fine. "So it's a family outfit, huh?" I asked. He smiled, paused, and touched my shoulder like an old political pro. "Brother, it's the best kind. I've seen them all, and it's the best kind."

I was at Apostles for the spring semester of 2012, on the two days a week I was not at Al Haqq (also two days a week) or Good Tree (at that point, one day a week for student interviews). On my first day there, I noticed a huge map of the world on the wall next to the elevator in the school's entryway. The map had pins in each place where students were from. There were more tacks than space for Puerto Rico and the Dominican Republic, and then lots of pins in Brazil as well. There were many more, though none as concentrated, in other parts of Latin America and then the rest of the world, though it looked like the biggest single area besides the Dominican Republic and Puerto Rico was South Korea. I learned that Apostles has around 200 students in its high school (it has grades K–12 on the campus), with a large minority of white students, a plurality of Latinx students, and substantial numbers of Asian Americans and African Americans as well. Also, like Good Tree, Apostles had around 15-20 non-Christian students from Asia (usually China) who wanted to be at an American high school.

I asked the principal, Sue Simons, about how the school admits non-Christians (the only school in my study to regularly admit non-members). She said that for a while she thought about being more aggressive about trying to convert her students, but she realized that if she and the teachers lived a Christian lifestyle, then that would not be necessary. "It just happens that most of our seniors, by the time they get out of here, they're saved," she told me. "But we don't set out to do that. We really don't." She said that one Korean student came up to a teacher after Bible class and said, "I'd like to get saved." She smiled.

CHAPTER 2

⌀

Politics and Public Schools

At my very first day at Apostles, I was invited to a faculty meeting, where I introduced myself to the school's quite welcoming faculty and staff. Pastor Jacob Johnson, who usually left the school matters to the school's principal (who also happened to be his daughter) had come through the hallway connecting school to church. He was there to address an issue of paramount importance: thinking of their work as a ministry. Dressed in a business suit and with bright white hair, he was charming and passionate: "We *cannot* fail," he insisted. "The school is a light in a dark place. We cannot close. There's no one else." We were sitting in the school's basement gym, which doubled as an auditorium. Pastor Johnson returned to this sense of isolation repeatedly: "We were talking to some Christians from Australia, and they have a Christian school with a thousand students, and another with 800 a few blocks away. We were talking to them about the rise of Christian schools in Australia, and because they have some help from the government—not everything, but they get some help—it's much easier to have Christian schools. We don't have that help. And so if a school closed in Australia, there'd be another one around the corner. But that's not true for us. We're all there is . . . . " That sense of moral necessity pervaded each school, leading to a deep conservatism, partially in its most obvious political sense but mostly in the broader sense of wanting to conserve something essential in their communities and, most preciously, in their children.

Agents of God. Jeffrey Guhin, Oxford University Press (2021). © Oxford University Press.
DOI: 10.1093/oso/9780190244743.001.0001

BOUNDARIES AND POLITICS

Someone who only knows about Muslims and Evangelicals from the news might assume the four schools studied here put politics, in its narrower, more governmental sense, above everything else. Both academic literature and news stories tend to portray Evangelical Christians as the Republican Party's loyal foot soldiers. Meanwhile, popular perceptions of Islam in America emphasize Islamist political violence and state-sanctioned Islamophobia.[1] While I certainly encountered many political discussions in these schools (some of which were on these very themes), these conversations were less prevalent than I had expected.[2] The Muslim students, perhaps out of necessity, were more politically aware than the Christian students: in addition to being Muslim in the New York City area around a decade after 9/11, both the Arab Spring and revelations of New York Police Department spying on local Muslim organizations occurred during my time at Al Amal and Al Haqq.[3] Yet even for the Muslim schools, politics in its explicitly governmental form was not something the students often discussed.

Yet politics still mattered, mostly because politics is about more than what the government does. It's about how people engage with each other and how they organize their lives together.[4] Education is a necessary part of this broader politics, as has been described from Aristotle and Plato on to Dewey and Du Bois.[5] Such education might entail the memorization of key civic facts (how a bill becomes a law, or the proper role of the Supreme Court) yet most political education is subtler and more local. How are students supposed to be members of their own communities? What is required of them, and what are they allowed to require of others? What are the practices they must continue to keep their communities alive, and what are the boundaries they must maintain to keep their communities safe?

BOUNDARIES: ESSENCE VERSUS ACCIDENT

Boundaries are things we say or think about how people are different from us. When we speak or think about those differences (or we hear others speaking about them), such speaking, thinking and hearing have real effects, in that they help to solidify certain differences we come to regard as natural and obvious. In more technical language, boundaries are habituated distinctions rooted in declarations, whether explicit or implicit, that often have important effects on inequality and social outcomes. Sociologists Michèle Lamont and Virág Molnár distinguish between *symbolic* boundaries, which are "conceptual distinctions made by social actors to categorize objects" and *social* boundaries, which are "objectified forms of social difference manifested in unequal access to and unequal distribution of resources (material and nonmaterial) and social opportunities."[6] Lamont and Molnár argue that all social boundaries are rooted in symbolic boundaries, but not all symbolic boundaries become social boundaries. The boundaries I will be describing in this book are largely symbolic, though sometimes with the social effects Lamont and Molnár describe.

What causes those boundaries can be hard to determine. How men have historically separated themselves from women, for example, is a social boundary with clear effects on inequality, yet it is not only men who claim that a woman's place is in the home, even if it might well be the system of patriarchy that ultimately explains these inequalities. Women's participation in their own oppression shows that boundaries are often *ideological*, which is to say that those whom boundaries have harmed and those whom boundaries have benefited might both think their boundary is a fine thing. Of course, others might provide counter-descriptions of the boundaries, or they might deny the boundaries' importance or even their existence.[7]

In any of these cases, boundaries are linked to power: both the power to classify, which sociologist Pierre Bourdieu would call "symbolic power," and the power to contest, agree with, or ignore that classification.[8] The cognitive (and therefore ideological) piece is critical here, as both individuals and communities participate in what is ultimately a declarative claim about difference. A boundary is an insistence that *they* are not like us in some specific way, such as politics, gender, or religion. Yet even these examples are a bit too broad: after all, gender, politics, and religion are all expansive terms, and even these are broken down into what I am calling "sites of boundary contestation," that is, the specific, practical locations of distinction.

These distinctions might well not be understood or experienced as structurally limiting in the ways that Lamont and Molnár describe. A woman who has made the choice to be a stay-at-home mother because of her belief in the "complementary" differences between men and women might not identify herself as being oppressed. She could instead insist that it is other women, those who refuse to recognize their primary role as wives and mothers, who are truly missing something fundamental. As described in Chapter 1, Aristotle's distinction between essence and accident is helpful as a way of illustrating this comparison. This woman might understand the true *essence* of being a woman as caring for her family. While some might classify her as a victim of false consciousness or of ideological misrecognition, she might argue the same about her opponents. In either case, there is a debate about what is *essential* to being a woman and what is simply accidental.[9]

As described in the introduction, a blue house is *essentially* a house; if it were to stop being a house, it would lose its identity. However, it is *accidentally* blue, which doesn't mean it is blue by mistake, but rather that being blue is not essential to its core identity. Were it to stop being blue, it would still be a house. Again, to be clear, such distinctions are fundamentally reifications, which means they are the social production of things that come to feel natural and obvious. Various philosophers have argued quite convincingly that "Aristotelian essentialism" does not accurately describe how things really are outside of human interpretation.[10] Yet what matters for my purposes here is what happens *within* human interpretation: determining what is felt and understood as essential as opposed to accidental is a helpful way to understand how people navigate their differences from each other. Some people see their differences as purely accidental and therefore unimportant; others see their differences as essential and therefore critical. Others might disagree about the nature of the difference itself, some seeing it as accidental and others as essential.

This analysis of how boundaries are experienced differently by different sides has important implications for the schools I studied: sometimes they felt boundaries were more their own work, and sometimes they felt boundaries were forced upon them. They often disagreed with how they were distinguished from the rest of the world, believing people got something *essentially* wrong about them. But they also felt—sometimes in agreement with mainstream America and sometimes not—that there was something essentially different about the rest of the country. Boundaries were often felt necessary not only as a means of distinction but also a means of protection, which in some sense explains the presence of these private schools when public schools are free and available to all.

The difference between essence and accident functions on a few different levels, just as boundaries (or authorities, or institutions) can be nested within each other: there are questions of what is essential and accidental about a certain identity (that we are a religious school, rather than a nonreligious school), and then within those essential differences can be still further ones, for example that our religious school is marked by prayer, or safety, or compassion.

In the rest of this chapter I will examine how the schools distinguished themselves from public schools, a distinction which helped them establish what was essential about their own communities and their politics. I will then turn to the more explicit engagement with politics that I saw in the schools. In discussions of both public schools and politics, community members described essential differences between themselves and the rest of the world, and they also expressed frustrations that outsiders thought differences were essential when the community members believed they were not.

PUBLIC SCHOOLS

In my interviews with students and teachers, I almost always asked why their school exists. Many immediately distinguished their school from public schools, emphasizing two themes: public schools are dangerous, and public schools don't care. A few disagreed; some students told me they wished they were at a public school, and a few more told me they were tired of so much separatism. Yet the students and teachers I met tended to agree that public schools lacked the essential characteristics of safety and compassion. What might appear to be the most salient difference between public schools and private religious school is *religion*, yet that concept is probably too broad as a source of distinction. Instead, what mattered were specific elements of a religion, such as prayer and wearing headscarves for the Muslim schools or not being forced to teach evolution for the Christian ones.[11] And even more than these, it was the sense that with their specific religious community came a sense of safety and a sense of care.

The Muslim Schools

Brother Umar Abbas is an intellectual, with an office full of books and good progress toward his PhD in education. He is, among other roles, Al Amal's assistant principal and high school disciplinarian. Probably in his 40s or 50s, he took on a parental role to the boys, and many told me how much they admired him. We chatted often in his office, and in one of our chats, he said that "you can only do so much good with whatever you're trying to do." This was after he told me you can't change everything: "Like at this school, when we started, we had all these theories about making the perfect Islamic student . . . but we realized pretty quickly that they [the students] are in an environment and that has an impact on them . . . . So what we were really trying to do here is to just create an environment with less damage."

When I asked about the nature of that damage, he emphasized the importance of gender separation, something he said you cannot do at a public school. But there were other dangers at public schools too: "Some of these schools, they make the school a place for drug exchange, and there are no drugs here. And there are bullies too, kicking people around. And that's how we're different from public schools. Parents know that here their students will not use profanity in any way, and that there will be no bullying."

As much as I respected Brother Umar, what he was telling me was not exactly accurate, and I would be surprised if he did not know that. A few students liked to tell me how often they smoked weed or got high. One student would sometimes tell me he was high right then, as we were talking. I had no way to verify if this was true, but his giggles and the red in his eyes made me think he was probably right. I had no way to check this, but my sense was that Al Amal boys (though probably not the girls) used pot and tobacco at about the same rate as other high school boys in the area, even if I doubt they used much alcohol. In contrast to Brother Umar's insistence that "students will not use profanity in any way," I heard many of the boys cursing quite casually. Of course, teenage boys across America say bad words, and teenagers in the New York City area often grow up with the f-word as a term of endearment.

These discrepancies between Brother Umar's claims about his school and what I saw his students do reveal the limits of the school's reach: as Brother Umar admitted in the beginning of our conversation, he can't change everything. How to reconcile this difference between what was said and what I observed? I think part of the distinction might be found in a claim I heard at all four schools, that teachers really *care* here, as opposed to public schools, where they're just going through the motions. So sure, there are drugs and cursing at Al Amal, just like at a public school. But, the teachers and students at Amal might say, *Here*, at Al Amal, we're *committed* to making it better and we really mean it, so those drugs and curses don't really count: they're accidental at Al Amal and essential at the publics.

I had a similar conversation with Ahmed Nagi, the biology teacher at Al Amal and one of the faculty members with whom I became closest. Brother Ahmed is about 5'10" and stocky, mostly bald with his remaining hair and beard trimmed short and neat. At our first meeting, he wore a white sweater, olive pants, and black shoes. The pants, like those of many teachers, had chalk marks on the seat. One day we were in the science lab, talking about how he had a certification to teach in public schools. He'd been at the school for 11 years, and he liked that his children were at the school as well. "The pay is terrible," he admitted, "but this way I can be close to my kids, I'm in a Muslim environment, I can pray every day, and my kids can go to a Muslim school too." He paused thoughtfully. "I mean, at the public schools, God knows what they're teaching them there, and what the boys and girls do with each other, and all the drugs. No. I've heard things. I'm glad my kids aren't in the public schools." Again, the essential quality of public schools is their danger, both related to gender and to drugs.

Those public-school problems might exist at Al Amal too. Yet the difference for the community members I worked with is that Al Amal teachers *really* care about fixing them. On another day, I had a conversation with four junior boys, all of whom were waiting for Brother Umar to talk to them about some disciplinary infraction. We talked about why they were at the school and, without prompting, they compared Al Amal to public school. "At public schools, they don't care about the students—here they really care about us," said one boy. One of the students, a boy who sometimes talked about smoking pot, nodded: "Yeah, if they catch us smoking at a public school, they'd just walk past, but here they'd pull you in and beat you, you know, make sure you're never going to smoke again." I asked if that's a good thing. "Yeah it's good—I don't like it at the time because I'm going to get beat but it's good." The other students all nodded in agreement.

To be clear, there was no corporal punishment at Al Amal (indeed at least two teachers complained to me regularly about this). However, as the boys described, there was a certain kind of moral discipline of the kind sociologist Emile Durkheim describes in *Moral Education*, a commitment to enabling students' own capacities for self-control and the best version of themselves.[12] Students at all four schools were ambivalent about this tension, sometimes annoyed by the extra work but also acknowledging the accountability was in their best interest.

Faculty and staff could also be ambivalent. One teacher at Al Amal complained to me that the board had stopped the school from doing collaborative magazines with a public school. She pulled one of the magazines off of her shelf, showing me a photo spread of the public-school girls trying on the hijab. "They had all these piercings and tattoos," the faculty member told me. "We were like, okaaaay—at first. But it was good! We were judging them, and they were judging us, but we got to know each other, and it was really good. But that was an earlier principal, and the Board stopped us from doing that." She complained, as did many at Al Amal, that the board micromanaged the school's life, steering everyone toward a very conservative direction. "They don't have any vision, they're more reactive than proactive," the teacher told me. She paused and looked frustrated. "They want us to choke the kids to make them very Islamic, but we're here [meaning the United States] and it's not like that." Yet this same faculty member would not want to give up on the mission of a Muslim school, or even the broader goals of time for prayer and proper interaction between genders. She shared the board's essential goal of running an excellent Muslim school and was frustrated by their confusion of essence for accident, of conflating Muslim education with conservative hypervigilance.

This ambivalence was on display at Al Haqq as well. I did tape-recorded interviews with students from each grade at Al Haqq, usually sitting outside on a bench beneath a tree, about a dozen yards from the main building. In one interview, a junior boy, Usman, told me that he thinks the faculty are generally on board with the religious goals of the school, even if his fellow students were not always so enthusiastic. I heard exactly this response whenever I asked these questions at all four schools: students almost always thought teachers were committed to the schools' religious missions, while their fellow students were a mixed bag. Different students gave different numbers, some more optimistic and some more despairing about the amount of other students who really cared. Yet the narrative was generally the same.

Usman used the word *force* to explain why some students attended Al Haqq, though he earlier insisted that his school's religious outcomes can only come from people freely choosing their commitments. That force is not universally felt, he argued, as many do not feel it as a coercion. In fact, even those who resent the imposition will appreciate it later:

> Some students are attending Al Haqq because they're—well at least they feel that their parents are forcing them. And however from—even though it's a small number—from the few alumni that I've met outside of school, they all—almost all say the same thing. That you don't appreciate it until you've actually left it.

I asked what the difference would be at a public school, and Usman replied that his mother taught at a public school and told him "about two girls almost punching each other, getting into a fight over a guy in sixth grade." Here, again, violence becomes an essential representation of public schools. Usman told me that hearing these things made him realize "whether or not I want to be in Islamic school isn't really the issue . . . this is the best thing for me."

Christian Schools

The Christians' distinction from public schools was more or less the same, emphasizing the real possibility of danger and the need for caring relationships. I asked a popular sophomore boy at Good Tree, Brent, about why he thinks Good Tree exists. "There were people that wanted to make a Christian school just because they didn't agree with the public school system or they thought other Christian schools in the area didn't really teach the correct [version of] . . . Christianity." He went on to say that "public school is definitely not a Christian point of view. I used to go to public school and just coming here for high school: there's a huge difference." Yet one of the things that was most striking for Brent, as with the students I described at Al Amal, was that at Good Tree the teachers *really* care. "Like the teachers at public school are nice too, but not the same way. Because they're also spiritual role models here, whereas in public school it's just like they're just nice because they have to be nice. But here they actually do care."

That phrase, "actually care," showed up regularly in my interviews with students about their teachers, always as a way of distinguishing them from public school teachers. Even the teachers made similar claims: in an interview, Good Tree's biology teacher, Carla James, told me that she and her fellow teachers were "able to have deeper relationships with the students." She emphasized how students could feel more open about prayer and their faith. "There's a lot of aspects that yeah, we're doing the same things that everyone else [at public schools] is doing, but we're doing it differently as well and that's an aspect of where we are in the world, but not of it." This difference also shows that even if public schools and private schools are both schools, my respondents often felt there was something essentially (rather than accidentally) different about the way they did things.

This commitment to being in the world but not of it was an explicitly Biblical commitment at the Christian schools, and the commitment was paralleled in the Muslim schools, where students regularly told me the purpose of the school was to create successful students in general, yet with a success that *maintained* rather than *avoided* Muslim identity. Yet it's also noteworthy that, in the paragraph above, Brent mentioned Good Tree's ability to teach a Christian "point of view." This is subtly different from the Muslim emphasis on specific embodied practices, whether making daily prayers or separating genders. A commitment to specific truth claims was especially important to many of the Good Tree interviewees when I asked them about why their schools existed. The importance of *practicing* those claims—to teach and learn them, to talk about them and share them—was something I saw repeatedly in my fieldwork, even if Christians might not articulate their experiences of orthodoxy in quite so orthoprax a fashion.

Of all the orthodox beliefs to care about at the Christian schools, evolution was often one of the most central. In my first week at Good Tree, I was hanging out in the lunch room with the school's chemistry teacher, who told me one of the reasons she left her job at a public school was because she didn't want to teach evolution. I asked one sophomore girl at Good Tree, Janet, about why the school exists, and without any prompting about evolution or science, she responded "I basically think it's here to—well, in some ways it's here to give relief from what we find outside. Because what we find outside is a bunch of people who teach children a theory and it's just deceit." When I asked which theory, she responded with one word: "Evolution."

Boundaries, I have argued, are rooted in either explicit or implicit claims about how we are different from others. Especially in the Evangelical tradition, those differences are often established in explicit claims people make: "sharing your testimony" is at once a key practice and a collection of words. The paradox of the Evangelical practice of orthodoxy is revealed in a story I heard from Asma, a first-year student at Good Tree. Both of Asma's parents are Indonesian immigrants and pastors, and, in our interview, she distinguished her experience at Good Tree from the public schools she had attended her whole life. "There was a lot of kids that did drugs a lot . . . like policemen started coming and ambulances started coming and then my parents were just like okay, you're not going there anymore."

These accounts of dangerous public schools are similar to those other students told me. Yet what seems to have upset Asma most was that she was punished for wearing a t-shirt with the phrase, "I love Jesus." "They were like if you wear it, like you could get detention and I was like okay. I kept wearing it though. It hurts because, you know, I had a friend that could wear her, she was a Muslim and she could wear her thing and I was like why can't I just wear a shirt that said I love Jesus." This was especially unfair, Asma believed, in "a country that's supposed to, like, know God."

For all four schools, this was the ultimate problem: America does not know God. All four schools believed that their practices were under threat: for the Muslim schools, it was the ability to pray, to wear clothing they considered appropriate, and more existentially, simply to be a member of the American nation who is not constantly under suspicion. For the Evangelical schools, it was the ability to proclaim, to say "I love Jesus" without fear or punishment, something they claimed a Christian nation had forgotten it once also believed. The expression of belief, in speech or even on clothing, is an essential practice that must be protected and preserved, even if that means spending money to go to a private school.

Asma mentioned the favoritism showed to Muslims, a regular complaint at Good Tree. When I talked to my Christian respondents about this, they said it was secularism that ultimately drove the tension. I interviewed the principal and founder of Apostles, Pastor Johnson, in a large conference room over the church. When our conversation turned to public schools, he said,

> I never felt so committed to schooling now that I really have come to see the demise of the school system . . . all these people that are living out here in their little bubble . . . when their kids hit the real world and they haven't been trained and developed and so on, the fallout—oh, some may go on like troopers but the fallout is very, very, very high. Very high because it's almost impossible, it's almost impossible to overcome the power of secular culture."

As with the two Muslim schools, these opinions were common but not universal at the Christian schools. Students at both Good Tree and Apostles complained to me about their schools, some even wishing they could transfer to a public school. I met one boy at Good Tree who explicitly identified as an atheist and a few others who, like him, would have preferred being at a school with more Advanced Placement classes (there was only one AP class, biology, which began in my second year there). Yet even these students generally appreciated the sense of community in the schools. The atheist, David, was a white boy well known for making strong claims in class. He told me he liked to discuss his opinions with Mr. Morgan, the senior Worldview teacher and debate coach, especially when Mr. Morgan was taking David and other students to debate tournaments.

Similarly, Jessica, a junior at Apostles, told me that she realized she was an atheist at age 14. She felt frustrated that some of the teachers at Apostles were hired for their Christian bona fides rather than their teaching credentials. She was especially frustrated by Mr. Lopez, the junior and senior religion teacher mentioned at the beginning of Chapter 1. She was upset that he hadn't finished college, and she felt his class was all-over-the-place. Yet, these atheist students often told me, folks around here really do care about us. In other words, even if these dissenting students disagreed with the schools about some fundamental things, they agreed that the schools were essentially different from public schools, not only regarding the standard fears of sex and drugs but the much more immediate concern that people actually care.

POLITICS

In a strictly governmental sense, these schools were intensely political places: they had to ensure students learned certain state-mandated information and developed state-mandated skills. They had to guide students through state tests, which a certain number of students had to pass lest the school's own status as a school be called into question. And these were only the most basic of requirements. There were also the responsibilities the schools felt to a broader sense of politics: teachers at each of these schools told me they wanted their students to be leaders in society, helping to guide America toward its best self.

Yet, here is where things get complicated. Because "America" is not only the name of a government; it is also the name of a *nation*, a term that refers to a people who have some common identity, whether linguistic, religious, or simply the fact of a shared government.[13] The politics of state power were certainly important at these schools, though its importance could sometimes be taken for granted, especially at the Christian schools. The bigger question at each school regarded the politics of national identity: who gets to be called American and what the term comes to mean. Of course, the state and nation interact in important ways; this was especially true for the Muslim schools, which felt their persecution and surveillance by the federal, state, and local governments was motivated by Islamophobic worries about what Muslims would do to the nation.[14] But persecution does not only have to come from the state, and people in all four schools told me how they felt they were persecuted and misunderstood by the rest of their nation. These distinctions show how "essence" and "accident" play out differently in the Muslim and Christian schools, with the Muslim schools insisting, against Islamophobic claims to the contrary, that their differences are simply accidental rather than essential. There is nothing essentially anti-American about Islam, they might have said, and part of the challenge was teaching their students to recognize what of their own tradition was "cultural" and therefore adaptable and what was a "religious" commitment that must not bend.

The Christian schools also focused on the difference between culture and religion, though with a much more tragic sensibility, worrying that the essentially Christian character of America had been lost. The Christian schools might agree with their secular critics that they have certain essential differences from the rest of America, but to the extent they do, it is because America has lost its way.

The Muslim Schools

For Sheikh Yusuf Siddiqui, the head of religious instruction at Al Haqq, the real goal of his school is to create an "enduring understanding." Sheikh Yusuf is a tall and skinny man with a neatly trimmed beard. He has a kind smile and always wears a small cap on his head. We were meeting in the Islamic Studies department office, a crowded room full of books, with posters of mosques on the wall. He told me how former graduates had gone on to schools like Columbia and MIT and "slipped a little into this dominant culture [yet] they kept the core aspects of their identity." I asked how, and he said the most important thing was to join with other Muslims, to maintain the required practices of Islam (especially prayer, fasting during Ramadan, and proper gender interactions and coverings), and, finally, to properly distinguish between what is *cultural* and what is *religious*.

"We try to differentiate between the culture and the Islamic rulings, the Islamic principles," he told me. "At the end of the day, this is something they can't compromise. If it's clear and fixed . . . in the Qur'an and hadith, there's little they can do." He moved his hand as if to acknowledge it's complicated: "We teach them to be flexible with the cultures and the existences between the cultures . . . when there are contradictions between the American culture and the Islamic culture . . . ." He gave the example, as he often did in class, of shaking hands with members of the opposite gender: it is not something he thinks is good, but it also creates even more misunderstanding not to do it, so it seems an acceptable compromise with American culture.

Note how Sheikh Yusuf makes Islam and America parallel categories, the first producing religion, the second producing culture.[15] This distinction is something I heard often at Al Amal, especially for teachers who said that the school was more *Arab* than it was Muslim. "That's dangerous," A South Asian English teacher at Al Amal, Sister Yara Qadir, told me:

> People with a little bit of religion are dangerous, it's like people with a little bit of knowledge. It's better to either have a lot or nothing. Because if you have a lot of Islam, if you understand all of it completely, then you would know that a lot of the things the [Arab leaders at the school] worry about are very small and they aren't [in line] with the religion.

Sister Yara felt this was especially the case for rules about the interactions between men and women. She told me about "a group of non-Arabs here at the school, and we talk to each other because it's hard sometimes." Another teacher at Al Amal, a Berber man who taught Arabic, told me, "There's discrimination at this school—like one time the principal said to me in front of the students, you're not an Arab. And I know I'm not an Arab, I'm a Berber, but I speak Arabic, and I teach it, and I'm proud of it. So why would he say something like that in front of the students?"

As was often the case, Sister Yara distinguished her version of Islam from people who are fundamentally mistaken: She said that "a lot of these Arabs don't realize is that what they're advocating, really, it looks a lot like *jahiliyyah*," a reference to pre-Islamic paganism, a harsh though not uncommon charge in Muslim debates. "Some of these men who say things about women, they don't even have a support for it, they have hadiths [accounts of the Prophet's words or actions], but they're not even strong hadiths, they're weak hadiths, and they twist them around to fit their culture . . . ." For Sister Yara, it was her kind of Islam that must win the day: "If Islam is going to work here, it's going to be our kind of Islam, which is the real Islam. And the thing is, the thing they forget, is we're not just inventing a new Islam, that's how it really was. It's not like we're changing Islam to move it to work for America." This claim, that American Islam is the authentic, *essential* Islam, is a common one well established in recent work on American Muslims.[16]

That is not to deny that America can be a threat. One of my interviews at Al Amal was with a Pakistani-American senior named Farhad. He told me that it's "becoming such a trend for Muslims to mix Islam with American ideologies . . . so I think to be able to keep yourself pure from all that, it's difficult because it's so easy to mix with them." When I asked Farhad what he meant, he became a bit more reflective, telling me there was more of a commitment to gender equality in America, which is "one thing in America that should be applied to Islam," though he then quickly corrected himself: "not Islam, to Muslim countries because they're missing that." Farhad's self-correction is interesting, because it reveals an overarching commitment to Islam itself being beyond reproach. When Muslims are doing things wrong, it is because of their culture (or their countries) rather than their religion. The accidents are cultural; the essence is religion.

In an interview with Brother Yaqub Rahman, the junior Islamic Studies teacher at Al Haqq, he told me that when students distinguish Muslims from Americans,

> I always jump in and say, "All right, what are you?" And that was the first thing I began my class with this year. And then some of them were kind of like in denial. They're like, "No I'm not American. I'm Palestinian." And then I would ask them, "What's your favorite food?" "Oh pizza and burgers." And then I would tell them, "Do you speak English or Arabic better?" "English." And then they kind of realized wait a second I am more American than I am Palestinian or Pakistani or whatever.

Yaqub is Palestinian, and the distinction hit home for him, telling me a story I heard from many second-generation immigrant teachers and students: "I mean it's very difficult. Like when I used to go to Palestine a lot of people would be like, 'Oh you snobby American.' So I wouldn't fit in there. And when you come here everyone's like, 'Oh you Arab terrorist.' So okay, I don't fit in here either. Where am I supposed to go?"

Brother Yaqub's beard and skin color marked him as a potential "terrorist." And this leads to another kind of boundary, no longer about how Muslims distinguish between "American" and "Muslim" and between "culture" and "religion" but rather how non-Muslims distinguish Muslims from other Americans, or, only somewhat less problematically, between the good Muslims and the bad Muslims.[17] Radi, a senior at Al Amal, related an experience similar to Brother Yaqub's: "One thing is the media. I'm a brown person . . . so for the media most terrorists are brown. I've got somewhat of a beard and most likely, if someone sees me, they'll probably—they'll know I'm a Muslim. They can easily just categorize me as a terrorist."[18] If the Muslims I worked with wanted to make the case that the American essence could include Islam, they felt that too many other Americans wanted to make the case that the Islamic essence contains terrorism. Indeed, this was a source of constant frustration for Brother Yaqub, a religion teacher at Al Haqq who hated the phrase "moderate Islam": "When you say moderate Muslim," he told students who would describe themselves that way in class, "what you're saying is that Islam in its full form is dangerous. And that's not true. Islam in its full form is peace. It's joy."

In a similar way, women who wore the hijab told me they often felt profiled and stereotyped before they ever talked to anyone. In an interview with Sister Jannat Shadid, a science teacher at Al Haqq, she told me, "I walk in the room as a hijabi . . . I have to prove that I'm not a terrorist. I mean, that's what they see. They see a hijab, they link us to 'them' and then they link it to terrorism." Sister Jannat went on: "So as a Muslim, it's trying to prove that I'm an American . . . I feel that in today's society, it's hard to be an American Muslim and feel that they [non-Muslim Americans] look at you as a member of society." While many of the students were quite young in 2001, Sister Jannat remembered the moment as consequential. "Pre 9/11, you felt like you were American. They didn't look at you and say are you Muslim? Okay you're not American. Post 9/11, you're a completely marginalized group, you feel like you have to prove yourself, prove your innocence, and until then you're completely guilty."

Note how the experience of 9/11 not only further bounded Sister Jannat from the rest of America, but it also made the hijab a boundary marker against her will, giving it a meaning she did not intend. There is a kind of unintended semiotics here, with the hijab intended to communicate one thing (religiosity, devotion) and then being read another way (extremism, terrorism), a process that has led some Muslims women to stop dressing in identifiably "Muslim" ways even if they wish they could, while others have chosen to wear the hijab as an explicitly political claim meant to counteract the stereotype.[19] For Sister Jannat, her hijab links her to something fundamental in her religious identity. Yet for other Americans, the hijab is also an essential marker but of something very different: a hijab indexes terrorism instead of religion, patriarchy instead of devotion. It remains an essential rather than accidental symbol—the hijab is much more symbolically important than, for example, the socks—yet the meaning of the symbol is entirely contested. Both sides agree the boundary matters, but they disagree fundamentally about its meaning, about what is essential and what is accidental.

Despite all of this, people at both Muslim schools were generally optimistic about the possibility of integration into the American mainstream. In interviews, students told me about important Muslim leaders and athletes or the recent election of a Muslim U.S. representative: "I do think it's gonna get better," one senior at Al Haqq told me. "There's . . . more people getting into government. The more we have people in office, the more people are going to know that we're fine. We're peaceful people. It's just a religion just like any other religion."

While this student compared Islam to "any other religion," the dominant metaphor of progress I heard was more often ethnic than religious, perhaps again showing the importance of an ethno-racial framing in shaping how both non-Muslims and Muslims themselves view Islam in America. In addition, the framing might have shared in a teleological model of American integration, rooted in how once-minority religions, like Jews and Catholics, become American by gaining the full rights of whiteness.[20]

For example, one Friday in early February, a Black man whose father had marched with Martin Luther King Jr. gave the *khutbah* (sermon, homily) at Al Amal. He called Muslims "the new Negroes today. As Muslims we have our own civil rights struggle." I looked at Brother Naguib during the *khutbah* and could see that he was uncomfortable. A Black man from the West Indies, Brother Naguib Faizan sometimes lamented to me in private how students made jokes about each other's race, often mocking a student for being dark-skinned. He came up to address the students after prayer was completed: "He made the comparison between—he used the word [Negroes] and I will not—Africans here in America and the Johnny-come-lately Muslims today." It is noteworthy that, like many post-65 immigrant Muslims—even people coded as "Black"—Brother Naguib did not reference the long-standing tradition of Black Islam in the United States.[21]

He went on, "We now have our own civil rights struggle, and because it is February, [it is] a time when we remember the example of African Americans in our country and the example of Martin Luther King—who [the imam]'s father marched with." Brother Naguib used the example of movements for *racial* justice as a model for a religious group's integration into America, a rhetorical move that perhaps recognizes the racialization of Islam in the United States. Yet Brother Naguib's comparison also obfuscates the experience of Black Muslims before the "Johnny-come-lately" immigrant Muslims and implies a kind of "color-blind ideology"[22] in his insistence that Black civil rights struggles have achieved a level of justice that immigrant Muslims could now also achieve.

A color-blind ideology refers to a specific way of thinking about and describing race and racism. It emphasizes a lack of explicit, interpersonal racism and looks for cultural and personal excuses to describe and legitimate racial inequality and marginalization. A similar color-blindness can sometimes be seen in recent immigrant Muslims' approach to Black Americans, including Black American Muslims.[23] In a similar way, a guest speaker at Al Amal's graduation urged students on their way to college, "As Muslim Americans, we have to represent ourselves . . . we have to do what the Italians, Irish, and African Americans all did before us, we have to challenge those stereotypes . . . for some people when you say Muslim, it means terrorist, and we have to challenge this." This guest speaker puts Black Americans in the same categories as Italians and Irish, a common move in color-blind ideology, making it possible to deny the central role of anti-Black racism in American history and using other stories of "ethnic uplift" to blame Black Americans for their marginalization. As such, when Principal Naguib described how the American dream once applied to the Irish and Italians and now it applies to Muslims, he implies a "teleology of racial progress" not only for Black Americans but also for increasingly racialized Muslims.[24]

It is also worth noting that, again, a Muslim identifies how they are marked as "terrorists," this time even by the very name of their religion. Both the hijab and the word *Muslim* thereby become sites of contestation. What do they actually index? What do they actually represent? A certain kind of social performance is thereby deemed necessary to "challenge" these "stereotypes," one that shifts, in this case, the relationship of terrorism to Islam from one of essence to one of inaccuracy or, at worst, accident.[25]

An anger at these stereotypes came to a head at Al Haqq, when it was revealed in the news that the New York Police Department had been spying on local Muslim groups. In one of Brother Yaqub's junior boys' Islamic Studies classes, he read a line from one of the police reports: "This is the 4th time a boy is praying today—it looks suspicious." The students all laughed, given that all Muslims are required to pray five times a day.

A boy said, "It shows how little people know about Islam."

Brother Yaqub was incredulous and visibly annoyed that day, an interesting shift given his usual neutral affect. While in most classes it was the students who did the talking, Brother Yaqub dominated discussion that day: "How is praying five times a day or putting your foot in a sink [required washing before prayer] in any way suspicious?" he asked. The conversation went on for some time, and one boy said, "Islam is growing, maybe they're saying we should keep them down."

"What is an American?" replied Brother Yaqub, his voice slightly raised. "Who is they? You're saying us and they. We're just as American as the blond haired, blue-eyed white guy who works for the NYPD."

Later in the conversation, Brother Yaqub said, "Whenever I go to a public school to talk about Islam, someone always asks about terrorism."

Ahmed, a very skinny short boy asked, "They don't ask about hummus?" The students laughed.

"Hummus is Arab, it's not Muslim," said another boy.

"No hummus is Muslim," said a third boy. Everyone laughed.[26]

Christian Schools

At the Christian schools, there was a similar worry about the relationship between America and the culture at large. Yet despite suffering more mistreatment and outright stereotypes, the Muslim schools were generally more optimistic about their capacity to make it in America: their worries about the outside world were about temptations and danger. In contrast, the Christians worried about war. I sometimes heard references to *jihad* at the Muslim schools, but really only in reference to internal struggle ("the greater jihad" as it said on the wall of one of the classrooms at Al Amal). Similarly, while Islamic theologians sometimes refer to Muslims living in non-Muslim countries as those living in a *dar al-harb* (land of war), I never heard this reference in the Muslim schools, perhaps reflecting Mucahit Bilici's insistence that American Muslims are gradually making the United States a *dar al-Islam* (land of Islam).[27]

In contrast, talk of battle was common at both Christian schools. Some referred to "spiritual warfare," or battles with Satan and demons, but secular society was just as much an enemy and often described as Satan's unwilling accomplice. The stakes were nearly always global and catastrophic: in a film in the "senior worldview" class at Good Tree, a large picture of Darwin was placed next to Hitler (a quite common link in these communities), and Good Tree's superintendent warned a community meeting that "Darius to Daniel, Hitler, Lenin, Mao—they stole their minds first. Look at China and the cultural revolution—they stole their minds first." At both of the Good Tree graduations I attended, the principal, Brenda Forrest, had students return to their parents to be "commissioned":

> There's a war going on out there, and it's a war we're sending these graduates out into. It's a battle in the spiritual realm that's lasted thousands of years, and nowhere is the battle raging more than in college campuses. You learned about this in your Worldviews class—it's a clash between the Christian worldview and the other worldviews out there. And so today, just like how in an ROTC commissioning, the parents pin a medal on their son and daughter, so now we ask all of you parents to pin the same insignia on your children so they can be a light for Jesus Christ wherever the battle takes them . . . they've been training for battle all their lives but now they're entering it.

At that graduation ceremony and in the one the following year, speakers mentioned three young Israelites in the Babylonian Captivity who "refused to bow" to a graven image provided by King Nebuchadnezzer (Daniel 3). The first year, when the speaker mentioned them—Shadrach, Meshach, and Abednego—I noticed the principal and students whispering the names to themselves. These three men were sentenced to burn alive in a furnace for their obstinacy, yet they escaped without even the smell of smoke on them. So, claimed many speakers and a visiting preacher at *Apostles*, would be the province of those who were strong in battle. And yet, as the Good Tree superintendent made clear in his speech about the Babylonian Captivity, Daniel was also respected for his adherence to laws and found success in a nation with different rules by being true to his God. Some integration is not impossible, yet Christians should always be on their guard.

The graduation at Apostles was much less focused on the difficulty of being a part of the outside world, perhaps because, unlike Good Tree, they admitted non-Christian students. Nonetheless, Tomas Lopez, the senior and junior Bible teacher, regularly told his classes, "if you're a Christian, the world is against you, like *literally* the world is against you!" The war metaphors were part of a school drama as well: during a talent show, a dance routine set to the high-energy soundtrack of an action movie had regular people being imprisoned by sin and then Jesus coming out in white and fighting them all away.

That hostility had much to do with cultural politics. I asked Bill, a senior at Good Tree, about Christianity in the United States as part of our tape-recorded interview. He told me that the United States is "an in-creasingly hostile environment and increasingly repressive." Yet things are better than in Europe, he said, admitting that "basically America is the last place where a conservative has a strong hold."

I said it was "interesting that I asked you about Christians and you started talking about conservatives."

"Yeah," he responded. "I mean, a lot of the conservative principles are derived from a Christian basis, so there's a lot of conservative principles that aren't really Christian, but . . . " He went on to defend why abortion was central to Christian political identity.

Another Good Tree senior, Kristy, agreed. A popular student leader with a big smile and confident, careful diction, she said, "This nation was founded on the Lord and now we're kicking Him out of everything . . . " Kristy said she often felt discouraged by "the antagonism" but she reminds herself that she is "still part of America": "I am still a citizen. I ought to be standing up for what I know is right. And just because everybody around can be falling into the world until the breaking point doesn't mean that I have to." She said that Adam Morgan's Worldview class really opened her eyes to the problems in the world, making her want to get more politi-cally involved. She acknowledged that no political party is the perfect rep-resentation of Christianity, "but . . . I'd say from a Christian standpoint it's the safest and the most logical rational way would be to stand for things like life and marriage. Like the values that we really know that God wants upheld based on the Bible."

Yet not everyone was as ambitious or as knowledgeable as Kristy. I asked a lot of students in interviews about politics in the schools. The words of one of Good Tree's junior boys, Sam, is representative. Sam is a tall white boy, with an athletic build and short blond hair. When I asked him about political discussion at the school, he told me "it definitely comes up every once in a while . . . you'll listen and you'll hear somebody say some-thing . . . I know I've heard like a lot of anti-Obama and, you know, stuff like that . . . . But, like, it's really not something we've ever talked about, like in a class." I asked if he identified as being political and he said that his family is Republican and that his parents had recently watched the Republican pri-mary debates for the 2012 presidential election. "But you know," he added, "we'll have different conversations and it doesn't impact, not impact but it doesn't really strike me or it doesn't really interest me very much, as much as it does the rest of my family." I asked who his family was then supporting for president in the Republican primary, and he said he didn't know.

Even if explicit governmental efforts were not described in class, there was nonetheless an ongoing education in the culture war. Mr. Joe Smith, the sophomore Bible teacher, was a charismatic and enthusiastic part of the school community, a warm presence who was always happy to have me in class. We had many wonderful conversations and he was, in the kindest way possible, somewhat concerned about the status of my Catholic soul. As a weekly assignment, he had students look up information about "Christian contemporary issues," in which they bring a copy of an article about a Christian issue and write a summary of the issue. The section of the class, every time I observed it, generally focused on three themes, in roughly the following order: most commonly, American culture war skirmishes, especially about the marginalization of traditional Christianity; followed secondly by the persecution of Christians in Muslim-majority countries; and finally feel-good stories about Christians doing well in the world. This order of things, for what it is worth, is not altogether dissimilar from various conservative Christian websites, radio programs, and television shows.

In an interview later, he told me that he gives the assignment to show that just learning about doctrine is not enough: "When you see that believing cost somebody his life *now* in another country, or is costing people a lot of grief in our own country, then it puts flesh and blood to theology. They're thinking, oh these people are putting their neck on the line for what I'm learning in my class." Being a Christian in America is "certainly easier than being a Christian in Iraq right now" but that might change. "Sooner or later," he told me with a world-weariness I heard often in these kinds of conversations, he will have to put his "neck on the line. Will the real Christians please stand up and be counted?"

Mr. Smith linked the persecution of Christians in Iraq to culture war clashes in the United States, arguing that people will eventually be punished in America—even killed—simply for being Christian. I asked if he thought that would happen soon, and he told me it would, largely because of the recent influx of Muslim immigrants. "Just look around. Suddenly, the Christians are browbeaten because there are crosses on buildings. Any other religion or group can practice virtually anything, but a Christian can't. At Christmas, they can't do public things. You can't— it's taken out of public schools. I mean, you can just see it coming right now." I responded that I wasn't saying he was wrong, but I did not understand how his argument worked, as there didn't seem to me to be enough Muslims in America for that to happen, even if all of them were committed to the imposition of a conservative theocracy. I asked him if he was actually more upset about secularism. "Well, Muslim or secular," he told me, "It's going to be anti-Christian."

Mr. Smith's boundary-work here is complex and ornate, separating "real Christians" from cowards who will not stand up for the truth. He also links various "anti-Christian" factions together as almost interchangeable, whether Muslim or secular. There is a sociological process here that is often noted in social-psychological work on boundaries: people link their enemies together and assume they're in cahoots, or, somewhat similarly, they assume that someone their enemy tends to support must also be their enemy.[28] The irony, of course, is that conservative Muslims have more in common with conservative Protestants than at least the latter might be willing to admit. In any case, there is a sense among these conservative Protestants that something essential to America has been lost. If the Muslims I studied were hopeful they might move from exclusion to inclusion, the Christians worried they had been moved from inclusion to exclusion, from an essential characteristic of America to an embarrassing accident.

Besides relative optimism about the American project, the other important difference between the Muslim schools and the Evangelical schools was race. There were obviously differences of racial identity, not least because Islam is itself racialized, but also because the Muslim schools were dominated by Middle Eastern and South Asian teachers and students. Yet it is not as though the Christian schools were entirely white: Apostles had a minority of white students (even if the majority of the faculty was white), and Good Tree also had a much smaller percentage of white students than is representative of the broader United States, even if it was roughly equivalent to its fairly diverse suburban area.

However, even if these Christian schools were not linked by particular racial identities, they were linked by a particular racial *ideology,* one that privileges the white experience of the United States as the relative baseline—what Sarah Ahmed has called an "institutional whiteness."[29] Scholars of American Evangelicalism have found similar racial ideologies in racially diverse Christian churches led by white pastors,[30] and while there has not yet been work on how such processes are reproduced in white-led Christian schools, I found similar processes in the schools I studied. Race was often simply not mentioned, and when I asked about race in interviews, students—including the students of color—emphasized how everyone basically got along.

I asked a few Black students at Good Tree about how they felt about race relations at the school, and most told me something along the lines of what I heard from Lana, a Black junior girl working in the school office with a friend on the seniors' graduation video. "Yeah, but we get along with everybody," Lana told me. I was working on my day's field notes and brought up that I saw the Black kids sitting together at the lunch table most days. The white girl working with her on the project, Ruth, said, "Wait, you all sit together? I never noticed that." "Yeah, we do," said Lana. There was an awkward pause and they went back to working on their video. This racial ideology—a combination of institutionalized whiteness and color-blind ideology—was almost never acknowledged, and neither, at least that I observed, were explicit discussions of race, except occasionally in Mr. Morgan's class. In both his lectures and the students' class presentations, when racial inequality did come up, it was described as the result of cultural and personal deficiencies rather than structural and historical causes.

To the extent race came up in my interviews, it inevitably intermixed with politics. I interviewed a white pastor in the Good Tree community who had a child at the school. In our meeting, Pastor Daniel told me that Evangelical Christians were *definitionally* conservative: "You've got conservatives, Evangelical Christians all on one side and the other side is exactly the same, you've got the liberals to the left. The Democratic Party has a different vision of what ought to be. Really those are 180 degrees out." When I asked about liberal Christians' commitment to the poor, Pastor Daniel did something that often happened at Good Tree when I brought up issues of economic justice. Nobody explicitly disagreed with me; instead they would emphasize that abortion, marriage, and other culture war problems are more important issues, that government aid actually just makes poverty worse, and, finally, that the real problem is souls. He lamented that there were some in his church, "especially those women who come from a minority background," who might acknowledge abortion as a "concern" but who believe "the Republican candidate doesn't care about the poor."

Pastor Daniel said he was not sure that was true about Republicans, but the more important point is a question of priority: "As bad as it is that people are starving to death—again going back to priorities, what is the priority? Temporal suffering, how does that compare to eternal suffering?" He worried about a recent book by Rob Bell that doubted whether God would ever send anyone to Hell. Mr. Smith often told me something similar at Good Tree, urging me to declare my belief in God in exactly the right way, a subtle distinction that might be my difference between Heaven and Hell. Which is quite the boundary. Yet this focus on souls and heaven can also allow Christians to look past not only economic injustice but also racial inequity.

Politics at Apostles were similarly conservative. They also extended a suspicion of liberals' rhetoric on race, though they also move into the slightly more paranoid. Tony Dominguez, himself a Latino pastor and also the freshman religion teacher, told me he was suspicious of some of his students' love of Barack Obama. "Do you think it's right to vote for a Black man just because he's Black?" he asked me when we ran into each other at the school's evening academic fair. He initiated the conversation on politics, eager to hear what I thought, and I would come to learn his suspicion of Obama was an important issue for him, a concern he discussed with his students and with other teachers.

In one of Mr. Lopez's senior classes at Apostles, a girl asked, "Isn't Obama Christian?" The teacher looked thoughtful. "He's a freemason as far as I know."

"Eeeeeee!" exclaimed the student, smiling in shock. She looked quite surprised.

"Obama as far as I know is a freemason. Does that mean that Obama worships the devil, that Obama is an Illuminati, that Obama is going to hell? That I don't know." He told his students "the perception" is that "in most industrialized countries, most of the leaders of these countries are freemasons."

Mr. Lopez manages to hedge his quite common claims about freemasons by often referring to "perceptions" about them—that they worship Satan and control much of the world, among other things—and by simply repeating what students say. "How many of you have ever heard of the new world order?" he asked his students in another class. He fielded a few responses and then answered his own question: "They're trying to bring the world under one leader, one currency, one everything." In my interviews with students at Apostles, many of them were not entirely sure about these claims and, at any rate, they thought Mr. Lopez spent too much time on them rather than actually getting to a systematic study of the Bible.

Both Mr. Lopez and Mr. Dominguez, the Apostles freshman and sophomore religion teacher, were especially worried that President Obama was going to force everyone to get a computer chip in their body that would track all of their moves. "If you don't wear the chip," Mr. Lopez warned his students, "you cannot buy anything or do anything, you cannot go to the doctor because they cannot scan you if you do not have this."[31]

Some in the class disagreed or worried this sounded too extreme. A few students complained to me about this in interviews as well. Nonetheless, one freshman boy told me in a taped interview, "Mr. Dominguez told us about the chip. It's something like the mark of the beast." He told me he thought the chip would be implemented with the rollout of Obamacare. Another student said in Mr. Lopez's class that Obama is probably not the antichrist, "per se" but he is the "set-up man" with the antichrist not far behind. I asked Mr. Dominguez about it and he said,

I mean somebody gave me a pamphlet today that said that the chip that's going to be out there is going to be barcoded with 666 on it. I mean where did they get that information? . . . I can be a radical Christian and be like, yes, this is the mark of the beast, they want to put it in your hand . . . . I mean it just—the list goes on and on and on. Is it technology that can develop into something? Yes. So I don't think it's something that you should just laugh off and say, aw, it's just another advance in technology . . . . What form is it going to take? Because it's very real and it's very true . . . I don't want to be forced by the government to do anything. I still believe in my right to do certain things.

Note his use of the word *still*, referencing a long-lost time, now under threat, when there was freedom, a possible predictor of Trump's "make America great again" mythology. In any case, what matters is an essential difference these teachers identified from the rest of America: America, they argued, is no longer a Christian nation, and it is vulnerable to grave dangers its Christians must steer it against.

CONCLUSION

In a wide-ranging (though untaped) conversation with Sheikh Yusuf at Al Haqq, he told me that the biggest challenge for his students was "the neg-ative culture around them." I asked him to elaborate: "I know their families are Muslims, but the dominant culture is affecting them everywhere, the time they log onto the Internet, the movies they watch, their phones, iPods, iPads, all this new media . . . " Hence, for Sheikh Yusuf, the impor-tance of a Muslim school.

And indeed, this was the reason for all four of the schools: they sought a space in which they could conserve something essential in their students, looking to bound themselves away from the outside world. Their primary distinctions were from public schools, those places of instruction right in the middle of secular America. Despite this negative culture, Sheikh Yusuf was not especially worried about any of his students abandoning Islam. He said it was "very rare" for a student to leave Al Haqq and then renounce Islam completely, even if some had significantly decreased their levels of commitment. Similarly, Brother Yaqub, also a religion teacher at Al Haqq, told me, "We don't worry about people not believing in Islam. The problem is the practice of Islam . . . as a youth teacher, I don't re-member getting a question about . . . people doubting their faith; it's al-ways about practice." I have no way to verify these assertions as empirical claims, but this idea was generally shared at the Muslim schools: nobody seemed altogether worried their students would stop being *Muslim*; the concern was instead about *how* they would be Muslim: whether they

would pray, wear hijab, fast during Ramadan, keep halal, and other required practices.

I think there are at least three possible explanations for this relative optimism in contrast to the Evangelical schools, where teachers constantly
lamented—often to the students themselves—that many of them would
eventually stop being Christian. First, Islam in America is racialized and
turned into an ethno-racial category, making it harder to stop being
Muslim even if you wanted to, in a manner somewhat similar (though obviously not identical) to how hard it is to stop being a Jew. Second, and
also like Judaism, Islam is rooted in specific bodily practices that are relatively autonomous from (even if related to) beliefs: keeping practices is
a more meaningful indicator of identity than being wholly convinced by
doctrines. In contrast, for American Evangelicals, the practice of belief is
by far the most important piece: if you struggle with your beliefs, then in
many varieties of American Evangelicalism your identity is itself called into
question.[32] This makes the existential dilemmas of every teenager trying
to work out what it all means much more troubling for young conservative
Christians.

Finally, and relatedly, there is a subcurrent of Calvinist predestination
in much Evangelical Christianity, meaning that in some sense it is not altogether surprising that certain people fall away. Maybe they were simply
unchosen. Of course, nobody at the Christian schools was ever so cavalier
about the perils of predestination, yet there were occasional references to
God's mighty sovereignty and the signs of chosenness at both schools, especially Good Tree.[33] Interestingly, the concepts of fate and God's sovereignty are also quite important in Muslim theology,[34] but neither Sheikh
Yusuf nor anyone else I encountered much emphasized this matter, with
the importance exception that "if God wills it" (inshallah) seemed to be
said about every ten minutes. People at the Muslim schools, like people
at the Christian schools, were much more concerned about surviving "the
culture." The difference was that the Muslim schools were generally more
optimistic about their students' capacity to do so.

Part of the reason for that optimism might also have something to
do with how these schools bounded themselves from the rest of their
country. All of the schools distinguished themselves from public schools,
emphasizing their safety and compassion in comparison to the danger and
indifference they said characterized public schools. Yet in a broader sense
of national politics, the schools were quite different. The Muslim schools
emphasized that the supposedly essential differences from them and the
rest of America were often simply errors (Muslims are not terrorists) or
accidents—things, like the hijab, that do not have to mean what people

think they mean. In contrast, the Christian schools agreed that there was something essentially different between them and the rest of secular America. They worried that America was moving away from the essential truth of Christ toward a secular worldview that was not so much an accident as a grave and essential error.

CHAPTER 3

ↀ

Differently Differentiating Gender

INTRODUCTION

Jenny Huang is an Asian American girl who won just about every award at
Good Tree's graduation—best at science, best at math, all around student
leader, and on and on. She was friendly, unpretentious, popular, and on
her way to one of the best universities in the country. In her valedictory
address, she listed her favorite Disney princesses, giving them as examples
of the love a Christian school might encourage, a love she and her fellow
graduates would need as they entered a secular world. "What does true
love look like?" she asked. "Disney princesses know best. We should be
like Belle, and study hard, learning everything there is to know about the
Lord. We should be like Cinderella, and work tirelessly without expecting
approval, and we should be like my hero Mulan"—the students applauded
and laughed—"and break the world's mold for you and fight for the glory
of your true Father."

Jenny's speech could be read as yet another example of Evangelical patriarchy. She extols a movie genre less famous for its feminists than for
its damsels in distress; she insists that everyone ought to serve some oth-
erworldly deity who happens to be male. Jenny's comments to me about
family life add to the case. At lunch one day at Good Tree, I asked a group
of senior girls what they thought about marriage, and the girls all said they
wanted a man who would be their leader, hoping they would have the humility to let him run their household. I told them I simply found that hard
to believe: these were impressive girls, the leaders of their school, and they
hardly seemed the types who would give up their autonomy. Jenny found

Agents of God. Jeffrey Guhin, Oxford University Press (2021). © Oxford University Press.
DOI: 10.1093/oso/9780190244743.001.0001

me later that day and said she had been thinking about our conversation. It's a problem of sin, she told me, referring back to Eve, that first woman who did not do what she was told. People don't listen. Even more importantly, it is the outside world that pressures women to go beyond their proper role, their necessary humility. As has been described in much sociological work on gender, women's lives and actions were themselves the boundaries of communities. Communities know they are different based on what their women do.[1]

Yet, women were to do quite a lot in these schools, both conservative and not. These girls were very much the products of the American middle class, interested in upward mobility and the tokens thereof. At each of these schools, I found that women's behavior served as an essential indication of their difference from the rest of the world, but with a key difference: at Good Tree (and, to some degree, Apostles), the essential difference was what women believed, especially about feminism. At the Muslim schools, the essential difference was what women did, especially in terms of what they wore and how they interacted with men. Women, in each case, were the basis of distinction: but the schools differed in their views and their practices of women's difference.

DIFFERENT WAYS TO DIFFERENTIATE

Jenny's concerns about her own ambition were not unique. Many of the female students I met at all four schools were impressive leaders who did not seem remotely interested in obeying their male peers. Yet, in different ways, there was pressure at all four schools that female students would, eventually, mind their husbands. That pressure varied in intensity between and within the schools, and it was most pronounced at Good Tree. The resolution is simple enough for Evangelical theology: husbands lead the home, and men lead the church, but males need not lead every social interaction.[2]

In many ways, the Evangelicals at Apostles—and the Muslims at Al Haqq and Al Amal—lived out what Sally Gallagher and Christian Smith call *symbolic traditionalism* and *pragmatic egalitarianism*: women do many of the things that might constitute leadership, but both these women and the men in their lives claim that it is the men who are *really* in charge. While younger generations of American Evangelicals are more ambivalent about these distinctions, at the Evangelical schools I studied there was still a real commitment to opposing feminism via a commitment to male leadership.[3] "Feminism" here is itself an important symbol, representing less the actual intellectual movement and more the changes in gender roles and gender expectations such a movement has been said to have brought about.[4]

Christians' boundary with America was situated at least ostensibly in what women do, yet it was subtler than that: it was what *we say* about what women do. That does not mean their boundary was only cognitive: saying is very much a form of doing.[5] Yet what was *essential* to the boundary at Good Tree kept to an old Evangelical commitment to interiority:[6] what matters is what one believes, and what is practiced (declaring your opposition to feminism) must be an accurate representation of what is inside (a real commitment to the "scriptural" model of gender). As this chapter and the next reveal, these beliefs have real effects, so they are by no means "only" symbolic; as activists and sociologists have long argued, symbols have real power.

The Muslim schools were pragmatically egalitarian in quite different ways. For them, the key concern was their students' gender separation and self-presentation, especially the girls but the boys as well. Yet these decisions were always framed to me as freely chosen,[7] going back to very old commitments within Islam about not forcing religious commitments, and dovetailing with long-standing American ideas about voluntarism in day-to-day life and in religious experience.[8]

Part of the explanation for that difference goes to the schools' different histories. As R. Marie Griffith shows in her recent book, questions about gender and sexuality—abortion, divorce, women's careers, birth control, and LGBTQ issues—have been central points of contention between conservative Protestants and their liberal antagonists. Conservative Protestants actually divorce at rates broadly similar to the rest of the country if not sometimes more often. Devoutly religious conservative Protestants are often less likely to have premarital sex, yet the difference from the rest of the world—while significant—is by no means absolute. But, at least in the schools I studied, what these Protestants *say* about gender and sexuality differs significantly from what one more often hears in secular schools.[9] Evangelicals' history of proclamation means their boundaries take on a different character, formed by opposition to ideas as itself a key practice over and above the more explicitly embodied practices of gender and sexuality.

The history of the Muslim schools I studied was somewhat different. These communities were full of immigrants' children and immigrants themselves, people who had brought certain traditional practices to America. As studies of immigrant religion have shown, recently arriving religious groups can become *more* conservative than they were in their countries of origin, especially regarding gender and sexuality.[10] Yet how that conservatism plays out can vary widely. While it was never described this way to me, it seemed as though hijab and gender separation could be interpreted by some conservative Muslims as a means of protecting women in the work force from crossing too far over to the side of secularism. Feminism is fine as long as it's a *Muslim* feminism, and what makes that feminism Muslim is a commitment to certain distinctive gender practices.

It's worth acknowledging here—as I did in the introduction—that these practices are not necessarily representative, especially not for American Muslims. There are American Evangelicals who call themselves feminist, and only four in ten American Muslim women wear the hijab. As I will describe further below, it also bears repeating here that many Muslims do not consider the hijab patriarchal, often including the Muslim women who wear hijab themselves. Additionally, this book is about private religious schools whose entire reason for existence, at least in some sense, is to be more conservative than everyone else. The question is what they are supposed to be conserving. For the Evangelical schools, it was ideological commitments practiced through acts of declaration, and for the Muslim schools it was a separation of genders and way of dressing.

This difference between the Muslim schools and Evangelical schools is about class as much as anything else. While the parents at the Christian schools were middle class as well, there were many more professional parents in the Muslim schools. As long as a Muslim pharmacist wears the hijab, that practice can be interpreted in a variety of ways. It is hard to interpret not being allowed to work outside the home as anything but patriarchy, but the hijab and gender separation can serve an important double function: they can simultaneously allow patriarchs to believe they are maintaining male dominance while allowing others to believe Muslim women are maintaining these practices for entirely different reasons.[11] A hijab, in this case, is simultaneously patriarchal[12] and feminist. Until an argument erupts, it can simply exist in the tension, a Schrodinger's cat neither alive nor dead. And even when there is disagreement, as long as the practices are aligned, a Muslim commitment to freedom of interpretation and a lack of compulsion puts much less emphasis on *right interpretation* than one might find in the Evangelical schools.

FEMALE DOMESTICITY AND MALE LEADERSHIP
The Muslim Schools

I interviewed a senior girl at Al Haqq named Amar Raad, and she told me that there are "some people" who think Muslim women "are just supposed to be married and stay home and please her husband." Amar is half-Pakistani and she has a big laugh. She told me her mom is a radiologist who took some time off to raise her children but will go back to work soon. "I don't necessarily think it's wrong for you to stay home all the time," Amar said, "but for me personally, I don't want to stay at home." I asked her if she felt pressure to be a stay-at-home mom and she told me "some people" think Muslim women should temper their ambitions, that wanting to be a politician or professor is "too big": "They think okay, you can become a pharmacist. You can become a teacher." She distinguished her ambitions from those who say women should "wait until your kids are grown." In contrast, Amar said "raising children has to be a mutual responsibility."

Not all girls at Al Haqq agreed with that kind of career ambition. In a taped interview with Leyla, another senior girl at Al Haqq, she told me, "It's very important for the mom, especially, to be at home raising her kids correctly, and how she brings up her family. Like the mom is the central part because she's always with them . . . and the father's always at work obviously to provide for them." Yet this was an unusual position for the girls at Al Haqq, most of whom told me about their plans for ambitious careers, often as doctors, pharmacists, or journalists. Leyla is short and quiet, and she sometimes seemed standoffish in class. I asked her if she felt judged for making that decision, and she said she did: "I mean a lot of people tell me, 'Oh, why don't you want to work? I mean you need something.'" She said this concern is why she is going to college, but she resents people saying she should be independent and not rely on her husband. "Your husband is like the man of the house . . . . Like a woman has her own rights in Islam, whether she wants to stay with her kids or whether she wants to work outside. But I feel like it shouldn't conflict with kids." Like some other girls I interviewed, Leyla told me that if a woman wants to work, she should not have kids.

Leyla's emphasis on women's freedom was something I saw at all four schools, and it paired with a conservative strategy common to Evangelicals and Muslims: rather than insisting women should not have careers because of a lack of capacity, there was instead an argument that raising children was simply too important and that a woman's place was ensuring young children's proper moral development. If a woman is going to have a demanding career, I heard, maybe she should not have children. "A woman has her own rights and decisions, especially in America," Leyla admitted, "[but] when you're going back to Islam . . . the kids are like extremely exposed to everything around them. So it's highly recommended that a woman stays with her kids to raise them." Leyla distinguished "going back to Islam" from

America here, and in a way that shows how, for her, gender roles bound Muslim schools from the rest of America, or, more starkly, America itself.

Leyla's position, while fairly common at Good Tree, was in the minority at Al Haqq, as Leyla herself acknowledged. It was in the minority at Al Amal as well, from what I could gather, though my conversations with students there were less systematic. I met a few girls at the Muslim schools who simply did not want to be parents, though even these students were open to changing their minds. Yet most of the girls with whom I discussed this told me they wanted careers *and* children, and they were not especially worried about being able to do both.

In a taped interview with Al Haqq's assistant principal, Sister Fatima Hanini, I asked her about the girls' career expectations. Sister Fatima was in some ways the heart of the school: always warm and kind, able to move between a joke and an order at a moment's notice. Like a lot of the teachers at both Muslim schools, she spoke with a noticeable New York area accent. She told me that the girls "are more successful than the boys sometimes, because they are much harder workers: more work ethic, more ambitious; very ambitious." She joked about her embarrassment that so many of the girls viewed the local state university as a disappointment. She attributed this change to the professional status of the students' parents, especially the mothers: "A lot of our parents, the mothers are very professional people, very educated people; not just the dads . . . . I can tell you off the top of my head that I think at least 50 percent of our mothers are very professional women, doctors, lawyers, and engineers. You name it." At Al Haqq's graduation, one of the board members addressed the girls: "When you go out there you need to compete in every field with your brothers. Marketing, medicine, and finance, whatever field you choose, you help to break the stereotype that Muslim women in any form are behind Muslim men."

There were exceptions to this openness at both Muslims schools. One of the science teachers at Al Amal, Brother Khalil Moosa, made clear to me he believed it was his duty to ensure the women in his life were dressed appropriately. He's skinny and tall, with a large beard that he told me gives him trouble on his trips to Palestine, where he grew up. We were talking about women's dress, and he paused, interrupting himself. "But the most important thing," he said, gesticulating,

And you should put this in your book!—is that a shepherd will be judged for how he took care of his sheep. So I am responsible for my wife and my daughters. And that is all. . . . There is a story that a woman is taken away by the angels to *jehenna* [hell] and she says, wait take my husband too. And a husband will be taken if his wife is not good, even if he is good."

This emphasis on male responsibility for his wife's behavior was much less common in the Muslim schools than Brother Khalil would have liked. But it was not absent. Indeed, one of the Islamic Studies teachers at Al Amal, Sheikh Khaled Farooq, wrote the following on the board in an Islamic Studies class: "Cooperation in the family: the husband spends on his wife and children and makes sure the children are trained Islamically and live as good Muslims. The mother obeys her husband and takes care of the children and prepares meals and trains her daughters to be good mothers in the future." To be clear, the girls respected Sheikh Khaled but also felt he did not quite understand them: he had studied in Saudi Arabia and did not grow up in the United States. One day, Sheikh Khaled saw me in the hallway and pointed to two female students. He exclaimed, "These two girls have memorized the whole Qur'an. They will bring their entire families to *jannah* [heaven]. Memorizing the Qur'an is not even easy for a man!" The girls thanked him and then looked at me, rolling their eyes and grinning.

Likewise, in all of my interviews with Muslim boys and male teachers, none gave as forceful a claim as Brother Khalil's. A few of the boys said they'd like to have a stay-at-home wife, but none said they would insist upon it or take it upon themselves to ensure her holiness. But then, in the beginning of that same conversation with Brother Khalil, he sighed while telling me his thoughts on the children at Al Amal: "They are lost," he told me, emphasizing how "American" Al Amal's students are. "But you know, as much as it pisses me off, I have to remember they are *kids*. It's the parents' fault."

That does not mean all boys at both Muslim schools were entirely open to female leadership. In a junior Islamic Studies class at Al Haqq, Brother Yaqub was talking to his boys' class about female leaders. "What if I were to tell you today that women can be prophets?" he asked the class, tilting his head as if to acknowledge the provocative nature of the question.

"Brother, I know exactly why not," responded Farid, a short boy with antsy energy. "We learned it from Islamic history that God only picked men."

Brother Yaqub, as usual, was calm and thoughtful in his reply. "I'm not saying I agree with this point. I'm just saying if you learned it in Islamic History, it doesn't mean it's true . . . . Imam Bukhari[13] believed that women could be prophets."

Farid was incredulous. "But is that allowed Brother?"

Brother Yaqub smiled. "You see how defensive he's getting?" he asked the rest of the class. "I'm not saying it's a majority opinion. I'm just saying there are people who disagree."

Farid leaned back as if in shock. "Brother. Prophecy is more fitting to a man."

"Who are you to judge?" asked another boy.

"Who are you?" responded Farid.

Brother Yaqub brought up the example of Miriam [Mary], the mother of Issa [Jesus]. "Did she spread the message?" he asked. "Did she have miracles? I don't want to argue the opinion about whether she's a prophet. I just want to say that . . . Islam is much vaster than 11th-grade Al Haqq. It's a huge, huge scholarly tradition out there, so what I'm trying to say is remember before you speak, there's so much you don't know."

Farid was still unconvinced. "Like women, they can't be leaders of high positions, because they get periods or whatever. That's not, like, their responsibility."

They discussed passages of the Qur'an and hadith [sayings of the Prophet] that seem to ban female leadership, and Yaqub said, "So there was a context to it. Everything has a context. In my opinion, that is not to be taken literally. Because in the Qur'an you have the Queen of Sheeba—"

Another student cut him off. "Does that mean she can't be in charge of a state or even like the president of an MSA [Muslim Student Association]?"

"No, in my opinion, she can be in charge of anything. In MSAs—you get to college, girls are much better than boys. There's more girls than boys . . . . The girls in my opinion are more responsible in this aspect."

"Woah, woah," said many of the boys, exaggeratedly. Some of them laughed. Brother Yaqub went on to invoke me as his witness, telling them, as he did on more than one occasion, that the boys took much longer to get ready for class than the girls. The boys were uncomfortable, continuing to laugh nervously, and the conversation moved on.

This distinction between male and female capacity was common at both Muslim schools, and at the Evangelical schools as well. I got the sense at all four schools that the girls saw a lack of academic focus as more of a stigma than did the boys. While the boys were impressed by the currency of good grades, it was the grades that mattered, and the "professional" presentation of self in the classroom was morally weighted differently for boys than it was for girls. In other words, boys were more rewarded by peer encouragement and less punished by teachers for acting up than were girls. At Al Haqq's graduation, a former religion teacher said that when he would assign a paper, the girls really worried about it, complaining it was too hard and asking for clarification. Meanwhile, the boys wouldn't worry about anything. "I was really impressed by the boys' calm," he said. "The sisters were really freaking out and here the boys were very calm and collected! No problem, brother they told me. I was really impressed! And then a week before the paper was due, I reminded all of them about the paper and the girls were still worried and the boys said, 'Paper? What paper?'" Teachers and parents laughed and nodded their agreement.[14]

Girls won most of the outstanding student awards at Al Amal at their graduation, and a member of the board said, "I'd like to see some of the boys competing here—we're getting whipped here guys!" Later at that graduation, the board promised eventually to have as many boys as girls in the senior year (at the graduation, the ratio was about two to one). Yet to achieve these numbers would be to change significantly why parents put their children into these schools. If the purpose of religious schools is moral formation as much as academic preparation, then the former especially falls differently on girls than on boys. These girls were being trained to protect their own purity and the purity of Islam, but along the way they were becoming leaders. While many of their parents and teachers—both male and female—were thrilled to see a new generation of women lead the community, they were also deeply concerned that women be kept from danger. Brother Yaqub once asked the girls in his junior Islamic Studies class if "parents really send their kids to have knowledge of Islam or is it just for them not to have boyfriends or girlfriends?" Various students answered, "It's both."

At both of the Muslim schools, it was rare to hear anyone using the word *feminist* to describe themselves, though their defense of the hijab often took on a feminist gloss and was pitched in response to feminist critiques. One senior girl at Al Haqq, Sally, told me she explicitly identified as a feminist. Sometimes a bit anxious in class, she had an easy smile and was often in the center of her group of friends. She was frustrated by what she called the school's "gender apartheid"—she told me it was "really stupid"—but she agreed that proper boundaries were important. "I wouldn't go out and hug a guy, and there are certain things I wouldn't talk about with a guy," she said, but that doesn't mean she couldn't be friends with one. She told me she doesn't wear hijab outside of school because she feels that she's "not at that level yet." She went on:

> I'll be quite frank. It's really hard, and just the way people will look at you. It's hard enough being a woman and to add that whole, it's hard enough to be a minority and then be a woman and then wear the scarf, if you screw up . . . that whole profiling of you as a Muslim woman in a scarf, I don't know if I can deal with that right now.

Yet her reasons for not wearing the hijab were rooted more in non-Muslim Americans' judgmental attitudes rather than her own feminist commitments. "I don't think the whole stance is anti-woman," she told me, "because I took a feminist Islamic course." She emphasized to me the importance of the hijab being a woman's own "personal choice" and her central concern was whether it would "hinder her getting a career or getting education." For Sally, it was others' Islamophobia that prevented her from maintaining the practice rather than her own beliefs about it. Whether or not the hijab is feminist is actually less important than whether or not she wears it and how the rest of the world will react.

The Evangelical Schools

Feminism was a bad word at Good Tree, and students were often shocked when I told them there were feminists who thought if a woman freely chose to stay at home and raise her children, that was entirely legitimate.[15] Seniors in Mr. Morgan's Worldview class all had to give a class-length presentation on a controversial topic of their choosing, and a few students (generally girls) always chose "women's role in society." Laura, an outgoing and vivacious girl with a huge laugh, was giving that very talk near the end of my first semester there. Wearing sensible white earrings and black heels, she introduced her topic:

"So my topic is women's role in society . . . this is important for us to talk about because when we get in to college we're going to meet a lot of feminists and we have to be able to defend our belief system. . . . God's word has clear instructions for what he wants us to do . . . . Also, for you guys, I want you to understand what feminism is and that it's not all bad." Laura went on to describe how she discovered two feminisms. There was a "conservative feminism" that she thought was attractive at first, especially because it did not support abortion, but then she "realized that if you're going to call yourself a feminist you might as well stand up for everything feminism stands up for, like lesbianism, abortion, and all of that, so I don't call myself a feminist." She then distinguished feminism from women's rights. "Just because you're not a feminist doesn't mean you don't believe in women's rights . . . a lot of women don't have rights, like Muslim women go through a lot and I don't think their problems should be overlooked."

As was the requirement for all the class presentations for Mr. Morgan's class, Laura presented multiple perspectives and used Bible quotations, presenting a PowerPoint slideshow of "Feminism versus Biblical Truth." She insisted, "We're under the authority of the males in our life—as girls we're under the authority of our fathers and then when we're married we'll be under our husbands—who will run our households." In contrast to feminists, who argue, "words such as vulnerability, modesty, and femininity suggest weakness," Laura argued that "when women were viewed as 'weaker' they were protected . . . modesty demanded the respect of men." Proper gender roles are good for women: "you have men who are masculine and women who are feminine and they help each other—I don't have a problem with a man being bigger and stronger than me. I want someone to protect me." That protection is necessary because "rape increases as feminism reigns in our society; the more women are liberated, the more they become objectified." While it might be tempting to dismiss Laura's argument out of hand, it is important to point out the power and confidence with which she gave her argument: she asserted leadership while also asserting the right to be led. There is a power—and a freedom—in submission.[16]

After the class, Mr. Morgan told me, "That's a topic where you'll really see a wide range of opinions—hers was more center right, but it can go in all directions." Yet, at least among the students and teachers I encountered, what Laura was saying was more or less the consensus opinion. Laura was careful not to come off as judgmental of working mothers: "I don't want you guys to think I'm condemning working women, because I'm not—I'm just saying that it's really hard, and that your children and your family have to be your top priority, and so there's less stress and guilt if you're able to stay at home."

Evangelical gender ideology is often marked by an outright dismissal of feminism and a focus on a woman's role at home.[17] Women in conservative religious subcultures (such as Good Tree) are more likely to hold negative views of feminism, and it remains a complicated empirical question how much those ideologies affect educational attainment, life outcomes, and marital decision making. It does appear to be the case that even if self-identified conservative Christians might not be as conservative as their reputation would lead you to believe, explicitly identifying with a conservative gender ideology tends to have material effects on future economic outcomes, sometimes because of a gap in education due to marrying at an earlier age.[18]

In her study of conservative Protestant gender roles, Margaret Gonsoulin suggests "that women who have intensive views of mothering and conservative ideals about sexuality and reproduction are less likely to perceive the need for educational achievement, but end up earning an income (perhaps a lower income) anyway due to the economic necessities of modern life."[19] An opposition to feminism in Evangelical high schools might seem more "symbolic" and less real-world than the Muslim focus on hijab and gender separation, but those symbols, as sociologists of culture have long taught us, can have powerful effects. To return to Laura's presentation, which I described at the beginning of this section, what is most emblematic about it is the *practice* of claim-making, a key practice of Evangelical Protestantism. All boundaries are at least implicit claims about who *we* are and who *they* are. As such, when Laura verbally distinguishes the good Christians in her community from feminists and those (however well-intended) working women who do their families harm, she is *practicing* a distinction that solidifies what is essential to her community. Perhaps more importantly, she herself then stands, as do other women who critique feminism, as herself a boundary between her community and the outside world. Simply because her practice of distinction is more expicility ideological and practically declarative than the wearing of a hijab does not make her body any less central to her community's distinction, nor her practice any less semiotically meaningful.

These kinds of declarations happen publicly and relationally, as was the case for Laura, but they are perhaps more important as the declarations people tell themselves, or which they relate in accounts about themselves. Annie is a senior girl I interviewed in my first year at Good Tree. She told me that she would prefer to be a stay-at-home mom and that she does not feel judged because of her decision. Like any other student, Annie was wearing the school uniform during our interview, her brown hair pinned up above her head. I asked if she felt that was a common decision at Good Tree, and she said she thinks it's about half and half. She still wanted to finish college because "you don't know what life is gonna bring." When I asked her about a man being the leader in the household, she responded, "I think girls especially our age in households they want to have a man lead the house in a spiritual way . . . . Like the man is the one who . . . ends up praying at dinner or something like that." She made clear that a woman *could* speak when it is time to pray and read the Bible, and "bring up things of God," but she thinks it is the father who should "be spiritually involved in helping their family grow." I asked if that leadership extended to finances or career choices, and Annie said she "didn't see that as much." While she acknowledges that the Bible "says the man is the head of the household and women respect your husbands," she said it's ultimately "biblical for it to be equal . . . . It's not let's go do this, this is the plan, it's we need to work this out together."

Most of the girls I interviewed at Good Tree said they wanted full careers outside of the home, though not as many as at the Muslim schools. However, even the girls at Good Tree who were excited about careers were unanimous in wanting to be home with children when they were small. I interviewed Rebecca, a junior girl at Good Tree in my last quarter there. She spoke with excitement and passion: "I really want to go into a field in psychology and work in either the FBI or in a mental asylum. So I definitely,

I would want to keep on doing that." However, she said it's especially important to be with her children when "they're really little": she worried putting her children in daycare would make her miss their childhood, robbing her of "the most important job in the world": "parenthood." She would then go back to working normally.

Rebecca's hesitation about daycare was echoed both in the Worldview textbook and in Mr. Morgan's lectures. In class one day in my first semester there, he was emphatic:

> This bothers me. I have a neighbor—she's an older woman, and she told me about how infants were brought to daycare and they would spend 6, 8, 10 hours a day at this daycare and they're not from single parent homes, they're from two parent homes, and yet they're just giving their kids to someone else. And this woman told me about how she's having all of this intense bonding—because that's what the kids will do, they'll bond—with someone else's kids. And that's before they're even potty trained! I really like this radio host Dennis Prager, he's not a Biblical Christian, but he's someone I would not hesitate to say you should listen to, and he's someone who is entirely sympathetic to the plight of modern women, but he would say that potty training is the cut-off point, that a woman has to be with her child at least until then."

Note that it is the woman who has to be with the child, rather than simply *a parent*, and note also the potential dangers of bonding with people who are not your parents. As should be clear, an ideological opposition to feminism has real stakes, even when it is simply talk. While "practical egalitarianism" can get conservative Christian women moderately far, it cannot get them all the way to actual egalitarianism. Which, for many, is precisely the point.

One of the most conservative teachers at Good Tree, Joe Smith, told me his church council had thought hard about female ministers.

> A lot of it's cultural, but the problem is that you can't go too far with that, because if everything's cultural then there's nothing there. But we realized that women aren't called—from everything we could see in the scriptures—to positions of leadership in the church over adults. With children it's a different story. But it's funny, because a woman gets up to sing a song right before the preacher, and that's just as moving, so I'm not sure . . . .

In that same conversation, Mr. Smith told me something everyone else at Good Tree told me: Brenda Forrest was doing a great job as principal, and her spiritual talks at school assemblies were excellent. Good Tree later had a female president of the Board of Trustees as well. So what to do with female leaders when society is coming to expect them and they're basically already leading anyway? The principal, I observed, can do what anyone might call preaching, but her community just doesn't call it preaching.

During lunch at Good Tree at my first semester in the school, I talked to a group of senior girls about being submissive to their husbands. Without prompting, Jenny—who, recall, was the valedictorian and en route to one of the top three schools in the country—said, "Sometimes I wonder why women go to college, because we're really not going to need it." Earlier she had said, "One of the reasons I would finish college is because I want to marry a man but you never really know when God is going to send you one, so you have to be ready to live your life in a certain way until that point." As I mentioned in the beginning of this chapter, that same day, Jenny found me in another class. "Mr. G, I've been thinking about why it's so hard for women not to submit to their husbands, and it goes back to Genesis 3—women are always going to try to dominate men, it's part of the fall, and it's a challenge we all have to deal with . . . " Jenny later told me that she struggled with her own ambition. She said that at the National Honor Society induction, Mr. Morgan read her a letter that warned her to be as careful about success in the afterlife as she is about success in this life. Jenny told me that if she realized she had a real talent she would commit herself to it, but she would be careful not to follow the "god of career," which would require her to be single. For Jenny—and for her teachers and peers—there is something *essentially* wrong with feminism, something that puts it in direct opposition to the goals and beliefs of a Christian school.

The boys I interviewed seemed equally wary of female ambition, even if more supportive than some of their elders. As one junior boy, Caleb, told me,

> To be honest, the Bible, it talks about husbands—"Wives, submit yourselves to your husbands." But I don't know how the verse ends, but what I know, like, that verse doesn't mean the wife has to be so humble and, like, down. Like, I have to demand this. There's equality between both of us. So we're equal . . . . So I believe, if my wife wants a job, and she can do it, then I'm gonna let her. I'm not gonna force her, say, "No, I'm the man. I have to bring all the money in the house." No, the Bible says equality between both man and woman. No one's superior. They come together. And it's basically, like, the case, like, if she can get a job, then I'm gonna let her get a job and get a babysitter, you know."

Note that Caleb still puts himself in the position of ultimate authority ("I'm gonna let her") even as he also insists on equality. Note also, as I will discuss in Chapter 5, that it is the Bible that speaks and acts with authority.

Apostles was a slightly different story, and for a few reasons. First, the school was more Pentecostal than fundamentalist in its history, and American Pentecostalism has often shown a greater openness to female leadership.[20] In addition, Apostles is a school in a much more expensive part of the New York City area, making it harder to support a stay-at-home mom for any but the most affluent of families. A Filipina senior named Mahali told me she wanted to have a meaningful career "because in my family it was more of the women who had to take charge, especially because my mom was the only one in her family to come here first. She had to strive and work to be a nurse and she was part of the first wave that came from the Philippines . . . ."

Yet, even if there were far fewer students who told me they expected to be—or to have—a stay-at-home wife, the tension was still there. I interviewed a girl named Samantha, whose dad is a pastor in the Bronx and whose mom is a stay-at-home mother. The dad's church is influenced by Pentecostalism though it identifies as non-denominational. Samantha's mother homeschooled her up until 10th grade, so this was her first year in the school. I asked her if she planned to have a career, and she said, "That's one conflict between me and my dad. [He tells me that] my first duty is to my family. And while it is okay for me to have a career, my career should definitely not interfere or not limit my ability to be a mother or a wife."

"And you disagree with that?" I asked.

"I don't—I disagree and then I agree," she responded. "I think that if you want to be a good mother and a good wife, you definitely should be devoted . . . so I think that if you're going to be a wife and a mother, you definitely should be devoted to your husband and your children because it's a full-time job. I know my mom is—she's a full-time mother."

Yet at the same time, Samantha wanted to be a CIA agent, and she felt confident she would be good at it. "I'm—I think that God gives gifts to people for certain reasons and I—I'm not saying being a wife is a waste but I have a true love for what I want to do and I don't think I should not follow it." Like Annie, the senior girl at Good Tree who wanted to be a stay-at-home mom, Samantha worried it was not really possible to have a career and be a mother. Unlike her father, Samantha thought women *could* have a career in historically male fields, and they could be quite successful (Annie thought that too); yet both shared with an older generation a wariness of working moms.

Apostles, in this sense, was somewhere between the Muslim schools, which seemed quite comfortable with working mothers, and Good Tree, whose adults (even if not all of the students) seemed more ambivalent. In a tape-recorded interview with one of the guidance counselors at Apostles, a Latina woman named Gloria Paloma, she told me that the girls in the school generally all wanted careers. "I mean, the principal and vice principal are both female. All the staff who are here are educated women who, some are married and have kids, but also have a career."

Feminism as a term in itself did not come up in my fieldwork and interviews at Apostles, and there was, in general, a greater openness to female leadership, as described above. As just one small example, in one junior Bible class, a girl asked the teacher, Mr. Lopez, "Does a woman really have to be submissive to her husband?" Mr. Lopez looked uncomfortable. "The Bible's pretty clear, women have to be submissive." The students looked warily at each other, and he quickly added, "But men have to be submissive too. There's nothing in the Bible about forcing." This sort of hedge was much less common at Good Tree. However, there was still, as also described above, a broader tension about what feminism was thought to represent: the autonomy and equality of women, and the degree to which such equality might undermine Biblical principles.

CLOTHING

All of the schools had uniforms for their students. At the Christian schools, these uniforms looked like generic high school uniforms: dress pants, pleated skirts, and collared shirts. At the Muslim schools, the boys' uniforms looked similar, though the girls had to wear *abayas*—baggy full-length dresses that cover a woman's body from ankle and wrist to neck. They also had to wear hijabs that covered their necks and all of their hair, though there was a bit more intensity about covering *all* hair at Al Amal than at Al Haqq: at the latter, I saw hair unproblematically peeking out onto the forehead, something which I saw corrected with quiet whispers at Al Amal. (A minority of students told me in interviews they did not wear hijab outside of school, but most said they did. Few wore abayas outside of school.) The women dressed similarly: the female teachers at both schools wore hijabs, and I would say a majority wore *abayas*, though it varied and I did not keep a precise count. No matter what, all women wore loose clothing, covering their legs and their arms up to their elbows. I saw women and girls wearing makeup at all four schools, though the Muslim schools technically had rules against it, and for each of the schools, makeup was usually quite subtle: a bit of blush and some eyeliner rather than a complete treatment.[21]

Appropriate dress at the Christian schools was a much less salient issue. Boys and girls at both schools got in trouble for not tucking their shirts in, or wearing jeans the color of uniform pants, or else girls might wear their blouses a size too small or roll up their skirts. In other words, the schools ran into the same kinds of disagreements that any American school with uniforms encounters (certainly they were the same at the Catholic all-boys high school I attended and at the Catholic all-girls high school where I taught).

The situation at the Muslim schools was quite different, especially given how important women's dress was within the communities. For some women, the hijab and *abaya* are simply markers of Muslim identity. For others, the hijab is about protecting their purity while helping men to avoid lust. The justification and explanation of the hijab as *autonomous* rather than *patriarchal* extended into boys' discussions as well. In an interview with Rahman Abdelnour, a senior boy at Al Haqq, he told me he

> love[s] the way the women walk around with so much self-respect. They don't need to show off their bodies. They don't need to show off their hair to look good. They know that when they cover themselves, they have that modesty. It feels like—you know, a lot of people think we're oppressing the women, but they're the ones who choose to wear it. They're empowering themselves. They're empowering themselves by saying we transcend physical looks.

This language of the hijab-as-empowerment was ubiquitous at both Muslim schools, and often, as with the quote above, in explicit contrast to claims of gender oppression.[22]

Now, it could be the case that such empowerment language is actually an ideological cover for patriarchy, yet recent work on the role of women in conservative religion makes it more complicated to argue these women (and the men who accompany them) are actually just dupes of a rigged system.[23] For the Muslim women and girls I interviewed, the ultimate proof was an insistence on *choice*.[24] While parents', teachers', and peers' pressure to wear the hijab was often so intense it made such choices difficult to make with real freedom, it was nonetheless the case that virtually everyone agreed choice was important. Even more significantly, *why* women wore the hijab was often left up to them.

While hijab was usually described to me as a question of Muslim identity and modesty, it was also defended as a protection from men. I asked a girl at Al Amal, Leyla, if it might be a man's duty not to treat you badly rather than your duty to wear hijab. She nodded thoughtfully, then responded in a pragmatic tone: "If you know how men are, it's not your job to prevent it, but if you can, why not? If you don't want to be treated like that, don't put yourself in a position to be treated like that. You just have to take care of yourself, and wearing a hijab is taking care of yourself." This was a teenager who did not seem particularly afraid of men or unsure about her ability to find a meaningful career in the workforce. As she understood the situation, she knew what men could be and wore an outfit that took the appropriate precautions.

A hijab is not only about protection from men. It is also about separation from a world where women are first judged (often by men) for their physical beauty. One Al Amal senior, Ghazal, told me that she liked not having to worry too much about what she was going to wear or having to accommodate herself to others' expectations. "I took off my hijab once because we had these people over," she told me. "They wanted to see what I looked like and they were like, oh you're so pretty, and I was like, I wasn't pretty two seconds ago?" I was in the college counselor's office another time, and Ghazal was discussing a recent college interviewer, who had started talking to her about her hijab. "Well, you'll stop wearing it soon enough," she told us he had said.

"That's rude," I said.

"Yeah," said Latifa. "I can't believe he said that."

Ghazal seemed embarrassed. "Well another guy asked me if I got sexually frustrated with that thing on."

Latifa was shocked and tried to get the name of the man who said that so she could make a complaint to his supervisor. Ghazal hedged about not being sure exactly about what he said and the conversation shifted.

The women and girls at the Muslim schools often had this two-pronged response to secular criticisms of the hijab. First, they claimed, these criticisms are bigoted and often linked to other Islamaphobic critiques, like that all Muslims sympathize with terrorism. Second, and perhaps more importantly, the criticisms are oversexualizing, insisting that Muslim women be sexually available in their appearance when they might not want to be. In that sense, being criticized for wearing the hijab is like being criticized for not wearing heels or not putting on enough makeup.

In an interview with Jenna, a sophomore girl at Al Haqq, she told me about how her experience of hijab differed when she wore it at a public school and when she wears it outside of Muslim contexts. She feels unfairly judged, but she also feels like she can gain a level of sexual respect she could not without it. "People look at me different when I wear hijab. I mean it's not always in a positive way but especially . . . when it's in a co-ed place . . . people look at you different. They know that no, I have to have respect for that woman." For her, that respect was worth the dirty looks she might get as well. "I mean like especially in America, the society's so male dominated that they feel that women are such objects . . . .I feel like if you

wear the hijab even though people might not look at you with the best out-
look, they still don't, like, degrade you like that."

By wearing the hijab, Muslim women put themselves at the boundaries
of their communities. Hijabs are often the first things both Muslims and
non-Muslims recognize; like the Jewish yarmulke, an ambiguously ethnic
person can become immediately recognizable as a specific category because of an article of clothing.[25] If I see you wearing a hijab, I might not
know anything about you, but I at least think that I do, in much the same
way that seeing you with a yarmulke or doctor's coat allows me to feel
safe about a few presumptions. In my fieldwork, both Muslims and non-
Muslims believed that what women wear gives them permission to make
assumptions about both those individual women and their communities.
Similarly, *not* wearing the hijab in these schools was often interpreted to
mean only one thing: that this woman was "not yet ready" for what full
Islam requires.

The hijab functioned as a boundary marker and, for many, as an indicator of what is essential in Islam. A teacher at Al Haqq used the hijab as
exactly this kind of metric of devotion: "You look at the parents coming
in, half are wearing hijab. If the family background is not having that *din*
[religion], what can we do?" This use of the hijab as an index of the religious seriousness of both the individual and her community extended to
how one ought to regard the faculty. The same teacher told me, "Even the
school, if you look at all the staff, you're not going to find everyone who's
at the same level of Islam, whether it's the makeup or the dress, you have
some differences." She made clear that prayer was her school's biggest concern, but appropriate gender performance was the second goal: "*Salah* [the
prayer made five times a day] is obviously the most pivotal, all of us know
people who pray all the time, they fast all the time, but they don't wear the
jilbaab [similar to an *abaya*]. Does that mean we're going to knock them
down? No, but they need work."

This pressure shows how complicated the emphasis on freedom becomes
when discussing a woman's choice to wear the hijab. I was talking to a
group of boys at Al Amal, and the subject of hijab came up. A sophomore
boy, Jibreel, said he would "make" his wife wear the hijab, and another
boy asked, "You'd make her?" Jibreel responded immediately, "No, I mean,
I wouldn't make her. It's her choice. But I wouldn't be with a woman who
wouldn't wear hijab." Women are free, but their free choices have real
stakes.

I encountered a particularly intense example of women's dress as a
measure of a community's religious devotion a few months into my fieldwork, sitting in the restaurant across the street from Al Amal. There were

three men, who appeared to be in their 20s, looking out the window at the table next to me. One of them was skinny, wearing a white cloak (or *thobe*) and hat (*taqiyah*). He had a small beard and was light-skinned. Another man with them was wearing jeans and a hoodie, and the last one was wearing a black *thobe*. They were eating their food and talking to each other, none of them being very polite to the older Arab man who worked there. "Is it ready yet?" they asked, impatiently. They didn't thank him. They were speaking in English without accents.

The one in the black thobe said, "I need to find a job. I'm thinking about Radio Shack, but women work there, right?"

"Yeah, there's women there," said the man in the hoodie. "But my cousin runs a garage, maybe he could find you something there."

"Women work there?"

"No man."

The man in the black *thobe* nodded. "I just wanna find a job that's halal, you know?"

The man with the beard nodded. He turned around and looked at the girls from the school. "Look at all these girls—they wear their tight shirts, and their American clothes. You can barely tell some of them are wearing an *abaya*."

The other men nodded. The man in the hoodie said, "They're more American than Muslim."

"Yeah," said the bearded man. "Look, they wear makeup too. And see, that one is talking to a man, right in front of the school."

The man in the hoodie said, "They're just American."

The bearded man shook his head and pointed at the school. "Do they even separate boys and girls at that school?"

The man in black said, "Yeah, they separate them."

"They do?" said the third man.

"Well . . . " said the man with the beard. His voice trailed off, seemingly disappointed.

Then the men noticed me writing things down and started whispering. I didn't hear the rest of what they said.

Overhearing that conversation helped me understand why the girls greeted me excitedly at the school but in that same restaurant, they pretended I did not exist—I go from being a friend to a potential mate. The girls felt frustrated that others were using their bodies to make an impression on the community as a whole, a problem of women's bodies as a community metric well established within feminist history and anthropology.[26] In this school and in many other locations, both religious and secular, women's bodies are a means of both indicating and maintaining a community's moral worth. No wonder people had a lot of opinions about what women should do.

At the SAT class I was teaching at Al Amal, I asked some of the girls about what I had seen at the restaurant. Faaiza, who wore a little bit of makeup and was more confrontational than most of the students said, "You see that—that's ridiculous . . . . You know who they are, they're probably right off the boat—they're probably from Yemen—no offense to anyone here from Yemen—but . . . these Yemeni guys, they come here, and they just want everything to be like it was. Well then go back home! Seriously!"

The other girls laughed nervously. One of Faaiza's friends, Noor, smiled at me and said, "You shouldn't have got her started on this!"

Faaiza went on, "It's like, they don't even really know Islam. Like, there's no rule that says we have to totally cover ourselves. And yes, some of us wear makeup, but they don't know our souls—some of the worst people, some of the worst people are the ones who are the most covered, you never really know . . . . Why are they looking at us anyways? They're not supposed to be looking at us . . . . This is the way things are in America, and they need to get used to it."

Like many other American Muslim women, these girls were in a double bind: they felt judged by Americans who considered them too conservative, yet they were also judged by Muslims who thought them not conservative enough.[27] Like the young Muslims John O'Brien studied in urban Los Angeles, these teens faced competing "cultural rubrics": urban American culture on one hand and Islamic identity on the other.[28] As described in the previous chapter, there was a constant tension in both Muslims schools between religion, ethnicity, and nationality, with parents, teachers, and students all insisting that what they disagreed with was *culture* and not *religion*,[29] the accidental and not that essential. That work often becomes most clear in questions of gender.

Disagreement on this issue was correlated with age and American identity, with older parents and immigrants tending to be more conservative. At Al Amal, a senior girl asked Sheikh Khaled, "Sheikh, is it okay for your husband to see you without your hijab before you get married?"

He nodded gravely. "There are many answers to this question. The Hanafis[30] [he held out his hands as though to keep someone from pressing up on him] they go too far, I cannot even mention it to some of you here. They agree, but only on the presence of family. Most other schools say only the hands and the face, but the Hanafis will allow you to see more—but only in the presence of your parents, or at least your mother."

A girl asked, "But what if he wants to see your hair?"

"Why would he ask?" asked another girl.

I heard the girls talking to each other about this, but it was hard to make out what they said because the girl next to me, a small string of hair slipping out from under her hijab, muttered to no one in particular, "What's so bad about showing your hair?"

"So you don't think that's a problem?" I asked, quietly, both of us leaning against the wall.

"No—you know, a lot of us don't wear these outside of school," she whispered. "I don't think it's a big deal." In my conversations with students, I learned that the majority of female students at both Muslims schools usually did wear hijab outside of school, but there were a few in each class who did not. I encountered no one who told me she had an explicit problem with the hijab, and those who did not wear some sort of covering generally described themselves as just not wearing it "yet."

Amar, the senior I interviewed at Al Haqq who insisted child care is a dual responsibility, told me she also does not wear the hijab outside of school. "People try to make me feel bad but I don't feel bad. I know I should, I will, but I don't think I'm ready to. I don't want to do it because I'm forced to." She said that she only knows of a few other students who do not wear hijab outside of class, though she feels "there's more to a person than wearing hijab or not." Besides, she felt that in some ways she is more committed to the values of modesty that hijab represents. Some of her classmates may wear hijab, but "they wear tight clothes outside. They talk to boys. I don't do any of that and I don't wear hijab. I wear modest clothes and I wear half sleeves [covering elbows is important for some Muslims] and loose clothing . . . ." To be clear, the hijab is not a problem for Amar. She simply interprets it as a free choice, and therefore does not want to feel compelled to wear it. She'll wear it eventually, she thinks, "when I reach that point where I think that I am spiritually secure. Then I think that'll be the cherry on top."

For Amar, the hijab has to be about freedom, and to the degree that it is not, it misses the point entirely. One of the science teachers at Al Haqq, Sister Leyla, agrees. "The problem," she told me, is that "the Islam that a lot of people are seeing is an Islam that has been tainted by its culture." In contrast, "Islam in is true form . . . really liberated women. Women were allowed to manage their business affairs. Women were able to have divorces and initiate divorces. At that time in Europe, women were considered property. Islam gave women a voice."

As I described earlier, some boys, like Rahman, the senior at Al Haqq, told me they "love the idea of the hijab," emphasizing the importance of autonomy and the transcending of looks. Girls told me something similar, even if many of them also sensed more personally and practically the cost such transcendence might require. One junior girl at Al Haqq, Zaria, admitted to me it was frustrating that boys in her class could go wherever they wanted without looking that different. Yet she insisted that wearing the hijab was not so much about male control as it was about Muslim identity: "Other Americans like, you know, Gothic people or something, they'll wear different clothes and they, like, dye their hair, but they take pride . . . that they look different. That's how I carry myself now; I just take pride that I look different from everybody else." There is an autonomy in Zaria's pride, an ownership of her difference.

Yet how far does such a description of autonomy go? For Rahman, and for many of the boys I met at Al Amal and Al Haqq, it goes much further than whether or not women should wear hijab. When I asked him about careers, he said, "I'm more liberal with it. I think that the wife should be able to do just as much as you could do. Like if you have the choice to go work outside of home, she should have the choice to go work outside of home if she wants to . . . she should have that right." The hijab works as a boundary separating men from women and boys from girls. Yet the reason for that hijab is not quite as important as a site of boundary contestation, and neither is the hijab necessarily understood as undergirding a patriarchy that would give men the right to make demands on women's careers. This does not deny that women's bodies are still used against their will as indices of a community's moral worth. It only means that, at least in the context of the hijab, women are afforded some level of interpretive freedom, even if those around them might not share their interpretations.

GENDER SEPARATION

I posed a hypothetical to the Muslim students sometimes: what if a boy and girl got caught at Starbucks, not holding hands but still alone on a date? Generally, the students told me the boy would get in a lot less trouble than the girl. "Was he with an Arab girl?" one of the boys asked me at Al Amal. If our possible Muslim boy had been with a Christian girl, he explained to me, it would not really be a problem. Besides the interesting conflation of Arab and Muslim (something I encountered quite often), the student reveals the real concern: female purity. This dichotomy—between "Arab Virgin" and "American(ized) Whore"[31] was a constant threat at these schools, with both students and parents aware of the possible danger and the simultaneously ethnic and religious logic undergirding the concern. It might bear repeating here that such problems are not unique to Muslims and that these Muslim communities are much more conservative, at least regarding gender, than the average American Muslim; it's also worth acknowledging that the policing of adolescent (especially female) sexuality is a common finding in studies of American immigration and American life more broadly.[32]

At both Muslim schools, teachers of both genders taught all students, though some male teachers tried to teach only boys if they could. At Al Amal, boys and girls were in different classes except for AP courses, where they sat in different parts of the room. At Al Haqq, the boys and girls were in most of the same classes together, except for religion classes (Islamic Studies, Qur'an memorization, and Qur'an interpretation), which were gender-segregated. However, boys and girls always sat in different parts of the classroom.

Both schools also had serious rules about "lowering your gaze" when approaching someone of the opposite gender, which, according to some, is the Qur'anic basis for separating genders.[33] Gender separation also probably explains why both schools had so many more high school girls than high school boys, as there was less concern about protecting teenage boys from the outside world than there was about protecting teenage girls.

I became much more aware of my maleness while in the Muslim schools, and I also became much more aware of the gender of the students with whom I was interacting, especially after I got in trouble for playing basketball with girls at Al Amal. When I was asked to stop my fieldwork at Al Amal early, it was partially because of these interactions.[34] Whether a student is male or female is probably something I always think about, but it became a much more active habit at these schools, where crossing gender lines is a constant source of danger. At both schools, a lot of the boys—some whom I had met and some whom I did not know at all—came up to shake my hand or say hello. At Al Amal, I had gotten to know a group of girls relatively well (though I knew a group of boys much better), but because the principal of Al Haqq asked me not to engage girls at all, I was sort of a big stranger to the female students there. At Al Haqq, when a girl said "Hi Jeff" to me, she would often do so at a distance, and I could tell it was a slightly risky action because the other girls around her would smile nervously or shake their heads or look down, as though embarrassed. Also, the tone in which the girls said "Hi Jeff" was a bit louder, more sing-songy, a bit more pronounced, making it seem like more of an *event:* it wasn't banal, like when the boys greeted me.

Such tension could be used as a weapon. In a science lab at Al Haqq, a girl, Muna, and a boy, Abdul, were disagreeing about a certain procedure in an experiment, despite being in separate, gender-segregated lab groups. (The male and female students often knew each other from dense social networks within the school community that overlapped with family ties, though I do not know how these students knew each other.) Muna was looking at Abdul's brewing beaker and Abdul said, "Did I tell you you could look at that?" Muna glared at Abdul and swatted his stirring stick as she walked up to the teacher. She asked the teacher what the correct temperature of the heater is supposed to be, and the teacher said something, though I didn't catch it. On her way back, Muna walked between the boys' table and the girls' table to get to her seat, saying, "I told you" to a girl and then, to Abdul, "I told you." Abdul looked angry and blurted out, "Don't talk to boys!" Immediately the other boys' table and his table started laughing. Some boys repeated it, snickering: "Don't talk to boys." The teacher either didn't notice or chose not to respond. All the girls looked uncomfortable as class moved on.

I became accustomed to the gender separation (at least in my time at Al Haqq), though I still ran into some problems. At each of the schools I became friends with secretaries, and Sister Abeer, the assistant to the principal at Al Haqq, was no exception. She saw me on the first floor one day when she thought I was out. She told me something funny and I instinctively touched her shoulder. She immediately looked uncomfortable, and the assistant principal, a joyful woman named Sister Fatima, noticed it, too. I walked back into Sister Fatima's room later—that's where I was coordinating my interviews—and I said you know the problem is that I'm this Irish Catholic guy, and I'm always touching people. Sister Fatima laughed and said, yeah, you did that to Abeer. I realized then that it was a big deal, and a few minutes later I went up to apologize to Sister Abeer, who was in her room by herself. I said "I'm sorry," and she laughed, saying, "It's no big deal." She then showed me the "Islamic high five" which is her holding up a clipboard like a hand and then me hitting it. We smiled and I left. (I've since become even more conscious of the need to ask permission for any form of touch, regardless of the context, even touching a shoulder at a good joke.)

Such rules about touch were often quite explicit. Brother Umar, the assistant principal at Al Amal and I were chatting in his office, and he described the benefits of single-sex education in general, assuring me that non-Muslim studies had proven their worth.[35] Yet Al Amal needed none of these external validations: "We started doing it before all of that just because it was part of what we do, it's part of our religion. For Muslims, there will be less interaction between the two genders, if you send your child here, you know he or she will not interact with a member of the opposite gender." Even an AP class that "has a few boys in it" has rules: "The boys enter from one side and exit from another, and they learn, one way or another, how to deal with the other gender, which is truly like a sister." Note how the object of concern here is primarily boys' interaction with girls, and the reference to how to interact with the other gender is not like a sibling but *like a sister*. In many ways, both the gender separation and clothing requirements were described as ways to protect women and girls.

If the goal was to treat people like siblings, that was not really what I saw. Siblings interact with each other in all kinds of ways that I did not see happening at these schools. People clearly knew each other, but when they had a question they were supposed to ask in a purely formal way without any intense greeting. The word often used to describe the interactions was *professional*, and the examples of appropriate interaction given—asking for a pencil, clarifying the homework—emphasize the utilitarian rather than relational character of appropriate conversation. As the students lowered their gaze and moved around each other trying not to talk, I was reminded of monks with a vow of silence maneuvering about each other in an abbey or, in the hallways when they were walking, of a crowded New York City street where friends greet each other and ignore the waves of others.

Not everyone thought this was a good idea. A non-Arab teacher at one of the schools told me she thought gender separation was a cultural obsession that had no basis in Islam. "Some of my best friends when I was growing up were boys, and I think by making the boys and girls [be] in separate classes you're just making them more excited," she told me.

> You should have seen the girls when the firemen came [for a fire drill the previous week]. They were so crazy. It's like, these Muslims, they think they're more Muslim than Muhammad—they forget that he let his wife go talk to men, she did business with men. It's ridiculous—it's not normal for boys never to talk to girls and girls never to talk to boys. I wouldn't raise my children like that. I wouldn't send my children to this school.

Another female teacher at one of the schools also took issue with her school being too extremist. As quoted in chapter 2, she said that "What a lot of these Arabs don't realize is that what they're advocating, really, it looks a lot like *jahliyyah* [pre-Islamic paganism], like what the Prophet was fighting when he started Islam." As with many, this teacher referred to the Prophet's wives—"teachers [who] men came to . . . for instruction"— using them as evidence that men who "say things about women . . . twist around weak hadiths to fit their culture."

The girls at both schools were generally open to more interactions with boys, with most of them conceding there should be some limitations on male–female interactions (not being alone together, for example) but that the rules should be much less draconian. The boys agreed. As one boy at Al Amal told me, "Once we walk out of the building we talk to girls." Another boy at Al Amal showed people pictures of a non-Muslim girl he was dating on his phone, talking about the photos in language that would not be described as pious. I sat next to a boy at Al Haqq during Islamic Studies day who spent most of the lecture texting a girlfriend. A teacher at Al Haqq complained to me that with cell phones and the Internet, there's really no way to prevent male and female students from talking to each other.

Even if the students did not see the need to be as restrictive as their schools required, most acknowledged it was something worth attempting, as revealed in the next chapter's discussion of cross-gender interactions on the Internet. Brother Yaqub, the junior Islamic Studies teacher at Al Haqq, often suggested a compromise position—that "work-related contact" was acceptable, and something like this was the dominant position at both schools. Brother Yaqub often gave the example of ordering drive-through. "If you come to the window and it's someone of the opposite sex, are you going to drive away screaming?" he asked, incredulously.

For the majority at both schools, gender separation really mattered, and, in general, it fell harder on women and girls than on men and boys. After prayer one day at Al Haqq, the principal told students that they had to get much better at lowering their gaze. She repeated the phrase often when addressing the girls, insisting they must learn modesty (or *haya*). She did not use the term *haya* with the boys, instead telling them they needed to learn responsibility for when they would eventually be heads of households. Yet Sister Fatima, the assistant principal, who was younger and, unlike her boss, grew up in the United States, spoke next, telling the boys, "Boys you have to do *haya* too, lower your gaze when you're coming down the halls. Girls we have to respect ourselves as young woman and girls."

I asked Sister Fatima about this later in a taped interview. "Maybe it's because I was born and raised here I really feel like. . . I have seen a lot of boys who have gone astray because the parents are thinking I have to take care of my daughter, my daughter, my daughter, and you're forgetting your son, your son, your son, who can also get lost in this world." As did others, Fatima distinguishes religion from culture: "If you look at an Islamic point of view it's equal. But the cultural point of view is a little bit different." There are boundaries here within boundaries: gender separation is a way of distinguishing Muslims from non-Muslims, and this is something Fatima agrees with. And yet she insisted that the *real* Muslim way of doing things, the *essential* way, is to emphasize boys' and girls' behavior equally. It would be an accident, she believed, to think otherwise.

CONCLUSION

Given my earlier description of the importance of autonomy at the Muslim schools, it might seem plausible to assume that Evangelicals' gender ideology has more significant material effects on students' lives than that of Muslims wearing the hijab and gender separation. As described earlier, it is certainly the case that the more conservative an Evangelical Christian woman is, the more likely she is not to make money outside of the home. In a series of papers, Eman Abdelhadi complicates my story here.[36] She finds that Muslim women's religiosity—as measured by mosque attendance, prayer, and importance of religion—has either a positive effect or no effect on having paid work. However, in another article she finds that Muslim women who wear the hijab are 31 percent less likely to seek work than Muslim women who do not wear the hijab. She explains one-third of this difference via demographics, human capital, and household composition, but the rest remains unexplained.[37] I would first say that, given what I have already described, it seems possible that women deeply committed to wearing the hijab—however they interpret it—might choose not to work out of concerns about potential Islamophobic treatment. It is also entirely possible that for some of these women who wear the hijab and do not work, they have a more conservative, anti-feminist gender ideology. Indeed, it seems intuitively more likely that Muslim women who are more conservative about gender are more likely to wear the hijab. My point is not that the hijab is *always* feminist, but rather that, at least in the schools I studied, it can be a relatively free signifier in a way that is harder to accomplish with an opposition to feminism for Evangelicals.

Feminism was not a concept that came up often at either Al Amal or Al Haqq, at least not explicitly, and it was often brought up only when I discussed the hijab and people felt a need to defend it as not opposed to feminism. Yet, something like feminism was common at both schools: that is, women should have the same opportunities and access as men. Of course, how to understand such distinctions is a subject of much debate, and there have been endless conversations about whether it can actually ever be feminist to wear a hijab.[38] Yet it is important that my Muslim respondents often saw nothing anti-feminist in the hijab, and nothing anti-feminist in Islam as a whole. This was not the case at the Evangelical schools. Good Tree was much more explicitly opposed to feminism (even if they practically agreed with much of it), and Apostles was somewhere in between. The boundary work here is complicated, especially because people at both Muslim schools recognized how they were often considered explicitly anti-feminist in the secular world.

These different framings of the hijab are fairly representative of most boundary contestations: the fight is never about just the issue in question but what the issue itself represents and the moral values that ought to surround them. Is abortion the ending of a human life or the preservation of a woman's freedom? Are certain immigrants "illegal" or "undocumented"? In any of these cases, there is often a need to acknowledge the other side's critiques, either disproving them or diminishing their importance, and then to emphasize both the factual accuracy and moral significance of one's own position. Yet what is key in each of these cases is an agreement about the relative site of contestation, and then a disagreement about what is essential and accidental within it.

CHAPTER 4

⌒⌣⌒

Sex and the Internet

In a conversation in his office at Al Amal, Brother Umar, the assistant principal, told me that his students "hear voices from all over, from outside of the school and outside Islam, and it all comes together in their heads." The Internet, he told me, was an especially threatening source of cacophony. There were all the secular influences, and then the immediately available pornography, and, perhaps most discussed, the chance to talk anytime with a member of the opposite sex. He worried, as did many at the four schools, that the Internet allowed for an undermining of religious authority, creating a democratization that was unhelpful to everyone. As I will describe in this chapter, sexuality was a key part of this fear: the Internet made many kinds of differences immediately available, but perhaps none was so threatening as the sexual experience pornography provided and the sexual possibilities the Internet could present.[1]

Brother Umar was doing his PhD (online, as it were), and we would often talk about research questions. He asked me, looking at his computer screen as we talked, "As a researcher, would you accept something from Wikipedia for your research?"

"No," I said.

"Of course not," he responded, turning around in his chair to face me. "But that is the whole Internet now. The whole Internet is Wikipedia. And that's especially the case for Islam. So holiness does not mean having a big beard, it does not mean you memorized a few short *sura* [chapters of the Qur'an] and can then make a pronouncement . . . the Internet is a means, like television, like the telephone. These are all means to an end, and what that end is, is up to us."

Agents of God. Jeffrey Guhin, Oxford University Press (2021). © Oxford University Press.
DOI: 10.1093/oso/9780190244743.001.0001

Unlike a distinction from public schools, the Internet itself was not a boundary but was rather a continual reminder of other boundaries, a way that community members were forced to encounter difference, or at least to know that difference was only a few clicks away. The Internet as a problem for moral formation had to be balanced with the many positive ends it could produce. Nearly everyone told me how useful the Internet was for them, both personally and professionally, for school, for leisure, for keeping up with family and friends. Yet it also had these risks. Sin was the first of these risks, most obviously pornography, though students were somewhat shy to talk about it. For the Muslim students, they also worried about their easy access to members of the opposite sex, not only for the conversations themselves but also for the unholy ends to which those conversations might lead. People at all four schools also wondered about the kinds of people the Internet makes them become: pettier perhaps—or crueler. Maybe the greatest risk was also the most existential: what if the Internet proved it all wrong? In that sense, the Internet was both a precursor and a warning for what might come after graduation: what if, like so many others, the students left their faith when they left their schools? Is the cacophony of the Internet an inoculation, or is it an infection?

But before discussing the Internet—especially because so much of the concern about it was related to sexuality—it is important to provide some background about how sexuality itself was understood at these schools. Discussions of sexuality at all four schools emphasized the importance of virginity, tending to emphasize female virginity more than male, a concern by no means unique to religious communities.[2] To the extent that discussions turned to same-sex marriage or LGBTQ religion, they were primarily emphasized as boundaries from the outside world, as things that Christians or Muslims are not, though there were boundaries within the boundaries regarding how people ought to relate to LGBTQ people and politics. All of this often intersected back with the Internet, in that it was through the Internet that students had access to sexual activity and ideas the schools would not support. In any of these cases, there was a continual need to emphasize what was essential about the schools' identities and a fear that the Internet could challenge these essential teachings.

SEXUALITY

Sexuality was contested in a variety of ways in these schools: first, there was the concern about the students' own sexual lives, and then there was the worry about how sexuality was experienced and understood in the world at large, especially online. In all these cases, sexuality, like gender, served as a boundary from the outside world, with various sites of contestation—notably same-gender and same-sex sexual attraction and sex before marriage—as flash points through which to determine what was truly essential in religious practice.

When students' sexuality at the Muslim schools was discussed, which was relatively often, it was rarely about sex itself but rather its threat. I heard continual references to the perils of the Internet and the risks of cross-gender interaction: sexuality was simultaneously not allowed and an ever-present danger, lurking behind any corner, virtual or real, in which an unsupervised boy finds an unsupervised girl. There were occasional references to gay Muslims, but they were extremely rare and much less common than at the Christian schools. In a wide-ranging group conversation on gender, a junior girl at Al Amal mentioned, "There's a gay mosque. We protested it. In Islam, it's completely outlawed. There's nowhere it says it's allowed." Nobody disagreed, and the conversation quickly moved on. I do not recall any conversation on trans or non-binary issues or identities at any of the schools, and I did not describe any in my notes. That obviously does not mean there were no trans or non-binary students at the schools, but I was not aware of them.

The strictness I've described in these schools does not mean that students never went against restrictive sexual mores at the Muslim school, though in my experience it was only the boys who admitted to doing so. It is certainly possible that the boys and girls at these schools were entirely different people off campus, both in how they practiced gender and in how they navigated their sexual lives, yet from everything they told me about themselves and about each other, my sense is that the students' distinctions between school and private life were a matter of degree rather than kind.

The Christian schools were a somewhat different story. They had no rules on gender separation, though Good Tree had a very loosely enforced rule on male-female contact. While the Christian schools also had similar strict commitments to saving sex for marriage, what counted for sex was somewhat unclear.[3] With the exception of occasional discussions in Mr. Lopez's class at Apostles, I never attended classes in which they discussed abstinence (though I know the schools had these conversations). I rarely observed teachers giving strict guidelines for how students could protect themselves from sexual temptation, as I observed at the Muslim schools, with the exception of Mr. Morgan's discussion of pornography at Good Tree and a few of Mr. Lopez's classes at Apostles.

Instead, what was most pressing at the Christian schools—at least in my observations—was the problem of what they called same-sex attraction. Efforts to legalize gay marriage were fully underway during my fieldwork at Good Tree and Apostles, and it was a real issue for many, especially as an indication of their communities' own moral worth. The principal at Apostles, Sue Simons, is a friendly blonde woman who was always eager to give a hug. Like many conservative Protestants, she sometimes talked about her concerns about gay marriage and the growing acceptance of the "gay lifestyle," telling a gathering of the school faculty that they're the only *real* Christian school in the area. "There's a Lutheran school in town," she acknowledged, "But they had gay teachers, they had lesbian teachers. It was just very different, and I know because we sent our son there."

At Good Tree, both Joe Smith, the sophomore Doctrine teacher, and Adam Morgan, the senior Worldview teacher, were deeply concerned about gay marriage, even if they worried students did not share their concerns. Adam Morgan and I talked about gay marriage laws in our taped interview, and he told me he thought it was interesting that students were increasingly convinced same-sex attractions was genetic, something he said would not have been the case even a few years earlier. While he kept the conversation theoretical, I got the sense he was as yet unconvinced about the genetic argument. The key piece for him was protecting the concept of marriage. I asked him if he thought students shared his concern: "They don't care about that . . . with a few minor exceptions you know."

However, as I found in my interviews, the fact that students rarely spontaneously discussed conservative positions on US culture wars does not mean that they disagreed with those conservative positions when presented with them. While what students discussed in their free time is certainly one interesting question, a perhaps more relevant question is how certain issues *activate* cultural and political commitments. As I found in my interviews and observations, it is true that the students at Good Tree and Apostles did not bring up culture war issues all that often. But when I raised the topics, they almost always had something to say, and what they had to say generally revealed conservative positions on sexuality, gender, and the fading Christian character of the United States.

Mr. McNulty, a junior New Testament and history teacher, was ambivalent in our conversations about these topics, opposed to gay sex on a Biblical basis but less troubled by it existentially. He asked one junior New Testament class if gay people should be able to marry.

"Honestly, it makes me angry," said Kathleen, a blonde girl in a pink sweater who would later go on to Liberty University, a conservative

Christian university founded by Jerry Falwell. "Marriage is something that God made, and it [gay marriage] is just another way Satan is distorting something God made."

Mr. McNulty nodded. "Okay." He sat in the front of the class on a chair turned backward.

Another girl said that she was worried about gay marriage because she's worried it will become a habit. "The more I see someone curse, the more I'll curse, I hear it around, I'll think about it more, if I see it around, it becomes normal to me, I don't want something I view as sinful to become normal and a part of my life."

The teacher nodded. He asked the class, "Who thinks it's okay to have a same-sex marriage in a church?" Nobody raised their hands.

"Right, I think we're all agreed on that. So I guess what I'm interested in is at what point do we as a church legislate our beliefs? I mean, we can all agree that what these people do is wrong—it's wicked. But then we believe that we're all wicked, right? We believe that we're all sinners." He launched into a pretty big monologue here:

> Marriage in the secular world really is not just about love, it's about insurance benefits, home ownership, and inheritances. These are rights for people who get married, and if you don't get married you don't have these rights. At one point do we deny them—the wicked, sinners—the rights they get in a society? Because we all know there are heterosexuals who are wicked, who don't believe, who sin, but they still have rights . . . so why is that? The question really is, should America be a Christian state? Is there a separation of church and state when we do that, or should we legislate our beliefs?

"Our country was founded on Christian beliefs," responded a boy.

"Yeah," said the teacher "but what about freedom of religion and the separation of church and state?"

There was a pause.

Mr. McNulty asked, "Is anyone here scared of turning gay?" Nobody answered. "So nobody here is worried that your time around homosexuals or hearing about gay marriage is going to make you gay?"

Kathleen said, "I'm scared of having a boy that's going to be gay."

Other girls nodded. One said, "Yeah, I'm worried my child would be gay."

Mr. McNulty said, "Okay, so what causes someone to be gay. Who here thinks it's genetic?"

Nobody raised their hand.

"So it's social. And what causes someone to be gay?"

Kathleen said, "Not having a strong role model, not having a man who they can identify with, a good Christian man who they can have as an example."

Mr. McNulty looked her right in the eye and said, "Kathleen, I just can't imagine that you won't have a husband who would be committed to you and who would help you set up a Biblical, Christian home. I can't imagine that."

He looked up at the rest of the students. "So is there still a fear of your children becoming gay—despite being in a Biblical Christian home?" Kathleen shook her head no. "I don't believe society is going to affect it if the child is gay," she responded.

Mr. McNulty said, "So it sounds like really we're afraid of being desensitized, but is that something you should fear? Or is that something you fear about your own walk with the Lord?"

This concern about being "desensitized" led directly into a fear about what the Internet might do, making people too easily accommodated to the secular world-as-it-is instead of the religious world-as-it-should-be. Yet it also shows why policing boundaries mattered so much, as students worried that gay marriage would challenge not only their vision of a Christian nation but also their own ability to maintain Christian lives and Christian families.

I only met one student at any of the four schools who identified as being anything but heterosexual, a junior girl at Good Tree named Evelyn Mitchells, a brown-haired, skinny girl with a goofy and ironic sense of humor. I interviewed her near the very end of my fieldwork. In the beginning of our interview, she told me that she has a boyfriend, but they "don't even hold hands." When the subject moved to gay students at the school—a subject she initiated—she told me that there were a few "gay kids" at Good Tree, though they are only out to a couple of people, except, apparently, a sophomore who "came out to almost her whole entire class this year" even though Evelyn believes the administration never found out. I never followed up on this claim with other students. Evelyn said that she sought out faculty who would provide "safe spaces" for students with questions about their sexuality, asking the teachers not to report these students to their parents or the administration. She said she found one teacher who said, "of course."

When I asked why these issues were so important to her, Evelyn told me she was bisexual. She said not acting on her same-sex attractions was "the hardest thing she has ever done" and while she primarily felt attractions to women, she was excited about her boyfriend, whom she believed God had put into her life. Yet things did not always seem so blessed. She told me that most of her class knows about her sexual identity, but not because she told them.

> I was a freshman and I was contemplating suicide. So I told people anyway because I didn't think it was going to matter. Yeah. One of the teachers here saved my life. She's not here anymore, but she told my parents just that I was contemplating suicide. That's all she told them. So they got me help.

She said she was picked on and bullied, though a girl who identified as a lesbian a few grades above her did take her under her wing, as well as the tolerant teacher who helped her feel a sense of safety.

Evelyn's commitment to Christian students figuring out their sexuality does not mean she is supportive of "the gay lifestyle," even if she is frustrated by how lesbian, gay, and bisexual Christians are treated by their communities. (We did not discuss trans, non-binary, intersex, or other queer issues).[4] She said she eventually wants to be a public speaker who helps young Christians also struggling with their same-sex attractions, and she wants, eventually, to marry a man. She told me she believes God can cure same-sex attraction through prayer, though she thinks "the church puts way too much emphasis—when they do talk about it—on that because most of the time that's not what happens." Nonetheless, Evelyn was especially inspired by a youth leader at her church who left a same-sex relationship to marry a man. "She still talks about how she struggles with that all the time," Evelyn said, finding in her a model for how to be a married, committed Christian woman who just so happens to be attracted to other women. I asked how she felt about gay Christians in committed, monogamous, same-sex marriages, and she said,

> I think that I would just tell them that like obviously I'm praying for them . . . I can be like: I've been there. Like not in a relationship, but I've struggled. Like even for a while totally considered just living that way, but God has brought me back. If God is going to bring them back, that's something He has to do in them. It's not something I can do. I'll just listen and be there for them and just be their friend completely all the time no matter what they're doing.

Like others I talked to at the school, Evelyn emphasized a distinction between the question of gay activity and the question of treating gay people unkindly. It was essential that a Christian not act on their gay attractions, but it was just as important that a Christian treat someone who has those attractions with kindness.

After hearing about her from Evelyn, I realized I had heard about this lesbian student a few grades above her from a few other people. At a dinner at Joe Smith's house, the two of us were chatting with Shane McNulty. Mr. McNulty told me—after nervously asking Mr. Smith about confidentiality— about "a homosexual student" at the school who was asked to leave because "she was totally unapologetic about the homosexual lifestyle and was completely open about it in school." I asked Joe about someone who's gay who's at the church and still acting on it, and he compared such sins to his own. "Now I'm celibate, but if you were to ask me, do I think lustful thoughts when I'm at the beach, of course . . . . But if this person is unrepentant and doesn't try to change, that's something we'd have to deal with . . . but again, I'm well aware of the sinner I am." Mr. Smith's framing of the issue parallels Mr. McNulty's: love the sinner but hate the sin.

Various queer theologians and LGBTQ Evangelicals have critiqued the "love the sinner, hate the sin" framework,[5] not least because it creates a false equivalency between celibate heterosexual life and celibate queer life. A celibate straight teen is still straight, giving them access to chatting about chaste celebrity crushes or any of the other subtle expressions of teenage sexuality I saw at all four of the schools. And the other problem is the political salience given to gay issues rather than other kinds of sin. Fred Dylan, a popular senior boy who played drums during praise and worship services, did a class-long presentation on homosexuality in Worldview class, one of the CAR-time presentations every senior was required to do. He emphasized—with agreements and thoughtful nods from Mr. Morgan— that it was not quite so clear that being gay was genetic, and that it might well be possible to convert people. Yet he also challenged his classmates to focus on other sins as well. "Why do we as Christians give it such a prestige in the sin category? The important thing we should be focusing on is not sex orientation but spiritual orientation . . . we shouldn't try to convince a person to become straight before they become a Christian." He went on that "if a homosexual person becomes a Christian, it doesn't mean they need to like women right away—it takes time. . . . "

At Apostles, I encountered far fewer conversations about homosexuality. In my private interviews, a few seniors and juniors told me about girls in their class whom they described as gay or bisexual, some of them "dressing like men." However, asking about gay students was not on my standard interview schedule, and when I did ask other students about whether there were gay students at Apostles, most told me they were not aware of any. There was a freshman who, when I was casually talking to students, asked me more than once what I thought about "the gay gene." I told him the science was pretty complicated, but it did appear that there was some kind of genetic connection in some cases. I was not really sure what else to say, and figured it was probably best not to get into the complications of politicized sexual dichotomies and the performativity of gender.[6] In a later interview with that same student, a Latino boy named Manuel, he told me that he thought a lot about homosexuality because he has a friend in his class who is gay, plus a cousin who was kicked out of his house for being gay. When I talked to Manuel about it, he said he tried to talk to them about God. "If you talk enough to a gay person, it's not that they were born that way," he told me. He said that the real source of same-sex attraction is a disconnect with how they connected to adults of the same sex from early on.

At one point, a guest speaker at an Apostles chapel service called students down for an "altar call" (an opportunity to affirm or reaffirm your commitment to Christ). He provided a litany of reasons to come to the altar: "You want your mom and dad back together, you want your brother to leave the homosexual lifestyle, you want your grandmother to get better, you want to save your house, you want your dad to find a job, just come down, come down." For this preacher, the "homosexual lifestyle" is not only a sin but is something that causes suffering to those around you, paralleled to a parent's divorce or unemployment, the foreclosure of a home, or the illness of a loved one.

I interviewed a freshman girl named Annie at Apostles and, while talking about prayer—and without bringing up anything having to do with gay people—she told me that one of her biggest challenges in her prayer life is a job she's had for three years, a summer camp which "allows lesbians and gay couples to have their kids in it." The camp, she told me in a sullen tone, has children's books about gay couples. Her father is the assistant director of the camp, and "it's kind of discouraging to be there and have some lesbian and gay co-workers and lesbian and gay parents to deal with." She worried she "should be talking more to these people about God. But at the same time that could possibly get me fired. And I'm not very good with talking to people. I'm kind of shy."

The only Apostles teacher I noticed talking about sex with his students was Mr. Lopez in his senior and junior Bible classes. He did not talk much about same-sex attractions, though we did discuss that in our interview.

In one junior Bible class, he asked the students, "How many of you know what the Bible says about sex before marriage?"

"It's bad" said one student.

"It's against the law," said another.

He showed the class a video that, among other things, compared pre-marital sex to rape. Daphne Hunter, a Black girl with short hair, seemed visibly frustrated. She said, "This is not a topic I wanna get into. Can I leave?

I don't like hearing this." In at least one other class I observed in which this topic came up, I actually saw Daphne pack up her things and walk out of the class. In this case, however, she did not.

"Well you're gonna have it on the test," said the teacher.

A long conversation ensued. Daphne seemed pretty bothered by the fact that someone might be sexually unsatisfied. She talked about how some people might have previous sexual experience and then be dissatisfied in marriage because it's not as good as before. "So that person has to go their whole life like that?" she asked. She seemed unconvinced.

Mr. Lopez shared his own story of getting married but then cheating on his wife.

Daphne looked exasperated. "Why are we talking about marriage when I'm 16?"

The teacher responded, "We have to start thinking about these things now because of all the influences around us. Look at the lyrics of the songs you listen to. Sex, violence, exploitation, abuse of women. It covers all these topics."

Daphne asked, "What if we just kiss?"

Mr. Lopez said, "Once again don't warm up the slot machine if you're not going to play the game."

"Are you serious?" Daphne asked, laughing nervously.

"And I'm not just saying this either. I wear this ring," he said, showing a purity ring on his finger, "because I can't just tell all of you to be pure and not be pure myself."

Daphne said, "So nothing? Nothing all?" She looks around at the rest of the class in shock. They were paying rapt attention to the interaction.

Mr. Lopez said, "I have no shame about saying this. Nada. But I have fear for the one who made me."

Daphne said, "I'm not gonna wait. I don't care. I'll just ask for forgiveness later."

The teacher seemed like he wasn't sure what to say. He paused. "Okay, well," he started, but then he was saved by the bell.

I talked to Mr. Lopez about Daphne when I did a tape-recorded interview with him. He nodded in recognition.

When you get her in the group, [she says] oh, you can't control that [sexuality], . . . But . . . there was a time after that double class, there was like six of them left, that she stood there. And her own friends came to her during the class. I was just sitting there listening. It had nothing to do with me. I was just sitting there. They asked her to stay. So I stayed there. They started asking her all kinds of questions about why you always lashing out when we talk about these topics? Why are you always acting like this? And everything goes back. Her answer is everything goes back to what happens in the house. Because like: I don't know if you were there the day I was talking about pastors' kids, how they're treated in the church and in people's eye view and other—and regular kids. And she's a pastor's kid. You know what I mean? So her whole life, she's expected to act a certain way. So when you push somebody so much, it's just like me. When my mother wanted me to go seven days a week in the church, I said, please, I ain't goin' no-where. Why? Because you're forcing me to go. You know what I mean? Now if you make her aware it's her choice, that she knows what she's not getting if she doesn't come, then she has her own choice to make . . . . So then I had a one-on-one with her, and she started telling me so many things that happened in the house . . . . So it all goes back to the root of the problem which is your back-ground or your house. You know what I mean?

Mr. Lopez emphasized the importance of choice—alongside the dangers of force—in many of his class discussions, and he emphasizes it again here. Yet what is most relevant for this discussion of sexuality is that Daphne's different opinion on sex was something to be explained, understood, and *distinguished*, both by her teacher and her peers. And the best way to make sure that students go the right way, that they are distinguished by correct beliefs and correct action, is to encourage and enable them to make the right decisions, referencing Scripture when necessary.

That strategy is what he said he would do if a student told him they were gay. "My job is not to condemn. My job is to—I'm going to follow Christ, so I'm going to show him exactly what Christ did, with love and care. I have to sit there." And Scripture should do the work: "I will sit there and counsel him and say, 'Listen, okay, your body is this, this and your body is the Temple of Christ. Okay. What do you do with your body is this.' And I will show them in the Bible. Listen, this is what God is saying. . . . But at the end of the day, I cannot force them into stopping that relationship or stop feeling that way. You know what I mean?" Mr. Lopez was suspicious he had power to force anything, but he was confident "The Holy Spirit could break that up out of the person," and the Holy Spirit would move through scripture and prayer.

Pornography

Students were understandably shy about talking about pornography, a ret-icence found in much of the literature on religion and pornographic usage.[7]

I sometimes said something open-ended in interviews like "pornography is hard for a lot of students," but few would take up the opportunity to describe their own challenges. The Muslim and Christian schools were virtually identical in this regard: there were occasional moments when teachers described the problem with porn, but they mostly did not address it. When pornography was addressed—by either students or teachers—it was usually in the language of addiction, with teachers or other adults insisting it is important to "admit you have a problem."[8] Masturbation was rarely discussed at all, except for one teacher at Al Haqq telling a roomful of boys that masturbation was not to be praised but was morally superior to looking at pornography or committing fornication if the students really felt they had no other choice. "But this is *not* to enjoy masturbation," he made clear, "which is a habit many young people have—they enjoy this as a habit. This is very harmful, especially when it becomes an addiction, like the addiction to pornography. You don't want to ruin your talents and your morals by this addiction." The boys, normally quite unserious, looked uncomfortably around the room, avoiding eye contact with each other.

Another teacher at Al Haqq, Brother Yaqub, sometimes fielded anonymous questions from students about their lives. In one junior girls' class, he pulled a note from the box in which a girl worried about her brother looking at pornography. "I think pornography's an addiction," he said calmly. "You don't want to embarrass them. Maybe tell your dad. You want to find a way to get him help." He suggested purifyyourgaze.com, a Muslim website for pornography addiction. While nobody at Al Amal was quite as explicit about pornography without me initiating the conversation, students and teachers there also admitted it was a problem and used the language of addiction to describe it.

Pornography functions here as what scholars of boundaries would refer to as "boundary markers,"[9] which have a wide variety of meanings but which tend to indicate a practice or characteristic that can indicate someone is definitely one thing but not another. This is not quite the same thing as the term I have also been using, "site of boundary contestation," by which I mean an area in which communities, alongside their antagonists choose to emphasize their distinction from each other. Sites of boundary contestation are always salient to identity, while boundary markers, at least as I am using the term, mark distinctions but does not necessarily indicate their salience. The consumption of pornography, in this case, is both: it is a site through which the school communities sought to distinguish themselves from others, and a practice that marked that distinction. To use pornography marked someone not only as a sinner but also as morally undisciplined and unserious, as doing things that good Muslims and good

Christians do not do. The *essential* promiscuity of public schools—and by extension, the secular world—is an important piece of this. Pornography is proof that the world outside drips with sin, and the Internet is a wall with many leaks.

When students did talk about their use of pornography, it was often in language reserved for grand battles and existential stakes. Andrew was a senior at Good Tree, a popular and outspoken student with boundless energy. He would sometimes annoy teachers with his jokes in class, but his big smile usually won them over. Without even bringing up the Internet, he told me, "We're constantly, being like bombarded with the world." I asked him what he meant, and the stakes got even higher: "Satan is here and he's trying to drag all of us guys down and he had his grip on me and basically I was a really good kid and the only thing I ever struggled with was pornography . . . for four and a half years." Yet all was not lost for Andrew, giving a narrative of struggle and eventual triumph common in various Evangelical stories of redemption: "He just dragged me down so deep and it's now that I've broken this bond I'm like, I have the Holy Spirit, like he [Satan] can't get in my head. It's like, like no more images will come up in my head. It's just like they're flipped off . . . ." The world, in Andrew's account, is a battlefield with Satan, a description I heard repeated at all four schools. And pornography is one of Satan's weapons. Whether or not the devil made anyone do anything, it is noteworthy that pornography here is not simply a private idiosyncratic struggle, like having trouble getting up early to exercise. It is instead a marker that separates "good kids" from a sinful world, a boundary marker of who is Christian (or Muslim) and who is not.

As did many, Andrew used the language of addiction to describe his use of pornography,[10] linking it to students' capacity to maintain their Christian identity when they left the school. When I asked him about some teachers' worries that students would leave the school and then leave their faith, he told me, "If you're not sound with God here and you leave this school . . . you're going to just get molded to the world and it's going to pollute you pretty much." I asked if the Internet had anything to do with the world polluting you, and he answered, "I think it's got a huge part. Like it took four and a half years for me so and it's like, I wasn't a bad kid and when someone is a bad kid and it's like oh my gosh, I just think of what it's doing to them. And it's just. . . back to the pornography." Note also how Andrew distinguishes himself from "bad kids" who have it even worse. Even good and wholesome Christian young people are at risk. The Internet thereby becomes not so much a boundary as an opportunity for boundary-work and the identification of boundary markers, a place to distinguish between Christians and non-Christians, good kids and bad kids. Porn—and sexuality more broadly—was an important site through which to work those boundaries out.

The other person at Good Tree who was open about pornography-as-a-problem was Adam Morgan, the Worldview and Scripture teacher. When I asked him about the Internet in our formal interview, he lamented that Christian churches, schools, and parents did far too little to engage the problem.

> They know pornography's wrong, right? But there is no—unless a father in the home is doing that or a very brave youth pastor—they're not getting any instruction helping to understand why pornography's bad, admitting that it's a huge temptation and they're all looking at it. Cause they all are . . . . Well it's something I've gotten to do in my classroom, and even in my discipleship group two years ago . . . . Every one of those boys, head down [said]: "Absolutely. It's a huge struggle for me."

Adam Morgan seemed primarily concerned about *boys* using pornography, and, as Samuel Perry notes about Evangelical discussions of pornography in his work, neither Mr. Morgan nor anyone else at the Christian schools talked about masturbation, though it is generally assumed that people masturbate while viewing porn.[11] On the first day of his Worldview class, Mr. Morgan encouraged students to cultivate their passion as a kind of "jet fuel" that will drive them to success. He told the students that the dark side of what happens with passion is that it can be "wasted," and it is wasted in different ways for the two genders. The three ways "guys waste their passions," he told the class, are sports, video games, and, "most guys will admit," pornography. "Girls," on the other hand, waste their passion on a relationship, vanity, and "being emotionally anxious about things that don't matter."

Yet, in our interview, these concerns come together in Mr. Morgan's concern about the Internet, not only because of pornography but also because of social networking: "The social networking also is causing them to be more vulgar and crass, and to learn how to be artful in slandering and gossiping." He said the school can be something of a "check" on this behavior: "We can't stop what they're doing but we can at least try to provide real instruction about things like pornography, and then like try to explain to them in the real world, what you say on Facebook gets out you know." For Adam Morgan, the temptation toward gossip and the temptation toward pornography are linked both in their common location online and in their tendency to lead children astray. I did not encounter quite as many explicit references to pornography at Apostles as I did at Good Tree, but people there, when I asked, also worried about pornography's effect on students, with some students acknowledging it in my private interviews as a major crisis for them.

The Wrong Kind of Talk

Mr. Morgan's concern about how students talked to—and about—each other was another fear about the Internet. Again, the Internet itself did not function as a boundary here but rather as a point-of-entry for the world outside, a means through which students could enact lives that would not be possible—or at least not *as* possible—in their person-to-person interactions at school and at home. As with fears about pornography, fears about the Internet reproduced anxieties about public schools and the world at large: if porn showed the perils of secular sexuality, then social media showed how the outside world doesn't really *care* about people.

This concern was more marked in the Muslim schools, where cross-gender interaction was significantly more policed. Yet the concern was not only about interactions across gender lines. Some of the students told me they called the chemistry teacher, Brother Nabeel Irfan, "Facebook" because they worried he "Facebook stalked" them. I asked him about this in our interview, and he told me he's not on Facebook and, in fact, he's "anti-Facebook." Instead, he searches students' profiles for what can be found publicly to show them the dangers of oversharing. "I'm trying to teach them about privacy. If you don't want this to be known by, let's say, your teacher, then don't put it online. . . . And I'm trying to bring it in a sense of not just Islamic point of view but even from a professional point of view."

In my conversations with them about the Internet, students often worried that they were wasting time and, less often, that they were oversharing. Yet much more common, at least in the Muslim schools, was a worry about how they interacted with the opposite sex. In an interview with Jasmine, a girl who had just graduated from Al Amal, she told me that at college she had begun accepting Facebook friend requests from male students at her college, but she accepted them at a different privacy level. "Now in college, I have some guys adding me and I don't really know—like what am I supposed to say. I don't add guys on Facebook? They're going to be like what the hell? I add them but then there is that boundary where you don't get too open with them."

Note how Jasmine herself used the word *boundary* to describe how she ought to relate to male students. How students interact with members of the opposite sex is not only *about* boundaries between men and women;

these interactions are also themselves boundaries between Muslims and the outside world. The practice of cross-sex interaction thereby becomes a key site of boundary contestation between proper Islam and the world at large. It also becomes a marker, like the use of pornography, which the Internet has made easier to access. As such, cross-sex interaction not only *marks* boundaries, it also *situates* them as places of contestation.

In one of Brother Yaqub's junior boys' classes at Al Haqq, some boys said the Internet made talking to girls too easy, a surprising claim for a group of young people who had otherwise described their school's rules on sex interaction as far too harsh. One wavy-haired boy named Saeed said, "Now people are on the Internet, and two people of the opposite genders . . . and even though they're not actually together, they can still do things they wouldn't do in front of others. And they can do *haram* [forbidden] things. So basically you're—"

Brother Yaqub cut him off. "Do you think it's halal [permissible] to be alone in a room with a woman?"

"Sheitan [Satan] is the third person," interjected many of the boys, a common saying I heard especially at Al Haqq.

A larger boy with big sideburns, Ubaeed, said, "Let's say . . . she sends you a picture naked, how is that different from just seeing her naked?" The boys then disagreed about the degree of wrong this action portended.

A quieter boy, Yahya, took the opportunity to become philosophical:

Now that Facebook has gone up and instant messaging has gone up, I think now the world has gotten so much smaller and the things that we can do and accomplish. Acquiring fame now is so easy. You can just be famous just like that. Talking to girls—the biggest example right now—you have that on your computer. Back then you couldn't do that, and right now the world has gotten so much smaller and it's so much easier to get these things. And you feel like there's not much in this world, there's nothing in the world.

Yahya's concern about how the Internet cheapens religious commitments and thereby the experience of life itself leads into the conclusion that the Internet might well challenge the school's existential commitments, in addition to its more piecemeal moral goals.

Like the Muslim schools, the Christian schools also worried about how students behaved on the Internet, though they had different ideas about how to police it. In a school assembly near the beginning of the academic year, Brenda Forrest, the principal at Good Tree, reminded students that their theme for the year was from Philippians 1:21, "For me to live is Christ." She lamented that too many people "compartmentalize" their lives, separating their spiritual lives from everything else. "It all has to be together," she insisted. "How you do in class, how you do academically, that's part of your spiritual walk." This commitment to checking students' lives went all the way to the Internet. "As I'm going to the computer, and posting things on Facebook, am I thinking, for me to live is Christ?" she asked them. "Are you communicating in a way that pleases the Lord? Are you not using foul language, not talking about each other?" She said she would not require people to turn in their Facebook passwords, and she would not be checking accounts all the time, "but just remember that when you're on Facebook, when you're anywhere, you represent Jesus Christ, you represent Good Tree and you represent your family too, and so it's important you know that, and that you know we'll talk to you about the way you behave." I talked to students who were frustrated by this threat and its implications, though I never actually met anyone who got in trouble for anything they posted online, even if I heard of other examples.

I heard from multiple sources about some students who had gotten in trouble the year before for posting about smoking pot on Facebook, though I never checked this with the administration. "They love us and they wanna take care of us," admitted Beth, a senior who had been at the school since kindergarten. In my interview with her, she told me that she worried faculty went a bit too far into students' "personal lives and stuff like that." She said she knows other students think "the only reason . . . is they're just trying to find things wrong with us and they're trying to pick at us and they don't like that kid so they're gonna try and get evidence on whatever, why they don't like him." She told me she doesn't think the faculty is quite that cynical, but she did "wonder if their motives are really to truly teach us about Christ and teach us to submit to authority or if they're just annoyed with us . . . ."

Another student told me about how the school's interventions into students' online lives created "a big massive controversy about whether or not it's right for the administration to become involved with your online social life. It was very much kids against teachers for a good couple months last year in regards to that."[12] Yet the student told me, "I agreed with the administration, because it's not a matter of: oh, you're trashing this person; you're going to hurt their feelings. It's a matter of your name is associated with Good Tree on your Facebook page." She worried that "small and finite" as an Internet comment might be, it could do real damage to the school's reputation, and "what a real Christian school is like—what real Christianity is like." Note here an important point about boundaries: they are not only about how we view and understand others. They are also about how others view and understand us. The concern, then, is that a student's sarcastic comment will be the wrong kind of boundary marker, miscategorizing the school—and by extension, Christianity—as something it is essentially not.

Unlike Good Tree's students, the faculty were more pleased with the policy, even if some took matters into their own hands. In our taped interview, Mr. Morgan told me Facebook is "not an environment that in any way encourages or builds up . . . the nobler virtues." He described how some students become attracted to the attention they gain for sarcasm and cruelty, and he had to deal with one student himself as the debate coach, someone who had become "very popular for their witty and insightful biting humor." This student became a "totally different person" on Facebook, Mr. Morgan said. "Former students would email me screenshots of what this nitwit would be saying and I know the kid . . . would never say those things around any other person . . . [and] probably never had in the past."

Unlike at Good Tree, there was no policy to police students' online behavior at Apostles. I spoke to the dean of discipline, Phil Rodriguez, who told me in a taped interview he was not involved in students' online lives, although sometimes material is brought to his attention. One time he saw a picture of a student "flipping the bird" on a Facebook post and punished the student, but he and the other faculty and staff are generally not that involved with what happens in the students' online lives; they're busy enough with the students' lives on campus.

Yet the two obviously intersect, especially in what Mr. Rodriguez called "subs," which he said was a reference to "subliminal" but I think might have referenced sub-tweets. In either case, "subs" at Apostles referred to when someone says something that is directed at someone but could plausibly be said to refer to someone else. He told me this occurred often on Facebook and then had implications for the school day. The other tension was what some students called "Facebook thugs," people who talk tough online but then do nothing in face-to-face interaction. Frida, a senior at Apostles, defined them for me in an interview: "A Facebook thug is a person who on Facebook, they say whatever they want, but in person they're not going to say what they feel." Frida's mom is a minister, and Frida takes her spiritual life seriously, even if she's worried a good half of her class does not. As she put it, "It's always the same people split in half, the people I hang out with and the hoes." She said it's this other group that can make Facebook so difficult. "They say on Facebook . . . it's of the devil. . . . Someone puts a status and you feel like it's about you so you go up to them and all this and then it starts more statuses and then more problems." Because so much of the class is Facebook friends with each other, "there are Facebook fights, a lot of Facebook fights."

In an interview, I asked another senior girl, Doris, about Facebook thugs, a term which seniors and juniors recognized, and sophomores and freshmen did not. Doris told me, "I think on Facebook when you have unchristian friends there—like here in this school . . . we go to Bible class every day . . . . But when you're out there on Facebook and you don't have Christian friends so you're not gonna be like God is my strength and dah, dah, dah, dah because you're afraid one of them is gonna comment on it like, 'Yo, shut up.' So when they get on Facebook, they are like, 'Oh, F this, F that, F the world.'" Note how Doris described the Internet as a place where it's hard to be a Christian, and that distinction is recognized by its boundary markers: cursing and aggression, as has been described before as essential markers of public schools, and then studying and quoting scripture as essential markers of Christians. Yet the problem with the Internet is that these essential Christian practices do not last: "Because the non-Christian friends and then the Christian friends, a lot of them aren't bold enough to say like, 'You know you shouldn't be doing that.' You're just gonna let it slide by or even like the status," said Doris. "So I feel like the Christians aren't bold enough, but the sinners are."

CONCLUSION

Worries about the boldness of sinners were the very reason these schools were founded, making those sinners entrée via the Internet particularly threatening. The nature of these threats was generally piecemeal and particular rather than total and existential, yet sometimes these worries hinted at a deeper fear. Remember Yahya's complaint that the Internet might portend a deeper nihilism, or Doris's worry that Christians become *essentially* less Christian because of Facebook.

People did not generally describe the Internet as quite so existentially threatening. Indeed, when I asked students in interviews if the they ever found anything online that made them question their beliefs, they almost always said no. Yet a few students did tell me something like what Yahya said. For example Frida, a student at Good Tree, told me she encountered the question of how anyone knows their religion is really the "right religion." "I'm like, 'Whoa, it's true! Why be Christian when I could be a million other religions that are in this world?'" She said the experience caused her a lot of anxiety, but she resolved it "through a lot of prayer. I said, 'God if you're real, show me this, show me that. Whatever.' And without fail, every time, He would show me what I needed to see. And I was like, 'Oh my gosh. I'm following the right thing.'" Note how, as will be described more extensively in Chapter 7, it is prayer that helps to answer a hard question and clarify a boundary between belief and unbelief.

For this was the biggest concern adults had about the Internet, that it could be a place that drove people away from their faith. And while sexual temptations were not the only possible problem online, they were much of what I heard discussed at the schools, both because of the problem of pornography and, relatedly, the possibility that students will discover other kinds of sexuality. As a teacher at Al Haqq told me, "I think there's a lot of dangers on the Internet period. I can look up something on the Internet about Islam, and I can find anything. I don't think you'll find a book that says being gay or lesbian in Islam is okay, but you'll find it all on the Internet." This teacher said that Sheikh Yusuf, the school's Islamic Studies teacher, was developing "a list of all the websites that he believes are sound Islamically . . . these are the sites I should stick to, rather than going onto a site that could lead you . . . into something that is *haram*. That's a worry. That's a fear."

Similarly, in a tape-recorded interview, Ms. James, the Good Tree biology teacher, told me she was concerned about female students saying they were "married" on Facebook. She believed the students weren't actually in gay relationships—"you're posting that as a joke because you're best friends or whatever"—but she worried about how the Internet encourages a lax quality in her students. "Because the culture in general has become so okay with divorce and homosexuality and being scandalously desensitized and all of these kinds of things, I think that a lot of our students are exposed to that as well because of what they see on the Internet . . . and so they don't necessarily think that it's bad to watch certain things or to view certain things on the Internet or whatever." This lack of concern about *viewing* certain things can lead to lack of concern about *doing* certain things. She went on that "because students are so exposed to these different lifestyles . . . or whatever in terms of the Internet . . . they can be like, oh well, that's not so bad."

It's this fear of relativism that was so important at all four schools, even if was not acknowledged as often as the more explicit fears of cruelty or sexual sin. When I asked him about the Internet, a senior boy at Al Amal, Mustafa, told me that it's dangerous. I assumed he was talking about porn but he said no, "[The Internet is] good and bad, good because you learn more about Islam and bad because you can see a lot of sites that can be dangerous for your faith, like, you see stuff about other religions, it might make you doubt." The Internet was not so much a boundary from the outside world as it was a place to encounter boundaries, to make continual decisions about whether to hold to them or cross them. It was often the

Internet that forced people to consider what was actually essential or accidental about their identity. As Ms. James described, the great fear these teachers had about the Internet was only partially that students would do something wrong; it was also that students would consider what the school thought essential as no longer important, that it was actually just accidental. And if the schools' essences began to fade, they worried, then so might the schools' authorities.

CHAPTER 5

cVᴏ

Scripture as External Authority

INTRODUCTION

During my time at Good Tree, some students started calling Dr. Martin Hawthorne "Doctor Doctor" after he received his second doctorate, earning a PhD in biblical hermeneutics to accompany his first in engineering. All of the seniors took his senior Bible class, and those I talked to about it appreciated the opportunity to learn scripture for themselves, a skill they were told would be necessary as many of them went on to secular universities.

In my second semester of fieldwork at Good Tree, I sat at Dr. Hawthorne's desk as he stood in front of the class, arms bent at his sides, hands resting on his hips. He asked his students to turn to Philippians 4:13 ("I can do all things through Christ who strengthens me"), telling them, as they flipped through their Bibles, that understanding any Bible quote required knowing what a passage meant in its time, reviewing its context within the passage, and recognizing similarities and differences from our own time. The goal was to find "a concise statement of universal truth" that could be applicable today.

"So," he said. "Because I can do all things through Christ, I'm just going to go outside and jump over building seven. I can do all things through Christ, right? Isn't that true?"

"I believe in you!" said a boy sitting in the middle of the class.

"Go!" said another boy sitting nearby.

Dr. Hawthorne laughed. "You don't believe that! You wanna see me hit the wall! You wanna laugh at me when I fail!" The students laughed.

Agents of God. Jeffrey Guhin, Oxford University Press (2021). © Oxford University Press.
DOI: 10.1093/oso/9780190244743.001.0001

He paused, waiting for an announcement to finish before he could continue. "First of all, what does it mean in context?" he asked, returning to scripture. "Here's one way to read the Bible—rip it out of context and say that this particular quote means this. But we don't want to just do that . . . . Instead, we have to read the Bible in—" He paused and looked at the students, his eyes slightly widened, encouraging them to talk.

"Context," said the students.

"Yes. So how might the context here limit 'I can do everything'? You all just took New Testament. Where was Paul when he wrote this?"

"Prison," said the class.

"Right. And was he able to just spontaneously leave the prison?"

"No," the whole class responded.

Dr. Hawthorne nodded. "So maybe what's going on here is not just anything but that I can make it through any circumstance because the Bible strengthens me . . . . "

Next, he asked the students to read Romans 16:16, not telling them the passage is about greeting each other with a holy kiss. A few girls giggled at each other as they made eye contact after reading.

Dr. Hawthorne waited for everyone to finish reading on their own. He then read the passage out loud, looking up from his Bible when he finished. "Wherever your minds may be going with this, it's a holy kiss," he said, sardonically. The students laughed. Dr. Hawthorne told the students that kissing is a part of some cultures, and one student volunteered that his new brother-in-law kisses people a lot.

Dr. Hawthorn nodded. "Your brother-in-law is from a culture where that's accepted. And for most of us, that's not something we would do when we greet someone. Do you see anyone around here doing this?"

"No" said the students.

"You'd get a NODA," said one of the students, which stands for a notice of disciplinary action.

After pointing out their Spanish teacher—called, simply, Señora, does greet people with a kiss, Dr. Hawthorne showed how cultural differences can vary widely: "It looks like the natural thing to do back then." He told his students, "Sometimes it looks like there's a cultural difference. Any other times we need to do exactly what the Bible says to do, even when it appears to be very different from our own culture."

There's a lot going on here. First, Dr. Hawthorne is encouraging his students to go to the Bible for advice about how to live, and to do so in a thoughtful way. But he is not only suggesting that the Bible is a resource for godly living. He is also describing the Bible as a kind of agent: the Bible is "saying" certain things, and Christians must "do exactly what the Bible says to do." Note that it is not God here who is making the request but rather God's agent, the Bible. Indeed, in an interesting slip, Dr. Hawthorne misquotes the passage he had been discussing with his students: instead of saying it is Christ who strengthens him, at one point, he says it is "the Bible" which strengthens him.

Yet this is not really such a misstatement. For, as we will discuss below, in all four of the communities I studied, scripture—whether the Bible or the Qur'an—took on an agentic and authoritative quality. The scripture did things and said things, communicating how to live, giving solace in adversity and clarity in confusion. In these schools, relating to scripture became a habit through which people formed the selves their communities (and their scriptures) understood to be ideal.

I am not arguing that the scriptures here actually have agency or a clear and obvious ethics, even if theologians have made these kinds of arguments. Instead, my argument is that scriptures are special kinds of texts that are felt and understood as having an agency over and beyond the people using and reading them. That agency is related to what various social theorists would call a reification, that is, the social creation of a thing.[1] Yet, as sociologists have long shown, nearly all of social life is one reification or another: a handshake has its weight not because of any natural cause but because of social conventions about what shaking someone's hand entails. Reification in this sense has a dialectical aspect: it is the result of social conventions, even as it strengthens those same social conventions as the reified thing is discussed, used, and experienced. The solemnity of each deal sealed with a handshake makes every future handshake that much more solemn.[2]

As scholars of scripture in religious studies and anthropology have made clear, the meaning of scripture is never obvious or clear absent a certain interpretive community to give its texts meaning.[3] This might seem too nihilistic and postmodern: it seems much easier, for example, to make a claim for reincarnation based on Hindu scriptures than Christian ones. While it is certainly the case that particular texts make it easier to claim this or that theological precept, what communities do with texts is often a creative application which might surprise others reading the exact same text. After class one day, Dr. Hawthorne told me that his graduate study of scripture was often somewhat shocking to him as a conservative Christian, because he found—like many who have studied the Bible—that the Bible is not as obvious a support for Christian theology as some might claim. He said that, when reading Origen's third-century commentaries on scripture, he felt as though the ancient theologian was describing another text.

Dr. Hawthorne was echoing something anthropologists of religion have long argued: scripture's meaning is always *social,* that is, the result of a community of people's meanings, often worked out in contestation and determined by those with the most power.[4] Yet what is perhaps most important about scripture is that even though its actual meanings are socially produced, those meanings often feel natural: that is, they feel obvious, plain, and untethered to any social interpretation. Scripture, in this understanding, just says what it is. And indeed, this *naturalization* of a social thing into the felt experience of a natural thing is the very definition of reification. When we shake someone's hand or pay someone with money, we might—if we have recently read some sociology—think that these are arbitrary social conventions, but that's not usually what we're thinking. And even if that is what we're thinking, it doesn't stop a handshake from being solemn or money from paying for dinner.

Yet if money and handshakes are what sociologists might call institutions, scripture is something subtly different than that, even if it can also fit into most sociological definitions of an institution.[5] Scripture is what I am calling an external authority, by which I mean something felt to be outside of people's lives that can actually compel particular kinds of actions and is understood to have a certain kind of agency to do so. In my fieldwork, I regularly heard people talk about how the Qur'an or the Bible "does" or "says" certain things. However, as I will show, given the subtle distinctions between how the Bible and the Qur'an bound their communities from outsiders, the Bible was felt to have much more "agency" as an autonomous agent than was the Qur'an.

As I here define it, what makes a scripture a scripture is that it is a text with stakes within what Pierre Bourdieu would call a field of power.[6] People might like *The Great Gatsby,* but it is not a scripture in this sense, even if something like psychiatrists' DSM (Diagnostic and Statistical Manual of Mental Disorders) might well be.[7] The DSM, like the Bible or the Qu'ran, is located at the center of a community that shares a common interpretation of the text,[8] and these interpretations—leveraged through the authority of the text—can then declare certain things about the social world and other people's place within them. There is a performative power[9] in scriptural reference that is unavailable to other kinds of texts. A psychiatrist can use the DSM to declare someone schizophrenic, and through that declaration she provides her patient with access to various forms of medical care and insurance payments. In a similar way someone can use the Bible to declare something sinful or the Qur'an to declare something halal in ways that make those texts uniquely powerful within their bounded communities. In making these pronouncements, people who acknowledge the scripture's authority both strengthen that authority and distinguish themselves from those who do not recognize the power of the text.

What makes scripture even more special is that it is more than simply a tool. The scripture is understood as itself making claims and commanding action, and, in the schools I studied, people understood themselves as agents of scriptures' authority.[10] Of course, that authority is not final: in the schools I studied, the Bible and the Qu'ran are understood as ultimately rooted in the authority and agency of God. Yet when people talked about the Bible and the Qur'an, they did not always talk about "God" saying certain things but rather the Bible or the Qur'an saying certain things, or, sometimes, a more intermediate framing of "God's word."

References to scripture's agency were much more common in the Christian schools, where I heard "the Bible says" all the time, though I still heard occasional references to the Qu'ran speaking or doing things at the Muslim schools. And, more importantly, the Qur'an was always understood to have an external authority over and above any one individual. The Muslims I met at these schools did not describe themselves as using the Qur'an to make a point: The Qur'an already had the point. They were simply illuminating it.

Yet, what is the source of that illumination? Here, there was a key difference between the Christian schools and the Muslim schools in that the meaning of the Qur'an was generally understood to be slightly more complex, requiring aid, instruction, and expertise. In contrast, at the Christian schools the Bible's meaning was clear and obvious. This difference only goes so far: nobody described the Qur'an as utterly inscrutable, and neither did anyone find it morally offensive to ask for help with the Bible. Yet there was still a key difference in how the Qur'an and Bible were approached both individually and collectively, creating a norm of interpretation that forms the shape of each scripture's external authority.

Scripture gains its authority in a few ways. First, it functions as a powerful boundary from other communities. Second, it is understood and described as an autonomous agent that acts in people's lives. Third, scripture maintains its power through its role as a habituated practice in people's day-to-day experience of relating to the text, especially reading and memorizing. I'll describe each of these here, after first providing some historical context to the authority of scripture in these schools.

HISTORY AND CONTEXT

Early Protestants—especially certain radical sects coming out of Calvinism—were convinced that Catholics wandered too far from the

Word.[11] The Protestant Reformation not only changed how Christians accessed the Bible; it also changed the role of the Bible in salvation itself. While certain Protestants—Lutherans and Anglicans, for example—are not that different from Catholics in emphasizing the role of sacraments and rituals in religious life, later generations of Protestants came to press more and more upon the role of scriptural understanding and pietistic reading as the central requirements of devotion. This was a complicated process with winnowing on both sides: on one end was a suspicion of Catholic tradition, ritual, iconography, and hierarchy; on the other was an increased emphasis on the role of the Bible in everyday life and a growing optimism in the capacity for everyday believers to come to know God through his word without any mediation. Out of those changes came the Pietist movements in Europe and North America,[12] movements whose emphasis on spiritual devotion and emotional affect had an important effect on Protestant history—with effects still visible in the Evangelical communities I studied here.[13] The Evangelicals I studied don't have sacraments, but if they did, their most important would be the Word.

Of course, Sunni Islam is also radically democratic, but as I will describe in the next chapter, its democratic accessibility is most obvious in prayer rather than the Qur'an. Even though the Qur'an was brought to Earth for everyone, it is often understood to require the aid of religious authorities to understand its meaning. Another complication to this comparison is that the Qur'an is theologically quite distinct from the Bible. If forced to find a parallel in the Christian universe, the better (even if still imperfect) analogy is that the Qur'an is more like Jesus (or like the Eucharist) than it is like the Bible.[14] The Qur'an is sacred not because it is God's revealed words through various prophets and scribes; rather, the Qur'an is God's word itself, spoken by God through the angel Gibreel (or Gabriel). Similar to the Catholic conception of the Eucharist as Christ's body come to Earth, the Qur'an is God's words come to Earth.[15]

Yet this difference between Muslim and Christian scripture is not as obvious as it might appear. Many Christians think of the Bible as the divine word of God, so while they might recognize the Bible as having multiple original languages and time periods, its author is ultimately one person, God. At the two Christian schools, it was God who wrote the Bible, or so I learned when people referred to the Bible as the Word, with that *word* obviously being God's. Or, when I heard in countless interviews and conversations that "prayer is you talking to God, and the Bible is God talking back." There is strenuous debate among Christians about the degree to which scripture is the "word of God" or the inspired word of God,[16] with the latter seen as more aware of the historical basis of scripture's production and the former more insistent on God's ability to speak through the book's disparate human authors to proclaim his actual words. The schools I studied fell much more in the former camp.

There is a somewhat similar debate among liberal and conservative Muslims about the Qur'an, although very few Muslim scholars would argue that the Qur'an itself was "inspired" rather than the literal word of God. Even the most liberal position tends to be that the Qur'an is the actual words of God, narrated through the Angel Gabriel to the Prophet Muhammad, who then shared what he had heard with his people. The people then saw to its composition and memorization, some time later creating the canonical order of books that we have today. While certain secular critics challenge whether the Qur'an was actually composed and canonized in the manner often described,[17] the larger matter of contention for both progressive Muslim scholars and their conservative critics is whether a divinity's words can ever truly be captured by human language, especially as that human language is located within a particular time and place.[18] Certain progressive Muslims do not deny God's words in the Qur'an but simply argue that those words are imperfect vessels for perfection, as any human language is necessarily limited by its historical context and its finite capacity.[19] While this debate has picked up steam in the modern era—driven both by the desire for political reform within Islamic interpretation and developments in the philosophy of language—the capacity of the Arabic language to hold the words of God has fascinated Muslim philosophers for some time, leading to the focus in Islam's classical age on Arabic grammar and linguistics, as well as an early insistence that Arabic truly is the most beautiful language and the Qur'an its most perfect expression.

And this gets at another important difference between the Bible and the Qur'an: while there is some debate about the historical origin of the Qur'an, most Muslim and non-Muslim scholars agree that the text we have today is more or less the same text that the Prophet Muhammad recited to his people. As a result, the Qur'an is marked by some kind of consistency, particularly of language, sociocultural context, and time and (general) place of composition.[20] In contrast, the Bible is marked by its amalgamation across genres and centuries: "a more heteroglossic, polyphonic, or dialogical work is hard to imagine," writes anthropologist James Bielo. Perhaps because of the centrality of the original Arabic text, there was not much focus in the schools themselves on which translation students used in the Muslim schools. In contrast, translations were quite important at the Christian schools as certain more "modern" translations were considered far too liberal. The Evangelicals in the schools I studied tended to use two common translations of the Bible, the New King James Version and the New International Version.[21]

Understanding these texts is not always easy. There is a normative commitment among conservative Protestants to understand the Bible as literally as possible, though they recognize this is often not possible for a variety of reasons, primarily, as Dr. Hawthorne laid out in the vignette that began this chapter, because some commandments were "cultural" and therefore not "religious" or universal. The Qur'an can also be quite complicated, and part of the reason for the gradual importance of the hadith (or accounts of the Prophet's words and actions) was their capacity to flesh out some of the more complex or vague elements of the Qur'an.[22] As various Muslim respondents told me, the Qur'an tells us to pray, and the hadith tells us how. "For us the two go hand in hand," said a staff member at Al Amal. "They are both necessary." There are complicated rules about which of these words and actions must be imitated, which should be imitated though it is not required, and which are simply cultural habits of the Prophet's that are morally neutral.

The question of how best to understand the Qur'an and the lives of the Prophet and his companions is the basis of Muslim law, or shari'a. Muslim scholars throughout history have debated how to understand the idea of shari'a (or "the way"), distinguishing between *fiqh* (legal interpretation) and *shari'a* (the religious law itself) with varying level of optimism about humans' access to the real law.[23] Yet the common basis for these discussions is the Qur'an, and the words and deeds of the Prophet and his companions. As with differences between Christians regarding the books of the Bible—Catholics have more than Protestants—there are significant debates between Shi'a and Sunni Muslims about the hadith. However, as with Christians, a critical mass of their "scripture" is the same.

Unlike Catholics, Orthodox, and mainline Protestants' commitments to certain authorities of interpretation and tradition, Evangelicals generally do not believe they need anything for their theological beliefs outside of the Bible. Church and spiritual leadership are still important for Evangelicals but more as a source of communal accountability. This is not to deny the massive industry of Biblical guidance and faith development in Evangelical media, whether in books, television, websites, or inspirational films. The Evangelicals I worked with chatted with each other and with me about these resources. Yet much more often, I found someone emphasizing their time "in the Word" as a private, unmediated experience, even if it was sometimes obviously guided by the latest insight from this or that Evangelical celebrity about "the Bible's relevance for your life." At both Christian schools, there was little if any focus on church history in religion classes (outside of what happened in the Bible). Good Tree did devote the sophomore year religion classes to the study of "doctrine," and its Worldview class for seniors served a similar function. Yet the other three years of religion focused on the Bible, and "Bible" was the simple name for all four years of religion class at Apostles.

In contrast, both Muslim schools paid significant attention to Islamic history. Evangelicals' emphasis on the complete sufficiency of scripture in some ways parallels more conservative Muslims' insistence that no innovation (*bid'a*) should be allowed in the shari'a, refusing to acknowledge a millennium and a half of Islamic thought in their argument that only the hadith and Qur'an are required.[24] However, I encountered very little Salafi influence in the schools I studied, even if such influences are increasingly common in the United States.[25] In some ways it was the Evangelicals, rather than the Muslims, who were *salafi*, at least in the sense of rooting everything in the original texts and insisting the true meaning should be obvious. At least in the Muslim communities I studied, the Qur'an and hadith were deeply important, but they were also recognized as complex and requiring aid in their understanding, aid that comes both from local guides and from centuries of tradition.

BOUNDARIES

Good Tree brought in guest speakers for most of its school-wide chapel services, and they were often young men like one particular preacher, speaking on a Wednesday afternoon like any other. He was a little under six feet tall, in a full suit that made him much more formally dressed than anyone else in the auditorium. While most speakers at Good Tree were friendly and approachable, this speaker was much more fire-and-brimstone, serious and solemn in his pronouncements. He did not smile much as he told the gathered students about the "signs of conversion." One of these signs was difference: "If you're the same as unbelievers, then it means you're probably not a Christian," he told them. "The first sign of conversion is God's word. Ask yourself that: do I love the Bible? If you don't, it's probably because you're not a Christian."

I often heard the phrase "Biblical Christian" at both of the schools I studied. The Bible was used to distinguish the unserious Christians from the serious ones, those who are untrue from those who are, in the guest speaker's words, "true." As Mr. Morgan told his students at Good Tree, "I call myself a Biblical Christian . . . . If people ask what that means—isn't Christian Christian?—I tell them there's a big distinction between me and some of my acquaintances who call themselves Christian but aren't aware of what the Bible says." For Mr. Morgan, the Bible becomes the essential marker of true Christianity, and an *awareness* of the Bible—which would also be evidence of an ongoing relationship with it—becomes a marker of this marker. The Bible and the practices associated with it—particularly the practice of interpretation and obedience—also becomes a key site of boundary contestations, determining who is truly Christian and who is not. Note also that the Bible is not only an authority here but also an agent: it says things, and what it says must be obeyed.

In contrast, I almost never heard the adjective "Qur'anic." My respondents at Muslim schools cared about the Qur'an: they would describe it as the very basis of Islam and its greatest miracle. Yet, such a phrase would still sound strange: too textualist perhaps, or maybe missing the broader understanding of Islam as a way of life. When I asked students at both schools what people should do to keep their faith strong, it was much more common for Muslims to mention prayer (which we will talk about in the next chapter). When I asked explicitly about the Qur'an, they almost always told me about its importance, and many described how the Qur'an is the basis of everything. As one student at Al Amal, Ibrahim, told me in a taped interview, "We recite the Qur'an in the morning [in the school's daily morning assembly] and then we recite the Qur'an when we pray. Everywhere you go at this school, you always find the Qur'an." The integration of the Qur'an into so much of daily life—rather than insisting upon a discrete, autonomous practice of reading scripture in private life— made scripture at once fundamental and yet less essential (even if quite praiseworthy) to *practice* at the Muslim schools as opposed to the Christian schools. As I will describe later in this chapter, such private reading of the Qur'an was indeed important to many I met at these schools; it was simply considered less necessary and essential than other elements of Muslim practice.

Teachers at both Christian schools were somewhat reflective about the central role scripture held in their lives. Adam Morgan, the senior Worldview teacher at Good Tree, and Mr. Dominguez at Apostles both made clear to their students that they should not defend their faith to non-believers using the Bible. In a conversation about intelligent design and the scientific basis of creationism, Mr. Morgan said, "When a student comes up to you and asks you to explain the Biblical worldview, I will jump off the chapel if you defend it with Genesis 1:1." The students all laughed. In the conversation about jumping off the chapel, Mr. Morgan was talking about how students would defend their beliefs at the local state university. This fear about how well students would stand up to secular scrutiny about their commitment was constant at Good Tree and existed to some extent at Apostles as well. The fear of 'atheist professor confronting Christian undergraduate' is a common trope, the basis of many facebook posts and at least one Evangelical movie series (God's Not Dead). The superintendent at Good Tree told a version of the story starring his brother who defended the Bible itself from a professor's attacks. After embarrassing the atheist professor with his confidence and getting him to acknowledge he is not Christian, the brother said, "The Bible is God's letter to the people of God. And that's what you get for reading someone else's mail!" The superintendent's audience all laughed, and he finished his story with a moment of triumph: "[My brother] said I can answer those questions if you give me equal time. And then [the professor] never brought it up again." The Bible was both central and essential: to attack it was to attack Christianity itself.

The sacred centrality of the Qur'an was just as marked—perhaps even more marked at the Muslim schools. Yet relating to the Qur'an itself was just one way among many that people interacted with Islam. There was much more emphasis on "Islam as a way of life"—a phrase that I heard regularly in my interviews—rather than "Qur'anic" ways of living and distinguishing from the outside world, perhaps because the various forms of Muslim revelation are themselves complex and have been rendered even more complex through generations of interpretation. As such, their boundaries from the outside world were rarely "Qur'anic" but were instead rooted in practices with a basis in the Qur'an and hadith. Again, that is not to say that students and adults in the communities ignored the importance of scripture and maintaining an ongoing relationship to it, as I will describe in the rest of the chapter.

In contrast, a Christian had to be "in the word." A taped interview with a senior at Good Tree is fairly representative of what I found at both Christian schools. When I asked a senior, Megan, about what she had to do to keep her faith strong, she responded almost exclusively about the Bible:

> Well, I think that it's a matter of how you give time to God's word like it's about—it's not just saying oh, I have faith because somebody can say it but it's more like your actions, your works to show that you have faith and truly be sincere and genuine about that so I think to keep my faith I think I would have to be fully committed to what I believe which is God's word, that's where faith is found and that's the only way people can receive that faith.

To be clear, other students at the Christian schools would also emphasize prayer in their answer and not only scripture, but this exclusive focus on scripture was not uncommon. At the Muslim schools, scripture revealed boundaries; at the Christian schools, scripture was itself the boundary.

SCRIPTURE AS EXTERNAL AUTHORITY
The Christian Schools

In his senior Bible class, Dr. Hawthorne started the year by telling students they would do three things, all of which he wrote on the board as he spoke: observations, interpretation, and application. About this last piece, he said application could be understood in two ways: "what should it do to me or what should I do with it." He told students, "I like the first way because it's more about the Bible, because I believe the Bible . . . should transform me. The Bible needs to change who I am." In the Christian schools, scripture was understood to work as an agent with an autonomous authority. Part of that authority stemmed from providing quotations to justify various positions, yet the Bible is not just a holy book to be considered and used in arguments and claims. It is an actual actor, whose authority is experienced as relatively external to any one individual in the community. Reading the Bible might make a Christian a better Christian, but it is not necessarily the reading (or even the person doing the reading) that does the work: to claim that the *reading* is what matters is to claim that it is the individual Christian who is the primary actor. To go back to Dr. Hawthorne's comment, it is to ask "what should I do with" the Bible rather than what the Bible should do with me. Instead, reading the Bible matters because of the *Bible*, which Christians understand as acting in the world.

This insistence that it is the Bible that acts showed up often in my interviews. One junior at Apostles, Chris, told me, "There is something more to the Bible than any other book I've read in my life. Like Harry Potter and Hunger Games, these are just books to me . . . . The Bible, it changes you. It changes who you are." In my first year at Good Tree, I taped an interview with a senior named Vicky, a popular student leader at the school and the daughter of one of the teachers. She told me the Bible "is sort of like the guideline book to how we should live our life. It's almost like a second conscience." I asked her to clarify, and she told me "when I'm struggling with something, I get advice from my parents . . . but [if] I'm still not sure . . . I would go to my Bible. I feel like God would just send me to this passage and it would be clear." Vicky acknowledges—as would anyone in the schools—that it is God who acts through the scriptures. Yet, in much of her description of the Bible, it is less God acting than the Bible itself, and even when God does act, Vicky describes herself as not going to God but going to the Scripture, which will then present God's wishes. When I asked her about how her knowledge of scripture affects her life, she again returned to describing the Bible itself as the agent of enforcement: "There's stuff that I don't do because I know that the Bible says it's wrong. I mean, back when I was, the last time I was in a relationship, I knew the boundaries because I knew that the Bible says your body is the Lord's and not yours."

Similarly, another senior in Vicky's class, Becky, told me in a taped interview that scripture is "final." When I asked whether scripture was important to the school, she said,

> I think Good Tree does go back to the Bible and say, "Well, what does the Bible say about this?" I mean, even if we don't always know as students, the teachers will direct us to that and say, "Well, look in this Scripture and see what God's word says about it." If God's word is what we believe in and what we believe is the ultimate truth, or the ultimate truth is found in there, then if we stray from that, how can we say that we're a Christian school?

For Becky, the Bible is the ultimate boundary marker. Yet what seems to matter most is not any one thing the Bible says but rather the act of going to the Bible itself. God here is subtly distinct from "God's word," in which "God's word" takes on the quality of a subject, a speaker who has things to say.

The Bible was just as active in a taped interview with Mr. Smith, the sophomore doctrine teacher. For Mr. Smith, Christians must believe "what it [the Bible] says is truth, whether you like that or not all the time . . . you have to make a bit of a stand that, yeah, I'm going to then base my character and behavior and world view on that this is an authoritative God-breathed writing." When I tried to get a sense of whether there was anything outside of the Bible that might define Christianity, I asked him if "there is a difference between teaching the Bible and teaching Christianity." He responded that "a secular atheist classroom" might teach the Bible as literature or history, "as opposed to the entire book that you will model your life after." There is little emphasis on tradition or authority, in Mr. Smith's account, about who has the right to make interpretations and who does not. Instead, we simply have the Bible. To be clear, other teachers at both Christian schools—including Dr. Hawthorne at Good Tree—were much more concerned about working out how we know what the scripture actually means. Yet the social construction of scripture's meaning was generally kept at arm's length and never really acknowledged, even in Dr. Hawthorne's class, in which students were promised they'd be able to read the Bible on their own by the end of the year.

The Muslim Schools

The Qur'an was certainly authoritative in the Muslim schools, yet it was somewhat less agentic. People did describe the Qur'an as doing and commanding things, but they did so less often than people at the Christian schools. For example, in a taped interview with Radi, a senior boy at Al Amal, I asked him why people should read the Qur'an. His response portrays the Qur'an with both agency and authority: "Because the Qur'an teaches us—it tells us what to do, what's right and wrong, and tells us our past history, stories about the prophets and everything." It is the Qur'an which is the locus of authority, rather than any specific individual. As Brother Simon, a white convert to Islam who taught at Al Amal told me, in reference to the Qur'an's authority, "It's just like in America, the President is not the boss, the Constitution is the boss."

The Qur'an maintains its status as "boss" by acting in these communities, providing wisdom and authoritative guidance. In one Qur'an class I observed at Al Haqq, Sheikh Yusuf was going over a famous passage of the *Surah al-Mu'minun* (the Believers). The passage, sometimes described as "the jewels of believers," describes the ideal Muslims by the actions they carry out in the world: humble prayer and turning away from evil, the paying of charity and the guarding of chastity, carrying out the required duties and making the mandatory prayers. These are the Muslims who will inherit paradise. The students were unpacking each Arabic word in the class, talking about its various meanings and how it might be translated. Sheikh Yusuf paused and smiled at the class. "These *ayat* [verses] are rich in meaning! . . . The Qur'an is always giving you something more, you get more and more each time. This is the book of Allah. It never fails you if you come to it." It is the Qur'an that acts in this case, even if as an agent of Allah. Yet what is most intriguing is that *reading the Qur'an* was not described as one of the jewels in this passage, while prayer (*salah*) was mentioned twice. As we will continue to describe, the Qur'an was certainly understood as having agentic capacities in the schools, but it was often understood much more as an authority than as an agent. And part of that difference from the Christian schools might have been that the Qur'an was understood more as an authoritative source of practices rather than a required set of practices in and of itself. This is not to deny the importance of reading and recitation, as we will describe further below. The Muslims with whom I worked *did* engage the Qur'an through key practices; the difference with the Evangelical schools was simply that these practices were framed as less central to their identity than was the practice of prayer.

THE POWER OF THE PHYSICAL ARTIFACT

At all four schools, reading and interpreting scripture was an important practice. People tend to think of reading and interpretation as more *discursive* (related to words) rather than *practical* (related to actions). Yet, of course, to speak, read, and interpret are to *do* certain things, and to do those things regularly constitutes a certain kind of practice. In a broad sense those practices were the same in all four schools: there was handling and interacting with the physical object itself; there was reading; there was memorization; there was interpretation by one's self and in consultation with trusted others.

In his monograph *How the Bible Works*, Brian Malley shows that Evangelicals tend to lack a normative concern about the physical entity of the Bible, emphasizing the verbal power of the words themselves rather than the materiality of the text in which they are contained. He interviewed respondents about whether they keep a Bible on the floor and how they treat the book itself, and while his interlocutors admitted that they did treat the Bible differently than other books, they made clear that the book itself was not a thing worthy of protection. I found a similar attitude among my Evangelical respondents, with the Bible respected more than most books (despite some messy classrooms, I never saw a Bible on the floor) but not much else. At Good Tree, I watched in a Bible class as a student threw a Bible at another student. "Who threw the holy word of God at me?" asked the victim, and all the students laughed. The person who threw it blushed. "I didn't realize it was the Bible!" Throwing a Bible at somebody (literally!) is wrong, but it's also kind of funny.

The Muslims with whom I worked did not share this lower regard for the physical artifact of scripture. This is sometimes hard for American Christians to understand, precisely because the historically Protestant country has inherited an anti-Catholic ideology that treats religious objects (like the Bible) as not that different from other things. Of course, many Protestant Americans have found other physical objects to venerate, including the American flag. As with the flag, there is a complicated set of rituals that must be used to dispose of a desecrated Qur'an. Passages from the Qur'an must be respected, which is why students at the Muslim schools often do not write the common Muslim blessing—in the name of

God, the most gracious, the most merciful—on their papers. This first line of the Qur'an was muttered continuously at the Muslim schools—as they began a class, as they prepared to eat their food, as they started a difficult conversation—yet it is not written on homework, as a science teacher at Al Amal explained to me, because someone might throw the paper away. To have such a quote end up in the trash would be terrible—a concern about sacred words I simply did not see at either of the Evangelical schools.

This difference is further reflected in the physical power of the two scriptures. The Evangelicals I met firmly believed in the power of prayer, and they also view scripture as central to the context of that prayer. Scripture, for them, is a necessary starting place for any ethical or moral decision, but it is not necessarily powerful as an artifact.[26] I encountered very few Evangelicals who talked to me about the things that the Bible or Bible passages can do outside of ethics or devotion. Memorized Bible passages, as I will discuss later, are important for both self-formation and spontaneous moments of friendly correction, but they are not seen as powerful outside of these settings. In contrast, I encountered many Muslims who spoke of the power of the Qur'an as a thing-in-itself, even if the belief in its spiritual properties varied tremendously, with many younger Muslims more suspicious of these older beliefs.

In an Islamic Studies class at Al Haqq, a group of boys was giving a class presentation about an early Muslim scholar named Ahmad Ibn Hanbal. The boy described (using a passage suspiciously similar to what I found on Wikipedia that evening!) how Ahmad recited a chapter of the Qur'an over a bowl of water, then gave that water to his son when he was sick. The teacher shook his head and shifted his weight, standing in front of the classroom. He corrected the students' account and then he paused, looking out at the students. "Do you believe in that?"

The girls, sitting on the other side of the room from the boys, paused and looked at each other. The boys stood up front and didn't say anything. One girl said, "I've never heard of something like this." Another said, "I never heard about it," and then a third looked at the other girls, turning around to say, "Old people do believe in that. It's part of their culture."

After a brief conversation the boys sat down again, and one of them asked, "Sheikh, have you ever cured someone?"

The sheikh shook his head seriously. "I don't like anyone to ask me," he said. "I don't want the Sheitan [Satan] to come in and put in thoughts that I have special powers . . . " Yet the students pressed him for a story, and he relented, sharing his experience of curing a non-Muslim whose family had come to him for help. "I made it clear that the Qur'an works for people who believe in it, so he could not have only believed to help him . . . I don't know his intentions then, but he's now a beautiful believer. I read part of the Baqarah [the second book of the Qur'an] and I read the Fatiha [the first book] seven times. . . . This is the Qur'an. It's not me, it's the Qur'an . . . . It could be I read the Qur'an and nothing happened. Sometimes I don't get the results I hope for. If it doesn't work, something is wrong with me. It's not the Qur'an. The Qur'an never fails . . . ."

Afterwards I went to the sheikh to ask him about the formative power of the Qur'an as a means of self-improvement. He eventually understood what I was referring to, and we had an interesting conversation, but his first response was to tell me about a research scientist who claimed to prove the healing power of the Qur'an in hospitals, reading it to patients who might not even be awake. Sheikh Yusuf's first thought was what he had just been talking about: the physical power of the Qur'an as an agent of immediate change within the world, rather than the capacity of its words to change hearts and minds. Of course, hearts and minds mattered, too: the Qur'an contains wisdom for any situation. Yet its power is not limited to its wisdom: sometimes simply the sounds of the words can change a life.

MEMORIZATION
The Christian Schools

Between the two Christian schools, Good Tree paid much more attention to memorization, with every year of Bible class requiring a "memory verse" quiz at the end of each week and a verse test at the end of the month. I talked to Shane McNulty, a junior religion and history teacher, who, along with Dr. Hawthorne, is responsible for choosing the memory verses each year. "We just meet and figure out what quotes we think would be helpful for them," Mr. McNulty told me, showing me that week's quiz from the pile of papers on his desk. "We try to go back and forth between the Old and New Testament, and we're really trying to take the pulse of the student body." The quizzes ask students to write parts of the passage out from memory and the tests ask them to fill in the blanks for the entire passage. The students are not tested for any oral command of the quotes. They are also asked to memorize from one of two translations: either the New King James Version or the New International Version, though the latter must be from its 1984 version and not the more "liberal" later version.

Memorizing Bible quotes is important because Bible quotes are important. They're everywhere: on professionally designed posters in the halls and massive banners in the gym, on printed handouts pasted to doors and decorated construction paper on classroom walls. Bible quotes are whispered throughout the day, shared in moments of struggle, scribbled on Post-it notes for further study. You can't escape the Bible, and its power is obvious. As Mr. Smith, one of the sophomore doctrine teachers told his students,

> Christ spoke of the book of Jonah and He used verses of Scripture to combat Satan . . . . The very fact that you are memorizing Scripture every week is a very good thing. You can tell your mother at the dinner table tonight [he looks at me] you can quote me on this [he looks back at the class] the best way to combat Satan and temptation is to use Scripture . . . guys when you have thoughts that are evil, that you know are dirt, take Scripture and replace those thoughts.

In an interview with him, Mr. Smith told me that memorizing scripture is different from memorizing anything else. Memorizing a Lewis Carroll poem might be fun, but "it doesn't change my life, Scripture changes life." Memorization, like reading, allows for the external authority of scripture to take shape: it give scripture space to act.

Scripture was just as central at Apostles—at the graduation I observed, an associate pastor read a specially selected Bible quote to each senior as they received their diplomas and hugs—yet there was much less of a focus on memorization. It would be impossible for a Bible teacher to avoid assigning memorizing scripture at Good Tree, while at Apostles it was only the freshman Bible teacher—Mr. Dominguez—who had his students memorize a weekly verse.

When I asked teachers at both schools why memorization was important, they often cited 2 Corinthians 3:3: "You show that you are a letter from Christ, the result of our ministry, written not with ink but with the Spirit of the living God, not on tablets of stone but on tablets of human heart" (NIV 1984). There are a variety of ways to interpret this passage, but the way it was usually interpreted to me was that Christians should live in such a way that the scripture is obvious to anyone by examining your heart. For them, memorization was not a necessary part of this process; it was simply a very effective technique. Yet it also shows how memorization helped to strengthen the role of the Bible as an external authority in the day-to-day experience of students.

Some students expressed concern to me that memorizing the Bible was just going through the motions. One freshman girl at Apostles, Allison, said she preferred to read the Bible and to make sure she understood it, which "gives you so much more than if you just know the words." A junior boy at Good Tree, Chris, was even more explicit, calling the required memorizations "a waste of time." This was not, however, because he didn't care about scripture but rather because he had a problem with the emphasis: "It takes away the true value of the verse that you're reading. I'm trying to memorize the verse word for word: I'm just memorizing the words. That's reducing the Bible from high to low." The Christian commitment to spontaneous action, to really meaning it when you engage God, made the memorization of scripture a possible problem.

The Muslim Schools

There were classes at both Muslim schools exclusively dedicated to memorization. The two schools are fairly different along these lines, with one class per day dedicated exclusively to memorization at Al Amal and one class per week at Al Haqq. There are two more Islamic Studies days per week at Al Haqq, plus one day per week dedicated to *tafsir,* or the interpretation of the Qur'an. There is an entirely separate period dedicated to Islamic Studies at Al Amal, meaning that, counting the Qur'an, Al Amal has slightly more than twice as many periods per week dedicated exclusively to Islam. (When I asked about coursework dedicated to Islam, many teachers and students at both schools mentioned the Arabic courses all students at both schools took each day, as the language is a necessary part of both scripture and prayer, and the courses often used Islamic passages for reading assignments). When I talked to teachers at Al Haqq about this difference between the two schools (without naming the first school), they often blamed the parents, saying they were more concerned about their children having AP tests and getting into good colleges than they were about a proper Islamic education. I heard similar complains at Al Amal, especially after one graduation ceremony where the prestige of students' college placements was mentioned much more often than the Prophet Muhammad.

Al Amal has a large gym that doubles as an auditorium, with a stage taking up most of one wall, save a yard or two on each side. On these remaining pieces of wall are written quotes in Arabic about the importance of memorizing the Qur'an and the names of students—boys on one side and girls on the other—who had committed the entire book to memory, thereby becoming *huffaz* (singular: *hafiz*). When I arrived at the school, a multiple copies of a poster were placed all over the walls congratulating a junior girl for having become a *hafiza*. Around the time of the graduation ceremony I attended later that semester, I saw chocolate bars with the image of a junior boy on them, a celebration of his having just become a *hafiz*.

The boy, Ra'ed Rahlis, had been taking his memorization work especially seriously, working with another boy in his class, Dafir Hatem, who was already a *hafiz*. Dafir had a thicker beard than most of the boys in his class, who were either clean-shaven or had some stubble. (There is debate among Muslims about whether men are required or simply encouraged to have some facial hair, with beards generally considered a sign of piety). I often saw Dafir and Ra'ed sitting on the stairs in the school's back lot, working on a passage together. Ra'ed's enthusiasm for Islam also extended to me: of all the people I encountered at all four of the schools, he was by far the most interested in my conversion. Dafir took his faith quite seriously as well, and for both boys there was some tension with the other boys in their class, who tended to be more attracted to the rap music and basketball of their neighborhoods. That's not to say that the other boys discounted Islam—I was always struck by how respectful even the most difficult students were at prayer—but it is to argue that the Qur'an was extremely important to certain students and to others it was just another thing they had to do, perhaps important in an abstract sense but not necessarily something to spend a lot of time worrying about.

I noticed this while observing Qur'an classes at Al Amal, where teachers worked with students on passages they had been asked to memorize. The pronunciation of the Qur'an—a system established shortly after the death of the Prophet and the formalization of the text—is critically important, and most of the corrections the students encountered were not about the words themselves but which vowels to add to which consonants and how long to hold these particular vowels, all of which affects the accuracy of the recitation as well as, occasionally, the meaning of the text. I asked one of the students at Al Amal what Qur'an class entails:

> So basically, the teacher asks you to recite what you had to recite the day before and he tells you if you did it right or not, and you work on that together, and then he has you read your new assignment and you say if you don't understand it or not, and he helps you with all the pronunciation—like a lot of people don't know how to lengthen the words right—and then that's what you memorize that night . . . it's pretty easy, it's not like you have to write things down, you just look at it and read.

In my time observing these classes at Al Amal, I found that they each took turns reciting passages with the teacher, and, when not doing that, they talked to each other, occasionally did homework for other classes, and basically hung out. Some classes were practically chaotic, with the teacher simply focusing on the one student he was working with at the time.

I don't want to give the impression that all classes at Al Amal were like this. In another Qur'an course, Brother Khalil, who also maintained the science lab and taught math, had far less patience for commotion. There were eight students in the class, and Brother Khalil sat in front, reciting passages for the students to repeat. Brother Khalil walked around at the front of the class, mostly having the students repeat him *en masse*, but occasionally calling on individual students. One had a lot of trouble with the Arabic Q, pronouncing a K sound instead. He never really got it, but after five or six tries to repeat it, the teacher just moved on. Three students were sleeping, and Brother Khalil gently flicked their heads as he walked past their desks. A boy quietly whispered along while the teacher worked with another student on his recitation. On another day I observed Brother Khalil's class, he responded to students complaining about all the errors of pronunciation not actually mattering: "This is the way of the Qur'an. If you read the Qur'an without all of this, it is not Qur'an." A student leaned over to me to complain: "I know the whole thing, but every little thing he noticed it. It was BS, man." The boy showed me the book they have to memorize from, which has English on one side and the Arabic on the other, and with explanations for all vocalization markers.

At Al Haqq, there was only one class per week for memorization, with another class in the week explicitly dedicated to the interpretation and understanding of the Qur'an. Sheikh Yusuf, the senior religion teacher and de facto spiritual leader of the school, made that call, telling me he wanted to reduce the amount of "mere memorization," worrying that if students memorized without knowledge, it would be "automatic memorization," which wouldn't "meet the point of spiritual education in this school." He went on: "We don't want to them to be ritualistic. We want them to be spiritually nurtured and enlightened intellectually as well, inspired, that their *din* [religion] becomes a motivating force for them on a daily basis. That's why we stress *salah* so it makes you a better person." The one memorization class a week that happened at Al Haqq was much better behaved than most of what I observed at Al Amal, though ultimately much the same process: students took turns reciting to a teacher. The difference was that all the other students were very quiet, either studying the Qur'an themselves to get ready for their turns or else surreptitiously doing other homework or looking at their smart phones. I only noticed one student with his phone out in the open, and he turned out to be using a website that helped with Qur'an memorization.

When I talked to students about memorizing the Qur'an, nearly all of them agreed it was important, but they were fairly insistent, like Sheikh Yusuf, that the most important thing was the relationship to Allah through his word. Some worried too much of a focus on ritual could miss the relationship. As Janet, a junior girl at Al Haqq told me, "I think [memorizing the Qur'an] is really important and a good thing, but I think it's more important to know the meaning behind the *ayahs* [verses] instead of just memorizing them." Another sophomore at Al Haqq, a sophomore named Usman, said memorizing the Qur'an without understanding its meaning was like "memorizing the Chinese alphabet." A senior boy at Al Haqq, Kareem, said something similar: "I'm not so caught up on the memorizing of the Qur'an . . . . They're convinced that you have to memorize, you have to memorize. Well, it's important to memorize but I feel like it's more important to actually understand."

Yet memorizing the Qur'an was not without its blessings, both in this life and the next. Various students told me something like what Fajr, a sophomore at Al Haqq, said when I interviewed him: "Sometimes, when I'm not strong . . . it helps me feel like a better person. It purifies me. It's like your backup Qur'an in your head. . . . But also, you have to memorize Qur'an because on the Day of Judgment . . . God asks you to read Qur'an and the more Qur'an you know, the more you go up into Heaven." This student—and many others—referred to hadiths that extol the virtues and heavenly blessings for those who have memorized the Qur'an, or even those who simply try quite hard at it. Nearly all of the Muslim students I interviewed told me similar stories about the virtues of becoming a *hafiz*. Nonetheless, many of the students I talked to did not identify memorization as nearly as important as a relationship to the Qur'an through understanding and reading.

In all of these cases the Qur'an had an authority in people's lives, and memorization was an important means both of accessing that authority and making it applicable in the day-to-day. From a sociological perspective, this commitment to memorize the Qur'an—and even debates about whether or not understanding the scripture is superior to memorizing it— played a role in habituating not only specific commitments to the text itself but, much more importantly, the *role* of the scripture as an authority in people's lives.

At the Muslim schools there was almost universal support for memorizing the Qur'an, even if students did not always live up to their professed commitments in memorization class. At the Christian schools, many students said they were ambivalent about memorization, which they recognized is probably a good thing but which they did not take especially seriously. They would rather just focus on reading. These differences probably have much to do with an ancient tradition of memorizing the Qur'an all the way back to Islam's first generation. Another possible explanation might be the commitment within Evangelical Christianity to a *spontaneous* relationship to faith: memorization, in this sense, might feel too rote and too forced, not living out the proper spontaneous, free engagement with Christian scripture. Yet it is important to note that this concern was not unique to the Christian schools: respondents at both Muslim schools also worried that memorization could make their experience of Islam too rote, not sufficiently attuned to the meaning and experience of God.

READING

The Muslim Schools

One teacher at Al Amal, Brother Ahmed, told me in a taped interview that he felt frustrated his school focused so much on memorization. "I don't know if the teachers are teaching as much as we should on application rather than memorization," he told me. I asked why that mattered. "I try to live my life by the book," he said, insisting that the Qur'an is the very basis of Islam. Yet when I asked whether he reads the Qur'an regularly, he told me he did not. He tries to do so in the summer, however. "The time that I have right now in terms of reading the Qur'an and contemplating the words of the Qur'an is very limited. So I try to make that up at least in the summertime and during Ramadan." The Qur'an was a required source of moral practices—Brother Ahmed later told me about how the Qur'an influences how he interacts with his students—but it is not necessarily itself a required practice, at least not in the sense of daily reading like I found for many of the Evangelicals with whom I worked. It is certainly quite different from how Brother Ahmed would describe the five daily prayers, which he would never put off until a few hours from now, let alone the summer.

Of course, the Qur'an forms the content of many other required practices, not least key elements of the five daily prayers we will discuss in the next chapter. Also, various calls to God and sayings throughout many Muslims' day come from the Qur'an (and the hadith) as well. The Qur'an matters throughout these schools' day, just not necessarily via the required practice of reading. In a taped interview with Issa, a freshman at Al Haqq, he told me that his school "doesn't really stress on reading the Qur'an, but they do stress . . . how important it is for the kids to still be connected with the Qur'an while taking care of their studies at the same time." To "be connected" might not necessarily mean regularly reading the scripture, and Issa described regularly reading the Qur'an as more a "side thing" to what's required in Islam.

Yet Issa's classmate, Tasmir, told me that he reads the entire Qur'an during the holy month of Ramadan (as do many Muslims), and he said "at least two or three times a week I'll sit down and read a page." He also said he often reads a passage of the Qur'an with his family before they go to sleep.

Similarly, a senior at Al Haqq, Muad, told me in an interview, "I want to improve my relationship with the Qur'an. The last four or five months I made a commitment to myself that every night I would sit down—maybe just 10 or 15 minutes—just read a portion of the Qur'an, know what it is, know the meaning of it, and try to apply it to my life." He told me he reads the text in both Arabic and English, and it has inspired him to push himself further, "knowing the struggles of the people of the past . . . and their efforts to please God and their worship made me feel like I have that room for improvement." I would say around half of the students I spoke with shared this commitment to regularly reading the Qur'an and understanding its meaning, with the other half emphasizing that such an action is obviously praiseworthy but not necessarily something they themselves do.

Emphasizing memorization can go alongside the importance of reading the Qur'an. For those who memorize, "they don't need a literal, a physical book to be with them for them to have the Qur'an. Anywhere they go, they'll be thinking about it . . . . Everything they see, it'll remind them of certain verses." The student who told me this, Yunus, was a senior at Al Haqq. He told me he struggled with memorization and that it was more important to be able to understand the Qur'an first. And that was entirely his goal. When I asked Yunus about the main thing Muslims should do to keep their faith strong, he responded that "one of the main things is to read the Qur'an, keep close with the Qur'an." When I asked why, Yunus told me "The Qur'an is the guideline to life. So the closer you are with it, the closer your heart to it, the more you're going to want to do good things." For Yunus, and for others who make a habit of reading the Qur'an, it functions both as an agent ("the guideline to life") and as an authority. Yet, even those Muslims who did not make a regular habit of reading the Qur'an still recognized its authority in their lives, as well as the role both reading and memorizing might have in honoring and maintaining that authority.

The Christian Schools

When I asked students at the Christian schools about what distinguished someone as a good or serious Christian, they would nearly always mention reading the Bible. Jim, a freshman at Good Tree, gave an illustrative answer:

I think it's someone that they walk in the faith that God has provided. Like, they believe Jesus Christ has died on the cross for our sins, that he came and rose again on the third day and that the only way into Heaven is by believing that Jesus came, he died, rose again for our sins and that there will be a second coming with a rapture and everything and their faith with God, they read the Bible, they do their devos.

Note how Jim first describes how someone walks in their faith, a common expression among Evangelicals to indicate that someone is serious about their Christianity. I often heard people talking about their "walk" at both Evangelical schools. His examples of that walk are statements of beliefs rooted in the Bible and then the reading of the Bible itself. To believe and to profess belief are both examples of action, but it is noteworthy again how focused the Christian schools were on orthodoxy and *saying and believing things* as forms of habituated practice.

When I asked Jim about what he means by *devos*, he told me "devos is when I read the Bible . . . usually I just open to a random page . . . and I read a few verses and then I just spend five to ten minutes thinking about it, thinking about what God is trying to tell me." "Do your devos" was a common phrase in both Christian schools, short for "do your devotionals," and it usually had this meaning of reading the Bible, either through a prepared set of readings or by simply choosing a passage at random.

To be clear, not everyone I interviewed read the Bible regularly. There were more people who claimed to read the Bible on a daily basis at the Christian schools than there were people who claimed to read the Qur'an on a daily basis at the Muslim schools, but there was also considerable peer pressure to claim you read the Bible every day. Given that, I was surprised by how many students admitted to not reading the Bible often at all. One student said she doesn't really read it, and when I asked why, trying to determine if it was a crisis of faith or something similarly dramatic, she said it was simply her social life. "Like the Internet. Like that's pretty much the whole reason why," she told me, when I asked why she no longer read scripture on her own. Other students admitted to trying to read the Bible a few times a week, but then becoming busy with sports or something else. One senior, Jessica, told me in an interview that reading the Bible regularly was an important theme in the senior's service trip to the Dominican Republic: "Half of my class talked about how they don't read the Bible. They want to now. I obviously don't know how they're doing since then, but they brought it back up at the wrap-up . . . . Just everyone talked about reading your Bible in the Dominican. So it was totally God." Reading scripture was an essential practice at Good Tree, and if students were not doing so, it was a problem that had to be resolved, apologized for, or excused.

One of those students, a boy named Caleb, said his time in the Dominican Republic had a significant effect on him. When I asked him what it would mean if I told him someone was a serious Christian, his first response that "they're really in God's word . . . like they're reading the Bible a lot, they're acting on what they're read . . . and they're speaking out about it." He said he did not consider himself a serious Christian before his trip to the Dominican Republic. He was moved by the connection he found to the children with whom he worked, despite not knowing their language. He was motivated by the bonding his class felt in their service projects and travels. And he was also inspired by a message they had the first night: "It was just, like this guy talked about [how] we need to be like reading the Bible every day and stuff, and that just kind of like: I felt like, well, I haven't been doing a good job of that. Like that's something I need to do." He said he's been much more serious about reading the Bible ever since then.

Students at Apostles said more or less the same things about the Bible as did the students at Good Tree. Not all of them read the Bible regularly—one of them admitted he knew the stories but he just didn't like reading—but those that did said something like what Michelle, a freshman at Apostles told me in our interview. She said reading the Bible had helped her through tough times, especially the example in the Book of Job. She said, "It's very important for any Christian to read the Bible consistently" because "it fits perfect with every situation you're going through."

When I asked Megan, another senior at Good Tree, what it meant to call someone a serious Christian, she said that "it means I take my beliefs seriously and I believe what I believe and wouldn't let anyone challenge that." When I asked what she should do to keep her faith strong, she told me "I would have to be fully committed to what I believe, which is God's word, that's where faith is found and that's the only way people can receive that faith." Reading scripture regularly thereby allows for the Bible to work as an agent of God's will, empowering God's authority and blessing serious Christians with faith: "You have to renew your mind and renewing your mind comes through the word of God, the way you read it, the way you apply it, it changes the way you think, it changes the way you carry yourself [from] how you were before to what you are now." Like Megan, many students told me they noticed a difference in themselves when they were not reading the Bible and when they were: they became kinder and calmer, more virtuous and capable of sharing God's message with others.

THE PROBLEM OF INTERPRETATION

In each of the schools there was always the danger that scripture would not be able to act, that its authority would be challenged. Mr. Lopez, the senior and junior Bible teacher at Apostles, warned that, "The Devil knows the Bible and he will use the Bible against you." A scripture can be less effective because a body is incapable of using it or because a willfully evil person misrepresents it. As Sheikh Khaled told his class at Al Amal, "The Qur'an will not benefit anyone who chooses to do evil . . . just because you memorize the Qur'an doesn't mean you are not evil; if you memorize the Qur'an and are still evil, it means you have not let the Qur'an have an influence on you."

Nonetheless, the biggest problem in using scripture was ignorance rather than evil. Scriptures are complicated, and they take work to interpret. This insight makes intuitive sense to the Muslims with whom I worked, who were quite comfortable with a tradition of scholarship that helps to explain how the hadith and Qur'an fit together. Yet it was something of a paradox for Evangelicals, for whom the plain, easy meaning of scripture seemed to bely the need for authorities to instruct in its proper reading. In all four of the schools, though, there was an insistence that scripture was really the authority that did the work, allowing adults and young people alike to insist that it is scripture that is acting (and enforcing) rather than anyone else. Any religious disciplinarian with good intentions is ultimately an agent of God, yet what was noteworthy in the schools was the degree to which scripture came to take on this role of intermediary agent. It was not God to teacher to student but rather God to scripture to student, with the teachers understood as simply showing what scripture says rather than forcing any belief. And when they *were* forcing belief, it was almost outside of their hands: they're just doing what scripture says, after all. Yet the challenge in everyone accepting such coercion is coming to a communal agreement on what scripture says.

At the Christian schools, I noticed a certain formula: the Bible might appear difficult, but given just a bit of background knowledge it is actually quite simple. The only teachers for whom this was not the case were Mr. Dominguez at Apostles and Dr. Hawthorne at Good Tree, both of whom stressed there are parts of scripture that are actually quite difficult. However, even these men stressed that this difficultly required a certain kind of expertise available to each individual. Following that early Protestant commitment, every person could still be a priest inasmuch as the most important job of a Protestant "priest"—at least at these schools—is to interpret scripture. The only real possibility of error here is misunderstanding something, as the Bible itself cannot be wrong. As Joe Smith, the sophomore doctrine teacher told his students, "I believe and Good Tree subscribes to the idea that the Bible, even though it is not the original autographs is still pretty much without error." He went on to insist that any of those errors could be easily explained.

As the Christian section of any bookstore will make clear, my Christian respondents still often asked for help in their understanding of scripture and how to access and implement its authority. I asked many of my interviewees where they go if they don't understand scripture, and many of them said they went to parents, teachers, or a minister. Yet there was nonetheless an overriding sense that revelation came through individual experience. I asked students in one of Joe Smith's Scripture classes at Good Tree about the problem of knowing what scripture means, and one boy told me, "I would say that if I have a question about a passage and I just accept someone else's opinion without thinking about it, then I'm a bad Christian. I need to figure it out on my own."

"But what about when you have a question or don't know?" I asked.

"I would try to figure it out on my own," he said. "I might ask my pastor for help, but I wouldn't take their word as law."

Another student said, "A lot of times I have questions and I talk to my parents or my pastor, but I need to make sure that I really bring it to the Lord myself."

Mr. Smith smirked. "You notice none have said my Bible teacher."

The students laughed, and one blurted out: "Of course Mr. Smith too!"

Mr. Smith's discomfort is an interesting depiction of the paradox of Evangelical education: on one hand, here is someone whose job is to teach how to read the Bible, yet what he is teaching should be easy and obvious. What does a teacher do if each student is their own priest? The challenge of giving scripture too much power is that it can make it impossible for teachers to claim any of their own. The way teachers at the Christian schools resolved this problem was by insisting that the *meaning* of scripture, even if plain and obvious, just so happened to accord with what they were already teaching, and if their students disagreed it was simply a question of insisting, as Mr. Morgan does in the beginning of this book's introduction, that the Bible has a coherent authority that just so happens to accord with what the teachers would like their students to believe.

Many students were already sufficiently aligned with the schools' conservative Christian commitments, such that getting them to agree about what the Bible really said was not altogether difficult even if there were disagreements on the margins—wishing the school had a prom, for example, or complaining about having to memorize Bible quotes. Students usually described the school as basically just letting the Bible do its work, as though no real interpretation were required. Even one student who did explicitly use the word *enforce* did not describe such force regarding "right interpretation." I did a taped interview with a student named Amber at Good Tree, and she told me that "here they do enforce Christianity." When I asked what that meant, she said "like that God has a purpose for your life and that certain things can't be tolerated . . . and the Bible does teach that and does enforce that, and the more you have a full understanding of it, the easier it is to tell what's right from wrong." For Amber, the force was not to get people to agree with a certain understanding of the Bible but rather to get people into Christianity, in which the Bible itself teaches and enforces. As Amy, a senior at Good Tree told me in a taped interview, "It's not that they're trying to enforce you to believe what they believe, it's something—it's more about who you are and how you accept what they're teaching you." If a student turns herself correctly, the truth will be clear and easy to accept.

Nonetheless, there were the occasional students who recognized force as something much more explicit. They did not share what sociologist Pierre Bourdieu would call the school's *doxa,* or implicit, unspoken beliefs and sense of how the world should work. One sophomore girl at Apostles named Leslie said she's no longer a Christian. She thought of Bible classes as arbitrary impositions, and, when I asked her what she thinks "this school is trying to do," she responded, "enforce God into our education." When I asked what that meant, she said "I'm not saying that everyone in the school is a Christian. They really can't force it into us. They're just trying to incorporate it." Leslie is a Latina girl who said her struggles with Christian faith had begun in the past summer, and they were confirmed when she got to know another atheist in her class, who convinced her to believe in evolution and support gay marriage. This crisis of belief was not rooted in what the Bible says but in Christian belief in general. For Leslie, as for many of the students and teachers I encountered at the Christian schools, the Bible's authority was all-or-nothing. As a result, the way people interpreted the Bible as straightforward and unerring simultaneously made it strong for those who believed and brittle for those who did not. Indeed, this kind of fixed Biblicism can explain why so many conservative Christians leave the faith in college, a topic regularly discussed with fretful faces by the teachers and staff at Good Tree and Apostles.[27]

When I talked to Muslim students about what they thought about an *ayah* in the Qur'an or a specific hadith, they would usually tell me what they thought, even as they would also acknowledge they were not entirely sure and that I should really talk to the Sheikh about the issue. To claim a lack of knowledge is a normative prescription in much of Islam, and so I met many very wise men and women who would insist they knew very little. While modesty was an important virtue in the Evangelical schools as well, I did not see this specific practice of well-read people emphasizing how little they knew about the Bible. Still, there is an important difference between saying that the Qur'an and hadith require interpretation and saying they are wrong. In one of Sheikh Khaled's classes at Al Amal, they were talking about inheritance law, and a junior, Hasan, questioned a law. A senior named Farid yelled in mock outrage "What? Are you questioning the wisdom of the Prophet?" Other students immediately joined suit, pretending to be deeply upset. A junior, Talal, called him a *kafir* (nonbeliever), and everyone laughed at this.

Sheikh Khaled said "No, no we welcome his opinion," not recognizing, I think, the students' sarcasm.

Hasan repeated himself: "It doesn't make sense to me."

The sheikh looked visibly shocked. "What? You have only one year to graduate, and you will never be an imam."

"I'm not saying that," said Hasan. "I'm just saying the numbers don't make sense to me."

The sheikh looked very stern. "So the numbers don't make sense to you and so it is senseless? You are calling the word of God senseless? If a Christian or a non-Muslim were to look at this," he said, pointing at me, "If *ustaz* [a term of respect; mister] Jeffrey were to look at this and say it is senseless, that would be his right, but you as a Muslim, you must accept the Qur'an."

Hasan shook his head. "That's not what I said. I said I didn't understand it."

"No," said one of the boys. "That's not what you said, you said it doesn't make any sense."

"Well, remember," said the sheikh, "that Muslims are those who believe in Allah even though they have not seen him."

I do not want to represent Sheikh Khaled as a complete literalist. In another class, he was talking to students about conversion and why certain Muslims were punished for leaving Islam. He looked at me, telling the class, "You all have to tell Ustaz Jeffrey that this is complicated. You have to give the hadith life! You have to give it flesh! Don't simply take the hadith when it is dry like, and just do what it says." Sheikh Khaled here is making clear that the hadith *acts*, making a demand on our action. Yet he is also insisting that there is a necessary process of interpretation to understand that action and take it into account. And perhaps most importantly, it is Sheikh Khaled who is able to make this adjudication, or if not Sheikh Khaled then people like him, scholars with real expertise. Yet that authority is still external, both to Sheikh Khaled and to his students. The authority is not simply contained in God, either. It is, at least partially, experienced as within the hadith itself, with a command that must be understood and obeyed. And while he was primarily discussing hadiths in these ethnographic scenes, I observed him making much the same claims about the Qur'an. In that sense, it was both hadiths and the Qu'ran that could function as agents of God.

CONCLUSION

It's worth returning to Dr. Hawthorne to describe scripture's capacity as an external authority. Dr. Hawthorne and I did four taped interviews in his office, discussing a wide range of issues. We occasionally talked about gay marriage, and he was characteristically thoughtful in his response:

> You listen to the politically active, conservative, Evangelical leaders; who's the problem? It's the gays . . . . It's the easy thing to point the finger. Oh, they're the problem when we're not really dealing with our own problems and then just the whole idea of hating the sin, loving the sinner; it gets completely missed whenever we start getting politically motivated that they're the bad guy. We're all sinners in need of a savior, and we have—I mean, and that's how I try to present the whole homosexuality issue. I mean, I wish I could say it was okay but I have to follow the Bible, and so I can say that I have to say homosexual practice is a sin. Do I believe that some people are born naturally tempted to that? Yes, just like I am tempted to look at other women other than my wife, and that's something that I can't say well that's how God made me so it's okay. That's something that I need to deal with. So I mean, it's—boy, I wish it was okay but the Bible tells me it's not.

In this interview, Dr. Hawthorne twice told me he "wished" he could say that "homosexuality" was permissible. What was preventing him? The Bible itself. It actually "tells" Dr. Hawthorne that being LGBTQ is not okay. As such, when Dr. Hawthorne teaches his students about gay marriage or anything else, he is simply acting as an agent for something that compels him: it is the Bible that acts here, an authority external to both Dr. Hawthorne and his students.

The major difference between the two Evangelical schools in this regard was the possibility of new revelations. The Bible was the end at Good Tree, while at least some teachers and students at Apostles seemed open to newer revelations, including a video the senior religion teacher, Mr.

Lopez, showed in his class in which a woman recounted her quite vivid and celebrity-filled visions of Hell. I asked the senior Bible teacher at Good Tree, Dr. Hawthorne, about people continuing to be influenced by the Spirit even after the Bible was written and he said, "There are some people who say that we're 'putting God in a box' by limiting Him to what he said in the Bible, but these are the words God gave us—he gave us these words to understand him—God gave us a box [which is the Bible]."

There was a sense at both Christian schools that this "box" is democratically available to all, even from someone like Dr. Hawthorne, who was quite aware of the historicity of the Bible. This was not the case in the Muslim schools. Muslim scripture was often rooted in a trust in authorities, which was less the case for Muslim prayer: even if the prayer itself was structured in authoritative rituals, Muslim students did not need an authority figure to pray on their own. In contrast, there was a real sense that teachers and other religious leaders—as well as history and context—were necessary to help someone understand the meaning and constraints of the Qur'an, the basis of its authority and agency. As Brother Yaqub told a group of juniors in his class at Al Haqq, "You have to be qualified in the tradition before you can say Islam teaches this." That emphasis led to the consecration of the Qur'an and hadith as the very source and foundation of Islam (rooted ultimately, of course, in God) but not necessarily its most important practice or its most visible distinction from the rest of the world. In the Christian schools, on the other hand, there was a continuous concern that students be in the Word, as what truly separates Christians from outsiders is the Bible itself and their ongoing relationship to it.

I had a lengthy taped interview with Brother Yaqub at a diner near Al Haqq. While this last quote might make it appear that Brother Yaqub was deeply authoritarian, he was often just as insistent that students "already know" what's right or wrong. The difference is in the discretion, but note that it is the authority that makes this discretion. I asked him about a boy who had been trying to figure out if a certain action was *haram* [forbidden], and he told me "[the boy] wanted me to give the answer that he wants." Brother Yaqub related a story about how someone asked a companion of the Prophet if there is repentance for murder and was told yes, and someone else was asked if there was repentance for murder and was told no: the difference was that the first wanted forgiveness for an action already completed, while the second wanted to be able to expect forgiveness for a murder about to occur. "So you had to understand the psychology of the individual," he said. "Maybe a Salafi [a conservative Muslim emphasizing the mandates of scripture] would say that there's got to be strict rules that have to be followed at all times. But if you really look at that hadith and

the way the prophets talk . . . so much depends on knowing the situation."
Brother Yaqub doesn't deny that there are rules: he doesn't believe "everything is contingent," and he recognizes there are certain claims for which
"there's nothing in the text that can help you with that."

There is a way that scripture is a "box" for Brother Yaqub in a way similar
to that described earlier for Dr. Hawthorne. Yet, given a tradition of scholarly interpretation, modeled both within Islamic history and the hadith
itself, there is more room in this box for different situations as they occur,
making the Qur'an, in some sense, less a box than a door. Yet whether box
or door, these scriptures had a felt authority in these schools, acting as
agents of God.

CHAPTER 6

ᴄᴧᴏ

Prayer as External Authority

I spent a lot of time in the basement of Al Haqq, observing Brother Yaqub's junior Islamic Studies classes. The classroom was sparsely decorated, and he had the students arrange their desks into a circle. The boys' and girls' classes were separated, and he often held the classes one before another, generally about the same theme. Brother Yaqub is a brown-skinned Palestinian American, the kind of young teacher who is young enough to be comfortable with high school students but confident enough not to care whether they think he's cool (which they did). He regularly challenged the students' complacency, whether liberal or conservative, encouraging them to recognize "Islam is much bigger than what you learn at Al Haqq."

On a day I observed both classes, he asked both the boys and the girls to write a letter to salah, the Muslim form of prayer that is required five times a day. "Okay," he told the boys, after expressing some frustration at how long it took them to get settled. "So we are going to write a letter to salah, as though salah is a person . . . you meet Salah face to face, and you need to have a conversation with Salah, and you tell Salah how you treated him or her, your relationship with Salah, have you been good to Salah, how you have been when you're hanging out with Salah."

He gave the students 15 minutes, asking two boys to leave for talking in the meantime. Brother Yaqub collected the papers, randomly distributing them to other students to read. The first, third, and fourth letters thanked salah for its effect on the writers' lives. The second and fifth were laments: in the second letter, the unnamed boy wrote, "Salah, I used to love you and focus my life around you and now I barely remember who you are. You protected me from hellfire . . . it's because of you my life is protected

Agents of God. Jeffrey Guhin, Oxford University Press (2021). © Oxford University Press.
DOI: 10.1093/oso/9780190244743.001.0001

and organized . . . now I only remember because I am scared of hellfire and not because I love you." In the fifth letter, another student admitted, "I see you five times a day yet I don't really know you." The rest of the letters alternated between these declarations of gratitude and inadequacy, admitting a lack of sufficient focus (*khushu*) or "standing you up" by not praying at the established times.

Brother Yaqub had the girls complete a similar exercise, and their letters had a slightly more romantic feeling to them, though they were ultimately quite similar, expressing both gratitude and regret, worrying that they're not praying enough or that they don't really mean it when they do make their prayers. "Dear Salah," one girl wrote. "I know how important you are to me, or rather how important you should be. I know that my relationship with you should be better . . . a lot of things get in between us . . . I hope you don't ever give up on me . . . ." Another girl wrote that, "Recently, I prayed three days in a row and I could notice immediately the difference. I felt like the black parts were scraped from my heart, but it's hard to keep it up. Lately I've been feeling a nagging in my head about you, one that I feel bad ignoring."

After reading each other's letters, both boys' and girls' classes asked Brother Yaqub a lot of procedural questions about salah: how to stand, how to hold their arms, how to concentrate. He answered these questions, yet while answering them he kept returning to a theme I heard repeatedly in my time at both Muslim schools: "Salah has a body and a soul. Sometimes if you only remember the body, you'll forget the soul."

Prayer has a kind of agency in Brother Yaqub's exercise, similar to what I described in the previous chapter on scripture.[1] As I noted earlier, scripture in the schools I studied could often take on an agentic quality, and in two senses of the word *agent*: first, in the sense of *agency*, scripture was understood as actually doing certain things; and second, in the sense of *being an agent*, scripture was understood as being an agent of God, an intermediary actor who, like an angel or prophet, intervenes between God and God's people. Of course, it would be heretical to call scripture an angel or a prophet in any of the schools I studied, just as it would be theologically nonsensical to claim that scripture gains its ultimate meaning from anything other than God. Yet there was nonetheless this *sociological* sense that scripture *acted* and was necessary for certain key practices and (practiced) beliefs. This is why I have been referring to scripture as an external authority: it is felt to have a kind of legitimate power, that is *authority*, outside of any one person or group and even relatively autonomous from God. Scripture, as I showed, *authorizes* key practices and prohibitions.

Brother Yaqub's exercise shows how prayer can take on an agentic, authorizing quality in these same ways. Prayer is understood to act on its own and is understood to be a kind of authorizing, autonomous actor—one that, for the purposes of this exercise at least, can be addressed as a being. While rarely as explicitly as in this class project, my respondents often used the word *prayer* as an actor in sentences, describing what prayer can do or accomplish, generally in connection to God's actions in the world but not always. I regularly heard that "prayer changes things," and indeed that very quote was on the back of a T-shirt Good Tree students made for themselves after a mission trip.

So what does prayer change? It can change situations: you can ask God for help with an uncle's illness or an upcoming exam. It can also change people, whether because someone requested the change in themselves or in others, or just because that's what prayer does. It's that second sense of change that is perhaps most important, because for nearly all of my respondents, prayer was not just a way to get something from God. Prayer was an intermediary between a person and God, and through that intermediary people changed. They became more virtuous, more present, more aware of themselves and their role in a vital narrative of religious renewal.[2] In that sense, prayer is an agent more in the second sense of an intermediate actor *between* two people. In a different sense, prayer can also be understood as a kind of technology, especially in Michel Foucault's sense of a technology of the self, in that prayer allows for a kind of development of particular virtues.[3] As one of the students noted above—and as we will see more of in this chapter—people notice a change in themselves when they pray, and they attribute that change to prayer.

As with scripture, this external authority is felt to have a kind of agency and authority within their communities, and that authority is maintained and made to feel natural and obvious through the maintenance of key boundaries and the continuation of key practices. This chapter will therefore be organized much like the chapter on scripture, beginning with a historical overview, then describing boundaries, going over how prayer is experienced as agentic and authoritative, and finally going over the practices that help prayer maintain its authority.

THE PRACTICES OF PRAYER (AND THEIR HISTORY)

The Centrality of Salah

For those Americans influenced by Evangelical Christianity, the word *prayer* tends to mean "just talking to God," or among American Catholics it might mean specific recitations, such as the Our Father or Hail Mary.[4] For

American Muslims, the term is often more complex. Most of my Muslim respondents used the word *prayer* to refer specifically to salah, yet they also sometimes used it to refer to *du'a* and *dhikr*.[5] To "make *dhikr*" means to remember (or make mention of) God, and this practice is often characterized as simple words or exclamations of praise throughout the day. Dhikr can also be enacted by spending a certain amount of time ritually repeating important phrases, such as *"La Ilaha illa Allah," "SubhanAllah,"* or *"Alhamdulillah,"*[6] sometimes using prayer beads as a means of focusing the mind. There are various guides for how to make *dhikr* that American Muslims can access online. To "make *du'a*" generally means to make a request, saying a memorized prayer as a form of supplication in a certain set of circumstances, of which there are hundreds if not thousands. As commonly understood, *du'a* is different from *dhikr*, and both are quite different from *salah*. As Al Haqq's director of religious instruction, Sheikh Yusuf, explained to me, "*Dhikr* are words that the prophets taught—part of the sunnah, the hadith. These are words that remind the one who says them of Allah, *subhanahu wa-ta'ala* [the most glorified, the highest; an honorific said after saying the name of God]: when they wake up in the morning, when they eat, after they finish eating, when they go to bed, when they come out of the bathroom, when it rains, when they see the lightning."

Du'a is subtly different: "The *du'a* is a central aspect of a Muslim's life," Sheikh Yusuf told me. "Asking of Allah, for whatever, in whatever situation you are in, whatever they need from Allah. *Subhanahu wa-ta'ala*, there are specific things to be learned here in terms of these words of Allah, how to follow these words of Allah, making these specific prayers. There are different kinds of prayers that cover almost everything." Lists of *du'a* are also easily available online. While it is often considered important to make *du'a* following the Prophet's example (or sunnah), Muslims in various Islamic cultures will supplement or replace these supplications with their own improvised prayers, as I have described in other writings.[7]

In virtually all Muslim communities—and certainly the two I studied—salah is the most important and emphasized of these three forms of prayer. However, these distinctions get complex: after all, there is a moment in salah in which Muslims make *du'a* themselves, almost always in their own words. Nonetheless, at least in the schools I studied, when people said "make *du'a*" to each other, they usually referred to the prayers said as separate from salah.

Salah is a physical process repeated five times daily, and it is the second of Islam's five pillars, preceded only by the *shahada*, or the statement of belief in Allah and the Prophet Muhammad. Salah can be done either individually or communally—though men are required to attend communal services on Friday afternoon. Certain interpretations of Islam discourage women from attending on Friday or are neutral about their attending, though the schools I was in required women's attendance each afternoon if they were not on their period.

Salah entails a series of opening rituals and then kneeling, standing, prostrating, and recitations, which, in one iteration, are called a *rakat*. The number of required *rakats*[8] varies slightly among the five required performances of salah each day, and the salah is generally performed early in the morning, in early afternoon, in later afternoon, in the evening, and shortly before bedtime (with an optional and encouraged prayer near midnight). Within the salah, Muslims recite passages of the Qur'an and have time to make their own intentions.

One of the main reasons for salah is simply its requirement: as many hadith attest (and as I continually heard through my fieldwork), Muslims' lives will first be judged by their prayer, and increased prayer will yield increased rewards in the afterlife (this extends to *du'a* and *dhikr* as well). The Muslim parents and children I encountered and interviewed during my fieldwork have been learning how to "make salah" since they were children, and for the high school students it had become second nature to them. This emphasis on salah extended to the Islamic Studies classes in both schools, where it came up regularly, in some ways simply because salah is complicated: there are certain rules and scholarly debate about when, what, and how much to do, how to make up missed prayers, how to clean oneself beforehand (*wudu*), and how to supplement one's prayers by additional devotions (*sunna*).[9] Yet it is also true that salah is challenging to do regularly and on time. Muslims in these schools generally acknowledged to me that salah was difficult, both because of its time commitments and also because of the necessity for concentration, or *khushu*, which we will discuss more later.

In her recent monograph on Muslim prayer, Marion Katz describes how salah has maintained its current form and importance with only subtle changes since the very first century of Islam. There have been— and continue to be—debates on the margins: different traditions within Islam might hold their hands differently or say subtly different prayers. While there is near universal agreement salah *should* be said in Arabic, there is some debate about whether salah *must* be said in Arabic, especially if the person praying does not understand the words she is saying.[10] There has been much more recent debate about how communal salah is gendered, that is, how men and women are asked to separate during prayer and how men are often understood as the only people able to lead other men or mixed congregations in prayer.[11] Yet these debates rarely engage the question of the content, timing, or central importance of salah itself.

Prayer as Just Talking to God

In my interviews with students and teachers at all four schools, I asked, quite simply, "What is prayer?" The Muslim students gave more complicated answers, but the Christians responses were generally quite direct. To quote Jonathan, a Good Tree freshman: Prayer is "just talking to God." I pressed Jonathan on this, as I did in many of my interviews. I wanted to understand the often implicit, unacknowledged bodily practices that went into Evangelical prayer.[12] "How do you—I mean, what does that look like?" I asked. "You just sort of chat? What does that talking look or sound like?" Jonathan shrugged. "There's no specific way to do it. You can do it however you like." I asked for more information about how he prayed. "Just like, close my eyes, and just like I'm talking to him. Like, he's right in front of me."

This focus on immediacy and relationality parallels what I found in the Muslim schools, albeit with a much more serious suspicion of ritual forms. The Muslims with whom I worked found ritual to be a means of focusing their attention and relationship,[13] while the Christians worried such ritual would become a distraction and an end in itself. Of course, ritual is harder to avoid than it may seem, as I will show below and have described in other writing.[14] Indeed, Evangelicals' lack of ritual form is itself a kind of ritual form, one that becomes habituated and socialized within communities.[15]

Unlike the Muslim practice of salah—which has been remarkably consistent since the beginning of Islam—Christian prayer has changed dramatically since the early church. This is even more the case in the United States, where Protestant prayer has shifted from formal structures to a form hostile to the idea of form. In her book on American Evangelical prayer, Tanya Luhrhann traces this change to the 1960s Jesus Movement, which brought forward the Pentecostal ecstatic experience of early 1900s Southern California, rendering it "palatable for white, educated, middle-class congregations."[16] While Luhrmann nods at previous religious awakenings in American history, she situates her respondents' ability to "just talk with God" as being part of a much more contemporary revival. There is surely something to this argument, made most famously by Donald Miller, that the 1960s affected religion as it did the rest of America, "democratizing access to the sacred by radicalizing the Protestant principle of the priesthood of all believers."[17]

Yet this movement is not nearly as new as it might appear. And while its origin might actually rest in seventeenth- and eighteenth-century German pietism,[18] the radicalization of the Protestant priesthood of all believers really took off, at least for Americans, in the Second Great Awakening that marked the nineteenth century's beginning decades.[19] Driven largely by revivals and spiritual entrepreneurs on America's then-western frontier, Christians combined a hostility for Eastern landowners with a suspicion of elites, criticizing anyone who flaunted their expertise, whether, medical, spiritual, or anything else. Anti-federalist ideology was mixed in with what Tocqueville described as Americans' remarkable obsession with the equality of all individuals.[20] And if everyone is equal, it puts on the same page not only preacher and parishioner but also God and Christian. God became identified more and more as the loving (and human) son Jesus rather than the wrathful and distant father, even as God-the-father also shifted from the Roman sense of a distant paterfamilias to a loving and compassionate American dad.[21] Stephen Prothero argues that "the more evangelicals associated God with love rather than wrath, the more God the Father receded and God the son stood out."[22] There is a democratic sense of access to God that comes most clearly out of the American (and, to some degree, European) series of democratic experiments, experiments that have been extended all the way into prayer.[23] That democratization of access for American Evangelicals is not all that different from the democratization of access for American Muslims, which, ever since its very beginning, has insisted anyone could simply kneel down and make *salah*. Yet it is the democratization and co-occurring suspicion of *form* that makes the schools so distinct in their attitude to prayer. For the Muslim schools I studied, anyone can pray, but the form is standardized; indeed, there was even debate about the required standardization of spontaneous *du'a*. In contrast, for the Evangelicals, form itself was democratized, or at least was claimed to be, as the inevitable tendency of habituated forms and structures led some of my Christian respondents to worry that a prayer with even a whiff of ritual was no longer really an authentic expression of their relationship to God.

BOUNDARIES

Salah is What Separates Believers from Unbelievers

In one of our conversations, a teacher at Al Haqq told me, "Prayer is a staple of our *din* [religion], one of the five pillars of Islam. Salah is the first thing you'll be asked about in our judgment, the difference between a kafir [non-believer] and Muslim is our *din*. If your salah is sound, everything else falls into place. For us as a Muslim school, the one staple of the school is we do provide that [salah]."[24] I encountered this emphasis on salah as an essential—indeed, for some *the* essential—marker of Islam in both of my field sites. It was prayer that was most necessary, making the absence of prayer an existential risk.

Near the end of my semester of fieldwork, Al Haqq had a special day for salah. The whole school gathered in the upstairs gymnasium, converted into a site for devotion and community, as it was each afternoon for prayer. The school listened to various invited guest speakers extol the necessity of daily prayer: a doctor described its medical benefits, a sociologist (me) talked about how ritual affects daily life, and many friends and alumni of the school described how the five daily prayers make for better Muslims and a better world, all while honoring Allah.

Speakers often mentioned Palestine on this special day for salah, which was not especially surprising. Many of the students and teachers at both schools were Palestinian, and the question of Palestine and its occupation was one of many foreign policy issues regularly discussed at both schools. One of Al Haqq's salah day speakers, a young man named Gibreel who had graduated from Al Haqq about a decade earlier, linked Palestine to salah, describing the powerlessness of Palestine—and the decline of Muslim power more broadly—as the direct result of a decreased focus on prayer:

Islam is a building built on the five pillars . . . . We left our home, the home of Islam, the home of modesty, the home of salah, so Allah *subhanahu wa-ta'ala* brings a catastrophe, like *al nakba*,[25] so now you are expelled from our homes. The corruption that occurs around us is simply a result of our own corruption . . . . Right now as you listen to this speech you're thinking of someone around you. But the real point of this speech is an introspective journey. You have to think, I have left this home, but if you come back to salah, then you are given the right of return. Because there are two creatures that have been expelled from their home. One was expelled and was told this is not your home. And who was that? Sheitan . . . and the other [humans] is given the God-given honor, called the right of return [this is a play-on-words, combining the same phrase for a return to paradise and return to Palestine] . . . . So remember when you leave the realm of Islam, you leave the realm of hijab, you leave the realms of salah, then you leave our homes. Once we return to our homes [prayer and hijab], then Allah will return us to our homes [meaning both paradise and Palestine].

Note a few things in this quote. First, Gibreel argues that both salah and the hijab are what I have been calling "essential" to Islam, that Islam ceases to be a "home" for anyone who does not carry out these practices (though, of course, it is generally understood that only females can wear the hijab). Yet more importantly, note how prayer is understood as having a kind of authority that makes possible both political and personal change.

While I did not ask him, it seems likely that the realm of Islam Gibreel describes is a reference to *dar al Islam*, a theological concept that describes where Muslims are home, as opposed to other potential locations in which Muslims could find themselves: *dar al ahd* (the land of accord), *dar al dawah* (the land of mission), and *dar al harb* (the land of war). As described in Chapter 2, sociologist Mucahit Bilici uses these distinctions as a framing device for Muslim immigration to the United States, arguing that Muslim immigrants who have entered since the late 1960s and early 1970s have gradually shifted from viewing the United States as a place of war, then mission, then accord, and finally, home.[26] Yet whether or not Muslims are at home in America, they are still distinguished from non-Muslims, and also distinguish themselves both from non-Muslims and from Muslims they are worried have lost something essential. Prayer, in this sense, helps Muslims to keep their Islam and to keep track of their fellow Muslims—those still with them and those who have left home.

Prayer as Separation and Solution

One morning in my second semester at Good Tree, I arrived at the school early to find people gathered around the flag pole in front of the school, praying "for our nation." I had to walk the mile or so to the school myself (usually I got a ride from the secretary or principal from the train station), so I missed the very beginning. A student council member that I recognized as the kangaroo in the recent production of *Seussical!* smiled at me and pointed at one of the groups where I could stand. I did not count the groups right away, and when I was writing my notes that evening, I thought it was around eight to ten, each composed of teachers, students, staff, and parents. The groups stood next to each other in circles of around five or six, speaking quietly so as not to disturb each other, all around the flagpole. My group had the physics teacher, Dr. Hawthorne (the senior Bible teacher), a 5th-grade teacher whom I had met earlier, and a junior boy in student council. He had been the elephant in the same musical alongside the girl who had been a kangaroo. There was also a Latina mother with her 10-year-old-son. She was the most profuse in her prayer, saying things like "Father God" with a melody and cadence that felt qualitatively different from the other prayers in the circle. The boy hugged his mom and, at least to me, appeared pretty bored.

They prayed about the school and then for the nation, and both the junior and the 5th-grade teacher mentioned decline. The 5th-grade teacher also talked about how "we've fallen away" from the "founding fathers." In contrast, Dr. Hawthorne prayed that we could be a beacon to other Christians, reminding other Christians about who we are and what we should be. Later that day, he stopped me in the hall and said that I should add politics to the questionnaire I was giving the students, because he was struck by the diversity of how some people want to engage politics and how some want to change other Christians. "Like in my prayer, I said that we can be a witness, but that's not the sort of politics you see from some of these students."

Dr. Hawthorne saw prayer as there to change hearts, while his co-prayers viewed prayer as a chance to change power. This tension is a common one among Evangelicals.[27] The "See You at the Pole"[28] event that Good Tree was participating in is generally designed for public schools, and, according to its website, part of the reason for meeting at a school's flagpole is not only because flagpoles are easy to find; it's also because "one issue that the teenagers [who founded the event] were praying about was the spiritual health of their country and its leaders." Because the day is designed for public schools, the website has various legal strategies making that possible, discouraging sympathetic adults from joining with students at the pole and providing contact information for various sources of "legal help." There was obviously nothing that confrontational when praying at a Christian school's flagpole, yet there was still a sense that these prayers had radical and controversial work to do: not just changing hearts and lives but changing America itself, and changing it back to a religious sensibility it must—for its own good—regain. While the majority of my conversations with Evangelicals were about how far society had fallen from the Bible, they worried about the shrinking space for prayer in America, too. Prayer held an authority to help America and also an ability to separate those who could really help America's godly potential from those who would continue leading the nation astray.

Yet, more importantly, they viewed prayer as an authority through which to get America back to the Bible. At both schools, I regularly heard people praying for "our country," asking that it might return from its sinful ways to its original Christian roots.[29] In my conversations with them, teachers, students, and staff at both Evangelical schools lamented the separation of their country's leaders from scripture and prayer, and they viewed prayer as an important weapon in a spiritual war they saw as continually ongoing. They felt this fight was new, an impending total war with secularists and their non-Christian allies, and it changed how they felt they had to pray. To be clear, I'm not sure anyone was advocating a theocracy per se: what they wanted—what they *prayed for*—was political leaders who shared their values and who would use those values to shape laws and institutions more in accordance with their own commitments. One way to see if that person was serious was to see if they prayed.

Which is not to say that prayer was necessarily required. The Christians I met were certainly comfortable saying certain actions were required, or others were always wrong, yet there was greater hesitancy about saying what was required in prayer, as any requirement could run the risk of getting in the way of an authentic, spontaneous relationship. Nonetheless, when I paid close attention I could see there were still important distinctions being made, namely that the best prayers were those that marked an imme-diate, spontaneous, and sincere relationship with God. For example, I was interviewing Ms. James, Good Tree's biology teacher, when the school sec-retary, Marie Shumacher, walked in. We were talking about prayer, and I shared some of what I had observed at the Muslim schools, especially the importance of mastering the form of salah. Ms. Shumacher, a short, brown-haired woman with massive energy and a big smile, paused thoughtfully. "When you talk about a Christian prayer . . . you're speaking from your heart to God. I mean there is—you're thinking about what you're saying but it's not just . . . it's more intimate than what you're saying." Ms. Shumacher dis-tinguished "Christian prayer" from any prayer that emphasizes form over intimacy, a dichotomy that other religions might reject, insisting that form is what makes intimacy possible. However, for Ms. Shumacher, it is the emotional quality that matters, which, while she might not recognize it as such, could itself be understood as a kind of form.[30] She described one "boy in particular" at Good Tree:

> [When] I hear this boy pray I am like right before the throne. I could cry. He is just—and it's not put on he's just so—like you feel like you stepped into this in-timate time between him and the Lord. And he's not showy, very humble, very quiet, but it's beautiful. It invokes that kind of a sense of, "Wow you've got it. You definitely talk to the Lord a lot" and you can hear it. It's intimate, it's per-sonal, you know me and you get to see a little window of that and he's just a kid.

Implicit in Ms. Shumacher's praise of this particular student is a judgment of students who *do not* pray like this: students whose prayer is too formu-laic or insincere. Prayer gains its authority at both Christian schools not only from its perceived power to change the world but also from the not-always-explicit norms that bound it off from other forms.

PRAYER AS EXTERNAL AUTHORITY AND AGENT

The Christian Schools

I regularly asked people in interviews if they thought prayer changed things and whether it had effects in the world, and nearly everyone said yes. However, their answer might simply be an artifact of the question, and in two ways: first, this might be an example of what sociologists call a "desirability bias,"[31] that is, a tendency to say what is desirable in a given social context. At a religious school, it seems likely people will say prayer makes a difference. That desirability bias only goes so far: it's worth pointing out how many students and teachers expressed disappointment about their school and themselves, admitting the school was an imperfectly religious place and that their own lives were imperfect examples of religious practice. Yet to express doubt about your organization or your own efforts does seem a bit less intense than to express disagreement about something as fundamental to Christian identity as the power of prayer.

So, even though I do have many transcripts with interviewees who insist "prayer changes people," I am aware that my framing of the question might affect the answer. Nonetheless, this was a statement I heard often enough at the Christian schools that its repetition in my interviews seems more the result of these schools' commitments than how I asked the questions. For example, in my interview with Mr. Smith at Good Tree, I asked him whether he thinks prayer changes people. "It certainly changes me," he responded. We were sitting at his desk, a messy pile of papers spread over it. He had pictures of bed and breakfasts he was thinking of visiting, something he and I talked about often. I asked for clarification, whether prayer only changed the one praying or whether it could change someone else, "like if you pray for me and I was an atheist and did nothing."

Mr. Smith had a habit of pointing his finger in the air when excited, and he did that here. "I believe we're told explicitly in Scripture to pray for each other and pray for somebody's salvation, that they'll come to the Lord, pray that they'll grow. The Bible says in Philippians to pray without ceasing, bring your petitions to the Lord. Certainty we're encouraged all through Scripture. Jesus constantly told people to pray."

Mr. Smith does a few interesting things here. First, as described in the previous chapter, he—without any prompting on my part—describes the Bible as both an authority and an agent, capable of "saying" things with a binding power that must be respected. And second, he describes how prayer has a certain kind of power relatively autonomous from God or the person acting. The person acting cannot simply wish something to occur for change to happen in the world; instead, that person must pray.

Yet while Mr. Smith talks about scripture in the subject position of the sentence, he does not do the same for prayer, treating it as a verb or an infinitive except in reference to my question, which did make prayer a subject. So even if turning prayer into a subject might be a result of the way I asked the question, I am not sure the *agency* of prayer as Mr. Smith describes it had much to do with me. It was clear that prayer's action *accomplished* things in the same sense that any verb in its gerund or infinitive form indicates accomplishment: "running" or "to run" mean that someone has moved, and that this particular movement would not have occurred without said running. There is a way that "praying" or "to pray"—these verbs that take the place of nouns—still have a kind of authority. Things become possible because they have been prayed about, and to pray is to gain guidance about what God wants. Yet prayer is nonetheless described in verbal forms rather than as a subject-noun (except when I introduce it as such), perhaps as a means of emphasizing, especially for the Christians with whom I worked, that prayer's power is fundamentally relational, rooted in God's power rather than in the form itself.

Forms nonetheless matter: to talk about tweeting something or calling someone on the phone emphasizes the relationality between the one acting and the one receiving the action, but it does not mean the action itself is powerless in the process. A phone call and a tweet are both different than a face-to-face conversation. I asked a girl named Jessie about prayer in my first semester at Good Tree. She was a popular student, passionate about a blog she had started for victims of human trafficking. Round-faced with brown hair, she smiled excitedly as we talked, answering emphatically that "it does" when I asked whether prayer affects her daily life.

> There are days when I walk outside and I'm just praying to God and thanking him for the beautiful day or something like that, and that really starts getting me encouraged and uplifts me throughout the day, and especially, like, I know that God is listening and I know that he will hear me, even if he doesn't say yes to some of my prayers. But I know that when I pray, there's power in that. And especially if I'm praying for a friend, something is going on, and there have been many times where I have seen my friends come through that because of prayer, and I mean, without prayer, they wouldn't have gotten through, like some of my friends who have been suicidal or been cutting and things like that, just going to God in prayer for that, and going to God in prayer together with them has also been something that I know has gotten them through, and without that they would still be where they were.

Note how Jessie's account here also moves prayer into a verb: I asked about "prayer" as a noun and she described how she prays. Yet she noted praying has a "power" over her emotional state and over the lives of her friends, and generally shifted prayer into the object of various prepositions: she talked about friends' changes "because of prayer," what they would be like "without prayer," and, twice, going to God "in prayer." Of course, for my argument, it is less important how Jessie or anyone else uses the word *prayer* in a sentence. What matters instead is the sense that prayer acts as an external authority relatively autonomous from either the people involved or even God.

For Jesssie, prayer provided a kind of authority through which to understand both God and the world. That authority most obviously arises from prayer itself. At Apostles, I interviewed many of the students one-on-one wherever we could find a quiet but still observable space—often a relatively still corner off from the gym, near a long line of folded rectangular lunch tables. I talked to one freshman named Veronica, a Latina girl who had been at the school since sixth grade. I asked her if it was important for her to pray every day. While most students I interviewed at Apostles said it was important to maintain such a practice, many admitted to me they did not do it. Veronica said she did pray five to seven days a week, because "if you really love someone, then you would talk to them every single day because you would have that communion with them and when people say oh I love God, but they don't pray at all, then it's like how can you love someone, but not talk to them?" Prayer, for Veronica, becomes evidence of an authentic relationship with God, and through this, an authentic Christianity. Indeed, she indicated earlier her frustration with students who don't take the school's Christian mission seriously, and her point of comparison was that these were the students who were unserious about prayer during the school's chapel services.

When I asked Veronica if she felt prayer made a difference in people's lives, she nodded, saying "mm-hmmm." I asked her for examples, and she described prayer as a "source that God has given us. It's like a weapon God has given us to go to battle . . . . So when you pray for someone, it's—because when you pray for someone and you start declaring things, those things are going to happen . . . . I was praying for my cousin, I started declaring that I declare over her life—I declare that her soul be saved and I said I declare it." Veronica's emphasis on the power of "declaration" has more in common with the Pentecostal wing of American Evangelicalism, and it is worth noting that her prayer is also marked by a kind of agency. This agency is relatively separate from either Veronica or, in fact, God, even if God is the ultimate source of the agency, its *rector* as the sociological theorist Isaac Reed might call it.[32] Yet if God is the rector of prayer-as-an-agent, then what role does Veronica play? In some sense she—or anyone else who prays—is an intermediary agent while simultaneously an *interacting* agent. Prayer in this case is almost like an agent sent by some mid-level functionary (the one praying) under the broad authority of some larger power (God). That agent might move between the functionary and the larger power, yet the agent might also go out into the world and engage those ostensibly outside of the meaning chain, bringing those people into the relationships or, as it might be put more theologically, into God's saving action.

I could also identify the authority of prayer in noting how the communities felt it was necessary to shape a body in a particular way for prayer to work.[33] Evangelicals at both schools often told me there were "no requirements" for prayer and that it's "just a conversation." However, when I asked them concretely what they did, most described closing their eyes in a quiet space. Of the two Evangelical schools I studied, Apostles was much more Pentecostal and therefore more open to ecstatic movements in its prayer life, even if most students limited their exultations to a raised hand or a shouted Amen.

At Good Tree, the physicality was subtle, distinguished most by still-ness, closed eyes, and bowed heads. Watching Wednesday chapel services in the school's sparsely decorated chapel (which doubled as the elemen-tary school gym), I was always struck by the phrase "Let's Pray" which might as well have been a hypnotist's command to sleep. Suddenly—and shockingly—all these boisterous students would bow heads, close eyes, and be quiet. I looked around from the back and noticed only a few heads above the crowd, usually teachers. While I would occasionally notice a trou-blemaking student twisting her head slightly left or right to see what was going on, generally even the kids I knew to be difficult respected the tra-dition. Closed eyes were an indication of sincerity. They were a sign prayer was doing something. Having your eyes closed is such a strong expectation that its absence needs to be explained. One speaker at Good Tree's Chapel Service said, "I pray with my eyes open when I drive the car! It's okay, it's legal, God doesn't mind." The students laughed.

In my first semester at Good Tree, there was one senior, Jarrod, who was always getting into trouble. Teachers and fellow students were frustrated with his lack of seriousness. Once, while talking to a group of students and the sophomore Bible teacher, Mr. Smith, about the commitment to Christian belief students must make to enter Good Tree, Jarrod shrugged and said he would just say what he had to say to get a good education. The other students looked uncomfortably at each other. Jarrod often slept in class and rarely participated in discussion.

So it was quite dramatic that he appeared to have something of a conversion at the school's annual senior service trip to the Dominican Republic. The trip to "The Dominican" is a vital part of the school's narrative about itself, and various students mentioned how important Jarrod's change had been on the journey (it was even mentioned in the valedictorian's address). How did they know Jarrod had changed? Well, he was kinder; he played with kids; he sang. And he closed his eyes. I asked a group of girls why that was such a big deal, and one girl, Sonja, responded, "I'm in praise band, so I see everything. I see when people don't pay attention or when they're really not into it, and this time, I could see that he was into it." Another student, Ebuwa, agreed. "When your eyes are closed, you can only think about yourself, your problems, and God. So, I mean, it's just easier to tell." Jarrod's prayer—especially its physical components—is both his own means of communicating to God and a sign through which others can read his relationship to God.

The Muslim Schools

At both Muslim schools, I often heard people talking about the power of prayer, especially salah and *du'a*. There was a poster at Al Haqq that said simply, "Never underestimate the power of duah."[34] As with the Christians schools, prayer was still relational and situated: its authority and agency come from God. Nonetheless, it had a kind of power all its own, as came up regularly in my interviews.

In a casual, untaped conversation with Brother Umar, the assistant principal at Al Amal, we were talking about prayer. The office has a large poster of the Dome of the Rock in Jerusalem and another large poster of the main mosque in Medina. "You know that at Islamic schools we are required to pray together, but that does not necessarily mean anything. If you memorize the Qur'an, it doesn't affect you if you don't have the right intention. There's a hadith that says if you give to charity or your intention is to impress others, then that is all, you have had your reward. If you are only praying with us but not at home, then it's just like any practice you might do, like at the gym."

Brother Umar provides a lot to think about. First, there's the recognition that the school encourages a certain kind of activity with the hope that it will lead to change, but there is no guarantee such change will occur. Importantly, it is not the school itself that decides on this enforcement: they are "required" to do so by some higher authority. Yet, more importantly, there's a recognition that the form of salah is just the starting point, that doing it without meaning it, without the proper *khushu* (or concentration) doesn't count for much.

Yet what's tricky is that Brother Umar almost immediately contradicted himself. We had just been talking about the Internet, which Brother Umar described as both good and bad depending on how you use it. I asked if the same was true of prayer, and his answer revealed a belief that prayer does, in fact, have a kind of staying power. "No, prayer is different," he told me. "There's a hadith, some people came to the Prophet, and they said that there is a man who keeps stealing and he goes to prayer. And they were expecting him to say, he shouldn't pray anymore, but instead they said let him continue to pray, and, over time, the prayer will change him."

"So even if the students are faking it, you don't care?" I asked.

He nodded. "They might be faking it at first, but over time, they will change. Now, certain people will finish here, they will neglect everything, we will have had no effect. But prayer does change people, it will affect people."

This sense that prayer has a relative authority was obviously always rooted in God's power, but it was nonetheless the case that prayer was often understood as a powerful agent. It might be worthwhile to compare two interviews with students I conducted at Al Amal, a senior boy named Ibrahim and a senior girl named Jasmine.

I asked Ibrahim how prayer affects his daily life, and he referred to a hadith comparing salah to bathing five times a day. "If you're someone that always prays, then you're always worrying about your next prayer . . . . So everything you do—I mean Allah, you always think about Allah before you do it, so it's always—He keeps you clean." Note how the question is about prayer, but the subject of the final sentence is Allah; it is God doing the work. In this sense, prayer is understood less as an agent than as a *technique,* a means of God connecting to Muslims and Muslims connecting back to God, like a phone or a telegraph.

Yet, as I have been arguing, techniques are not without their own power. It is the salah that *authorizes* a connection to God, even though Ibrahim's account—unlike some of the others I heard—highlights the centrality of God in this process, as well as the right intention of the one doing the prayer. "It's all about intention when it comes to Islam," he told me. "No matter what you do, it's all about intention." Prayer, as he described it to me, is "pulling everything back, everything in this world. You move everything back and you step in front and you talk with God. You and your God are isolated and you're talking with God. That's why you pray."

It is prayer that makes this immediacy possible. Relatedly, I asked Jasmine, also a senior at Al Amal, why someone should pray. "Because it will help them or because—"

She cut me off. "From my point of view I realize that prayer is . . . when you feel like you're just lost and there is no one there, there is always prayer." She told me about how her prayer life grew stronger during her mother's illness, especially as she was often the primary caregiver. "I guess prayer is something that God is, you can always turn to God. So, it helps you know that there is always someone there." For Jasmine, as for Ibrahim, prayer is ultimately about God, yet it is not itself God nor reducible to God. Prayer authorizes a relationship to God, making possible a kind of connection with important stakes in individual lives and in the world at large. It is in this sense that I describe prayer as having a kind of agency in my respondents' lives.

GETTING BETTER AT PRAYER

The Christian Schools

When I asked Christians at both schools about learning to pray, they often gave the example of the "Our Father"—the prayer Jesus gave to his apostles when he taught them to pray. Shane McNulty uses the prayer as an example of a perfect prayer in his junior religion class at Good Tree, and most of the prayers I heard at both schools model its emphasis on praise and reverence before asking for certain petitions. So, for example, when teachers at both schools began classes with prayer, they would usually precede the prayer by asking something like "what should we pray for today?" and students would shout out prayer requests, often for family members or friends who were ill, but also for games, tests, or vaguely labeled "personal intentions." Then the student praying—sometimes a volunteer, sometimes cold-called by the teacher—would begin by saying something like "God you are truly great" before getting to the class's petitions.

Besides highlighting the Our Father as a template (but not a recitation), I did not notice my Christian respondents discussing the right way to pray all that often. For example, "how to pray" almost never came up in a class at either Christian school, even if how to read the Bible came up all the time. When I asked some of my Christian respondents why that was, the question usually took them aback. A few of them responded that "maybe we should teach prayer more," yet most replied that prayer is a relationship with God that takes work but not necessarily instruction. I talked to some sophomores in Mr. Smith's Scripture class at Good Tree, and one of them told me, "I'm not sure [how I learned to pray] . . . I just started one day, picking it up, not learning anything . . . I wasn't taught how to do it—you just learn from observing, but one day I just started talking with God." A nearby student agreed: "We're not taught to pray. We're taught what to pray for—like pray for this person, or give thanks—but the prayer itself is a relationship." Even someone like Mr. Lopez, whose prayer life seemed much ornate and ritualized than anyone else I saw at the two Christian schools, still insisted that anyone can pick prayer up without much instruction. It takes practice to get better, but it does not necessarily require explicit training. And in fact, to coerce someone into prayer would be, for Evangelicals, a contradiction in terms, like the forcing of spontaneity.

When I asked about learning to pray in my interviews with students at Good Tree and Apostles, most of them shared stories of learning the form by either imitating their parents or gaining explicit instruction from them. Yet they also emphasized—as did their teachers—that prayer is most important as a *relationship to cultivate* rather than *a set of forms to master*. In my first semester there, I interviewed a senior, Jessie, who made this contrast explicit in her description of prayer in her family. She told me she didn't know if she's ever "really been taught how to pray as much as when you're a Christian, it's just something that you desire to do, or if you really care about God you just want to talk to him because it's natural and you tell him things." She went on to emphasize she didn't think there was one "strict way" to teach prayer.

As is sometimes common among Evangelicals, the ultimate opposition to spontaneous and heartfelt prayer is the rote memorization of Catholics, a distinction with roots all the way back to the Reformation. Jessie told me that her Catholic grandmother had gone blind in a car accident. The grandmother's son, Jessie's father, asked why she didn't pray, but the grandmother prayed "all the memorized prayers that she had learned." And then, Jessie recounted,

> . . . my dad told her, "No, don't pray those, just pray from your heart, because that's what's going to matter," and she really took that to heart, and the more she did, the more she got out of those hard times, and she began to praise God instead of just complain and weep and be sorry for herself, and she was actually really uplifted. So I think especially it doesn't matter how you pray as much as what your heart is in praying.

As this quote shows, prayer is not utterly spontaneous. However, its formal requirements are paradoxically anti-formal, and to learn to pray better is to learn, most of all, a certain emotional sensibility, an affect. As Mr. Smith told me in that same conversation in his class, "It's the same way you started talking to your wife, it was probably a bit formal at first but over time it became comfortable and casual. The closer you become the more intimate your prayer life becomes." Just as a marriage relationship works based on trust, ultimately changing the very nature of the spouse, so a healthy prayer life will make a new person. Prayer, in this sense, functions as an agent and authority even if it is rarely recognized as such. God is understood as the one who is acting, to be sure, but prayer is a necessary conduit for the relationship between the one praying and the one who receives and acts upon those prayers. As a result, as we see in Jessie's story, a person's emotions and virtues—their humility, kindness, openness, and sincerity—are at once the starting point and the result of successful prayer.[35]

That commitment to certain virtues, especially sincerity, can have stressful effects on those praying. After I finish my conversation about prayer in Mr. Smith's class, I was walking out the door when a blonde sophomore, Cindy, walked next to me, insisting she had something important to say but Mr. Smith had not called on her. "I'm going to tell you now and I don't care if I'm late," she said, as we walked past roaming students in the passing period. I agreed to follow her to her biology class, as she told me,

> For me, I have to believe what I'm praying, so I don't like it when other people pray for me, like when they say "We thank you for this day" because then I'm not really thanking God for this day, so I have to then tell God, Lord, I do thank you for this day, because I have to mean it. That's why I don't like praying before we eat because all I'm thinking about is the food in front of me, and I'm not actually thinking about God, and so I don't feel like it counts as a prayer. I really have to feel like I'm totally into the prayer, that's why I usually kneel when I pray—because I know I'm just going to cry anyway—but when I'm kneeling I'm able to focus on just God.

Note how a kind of physicality—kneeling—becomes important for Cindy, but not in a necessary way. Kneeling simply allows her a better capacity for focus—and with that focus, the virtues of sincerity and openness that prayer both engenders and requires, often facilitated through intense emotional experience. Note also that Cindy's "learning"—at least in this account—is a process of trial and error, of the self observing and better calibrating the self.[36] Parents and teachers might model prayer, but its authority and agency come most clearly when they are supported from within each Christian heart.

The Muslim Schools

Unlike at the Christian schools, where "how to pray" was rarely a subject of conversation, I encountered countless discussions about prayer in classes at the Muslim schools. Some of these conversations were simply about requirements or formal characteristics: how or if to make up a salah, which *du'a* to say when, why congregational prayer is superior to the prayer of an individual.

Yet prayer was often present for another reason: no time at the school was that long from a time to pray, whether having just prayed that morning, getting ready to pray at mid-day, or, when I was around after school, getting ready for a third prayer in the afternoon. The disciplining quality of prayer is something both students and teachers told me about: it was hard to be too sinful if you were always a few hours past one prayer and a few more hours away from another one.

I got to know a group of junior boys at Al Amal pretty well, and I was charmed by their constant hijinks. So it seemed more of the same when I saw them in the hallway behind the cafeteria that doubled as the school's masjid (or mosque), putting down small rugs as they joked around and shoved each other. Just like every Friday afternoon prayer around the world, able-bodied Muslim men were required to attend, and a sheikh gave a khutbah (a sermon). These boys were back in the hallway—unlike afternoon prayer every other day—because so many other Muslim men had walked into the gym. On Fridays, the cafeteria became the neighborhood masjid for local men (just as the gym one floor above became the masjid for the school's women), and I would stand in the back as men in business suits and men in mechanics' outfits blended into the lines. Yet what struck me even more than the school's sudden diversity was the dramatic change in my troublemaking friends: "Did it start?" one asked. "Yeah I think it started," said another, and then it happened: suddenly they became very serious, all of them bowing at the same time, respectful and silent. And then when they were done, they were quieter, more subdued. They shook hands with those around them, greeting each other with *Asalaam alakum* [peace be with you] and responding with *walakum asalaam* [and with you, peace]. As one of the Al Haqq teachers told me about another difficult group of students, "They're only well behaved at salah."

There are a lot of practices to learn besides the prayer itself. When I observed daily prayer at both Muslim schools, the men and women prayed in separate rooms at Al Amal. At Al Haqq, the women prayed behind the men, as is required in most interpretations of Islamic law. What was most difficult for the students was simply staying in line. Keeping the lines of salah straight is an extremely important piece of communal prayer, one which the Prophet himself insisted upon.[37] At both of the schools, students and teachers shouted "get in line!" as older boys told younger boys to calm down and settle. Shouting "Straight lines!" shows the power of communal bodily practice for Muslims, as everyone prays together, perfectly arranged in time and space. The focus on straight lines at prayer goes all the way back to the Prophet, as students heard in more than one khutbah. Yet it also shows the power of prayer to form both emotional and physical comportment.

Another important element of the school's daily life was *wudu*, the physical process of cleaning before prayer. The hadith is full of different recommendations about how to do prayers, and something that comes up regularly is the importance of ritual cleanliness. The time for prayer was an important moment in the school's progression, marked first by teachers shouting to their students to "make *wudu!*" Whenever I was unlucky enough to be caught unaware in the men's room when prayer was starting (before I figured out where the faculty bathrooms were), I would be besieged by dozens of boys, throwing water on their hands and feet, drying them without a towel, whispering a blessing, and running out the door. "Hey Jeff!" they'd often shout, as I stood in the middle, a tall and awkward witness to an important ritual.

Yet learning these physical requirements is not necessarily so difficult. In my taped interview with Brother Noori, a religion and history teacher at Al Haqq, I asked him about how Muslims come to realize they are praying correctly. "I think that even the youngest children learn very quickly the physical aspects of the prayer, where to have the hands, you know, how to make the lines straight, it's all part of the prayer." For Brother Noori, a Muslim must be "thinking about the words . . . really engaged with what you're saying . . . and feel it in your heart." It is only when prayer is done from the heart that it can change the heart. So if you sin after having prayed, if "you walk out and . . . you're supposed to be lowering your gaze, but you still look [at the opposite sex] . . . [then] prayer hasn't really changed your heart." That change of heart comes from focus, from an awareness that, as Brother Noori told me and I observed him telling his students, "When you actually pray, and if you do it right, it's as if you are standing in the heavens and actually having a conversation with God."

That internal attention, or *khushu*, was, for the Muslims I met, the most difficult part of prayer.[38] *Khushu* was in many ways even more difficult than getting up early for *fajr*, or sunrise prayer. Getting up is simply a matter of getting up. It's something you either do or do not do. Yet *khushu* is not such a straightforward question; it is a matter of how you *experience* prayer and, just as important, how your prayer is received by God.

Classical scholars might distinguish *khushu*, which means something like a gentle humility, from the other emotional states and personal qualities that salah at once requires and produces.[39] However, at the schools I studied *khushu* tended to have a broader meaning, a sense of concentration and humble reverence that served as a natural channel. *Khushu* was created by certain virtues and emotions and then, via the authority of salah, it made those same virtues and emotions easier to maintain. In this sense, *khushu* is similar to the sort of virtues my Evangelical respondents sought in their talks with God. Like the Evangelical focus on relationship, *khushu* is a certain kind of humility, openness, and vulnerability founded on complete trust. A speaker at a special day dedicated to salah at Al Haqq told students that *khushu* is "talking to God" and Sheikh Yusuf, the school's primary Islamic Studies teacher, regularly told students about the importance of both *khushu* and "a personal relationship with Allah."

In one discussion about *khushu* in Sheikh Yusuf's class at Al Haqq, a girl said that "when I have the *khushu* I feel spiritually everything is coming together, but when I'm not I feel like what's the point?" Another girl agreed. "I definitely have a problem—salah is a physical process and I do all the physical parts, but it means nothing if it's not much more than that—like even someone who's paralyzed, they can still pray, so it's not about just the movements—you have to mean it." The teacher said "Yes, this is very important . . . . Anytime you approach your salah, ask yourself this question, the moment you lose sight of this question, you lose *khushu*: what is the point of salah—why am I praying? If you're able to successfully answer this question, you'll be able to pray successfully."

UNDERSTANDING PRAYER

One of the problems with asking God for things is that God often says no.[40] How to make sense of God's refusal is a classic problem in many theologies and it's also one of the thorniest moral problems the authority of prayer presents. Can a prayer be wrong? Is the prayer not part of God's plan? Is it a problem with the person praying? When talking about miraculous healings, Mr. Lopez, the junior and senior Bible teacher at Apostles, hedged his bets: "I'm not saying that everyone will get better. It has to be in their heart too." "It has to be God's will," said a girl. "If it's God's will," the teacher agreed. Mr. Lopez argued at first that prayer's effects depended upon a person's heart, but then, in agreement with a student, he threw in another variable: the will of God. In a nutshell, this is one of the central problems in the theology of prayer: how much do humans' prayers actually change anything, and how much has already been determined by God's all-knowing plan?[41]

I sometimes posed this theological puzzle to teachers I was interviewing, asking them about two imaginary women in hospital beds, one with many people to pray for her, and one with nobody to pray for her. The women are equally devout, with equally good hearts. Would God reward the woman who had more prayers for her? It's a more targeted way to ask about prayer in theodicy, or why an all-powerful, all-loving God would let bad things happen to good people.[42] The responses I received in all four schools were usually similar, emphasizing that we cannot know God's will, that not all prayers are equal, and, most importantly, that God's loving mercy is more powerful than any theology we might describe.

I asked this question to Mr. Cassidy, the biology teacher at Apostles, while we were getting drinks at a bar. He nodded thoughtfully and paused to gather his thoughts. He insisted that part of the problem was a kind of theology that promised certain behavior would guarantee certain result, describing a theological position not altogether dissimilar from Mr. Lopez's insistence that a prayer's effectiveness was related to the heart of the one praying (or longstanding Protestant criticisms of Catholicism). Like many young intellectual Evangelicals, Mr. Cassidy was interested in the resurgence of Calvinism, insisting primarily on the sovereignty of God to do what God wills. "It's probably just nothing worse than to be in that situation," he said, referring to someone who suffers pain and feels as though God does not respond to their prayers. "But I feel that knowing that your sins are forgiven and knowing that you [are in] fellowship with God—that's the best thing to be provided for anyway, to have that guarantee." Prayer, for Mr. Cassidy, is more than anything about a relationship to a loving and forgiving God, and to measure it by any material effects on the world is to misrecognize the real power of God as well as to undercut God's sovereignty. An all-powerful, all-knowing God does not alter plans based on requests.

Yet, in my interviews, most students and faculty at all four schools were clear that prayer did a lot more than just help their relationship to God. It did things in the world, even if because of God's almighty power. Prayer healed family members, brought surprise conversions, and soothed long-strained relationships. It brought confidence, peace, strength, patience, joy. And prayer also brought answers. How to reconcile the power of prayer with God's sovereignty is a complicated theological problem, but I never really noticed people worrying about it. (It was much more common to worry about why God seemed not to answer prayers).

Nearly all of my interviewees told me that they regularly prayed for guidance, and I asked them how they recognized God's answer. When I asked a senior girl, Kristin, that very question in a taped interview in my final semester at Good Tree, she responded that she hears God's answer to her prayers "through what other people are saying or just something in my brain sort of sticks out so that I know that's what He wants and I can't stop thinking about it." She paused, making eye contact with me: "I'm like okay, that's definitely what God wants."

I smiled at her, leaning back in my chair. "How do you know that's God's voice and not your voice?"

Kristin shrugged. "I don't always, but a lot of times it comes with a real sense of peace."

"How did you learn to figure that out?" I asked.

She paused. "I just kind of figured it out I think."

Kristin's story is similar to that of many of my respondents at the Christian and Muslim schools. They told me that when they pray about their uncertainties, God answers back by acting in the world. A few Christian students told me they did hear God's voice, but this was a quite uncommon experience, even for those who told me God spoke to them directly. (None of my Muslim respondents told me they heard God's voice.) My respondents nearly all understood God's answers as legible through a particular reading of the world and their emotional reactions to it.

Yet, especially for the Christians with whom I worked, one of the most important places to find God's answer to your prayers is through scripture. As I heard countless times at both Christian schools, prayer is you talking to God, and scripture is God talking back. According to my Christian respondents, scripture tended to function in two senses as a means of constraining and channeling prayer. First, scripture limited what God might ask someone. A true answer to a prayer would never ask anything "non-Biblical." But second, and perhaps more importantly, the scripture itself would fuse with an emotional response to provide a sense of certainty about the right course of action.

In my first semester at Good Tree, I interviewed a senior, Jessie, whom I have already quoted a few times. When I asked her about recognizing God's answers, she told me she "definitely" does not hear an "audible voice" when God speaks. Yet, she made clear, one way to know for sure it's God's voice is "to always stay within God's word." She also suggested going "to people that . . . have a strong relationship with God and are wiser in the faith." She went on: "A lot of the times what happens is, I will get the same exact message from the Bible, from my advisors, from my friends, from the preacher, and from a bunch of different things within just like a week . . . . And I'm like, 'That has to be God.' Because it's not a coincidence." Jessie understood God as being the one who sent these messages, yet it is prayer, acting as God's agent, that attuned Jessie to noticing that prayer's potential answer. These connections and seeming coincidences were, for her, not coincidences at all. They were the messages of God, answers to the agency of prayer.

When I asked about how to understand God's response to prayers at the Muslim schools, I got similar answers, usually emphasizing the importance of feelings. A junior girl named Zaria told me, "You just feel it." She said the thing you ask for may or may not happen, but the important thing is "this feeling inside of me that like, God answers." My Muslim respondents also often told me about the *salat-al-istikhara*, a specific prayer for seeking advice.[43] As my respondent described it to me, upon saying it you should have a better sense which of your choices is the one to do.

Which is not to say that the prayer always works as it is intended to. A sophomore girl at Al Haqq, Khadija, admitted to me that when she made *istikhara* it was not always as successful as she would have liked. In our interview she told me that one time, she "made *istikhara* a few times" when she was facing a "really tough situation." She said when she finally made a decision, she was relieved. "I don't even think twice about it," she said. "But another time, I made an *istikhara* and then I even made it out, 'Please, give me some kind of answer in my dream or something. I don't know what to do.' And I didn't really get any answer."

I must have started to ask a question, because she almost interrupted herself. "It's not that I don't believe it's being—it's not being heard. I don't believe that it's not being heard. Maybe I did get an answer but not in the way that—not something—in something that I can see." She went on to say that the most important element of prayer is not its ability to answer her questions or grant her requests but rather the emotional effect it has upon her, somewhat paralleling Mr. Cassidy's (the Apostles biology teacher) emphasis on the importance of prayer as relational rather than as petitionary. In Khadija's words,

> I think, also as to what you were saying before with having a conversation with God and knowing whether or not he's answering you, I—I think a major part of not Islam, but my personal take on Islam is like, I don't really know, but when I'm done I feel good. I feel relaxed. I feel like I just let a huge load off my chest.

For Khadija, as for nearly everyone I worked with at all four schools, the most important part of understanding God's will is an emotional capacity

that is both evidence of God's work and indication of the virtues underlying one who prays and one who has been acted upon by prayer. In the
words of one of the guest speakers at a school-wide assembly dedicated
to salah at Al Haqq: "Salah is not this ritual we do five times a day, but
it's also linked to the deeds that you do . . . . Salah should train us just as
we train for a game or an exam." He made clear that the love of Allah that
salah encourages and requires becomes a personality trait, "not an emotion . . . not a feeling." It is in this sense that prayer works as a kind of agent
of God, moving its practitioners toward a certain kind of self even as it
helps them move through the world.

CONCLUSION

To talk about how prayer works, for my respondents, necessarily meant to
talk about what God does. The power of prayer, as I came to understand
it, is always a function of the power of God. Yet, as with scripture, this
is somewhat complicated. After all, it is the person praying who engages
the prayer and whose virtues and techniques make the prayer more or
less acceptable. My Evangelical respondents often told me that prayer is
us talking to God, and scripture is God talking back. To maintain that description, then if scripture is a kind of agent of God, prayer becomes a kind
of agent of God's people, sent up and beyond to connect to someone else.
Yet that is not precisely right, because the authority of that prayer is not
understood as coming from those praying but from the one receiving those
prayers, God, so it is almost as though prayer is God's agent returning back
from a mission with new information. The analogy is imperfect not only
because the communities I studied believe God is omniscient, but also because the authority of prayer is felt to come not really from God or from the
people praying but from the relationship between them, the connection
itself. I asked almost all of my interviewees to define prayer, and nearly all
of them—both Muslim and Christian—said it was something like "connecting to God." It's that connection that has a kind of authority, felt as
something that contains those who pray, yet also located to some degree
outside of them.

CHAPTER 7

cⅣᴐ

Science as External Authority

Shane McNulty has bright red hair and a wry, sardonic sense of humor. He teaches New Testament and history at Good Tree and, one day in my second semester at the school, I was sitting, as usual, at his desk in the back corner of the room while he leaned against his podium. As he and his students were discussing the miracles of the New Testament, one student, a girl named Larissa asked, seemingly out of nowhere: "Should we believe in science?"

Mr. McNulty took on a very serious face and sternly replied, "Absolutely not." Some students laughed nervously. The teacher laughed to break the tension. "Of course!" he shouted. He looked at me as he said, "Science is not the end-all be-all—we have to recognize it, it's a gift God has given to us, and it's important, but it's not the end. Scientists will tell you we don't know where the universe came from. I know where the universe came from: God created it. Scientists don't know what's true about where the universe came from, they have all sorts of debates, but they know one thing that isn't true—God. They know that's not true, and I disagree. Oftentimes, science is a greater leap of faith than religion, but they don't recognize that they have faith. They think they just have theory." It's noteworthy that Mr. McNulty quickly leapt from *science* to *scientists*, pouring most of his scorn on scientists even as he occasionally shifted back to discussing science. And it's also interesting that the category of scientists seems almost monolithically atheist. But what if a Christian wants to be a scientist?

In my first semester at Good Tree, I got to know an Asian American senior named Phil. The salutatorian of his class and planning to become a biologist, he was also a Young Earth creationist, convinced that evolution

Agents of God. Jeffrey Guhin, Oxford University Press (2021). © Oxford University Press.
DOI: 10.1093/oso/9780190244743.001.0001

was false and that the universe was created in six actual days, no earlier than a dozen or so millennia before Jesus walked the earth. In our tape-recorded interview, he told me that "if a scientific discovery seems to go against the Bible, it's either wrong or we need to look into it further." I asked if he was worried about being ostracized by fellow biologists. He said he certainly was concerned that he not come off as rude to his colleagues, but "if I'm just ostracized because I believe that the theory of evolution doesn't apply on a large scale to multi-cellular organisms, then that wouldn't really concern me, and I feel I can defend my viewpoint well enough. . . . I like apologetics, so it's very interesting to me, scientific arguments for why this is true and why this is false and whatnot." Note the adjective describing Phil's apologetic arguments: they're *scientific*. How do you defend against scientists who doubt the Bible? You use science.

Like Phil, most of the people I met at all four schools were creationist, even if the faculty and students at the Muslim schools were often more moderate about creationism, perhaps because opposing evolution was just not as important to them.[1] Yet, also like Phil, nearly everyone I met liked science as a thing in itself. As it is for many Americans, science was simply a way we learned about the world, helping humans to ease suffering, solve problems, and adjudicate claims. When I asked those I interviewed at any of the schools about a conflict between science and religion, they often distinguished, like Mr. McNulty, between neutral science and atheist *scientists,* sometimes also using the term *evolutionists* as an indicator of a contrary religion. To call people *evolutionists* was to insist upon their reliance on a belief system rather than the accretion of observations about the natural world.

Good Tree's biology textbook was one of the few in the school that was from a religious publisher, Bob Jones University Press, rather than a mainstream secular press. Near the book's opening, readers learned "It is wrong, therefore, for a Christian to condemn science as being anti-God or to fear science, believing it can destroy man's faith in God. It is also wrong for a Christian to ignore science."[2] This was the same biology text that explained, in intricate detail, all the errors in evolution. In a similar way, the famed Muslim creationism advocate Harun Yahya[3]—whom staff members and administrators at both Muslim schools insisted I read, and whose video was shown in biology classes at Al Haqq—argues that evolution is scientifically false, the result of a "blind superstitious faith."

Science's importance outside of these schools means that it cannot simply be rejected. It might be easier for a certain kind of creationist to simply insist that science's criticisms are irrelevant. One could imagine, from the perspective of sociologist Pierre Bourdieu, a creationist insistence that science is the wrong thing to care about, and that what we really should care about is the claims of a certain religious belief. In other words, a creationist could try to leverage symbolic power to change the rules of the game. Yet, that kind of rejection is impossible.[4] Science is too powerful, too useful, and too historically relevant to both Christianity and Islam. Too powerful because you cannot avoid science and still consider yourself a modern American. Too useful because science is not an all-or-nothing deal, and so anyone can take the science they like and reject what they don't as the misdeeds of particular "scientists." And too historically relevant because "science" has been an important part of Protestant[5] and Sunni[6] identity for centuries.

As I described with scripture and prayer in the previous two chapters, science was understood as a kind of actor in these schools, authorizing certain practices and forms of knowledge. Yet science was also distinct from these other "external authorities" in that it was an authority shared with—and often leveraged by—secular opponents. Of course, scripture and prayer extended beyond these communities as well, and they were also the subject of intense debate. Yet of the three, it was science that seemed the most neutral in these schools, a general authority rather than a local one. As such, science gained its authority in these schools in subtly different ways than scripture and prayer did. As I described in the previous two chapters, scripture and prayer gained their authority primarily via the practiced *habituation* of certain ways of engaging their power. In contrast, science gained its authority in these schools through a more complex and ornate network of authorizing practices and arguments, seen most clearly in the roles of teachers and tests.

Prayer and scripture have a certain agency in the schools I studied because people can see their effectiveness. And on some level, this is true of science as well: various students in interviews reminded me they believe in gravity for good reason. Yet, that effectiveness was also somewhat remote. If scripture and prayer were habituated as authorities that people can leverage to solve problems, science was habituated through the authority of other individuals and institutions, especially teachers, tests, and particular scientists or scientific claims. To hold to creationist science was to situate oneself within the network of various kinds of scientific claims and authorities, attempting to leverage certain authorities against others. And it was this kind of contestation—what John Dewey would call an engagement with fixed habits—that created within my respondents a more robust sense of science as an agent and authority in their own lives.[7] Perhaps ironically, it was in disagreeing with the scientific theory of evolution that science—or what they thought of as science—became most obviously an agent capable of action in the world.

WHAT IS SCIENCE?

Regardless of how comfortable my respondents might have been with describing science as a thing in this world, the concept remains a tricky one to pin down. Philosophers of science are quite divided on exactly what science entails, and debates among scientists and those who study them about what scientists actually *do* all day form a significant portion of science and technology studies. In some ways, it would be easier to talk about "science education" in the schools where I did my research, yet something called science had a power outside of the textbooks and classrooms. It was an external authority in the ways I've been describing scripture and prayer, a felt agent with a certain capacity to act and demand.

The sociologist Robert Merton described science as a set of institutionalized practices with particular moral and emotional claims. Science, Merton argued, could be recognized as the methods we use to gain and certify knowledge, as well as that knowledge itself. Yet it was also an "ethos," "a set of cultural values and mores governing the activities termed scientific."[8] For Merton, science was marked by certain moral commitments that had emotional and practical implications. Scientists are to be at once humble and courageous, committed and dispassionate. This is not to deny that scientists themselves were better thought of as regular people rather than ascetic seekers for truth. Indeed, as historian of science Steven Shapin argues, the idea that scientists "are human too"—that is, morally equivalent to non-scientists—was a twentieth-century innovation, articulated in no small part by Merton, the result of scientists' increased dependence on government and industry, which led them to be perceived as just another interest group.[9]

Later historians and sociologists of science have continued to challenge the idea of a homogenous thing called science across space and time: science hasn't always meant the things we think it means, and even for contemporary working scientists, how they describe their work varies tremendously both between and even within particular fields like chemistry, physics, or biology.[10] Yet, even if science is a hard-to-define category for scientists and those who study them, it remains an important category for non-scientists, and not only at the schools I studied. There's a thing called science that governments fund, surveys and polls ask about, and schools teach. And even if the figure of the scientist is just another human, there is nonetheless a sense within society that science is more than the sum of its imperfect human parts. In the schools I studied, science was often portrayed as a cumulative, self-correcting authority that seeks truth and (eventually) corrects error. As I have been discussing about scripture and prayer in the previous two chapters, science in this sense also acts: people describe science as showing things, saying things, doing things. Science is often regarded as a coherent authority through which we gain access to trustworthy knowledge.[11] That doesn't mean scientists can't be wrong, or that laypeople can't disagree with scientists.[12] But, interestingly enough, at least in the schools I studied, science as such is often considered by definition not at fault. The word was often interchangeable with rationality.[13]

Of course, there is a large literature—indeed, there are "wars"—about whether or not what scientists do all day is a gradual revelation of reality itself. While there is much to admire in Ian Hacking's distinctions between the contingency of the question and the contingency of the results, we can safely bracket these conversations for my argument here.[14] My point is that whether or not scientists uncover what's real, by the time their often counter-intuitive arguments get to non-scientists (or even working scientists in other fields), what is left are basically arguments from authority (or authorities). If we had the time, interest, and capacity, we could trace those authorities back to their roots,[15] yet most of us aren't going to go to that much trouble. We accept on good authority the existence of electrons, the reasons for precipitation, and the Earth's distance from the sun. We have not done the experiments ourselves. We probably wouldn't know how to do the measurements if we wanted to, and even if we did, we would generally be forced to repeat someone else's methods, with all the resulting possibilities for repeating another's implicit errors.[16]

High school lab experiments, then, are at best an appreciation for others' scientific work, yet the possibility of discovering something new or even falsifying something else is rarely if ever entertained. As a result, science can often function as an authority in these schools in a manner that is experientially distinct from that of scripture or prayer: instead of becoming an authority via habituation, it is sometimes an authority via authority, through the assurances by tests or teachers or other experts that we know the world is, in fact, a certain way and that *science* is the means by which we gain this knowledge. It is only when those assurances butt up against something important that they become worth concerning oneself with, thereby actually habituating a sense of science as an agent with more immediate relevance.

ON CREATIONISM

All four of the schools were creationist, emphasizing three key strategies to counter evolution: the centrality of lab science, a pragmatic focus on the here and now, and intelligent design. All three strategies took for granted that science is a kind of authority and that its language and form must be respected, even if the goal is to oppose the overwhelming consensus of biologists.

Each strategy uses a distinction between microevolution and macroevolution. Biologists often distinguish between macroevolution, or evolution between species, and microevolution, or evolution within species.[17] Ken Ham, founder of Answers in Genesis and the Creation Museum, says the distinction is between "kinds," which gives him a bit more wiggle room to explain genetic diversity.[18] That focus on *evolution we can see* allows creationists to hold that humans did not evolve from another animal while acknowledging that bacteria can adapt to antibiotics.

Yet showing there are some unanswered questions about evolution is many degrees less difficult than arguing the earth's age ought to be counted in thousands of years rather than in billions. Young Earth Creationism insists that the Earth's age is whatever age the Bible gives it. (There is some debate about the Biblical age: some claim the Earth is as young as 6,000 years, and I have heard as old as 15,000.)[19] While a relatively new orthodoxy in American Christian history, most of the students and teachers I met at both Evangelical schools not only believed in creationism but also in a young Earth, in contrast to competing schools of thought such as the "gap theory" or "old Earth creationism."[20] The biology teacher at Good Tree, Ms. James, taught all of these competing Christian beliefs about creationism in her unit on evolution. While she claimed to be open to students' believing whichever position they chose, she seemed to favor Young Earth Creationism in her presentation and tone. The Bob Jones textbooks used for science classes at both Christian schools are Young Earth creationist. While passages in the Qur'an also say the Earth was made in six days, Muslims are generally much more comfortable thinking of those days as metaphorical. I met no Muslim in my work uncomfortable with the scientific consensus on the age of the Earth.

Emphasizing Lab Science

Evangelical creationists tend to insist that all science must be falsifiable lab science, so it is relatively straightforward for them to argue that macroevolution is not "scientific."[21] An example of this preference for falsifiable lab science comes from an essay collection edited by Ken Ham, who gave a talk near Good Tree that the principal invited me to attend with a group of students and teachers. We all got into buses and went to hear the great creationist speak, and in his talk he said something much like this quote from his edited volume: "Any conclusions about things that are not testable in the present must be based on improvable assumptions about the untestable past."[22] This claim might not be "science" as some would describe it (what is being proven via scientific method here?) but rather a quite dogmatic form of philosophy of science. Yet, again, whether or not this is real science is not the point: What is important is that the creationists with whom I worked understood a thing called "science" as making demands they had to respect, and which they could demand from others.

Similarly, a key text in the contemporary intelligent design and anti-evolution-but-not-necessarily-creationist movement is Michael Denton's *Evolution: A Theory in Crisis*.[23] Denton writes that "Darwin's model of evolution is still very much a theory and still very much in doubt when it comes to macroevolutionary phenomena. Furthermore, being basically a theory of historical reconstruction, it is impossible to verify by experiment or direct observation as is normal in science." He goes on to nod at philosopher of science Karl Popper, using his emphasis on falsification to argue that evolution cannot be considered a legitimate scientific theory, which is a relatively common move in creationist literature and something I heard in conversation with adults at Good Tree.[24]

Focus on the Right Now

There was another, less philosophical way to approach this focus on microevolution: focus on the right now. In contrast to other biology classes, which would probably describe different physiologies as the result of evolution, all four schools' biology classes tended to describe physiological differences as just there. They came to the same synchronic place: form meeting function was a cornerstone of each biology class. The question of *why* form meets function was the primary difference from a secular biology lesson: at Good Tree, the "why" was clearly God's design. At the other three schools, the "why" was also God, though not quite as vocally defended as at Good Tree. At one biology class at Apostles, the teacher just classified the plants with his students, explaining how to distinguish between the various phyla without ever really discussing why or how these phyla developed. In a similar discussion in an AP Biology class at Al Haqq, the teacher said, "So if you were to look at the evolutionary perspective, we have the charopytes, bryrophytes, pteridophytes, gymnosperms, angiosperms," pointing at each name on the board as she spoke. Even though she did mention evolution at least twice in the lesson, the overwhelming emphasis was on the synchronic appearance of difference rather than these diachronic causes.

This subtlety becomes complicated when the differences between phyla are otherwise used as evidence for evolution. While teaching a regular biology class at Good Tree, the biology teacher Ms. James wrote the following characteristics of phylum chordata on the board, mentioning that "the vertebrates will develop bone instead of using a notochord" and that pouches develop into gills for fish, as she wrote on the board that "folds in the neck region of the embryos . . . develop into structures of the head and neck."

A student asked, "Does that mean we all come from monkeys?"

"Actually, that's not really what evolutionists teach," Ms. James responded calmly. "We would come from a cousin of monkeys, but really, we would all come from a common ancestor, something more like a bacteria. What happens is that when they look at the all the embryos and the stages of embryos, they say, oh look, they're similar. But if you look at the gills in embryos, those do eventually become *gills* and so the structures actually are not similar at all." What's important here is that Ms. James is not discounting the many tools of modern biology, all of which are generally used to support the theory of evolution. Embryology, phylogeny, ontogeny: all of these are fine in and of themselves. It's just wrong to say they support evolution. Just as importantly, Ms. James seeks to show how evolutionists are wrong *scientifically*, arguing they cannot actually support their claims, rather than simply asserting that the Bible says they are wrong.

At both Christian schools, students did a lab experiment that was part of the test workbook for Al Amal and Apostles. "You're going to be simulating what's happening in natural selection," Ms. James told her students. She had many multi-colored paper dots, made, I guessed, from punching small holes in construction paper. And alongside theses dots were small pieces of fabric, each about the size of a place mat, all of them different colors and patterns. She had the students drop twenty of the colored dots onto the cloth in various "generations." The students then looked quickly at the cloth, took the first ten they could see away, and then doubled the remaining ten that were left. They kept doing this through a series of "generations" until they saw what had been "naturally selected."

The lab maintains a theme Ms. James suggested when she taught evolution to her students, describing how darker moths survived the pollution of the industrial revolution better than brighter moths, as the darker moths were better able to adapt to the new, more polluted, and therefore darker trees. It's a historical example of a change within a species but not a change from one species to another.[25] The focus on microevolution allows students to imagine careers in biology and medicine, as the study of certain cellular processes or the performance of an appendectomy need not *require* a belief in evolution, particularly if you have microevolution to explain those obvious changes in viruses and vermin. In another conversation with Phil, the Good Tree salutatorian I mentioned at the beginning of this chapter, I asked if he was nervous about studying biology at the secular university he was going to attend. He nodded thoughtfully, as though he'd given this a lot of consideration. "Yeah, because I'm doing cellular biology, I don't think I'll have to deal with that [evolution]. I mean, they might have some of that origin of life, first cells garbage but I can work my way around that. I mean, we believe in microevolution, and that's mostly what I'll be working with, not macro."

Intelligent Design

Michael Behe is a biochemist who has challenged certain assumptions about various biochemical cellular mechanisms.[26] By doing so, Behe helped develop the concept of "irreducible complexity" as an alternative argument, galvanizing the intelligent design movement.[27] Something so irreducibly complex, the argument goes, must have an intelligent designer. Irreducible complexity is a centrally important concept in the textbook Adam Morgan teaches the seniors in his Worldview class at Good Tree.[28] The entire first quarter of the course is devoted to creation, intelligent design, and a Biblical understanding of human origin. "I'll ask about [irreducible complexity] on the exam, on the midterm, and on the final, and throughout the class because you need to be able to explain this at a detailed level," he told his students. This focus on intelligent design came, for Mr. Morgan, to symbolize how science itself must be separated from the philosophical presuppositions that color it, as well as how Christians must defend their own intellectual (and scientific) capacities: "Obviously Colson [the co-author of the textbook] is not saying science is bad," he told his students. "All commentators talking about science separate what is genuinely science from philosophy."

The role of intelligent design in Mr. Morgan's course illustrates the paradox of the movement, which is dominated, financed, and pushed forward by believing Christians and yet touted as a secular, nonreligious struggle. Thomas Woodward,[29] an Evangelical Christian and important historian of intelligent design, gave a lecture at Good Tree at which he kept repeating the names of atheist and agnostic allies, a very common rhetorical tactic among supporters of intelligent design. It's particularly well used by the Discovery Institute, which tended to be where Mr. Morgan got the films he showed in class. When I found out that Mr. Morgan was showing a video by a Young Earth creationist (Dr. Lisle) in class, I asked, "He's with Answers in Genesis, right? I thought you used Discovery Institute."

"That's true. Dr. Lisle is the one time I use Answers in Genesis. Most of what I use is secular."

"Would you really consider the Discovery Institute secular?"

"Well they have a wide variety of kinds of people working for them, and certainly not all of them are Biblical Christians. Most of the people on the films I show in class are secular and from secular universities."

"Right, but the people they actually employ, most of them are Biblical Christians. Like Nelson, the philosophy of biology guy, he's a Christian."

"I never really knew if he was or not. I always suspected it by the way he talked about things."

"And the rest of the people who actually work at Discovery, my hunch is most of them are Biblical Christians, right?"

"I'm not sure, honestly."

Unlike Answers in Genesis or other creation science media, Discovery has high production values and the veneer of secular science. Of course, some of the people in these videos are in fact non-Christian, and even non-theist, but the fact that many of them are Christian is left unacknowledged. Yet while this might well be evidence of a rhetorical sleight-of-hand, it is also an important indication of the authority of science and its capacity to make certain demands of how creationists must proceed: they cannot simply demand that scripture be respected. They instead must show why science proves them right, or at the very least why it has not, in fact, proven them wrong.

THE BOUNDARIES OF EVOLUTION

While opposition to certain elements of science—almost always the theory of evolution—showed up at all four schools that I studied, it was most salient in the Christian schools. I go into the reason for this salience in other work, yet evolution's relative function as a boundary is worth elaborating here.[30]

Before I began my fieldwork I didn't realize that many Muslims in the United States, Europe, and in predominantly Muslim countries also don't believe in evolution.[31] According to Pew's 2014 US Religious Landscape Survey,[32] 41 percent of US Muslims believe humans have always been in

their current form, though I found far fewer Muslims willing to acknowledge human evolution in the schools I studied. When I learned how few
of my Muslim respondents believed in evolution, I was standing in the
counselor's office at Al Amal. I leaned into the doorway and asked the
counselor, Latifa again: "Really? You don't believe in evolution?"[33] Latifa
looked at her friend, a teacher sitting in the office with her. "That we came
from monkeys, right? We don't believe that, do we?" "No," said her friend,
shaking her head. Latifa looked back at me: "No, we don't believe that."
What I came to realize, as this anecdote might indicate, is that Muslims
simply don't make a big deal out of this disbelief.

Some might argue that this difference is because of scripture alone.
They could claim, as scholar of Islamic creationism Salman Hameed once
did, that "in the context of evolution, the Qur'an does not end up playing
such a central role for Muslims as the Bible has done for fundamentalist
Christians."[34] While this might or might not be true on a global scale, in
the communities I studied the Qur'an *did* matter as a means of opposing
evolution, though through the mediating authority of trusted scholars. The
central difference is less what the texts say than what the authorities say
about the texts *and how to use them.*[35]

These fights are always historically situated, and for American
Evangelicals the famous Scopes "Monkey Trial" was one of many key turning
points through which evolution became a constitutive battle line in already-
established debates on the nature of scripture. Activists and intellectual
leaders linked German Higher Criticism and the "European" theory of evolution to German aggression in World War I. As the century progressed,
creationism became an increasingly important way for fundamentalists
to distinguish themselves from secularists and religious liberals, especially given increased federal and state efforts to teach evolution in
schools, the decreased importance of conservative religion in the older
Protestant denominations, and the dramatic success of "flood geologists"
who attempted explanations of the literal truth of the Bible's flood account
(and the rest of the Bible's creation narrative) through geological evidence.[36]
Yet all these efforts are descended from the nineteenth-century marriage of
a democratic understanding of the Bible's accessibility with an earnest optimism about scripture's relationship to science.[37] Of course, Muslims also believe in their scripture's literal truth and in their religion's compatibility with
science, yet, as I described in the previous two chapters, their practical focus
during the day tends to be more rooted in prayer than in the literal reading
of scripture. In addition, the Muslim understanding of scripture, at least in
the schools I studied, tended to be more committed to the interpretations of
trusted authorities and more aware of certain ambiguities.

Perhaps more important for the sake of comparison, the primary concerns I observed in American Muslims' relations to the outside world was that they were either sexist or terrorist, making their commitment to peace and women's empowerment a constant refrain in my interactions with them. In contrast, the Evangelicals I worked with were worried that people thought they were hateful and dumb, especially about science. As the sophomore Doctrine teacher at Good Tree, Mr. Smith told his class, "The media just does a number on Christians and just makes us look like buffoons every chance they get."

The threat that evolution would lead to nihilistic atheism was another litany I heard continuously, and for many it was the marker of Christian faith itself. At lunch one day at Apostles, I asked some freshmen in Mr. Dominguez's class about a hypothetical Christian scientist who believed in evolution as we sat together in the cafeteria. "Then he's not a Christian," a few of them said at once. When Dr. Hawthorne, the senior Bible teacher at Good Tree, mentioned that a particular Christian college teaches theistic evolution, various students in the class turned and looked at a girl about to go to that college as though someone in her family had died. "Oh Bethany," a girl said, with deep concern in her voice. "It's okay," said Bethany, grinning nervously. "I just won't take biology." Dr. Hawthorne immediately responded, "If you're saying theistic evolution is bad, you're missing the point." He told me earlier in a one-on-one conversation that the most important thing for him was that the world was the result of God's creation: "Now the mechanics of how the sun got there and how old it is, that's less important. But I have to be careful here. I'm in the minority."

Even people more representative of the majority opinion—such as Mr. Dominguez, the freshman and sophomore Bible teacher at Apostles—would generally not go so far as to call theistic evolution a "heaven or hell issue." Nonetheless, they still felt it was deeply wrong and corrosive inasmuch as it gives more space to a theory that is both incompatible with the Bible and destructive of humanity's sacred understanding of itself. As Mr. Dominguez told his students, "Guys, I'm sorry but Satan has used the evolution philosophy to deceive mankind . . . . He has given a big giant lie [that] you evolved from this primordial soup and now you are here today with absolutely no purpose in life . . . ."

Evolution was a less intense issue at the Muslim schools. I asked the principal at Al Amal what he thought about animal evolution, and he responded in no uncertain terms that he didn't believe in it, using much the same argument as many Christian creationists that it is hard to find examples of such radical change in daily life. "I think that Harun Yahya got it right," he told me. "If it happened once, why hasn't it happened again? . . . If you look at a bird, it looks the same to me as it did to my grandfather—it hasn't changed since when I was born to now when I am 45 . . . . Even in Christian schools, they don't believe in Darwinism." I asked him about state exams that required knowledge of evolution, and he nodded: "When you teach it to students to study it, it's different from teaching them to believe it. It's like when you teach students about World War II. It's history now. It doesn't affect them. It's just something they have to know." Evolution might have been wrong, but it wasn't something to worry about.

The students made similar distinctions, with one group of girls at Al Amal drawing a line at human evolution but then, when I asked them about the evolution of animals, they looked at each other somewhat confused. One said to me, "I'm not sure—maybe we should ask Sheikh Khaled. We're actually not sure about that." This lack of certainty extended even to Al Amal's biology teacher, Brother Ahmed. I asked him in the hall after one of his biology classes about human evolution. "That's where I draw the line," he said. "I draw the line between microevolution and macroevolution. I don't really go into the details with the kids, but it just seems pretty clear that there are genetic variations inside populations. But in terms of macroevolution— did reptiles come from amphibians? I don't know, and I don't know where Islam falls on that—I really don't know." I asked him why he didn't talk that much in class about evolution's religious implications, and he said, "First, I just don't know about it, it's not my subject area. I mean, I'd like to learn more about it, but for now, I just don't know . . . . But also, I tell the students that there's just evidence we can easily see, something like a bacteria, where it's clearly evolving and getting more drug-resistant."

In some ways, Brother Ahmed has the same strategies Evangelicals do, in that he uses examples of microevolution to create a pragmatic accommodation to the world at large, acknowledging those bits of evolution that do not contradict necessary and essential beliefs. Yet it is hard to imagine an Evangelical at any of the schools I studied—particularly a biology teacher— claiming not to know what their religion teaches about evolution. For the Evangelicals, evolution was an issue of such profound moral salience that ignorance could be no excuse.

The two biology teachers at Al Haqq were much more insistent that macroevolution was impossible: one showed a Harun Yahya movie over a week because, as she told me, "Yahya gives you all the scientific facts." When I asked what the school thought about evolution, she said it's "such a minor issue, it's not something that we're even entertaining." I asked if belief in evolution was *haram* [prohibited] and she paused. "You don't just throw out [the word] *haram*, that's why we have *makruh* [discouraged], but I've never even heard someone mention *makruh*." As is the case for Evangelicals, there is a concern that a belief in evolution is related to atheism, but, unlike for Evangelicals, that concern does not morph into a fear of conversion.

When I asked the head Islamic Studies teacher at Al Haqq, Sheikh Yusuf, what he thought about evolution, he paused, muttered a quick prayer, and gave a long explanation as to why it was dangerous and wrong. In a senior Islamic Studies class he had told the students, "Science helps us disprove evolution." In the interview I asked him what he would think about evolution for all life except humans and he scoffed, "This is just a theory, but there's an implicit thing in the Qur'an, that other creatures were created in that moment as well." Yet, when I then asked what he would think about someone believing Allah had guided evolution, his whole expression changed. "Oh," he said, "this is fine, they're trying to accommodate the theory, and they are trying to be scientific, well they evolved, and God is the one who is behind the evolution." Sheikh Yusuf hadn't assumed that theistic evolution was possible, and when it was suggested, he was not threatened by the idea, though he did not agree with it.

Even the most conservative of the Islamic Studies teachers I encountered at the four schools, Sheikh Khaled, was not willing to call someone un-Islamic for believing in evolution (again, provided we separate the evolution of humans and insist that God guided it). The Sheikh generously let me occasionally pose questions to his class, and I asked one group of about ten junior boys what they thought about evolution. The Sheikh nodded, "This is a good question—I will have my cane behind you for anyone who said Darwin did something good. Do any of you believe in Darwin?" Most of the students mumbled agreement. "Good—I will hit you with ten lashes."[38] The students laughed and the teacher smiled at them.

I asked them if they could understand Darwin together with Islam, and Dafir a student with a neat beard who, recall from chapter five, was already a *hafiz* and was training a friend to be one too, nodded. "I think so," he said. "Like, it just makes sense—you look at what Darwin figured out with the finches"—he proceeded to explain to me for about two minutes Darwin's discovery about finches in the Galapagos—"and that just makes sense. But it doesn't work for humans, because humans live together and live in packs—they don't leave their weak alone."

Other students chimed in, basically agreeing, and Said, a confident boy sitting in the middle of the class, looked me in the eye: "We all say humans no, but animals, we don't know." He went on: "To be honest . . . I don't care about if animals evolved or not. It's just not something I think about a lot. Allah made the whole world and how he made it, I don't know."

"Yeah, same here," said Dafir. Various other boys nodded.

The teacher nodded as well. "Remember that the Qur'an tells us exactly how Allah made the world and that humans were created on a *Friday* . . . . Anything that Allah says [in the Qur'an], we say. No matter what the scientists say. They'll say something and later on they'll change their mind." He later told Dafir, "I will give you ten lashings for what you are saying about Darwin." Dafir smiled nervously and the other students laughed.

Sheikh Khaled did not tell Dafir that his belief is *haram* or that it will necessarily lead to atheism. The sheikh was clearly frustrated by the belief and, as the students mentioned they did not care about animal evolution, he looked surprised, even if he then nodded when Said insisted that all creation came from God. Perhaps more importantly, *I was the person who brought the issue up.* Evolution came up regularly at Bible and science classes at Good Tree and Apostles, while it only came up twice without me bringing it up at Al Haqq and never at Al Amal. Even in biology classes at the Muslim schools, the religious significance of evolution was usually glossed over and only cursorily acknowledged, if at all. I asked a teacher at Al Haqq about this, and she said she tried to make the distinction by saying "scientists say" or "evolutionists say" when discussing the theory of evolution; the Evangelical biology teachers opted for less subtle strategies.

I thought maybe I had found a negative case for this argument when I started at Apostles. I was shocked to learn that that the biology teacher, Joe Cassidy, was a theistic evolutionist, someone who believes that God guided evolution (usually also including human evolution). In his first year at Apostles, he liked that Kenneth Miller, a famous Christian apologist for the coexistence of science and religion, wrote the school's biology textbook. (It was changed to the Bob Jones book used at Good Three the following year.) Mr. Cassidy told me more than once that he was nervous about teaching at a school committed to Young Earth Creationism. Later on in the year, Gabe Simons, the principal's husband who had earlier been the biology teacher, was looking for something in the lab at the back of the classroom during one of Mr. Cassidy's biology units. Mr. Cassidy was worried he was being supervised because he had sent an e-mail about wanting to show a video on theistic evolution. When I talked to Christians at both schools about theistic evolution, most of them were perplexed at the idea, and quite a few of the students had never heard of it. Evolution, as I have already described, is almost always framed as creationists versus atheist evolutionists, with evolution nearly always understood as a proxy for atheism. In response to the e-mail he sent, Joe got another that told him the school could not teach anything that went against the Bible. He was asked to show his biology class two creationist DVDs instead. Mr. Cassidy left the school at the end of that year. When I talked to the superintendent of the school, he told me that when he asked Mr. Simmons to teach biology, he told him the most important thing he could do was ensure that all of the children learned about creationism. The principal informed me that the year after I left, the school would start using creationist textbooks from Bob Jones University Press.

TEACHING SCIENCE

In the biology classroom at Good Tree (which is where I heard the most creationist rhetoric of the four schools), I noticed that the only reference to God in the room was a picture of space and DNA on the front desk, a large, four-foot by four-foot poster with a quote in the top corner saying, "the Heavens Declare the Glory of God." On the walls were students' drawings of cells and multiple periodic tables. There was also a large timeline wall poster giving a history of science with big pictures of important scientists like Galileo and Pasteur, and, shockingly enough, Darwin, who says, "Well I'll be a monkey's uncle." A monkey standing next to Darwin responds, "Cousin, actually." Darwin wasn't being lampooned in the picture: he was just there. Darwin is everywhere, yet getting around him might not be as difficult as it appears, particularly because creationists reject the idea that rejecting Darwin means rejecting all of science.

But how do students actually access science, particularly in a class for a grade? In a science pedagogy textbook, Wendy Ward Hoffer highlights the importance of *inquiry* for science learners, a trait that various science organizations have emphasized as well, including the National Science Foundation, the National Research Council, and the American Association for the Advancement of Science. Science class, these reformers argue, should be more than memorizing facts. Students should act as scientists: curious, methodical, active. Hoffer offers the following example:

> Science teaching and learning, then, must include the excitement and wonder, the stresses and struggles experienced by professional scientists in their work . . . . When we teach science through student inquiry, we prepare learners to understand not only science *content* but also science as a distinct way of *knowing*—one that expands from curiosity, requires active engagement, relies on evidence, and takes place in a community of discovery.[39]

While it's not at all impossible to encourage students to treat their science class less like an assignment and more like an inquiry, it's a hard thing to pull off. I certainly observed many moments of students excitedly discovering something at all four schools. Yet most of what I saw in classrooms was students doing what they had to do. The very existence of grade books and standardized exams—whose right answers require the repetition of previous discoveries—shows that high school science is often more about showing you understand what the authorities say is right than it is discovering what is right yourself. Of course, a good science class allows students to repeat this process of discovery, figuring out in labs what other scientists have already discovered. Yet this is not so much blazing a new trail as walking an older trail already dotted with historical markers and informative kiosks. The authority of science as an institution is diffused between various nodes, and there is a huge gap between the original authority of science's relationship to reality (complicated as such a relationship might be) and what high school students and all the rest of us end up learning, discussing, and using as mechanisms of authority.[40]

In Brother Nabeel's girls' chemistry classes at Al Amal, he asked his students about how they measure mass in science lab. One girl shouted out, "Brother Khalil!" (Besides also teaching some math and Qur'an classes, Brother Khalil is the lab technician at Al Amal.) Other girls laughed at the joke, and Brother Nabeel looked for someone else to answer the question, yet nobody could. "Wow," he said, shaking his head. Then, referring to their 8th- and 9th-grade physical science and biology teacher, he added, "Brother Ahmed is going to be mad." Science is taking on a variety of different characteristics in this vignette. "Science" in its broadest sense is only partially involved: what is being discussed is instead a discrete question—how to measure mass. Yet that question is a part of a class and a department, *science*, which is itself divided into disciplines: in this case, chemistry. Its authority is also divided. There might well be an autonomy to the method of measuring mass that Brother Ahmed taught the students, Brother Khalil now practices, and Brother Nabeel seeks to refresh, yet what becomes clear by watching the students engage with this piece of science is that, for them, the authority of science is nested within the teachers. Who seeks confirmation of the students' knowledge and will grade them according to its presence or absence? A teacher. Who might they disappoint by their lack of knowledge? Another teacher. And who do they cite—even if jokingly—as a replacement for the knowledge itself? Yet another teacher.

Science educators—including those with whom I worked—often admit that much of what they teach is sort of wrong—not malevolently so, but simply as a matter of necessity.[41] As Brother Nabeel told a group of students how he had to simplify an earlier discussion of atomic bonds, he described how that earlier description he gave them was "not real." He went on, "So, in a way, I lied to you. I didn't want to, but I had to." Even if there is a tremendous tension within science studies between studying what scientists do as opposed to the knowledge they produce,[42] for the non-professionals I studied it was this knowledge that was most important, specifically as it was filtered through textbooks, teachers, and the media.[43] In a high school, teachers provide the primary interpretation of science: its source and adjudication, its moral approval and opprobrium, even its functional equivalent. Textbooks obviously matter as well, and so do labs and the physical objects they use. Yet it is often teachers that make them matter.

During one AP Biology class at Good Tree, students worried about the specific temperature of liquids they were using, only to be told it really didn't matter. However, they didn't worry *enough* about the quantity of a specific chemical they were putting into those liquids at a later stage in the experiment, and then they had to do the entire exercise again. At Al Amal, during one chemistry class, one group of three students was measuring the volume of ball bearings and forgot to make a specific measurement. Rather than go back and do it again, they guessed "10" which turned out to ruin the entire measurement. A few days later, another group of students had faked another lab and it had gone totally unnoticed by the teacher. I watched as the girls lied to the teacher, winking at me, and I realized what most high school students already know: you don't have to do science at all. You just have to convince your teacher you're doing science.

TESTING SCIENCE

Of course, it's not just teachers who are the authorities. As a former high school teacher, I knew well the constant questions: "will this be on the test?" or "will we be graded on this?" It was only when I became a teacher that I realized how much these questions dominate a teacher's lesson planning as well a student's concerns. I also realized that what's on a test often has little to do with the teacher's own prerogative. Particularly at the schools with state science examinations (Al Amal and Apostles) and the schools with AP tests (Al Amal, Al Haqq, and Good Tree), the "tests" were a constant source of pressure on both teachers and students. Getting students ready for state and national tests was a regular point of discussion among teachers and between teachers and students (as it was when I taught high school English in New York City). Testing has an important role in shaping not only what kinds of science these students learn but the shape and source of science's authority. The teachers' own tests reassert their power over the students' interpretations, and the tests from state governments and academic organizations (like Advanced Placement) help establish a coherent, national vision of what science should look like.

This question of authority—particularly regarding standardized tests—becomes even more relevant when the school communities disagree with the tests. Of course, for most questions these tests might ask, the schools really have no problem. As sociologists John Evans and Michael Evans describe it, the conservative religious critique of science is often ethical rather than epistemological.[44] It was only evolution—and for some at the Christian schools, the age of the Earth and the universe—that challenged previous beliefs. When I had my first real meeting with the principal of Apostles, I asked her about evolution. She said, "No, we believe what the Bible says." I asked if that was a problem considering the state exam and she shook her head. "There's only three questions on it."

"So you teach both sides?" I asked.

"We teach both sides," she said. "But we have some great books about it. We'll show them to you. You'll be blown away—we just want students to know the facts, and when we show it to them, they really get into it."

There's a sense here that the test's requirements are neither too imposing nor particularly intellectually difficult. This confidence is harder to maintain for AP classes, particularly considering how virtually every secular biology textbook centers its presentation of biology on the theory of evolution. At the three schools that had AP Biology classes—Good Tree, Al Amal, and Al Haqq—each handled this tension slightly differently. At Al Amal, it wasn't much of a problem at all. As I described earlier, Brother Ahmed taught the students about evolution, making clear that it obviously does occur, even if he told me in conversation that he did not believe in human evolution and was skeptical about some forms of macroevolution. I asked the AP Biology teacher at Al Haqq about her strategy of simply saying "evolutionists say" when making more controversial points. She told me, "There are clear adaptations—in stories of the prophets, we learn that people's bodies were bigger, but each organism has its own DNA, and a species couldn't change into another species . . . there are big gaps in the theory of evolution. Where's the link between species?" I asked about making decisions about what to teach regarding evolution, and the teacher told me that the school's Sheikh is often involved in the decisions, making it clear to her that every species was created separately. She said that creates a challenge, because "the way biology textbooks are set, they're all set to mention evolution, they don't say Darwinism, but still, the way biology or life science are structured has to do with evolution." After the AP Biology test was over, she showed her students a Harun Yahya[45] video about evolution.

The AP teacher at Good Tree—Ms. James—regularly discussed the textbook's evolutionary assumptions with her students. I observed her first day of AP Biology—the first time the school had ever taught it. She told the students,

> Evolution is a central feature in this book, the whole book is centered around it, and as Christians, we have a different perspective on this. Genes can change—there are mutations, organisms can survive in different environments . . . . But the textbook talks all about this, and there are some contradictions you might see in there. The AP course is centered around the themes of evolution. I challenge you to look at that with critical eyes. You need to ask: is what they're saying on this page the same as what they're saying on that page? I'd challenge you to think critically about what you're reading.

This focus on critical thinking is an intriguing one, because she did not ask for a similar sort of criticism of anything else students take on authority—say, descriptions of white blood cells or mitochondria. And while she encouraged her students to "think critically" about evolution in a way that neither of the Muslim AP teachers did, she did not want students to ignore it.

In a separate conversation, Ms. James told me about how an AP grader she met was frustrated by students who would not answer questions about evolution. "You shouldn't just not answer," she told me. "You have to say what the theory says."

Her students did exactly this. One of the AP students, Michael, lent me his exam on evolution. Below are the essay questions. Note how Ms. James structured the questions, and Michael structured his answers, to get everything right, but without ever actually claiming evolution is "true" or that they believe what evolutionists claim.

Essay Questions:

1. Explain the relationship between fitness, as Darwin understood it, and alleles present in an individual. How do the collective alleles in a population explain the changes in a species observed over time? (10 points)
2. Evolutionists consider their idea to be a major unifying concept in modern biology. (10 points)
   a. <u>Explain</u> the mechanisms that lead to evolutionary change.
   b. Describe how scientists might use each of the following as evidence to support the theory of evolution.
   - Bacterial resistance to antibiotics.
   - The fossil record.

Michael's answers:

A) There are several mechanisms that can lead to an evolutionary change in a population. Mutations can occur in genes that can change certain characteristics that cause the population to evolve over time. Genetic drift can occur when certain characteristics become extinct in a population over time because of predation or natural disaster. And, selection can occur when certain characteristics are chosen over others because they allow the population to survive.

B) Scientists will say how bacteria can resist antibiotics supports evolution because they will say how that resistance shows how [in green pen, teacher has underlined "how" multiple times and then a line and arrow out of the paragraph to "by mutation" written next to it] organisms can evolve over time, which demonstrates how evolution occurs. Scientists will use the fossil record by saying that they find organisms that are the ancestors or predecessors of modern day organisms. Then they will claim that this demonstrates evolution because organisms have changed over time and their characteristics have changed.

Both Ms. James and Michael use a perspectival rhetorical device by always premising statements with "scientists say." A non-creationist might have simply written the sentences without the perspectival positioning at the beginning. Yet by prefacing that "scientists" make a certain claim, rather than making the claim himself, Michael is able to manifest his awareness of what the right answer "should be" while simultaneously distancing himself from the scientific establishment's claims. I was continually surprised by how easily the students managed to maintain this distinction. I interviewed all but one of the students in the AP Biology class, and every single one was convinced evolution was wrong. Nearly every one of them told me how learning more about evolution showed them it was really just a theory "with a lot of holes."[46]

DEBATING SCIENCE WITH SCIENCE

In interactions with both tests and teachers, most students in the schools I studied treated science at something of an experiential remove, a power that must be placated rather than an authority to engage. Which doesn't mean science was unloved. I met many students who were passionate about science, as were their teachers. For example, I interviewed June, one of the students at Good Tree who took Ms. James's AP Biology class in my second and third semester at the school. "I love science," she told me in our taped interview in Good Tree's spare room. She smiled as she went on: "Like randomly, I'll be driving, and I'll wonder how long it'll take me to stop if I gently press the brake, as opposed to if I just press it just a little bit harder. And I wonder what friction is going on with the tires." In the interview, she casually mentioned the many ways her mind wanders to scientific explanations of this or that piece of her day. June showed exactly the kind of scientific curiosity science educators are looking for, a sense that the world is brimming with randomness and regularities both calling out for our explanation.

So it might be surprising to a certain kind of secularist that June was wholly unmoved by her AP Biology textbook's presentation of evolution.[47] When I asked her about whether taking AP Biology had had any effect on her, she responded that "learning about evolution's really frustrating, because it kind of blurs the line of how true do you think your Christianity is, as opposed to how true evolutionists think that their theories are." She repeated a line of argument used by many in the Christian creationist community, and which I heard regularly in Mr. Morgan's Worldview class at Good Tree: the difference between evolutionists and Christians was philosophical rather than scientific. The move is clever in a few ways. First, it is a way of situating true Christianity as creationist, proving no acknowledgment one could believe in both evolution and Christ's resurrection, even if many Christians do.[48] Yet even more clever is the insistence that evolution depends only on first principles rather than on falsifiable scientific claims, a position that virtually any working biologist would contest. June told me that evolutionists "completely ignore the Cambrian explosion and then they take fossils from here and here, and on this side of the planet and that side of the planet, and they say, 'Oh, this was—must have been the intermediate of this.' And it's a lot of supposition." This focus on the Cambrian explosion was mentioned in the introduction of the book; it is often returned to in Christian creationist literature, as it is alleged to prove a spontaneous creation in the fossil record. Whether or not June is correct in her depiction of scientists' arguments (or lack of arguments), what matters here is that June is attempting to use science against scientists, to claim that her side—rather than theirs—is scientifically correct.

It might seem heretical to describe what June is doing here as science. Indeed, creationist attempts to shoehorn scientific claims into whatever fits with their particular understanding of sacred texts seems to have more in common with astrology or vaccine denial rather than biology, chemistry, or physics. Yet my argument here is not a philosophy of science examination of exactly what an accurate representation of the world would look like. It is instead a local study of how particular people understand an authority called science and how they enact that authority in their lives, experiencing science as exerting a particular agency to describe and make demands of the world.

In this sense, I draw on sociologist of science Thomas Gieryn's distinction from essentialized definitions of science, which "privilege analysts' representations of science," choosing instead to focus on "how people in society negotiate and provisionally settle for themselves the borders and territories of science." The definition of science therefore becomes "local and episodic rather than universal; pragmatic and strategic rather than analytic or legislative; contingent rather than principled; constructed rather than essential."[49] With some notable exceptions, the majority of creationists—even those for whom creationism is a full-time occupation—are not themselves working scientists in the sense that academic departments use the term (e.g., scholars who regularly publish their findings in peer review journals). Rather, they are a mix of all sorts of people. The more educated among them tend to be historians, lawyers, medical doctors, and engineers. Those with training in the sciences tend to have no professional need to use evolution as an explanation for their work. A creationist doctor can deliver a baby or remove an appendix as well as one who believes in evolution. The same is true for an engineer building a bridge with stone he believes is only 10,000 years old. In addition to this more intellectual vanguard, there are also all the hobbyists, some of whom are community members I met at these schools: people who really do love science and figuring out how things work, and who also love their holy books and the promise of a grand conspiracy to keep the truth of creationism away from the rest of us. It is outside of my capacity to determine whether or not these people are actually doing *science*, but what matters here is that they are engaging in something they think of as science, and they understand science to have real weight in their conversations and interactions. It was in these interactions that science became an external authority in the ways I have been describing—even if it was a science that those outside of creationism might not recognize as such.

Authority at a Remove

Yet for many students, science was not habituated and engaged in the ways I have been describing. It was simply an authority at some remove. For example, I had an interview with Simone, a Good Tree student I had observed not paying much attention in science class. I asked Simone—as I did many students—whether "evolution is a big deal at this school." She responded that "if you don't believe in the six days of creation and Genesis 1, your whole philosophy of the Bible is flawed." Simone is a junior with a family history at the school; I saw her father often at school events and met her older brother at a school board meeting. She told me she wanted to be a homemaker and raise children when she got older. She said if she did get a job it would be as a nurse, but she did not mention any of the scientific elements of nursing in her explanation for why she would find the work attractive. For Simone, science seemed to be something she just had to do.

Yet science was also an authority with leverage she could use, even if not so ably. Simone tended to defer to the *religious* defense of the book of Genesis and its account of creation. In our interview, Simone told me her father used to teach a course on the book of Genesis, so it might not be surprising that she had a lot of opinions about the text. As I did with many students and teachers, I asked Simone why she thought so many people get evolution wrong. Why are otherwise thoughtful scientists so deceived? "I don't know," she said. "I think they find it harder to believe that God would create everything and they just want to believe that things just randomly happen, and that's just the way it is. I guess that's easier for them to believe than wanting to be saved and Christianity requires you to do something and to act a different way, so evolution provides a different avenue where you don't have to do anything."[50] For Simone, as for many people I interviewed, an opposition to the Biblical account of creation was ultimately not about science at all; it was about an ethical conflict, a permission to go against God's word. When I asked her if you could be a Christian and believe in evolution, she told me something I heard often: "If you believe in Christ . . . then you'd need to believe the whole Bible . . . you can't just believe sections of the Bible and say that you're a Christian." For those Christians who continued to believe in evolution, she would "have to wonder if your belief in evolution is stronger than your belief in Christ."

When I asked questions that were much more explicitly about science, she was less articulate and much vaguer than she was about prayer or scripture. She referred to authorities at a degree of remove, making general statements not necessarily rooted in her own experience. "Science is proven, except for evolution, so in other areas I'm sure, but science and religion can't really be on the same page," she told me when I asked whether she believes there is a conflict between science and religion. I asked her to go on, and she paused, appearing to think through her answers in ways she did not for other questions. "Like the Bible, there are things in the Bible that can be scientifically proven, but there are things such as evolution that can't be proven. I don't know if I'm answering your question exactly, but—," she paused, looking a bit lost. "Science and religion right?"

"Yeah," I said. "Yeah," giving her an encouraging nod.

"So I don't know. It's very difficult—I don't know," she told me, looking a bit lost.

"You're doing fine so far," I said, smiling.

"So, let's see. Science is provable, but there are aspects to it that have tried to contradict religion and it's never been I guess strong or I guess never been proven. Like there are aspects that cannot say that religion is false, so Christianity is false. But Christianity is strong; I guess that's what I'm trying to say. Do you understand what I'm trying to say?"

"Sort of."

"Okay, so Christianity is like there's nothing that's been contradictory of the Bible that has been proven, and everything that they have tried to say that makes the Bible false has failed." Simone could not be much more specific than this, and I smiled and moved on in the conversation.

Note that for Simone in these conversations, science does not function as an authority in a way that she explicitly engages and habituates, something quite distinct from how she and most of her fellow students talked about scripture and prayer. Simone is quite forced and polished in her responses about scripture and prayer, as well as about the scriptural problems with evolution. Her lack of familiarity with scientific arguments does not prove a lack of intellectual capacity but rather a lack of intellectual engagement; science just isn't an authority that has to be practically engaged, even if it is an authority that has to be accepted and acknowledged. At all four of these schools I saw this same tendency to often treat science at some remove, as an authority learned and handled via the authorities of tests and teachers. When science was a problem—and it usually was not—it was dealt with via scripture rather than via science.

The Creative Application of Science

Not all students were so unwilling to engage science on its own terms, or at least on the terms they understood science to have. In his senior Worldview class, Mr. Morgan had students give period-long presentations to the class about a controversial topic. One senior I got to know well, Janette, gave her presentation on a topic that Mr. Morgan discussed a few times in the months he dedicated to a discussion of Biblical creation: distant starlight. Janette was tall and cool. She had straight brown hair and, while I have no idea if she had ever sampled any, she was interested in wine. She loved science and loved, like a lot of teenagers, to geek out over the meaning of everything. The only difference between her and a more secular teenager is that her effort to understand the meaning of everything required that she link it all to the earth being created by God in six days anywhere between 6,000 and 15,000 years ago.

Science became an authority in a much more practical way for Janette than it was for Simone. Science had rules she had to respect, and which could exert certain kinds of power, but as with prayer and scripture, she could also use those rules to accomplish work on her own. When I found out about her project, I honestly had never considered starlight as a problem. For most of the history of creationism (which began in earnest with the developing fields of geology and Darwin's discovery of evolution), it was geology and evolution that most challenged the idea of a young Earth. "Oh, right," I said, thinking out loud. "Because according to a Christian Young Earth theory, the earth can't be millions or billions of years old, right?" As the film Mr. Morgan showed in his class about the "distant starlight problem" made clear, if what we know of the physics of light is true, the light we see in the night sky has traveled billions of years to get to our eyes. How to reconcile old light with a young earth?

"It's really complicated," said Janette as we sat down at our desks, getting ready for Mr. Morgan's class. "I'm trying to simplify it a bit for my presenta- tion. But I watched a really interesting debate between two creationists— one of them believes the earth is billions of years old and the other one doesn't believe that." She thought she had reached a compromise in "gravi- tational time dilation theory" and she explained to me that using Einstein's theory of relativity, and because of where the earth is in the universe, cer- tain stars will be significantly older than the earth "so they're both right." At the end of her presentation—at which she claimed to find a compromise by saying that the Earth had not aged while the rest of the universe had because of gravitational time dilation—she told her fellow students that these discussions of space are important because they "show we have a de- fense, we have an answer to these questions that scientists say we don't have an answer for."

Whether or not Janette is right is actually less important than that she believes she can use something she identifies as science and that her practice of using it becomes habituated as a strategy she can use to solve problems she encounters in helping her world make sense. Science functions for her as a kind of authority that makes certain demands (con- sistency, plausibility) that coexist with other demands, namely the literal truth of her community's understanding of Genesis.

Janette might well have gained this interest in "the problem of distant starlight" from Mr. Morgan's Worldview class. "For people who are Biblical Christians and defend a literal reading of the Book of Genesis, for those who believe in a literal Biblical canon and that is their actual model for how old the Earth is, then the greatest challenge is starlight and time," Adam Morgan told his seniors. "What is the problem with starlight and time for Biblical Christians? If the earth is young, or as young as the Bible describes it, then how is it that we see light from cosmic bodies millions or even billions of years away? It appears to be a contradiction between science and the Bible."

Adam Morgan believed, like many Young Earth Creationists, that geology was not much of a challenge, primarily because of supposed errors in radiocarbon dating and the fact that the after-effects of the Mount St. Helens explosion could look as though they happened much earlier than they actually did, therefore proving that old-looking geological formations could happen much faster than expected. Biology was challenged primarily through intelligent design. In both cases, the strategy is much the same: peculiarities in a grand theory—whether the age of the Earth or evolution—are used as evidence that the entire theory is ineffective and must be replaced by the Christian worldview, or at least, by intelligent design.

Jason Lisle holds a PhD in astrophysics and has published peer-reviewed work in astronomy journals.[51] Like other creation scientists—and, for that matter, Richard Dawkins[52]—Lisle is an expert in a certain specialized area of science and then expands his focus to a broader philosophical and theoretical critique, without the empirical or theoretical acumen to make the larger claims. While his lectures are much more polished than Janette's, his logic is similarly circular and ad hoc, and one could read his efforts as nothing more than using bits of scientific fact to buttress a pre-existing commitment. That rhetorical cleverness is surely part of the story, but what is most interesting is the authority science claims both in Lisle's accounts and in the reception of Lisle's work at Good Tree and places like it. Science has an authority that must be respected; it makes demands that should be met. And the best way to answer that authority, to meet those demands, is with more science.

Mr. Morgan made sure his students knew the science, even if I'm not sure he represented it as such. They read Richard Dawkins as well as Stephen Jay Gould, and they applied them—especially Gould—in ways that the authors themselves might not recognize. For example, instead of emphasizing Gould's concept of non-overlapping magisteria (the insistence that religion and science are basically trying to get at different things), he instead focused on Gould's most important scientific contribution, the relatively heterodox evolutionary theory of punctuated equilibrium (or the idea that organisms could evolve suddenly rather than gradually).[53] Creationists cite this theory to explain how the fossil record could be used to support a Biblical account of creation.

When I talked to Mr. Morgan at the end of a class on Gould, he repeated that "the main things I want them to get out of Gould is the idea of punctuated equilibrium, which is a helpful idea to contrast with the gradual development you usually hear about it in evolution. And the other thing is how he talks about God as an idea that isn't necessarily a bad one but that doesn't belong in the classroom."

"So that would make you opposed to something like creation science, because it sets out to prove what it assumes?"

"Yeah," he said, somewhat hesitatingly. We were standing by his bookshelf because he was lending me a science fiction book. "That's why something like this"—he pointed to Meyer's *Signature in the Cell*,[54] another book that helped spearhead intelligent design—"is really effective, because he avoids that word completely, and instead he uses design." Note the use of the word *effective*: part of this really is a story about rhetorical strategy. But right after that, Mr. Morgan told me, "I really think that something that people are noticing is the importance of information. People are eventually going to think of it as something like energy or matter." He referenced here a growing theory among creationists that God's design will soon be recognizable as information (a theory paralleled in certain futurist circles), yet in so doing he also showed how the emphasis on science isn't just a debate tactic: it's a real commitment to an authority external to himself and his community.

CONCLUSION

In a khutbah (or sermon) at Friday prayer, Al Amal's first principal told students the story of the *mir'aj*, or the Prophet Muhammad's miraculous trip to Heaven from Jerusalem. "It happened," he said. "If you do not believe it happened, then you are calling the Qur'an a lie." For Principal Naguib, a key part of the tale is that when the Prophet came back, "his bed was still warm!" as he emphatically put it. "It was as though no time had passed at all! . . . So scientists and . . . scholars are trying to understand how the Prophet could have done this, perhaps it was a portal, like on the shows Stargate SG-1 or Battlestar Galactica. If you have seen those shows then you know what I am talking about . . . ." Secular science fiction, religion, and science all combine here, and what is most fascinating is not the principal's insistence that this is actually true but rather the assumption there is a scientific explanation for it that scientists could understand, and which science fiction authors might already have predicted. Science and religion will eventually work together. There's no real conflict, just a misunderstanding of the truth from certain secular scientists.

Because to say "science," ultimately, meant to say "truth." And the truth of science could never contradict scripture. In a freshman physical science class, a teacher at Good Tree who taught both scripture was telling his students about the scientific method and its faulty applications in the past. In a discussion of spontaneous generation, he asked students "why and how the Bible would support this idea."

"Man coming from dust," said a student.

"Good," said the teacher. "Adam came from dust, but they forgot that *God* made Adam, they forgot that God is all-powerful and all-knowing and people thought that spontaneous generation could just happen randomly . . . . At various times in history people thought what was said in the Bible proved something that wasn't true but we *know* that that's actually *not in the Bible*. And it could happen that we encounter something that's in the Bible that appears to contradict science, but then we just have to think critically about it, because we know that everything in the Bible is *true* . . . ."

Thinking critically here meant trying to find what you can in the science that you like in order to contradict the science you do not like. That might appear the very opposite of critical thinking and of science, or at least the scientific method. Yet what is striking in the fight between creationists and evolutionists is not their separation but how close they've actually become. Creationists have accepted overwhelmingly the rules of the game,[55] and the important half of the term "creation science" is not creation but *science*, showing the degree to which communities in opposition to mainstream commitments still feel a real need—not just rhetorical, but *moral*—to justify themselves as true by using the scientific language they have come to understand as best suited to the task. And indeed, the movement is not very far. As John Evans points out, most of the claims of modern science "do not contradict any religious claims."[56] Creationists don't mind meiosis. They don't deny momentum. They have no problem with molarity.

While some might want science to be an all-or-nothing deal, my work in these schools suggests that lay acceptance of scientific authority is much more pragmatic and situational.[57] Careful studies of survey research find similar results. Sociologist Micah Roos[58] has shown that creationists have *knowledge* of science; they just disagree with certain elements of it. Similarly, Cosima Rughiniş[59] has shown that agreement has less to do with scientific knowledge than whether certain concepts are "animated." Instead of thinking of creationism (or, by extension, the positing of a link between vaccinations and autism or the denial of global climate change) as a denial or ignorance of *all of science*, it might be more useful to think of it as a form of "motivated reasoning"[60] through which certain people act more and more creatively in a simultaneous effort to leverage and to pay fealty to the authority of science.

CHAPTER 8

ᴄᴠᴐ

It's Dangerous Out There

In almost all of the interviews I conducted at the four schools, I asked students and faculty something like, "Why do you think this school exists?" Sam was a senior at Al Haqq when we sat down for a taped interview. He had been at the school for six years, two years of junior high and four years of high school. His mom taught at the school, and while both of his parents are Arab, his father was born overseas while his mother was born in the United States. Like a lot of the students I talked to at the Muslim schools, he sometimes felt a tension between his parents' nationality and his own. For example, when he went to visit his parents' family, he was frustrated about how present he always had to be to everyone involved the entire time.

Sam told me he "loved" Al Haqq. "It doesn't have all the stuff that other schools have," he admitted, telling me about how he had to teach himself to draw and paint. He also acknowledged that some of his courses could have been better taught. But "the goals here are to not only to teach us education things," he said. "They want us to live in a Muslim environment, so we kinda grow up with our religion, so when we're older, we'll be able to spread our religion." He distinguished Al Haqq from a public school, where "you won't have a whole gathering of all your Muslims, and you pray together, and you will learn to honor Islamic studies."

This distinction from public schools was something I encountered often in my fieldwork, usually without me bringing it up (see Chapter 2). The Christian schools were similar: students and faculty alike told me the schools existed to provide students with a space that was distinct from public schools, often also repeating the word *environment*. In my taped

Agents of God. Jeffrey Guhin, Oxford University Press (2021). © Oxford University Press.
DOI: 10.1093/oso/9780190244743.001.0001

interview with Barbara, a senior girl I sat down with in my last semester at Good Tree, she told me she hadn't really thought about the purpose of her school, though she guessed "it's to provide an education for students but within a Christian environment—as opposed to public school." When I asked whether she noticed the school's distinctly Christian identity, she told me she did. "Teachers often will pray in class and . . . it's easy for them to take any kind of circumstance and turn it back into some kind of Christian Biblical kind of view or some kind of lesson."

Both Sam and Barbara highlight what I have been describing in this book. Both emphasize differences from the outside world, and they make clear how these differences reveal certain *essential* qualities that separate their communities from outsiders. Both also emphasize certain key authorities in their own lives. Both talked about prayer, and both talked about texts, even if, as was discussed in Chapter 6, the textual tradition is more complex in the Muslim schools I studied. It makes sense that the Muslim student talked about "Islamic studies" as a more diffuse textual category while the Evangelical student simply mentioned the Bible.

Perhaps most significantly, both Sam and Barbara emphasized the importance of a religious "environment" where young people can grow and develop as members of a particular community. These communities might be thought of as locations for what sociologist of religion Peter Berger has called "plausibility structures," that is, situations and social contexts that make certain beliefs seem plausible. If you're around enough smart and sensible people who do a certain thing, then it makes sense that not only would you do that thing, but that doing that thing would just make sense. These plausibility structures provided what Berger called a "sacred canopy," a way to protect religious believers from recognizing just how arbitrary their beliefs actually are. For Berger, the world can all too easily become a howling void, spreading meaninglessness and anomie unless communities insulate themselves from the chaos waiting outside.

Berger's argument has been much debated, not least by Berger himself.[1] In his study of Evangelicals' "distinction with engagement," sociologist Christian Smith argued that Evangelicals do not need everyone in society to agree with them in order to maintain their communities: they simply need environments in which most around them agree. They need "sacred umbrellas" rather than "sacred canopies."[2] Studies of religious communities since then have largely maintained this insistence that communities work together to make a religious world make sense. Whether it is studies of religious schools, neighborhoods, communities, or social groups, scholars have usually emphasized how meaning-making is collective, communal, and ongoing, and also that it does not require the total commitment of a society.

However, there are two important concepts sociologists have used to understand religious communities since Smith's work. The first is something that Smith's study already contains: boundaries. After all, Smith famously studied how Evangelicals "distinguish" themselves from others. In this book I have tried to build upon Smith's and others' insights into how boundaries work, and I have done so through emphasizing two developments. The first was a focus on boundaries' *practical* quality and the second, drawing from philosophy and recent developments in psychology, was a focus on how people distinguish between what is essential and what is accidental in community life.

Another important emphasis in the sociology of culture (though less so in the sociology of religion) has been a shift away from the study of beliefs and toward the study of practices. Within both Berger and Smith's work, the emphasis tends to be on people's ability to hold on to certain key beliefs, which makes sense given their empirical focus on Protestants, whose religious identity tends to be centered on belief statements. Yet, as Michael Strand and Omar Lizardo have argued, beliefs are themselves actions that people do in the world. Saying what you believe is an action; even thinking what you believe is a kind of action. Part of the problem, then, is a Protestant theological focus on the centrality of belief that has affected how sociologists study not only Protestants but all religious groups. An emphasis on beliefs in theology has led to an emphasis on beliefs in sociology.

In contrast, recent studies of religious communities—even Evangelical communities—have emphasized their practices. People's identities are formed not so much because of what they believe but because of what they do. Unlike beliefs, which can be thought of, again via Protestant theology, as rather dichotomous (one believes or one does not), practices can be all over the place. People might do a certain practice in certain situations but not others, and those practices might or might not have important implications for the identity of an individual and a community. Just as important, as I have shown here, beliefs are themselves acted out, practiced, and habituated.

In this book I have tried to show how practices matter in religion in three ways that are not so often discussed. The first point I have made about practices has been to push against an old tendency to describe Islam via a Protestant focus on orthodoxy (or right belief). Instead, I have tried to show how Evangelical Protestantism, despite its consistent suspicion of practices and ritual forms, is actually just as rooted in orthopraxy (or right action) as the religions from which it has historically distinguished itself. While this argument is somewhat new in the sociology of Evangelical Protestants, it is not at all new in the anthropology or history of Christianity, both of which have seen a flood of recent research on the practices of Protestantism. However, I hope that the *comparison* of two Muslim high schools and two Christian high schools has provided a productive study of how the practices of gender performance, scripture, prayer, and scientific knowledge are actually not altogether different in "orthodox" and "orthoprax" religions. This is obviously not to argue that there are no differences between the Muslim and the Evangelical schools I studied. Yet those differences are revealed less in whether it is practices or beliefs that matter, but rather how those practices and beliefs matter in different ways.

The second point I have made about practices emphasizes the way that boundaries are themselves practiced by individual and communities. By "practicing boundaries" I mean that people don't just take for granted their differences from others. Instead, these differences are repeatedly brought to the forefront of consciousness. People emphasize those differences they consider essential to their identity by talking about them more often, noticing them in others, and worrying about what losing those characteristics might entail. In contrast, there are other differences that some philosophers and psychologists might call "accidental." That doesn't mean those differences happened by accident bur rather that they are not necessary for identity in any meaningful sense. I developed these arguments in chapters on politics and public schools, gender, and sex and the Internet, using each to describe how boundaries help these communities to maintain a space for their identities.

Finally, the third point I have made about practices has been to emphasize their role in what I have been calling "external authorities," which is how I described prayer, scripture, and science. Drawing on the institutionalism of John Meyer and his coauthors, the "inhabited institutionalism" of Timothy Hallett, and recent writings on agency by Isaac Reed and Julia Adams, I described how prayer, scripture, and science were all felt to have a certain kind of agency and authority relatively autonomous from the people engaging them. As such, prayer and scripture function as "agents of God" in two senses. First, scripture and prayer are described as agentic; prayer, the Bible, and the Qu'ran were understood and felt as doing and commanding certain things in the world, relatively autonomous from the people who used them or even from the God who guided the scripture or received the prayer. Scripture and prayer are not simply tools, at least not in the sense of the easy use of tools that have no effect on the tool user. Instead, they are agents. Yet they are agents in a second sense as well, as when what Isaac Reed calls a "rector" sends someone as an *agent* to communicate something or accomplish a task. Whether or not scripture, prayer, or science are agents in the same way that humans are agents is a separate question for future sociological and philosophical work. What matters here is that scripture, prayer, and science were *experienced* as agents and that this experience and description had social effects.

One of these effects was that teachers and other adults were able to off-load any perception of force in the work of social reproduction any school community requires. To be in a school—especially a religious school—means to be in a place where adults expect young people to change in some way, and that change is almost always directed toward becoming more similar to the adults. Math teachers want students to know more math; English teachers want students to know more literature. Maybe those teachers also want students to love their subjects. Teachers at religious schools are no different. Indeed, the purpose of the school—as Sam and Barbara describe at the beginning of the chapter—is to provide an "environment" in which young people become religious adults.

There is, almost inevitably, some level of coercion in this process, something difficult for students to experience even in a religion like Catholicism that has historically had little problem with using force to impart belief. Yet this tension is even more marked in the four schools I studied, each of which emphasized the need for freedom in religious commitments. Whether or not Protestantism or Sunni Islam have always had such commitments to free expression of belief is not important for this argument, which is about four specific schools and how they consistently emphasized elements of their traditions that stress the importance of free, uncoerced commitment.

External authorities make this process a bit easier. Instead of a teacher commanding a student to do or believe a certain thing, the command comes instead from some other authority, one that is external to either the teacher or the student, or even the community itself. To say the Bible or prayer or science demand something is to externalize a demand, to make it possible to think of the teacher as just as beholden as the student to an authority more powerful than either of them.

To some degree, what I am describing here is simply the old sociological concept of an institution, something also important for Peter Berger's sociological theory of religion. Yet there are a few important differences from institutions here. The first, and perhaps most important, is the explicit agency and authority that these "external authorities" are experienced as having. Whether or not all institutions have such authority and agency is an interesting question others might explore in future work. For example, what does it mean when someone says that "I have to do this because we're family"? What does the institution of family demand there? Is it agentic in the way I have been describing scripture as agentic? I am not sure it is, mostly because I have data of people describing scripture (and prayer and science) doing things in the world that people might not say about family or other institutions, like masculinity or whiteness. But these are empirical and theoretical questions others might take on.

Another important difference between what I have been calling "external authorities" and what many sociologists have described as institutions is that my definition is much tighter. One of the problems with the word *institution* in the social sciences is that a lot of people aren't entirely sure what it means, or, more to the point, the definition is so expansive they are not sure what it might *not* mean. In contrast, I have tried to show that an external authority is a symbol, artifact, or concept within a community that is understood to have a performative capacity to make demands and claims about the world. In the communities I studied, "science" says and does things, as do "prayer," "the Bible," and "the Qur'an." Importantly, though I was able to study these external authorities partially through how people talked about them and what they said about their beliefs regarding them, these beliefs as such were only important as evidence of *practices*. It was practices that helped to maintain the authority and agency of external authorities, whether through engaging in scientific debate, praying the salah, or memorizing Bible quotes. In any case, repeated practices helped to habituate the authority and agency of these external authorities, maintaining both their plausibility and their felt agency and power.

These authorities were also *bounded*. In each chapter on external authorities, I describe how certain boundaries helped to create the space in which these authorities were understood to have their power. As I described in the chapter on scripture, only in certain Muslim communities do the Qur'an and hadith become *external authorities*. In other contexts, they are simply texts. Likewise, in certain contexts the psychiatrists' "bible," the Diagnostic and Statistical Manual of Mental Disorders is just a book, yet in other contexts it is the difference between insurance care and paying out of pocket, between being troubled and being legally insane. Boundaries make certain texts into texts with stakes. The same is true for any external authority: the repeated practice of boundary work both demarcates and helps to maintain their authority.

Habituated practices are another key part of this story: scripture and prayer maintain their authority because people habituate that authority through repeatedly engaging it. As I found in my work on science in creationist schools, it is only when science is *practiced* via an engaged effort to disprove evolution with science that science itself begins to function as an external authority in the way I described scripture and prayer. Otherwise, science's authority in the schools I studied is more diffuse, spread out upon a network through various nodes of tests, teachers, and textbooks.

In calling scripture, prayer, and science external authorities, I am obviously indebted to the sociologist Max Weber's own description of three forms of authority, as well as the huge literature on authority that has followed in the hundred years since. There is not sufficient space here to work out all the ways that my theory is different from Weber's, though future work might examine how the external authorities I describe here might work alongside and within Weber's forms of traditional, charismatic, and legal-rational authority. Following the work of John Meyer, in Chapter 1 I provide a brief analysis of how these "external authorities" depend upon a certain kind of routinized charisma. Yet there are still many questions to ask. How is the "law" itself a kind of external authority in the ways I have described, especially when the law can be consolidated into a semi-sacred text like the United States constitution? How does traditional authority help to maintain itself via the external authorities I have described? How might fights within traditions take advantage of the "external authority" of a scripture to leverage both conservative and progressive arguments? How might those who leverage charismatic authority situate their claims through the external authority of other entities, and how much might they insist their charisma is entirely their own?

WHAT COMES AFTER

Important as these theoretical considerations are, this book is as much a study of the schools themselves as it is an analysis of the theories I developed through studying them. As such, it might be helpful to end by returning to what Sam and Barbara were talking about at the beginning of this chapter: these schools exist to keep people religious. However, despite these goals, teachers and students at all four schools were realistic about what they could actually accomplish. Many of the Evangelical teachers told me, resignedly, that their students only had about 50 percent odds of staying Christian after they left the school—a concern not really shared by Muslim teachers, who might have been worried about students' practice of their faith but not really about them abandoning it (see Chapter 2). Nonetheless, as Brother Umar, the vice principal at Al Amal told me, "You can't change everything."

It is worth reflecting here on a skit I observed near the very beginning of my research at Apostles, one of the two Evangelical schools where I did fieldwork. Tomas Lopez, the junior and senior religion teacher, prepared the students to leave their overwhelmingly Christian environment by enacting what he called "scenarios" two or three times a week. He told me in a taped interview that his "goal is to basically get them to, in whatever situation, to be able to react the same way that Jesus would . . . . Because if you're able to practice it in your lifestyle, if you're able to practice when mom gets mad at you, if you're able to practice when your girlfriend gets mad at you, okay, it becomes part of your lifestyle. So now it is in your daily life."

Yet when I watched one of these scenarios, it was not altogether successful. In the junior class I observed in the high school's gym, Mr. Lopez had students stand on the stage and role-play an effort at evangelization. This was less a defensive effort at keeping your faith and more an explicit attempt to gain conversions, something that wasn't quite as common at the other three schools, all of whom seemed more concerned about just making sure their students kept the identities the schools had worked so hard to preserve.

"Get on stage," he told a group of students. "It's your time to shine." The group he was speaking to didn't look as though they were particularly focused on getting ready for the skit. It didn't appear, in their conversation, that there was really any preparation, and what emerged onstage was basically an improvisational comedy. There were five "unbelievers," two girls and three boys, all of them Black. The believers were one Asian American girl and four boys, two of them Latino and two of them Black. There was a nervous energy, and one of the believers joked, "We're all Black. We could be brothers and sisters." They were pretending to be at a picnic and the "believers" approached them, saying, "We're followers of Christ."

Janet, one of the Black believer girls, said, "I used to go to church when I was ten." She was wearing blue eyeliner that matched her outfit.

The whole time they were performing, Mr. Lopez was literally biting his hand. He finally interrupted them, almost shouting. "She just said I used to go to church when I was ten—that's your opening, this is your chance!"

One of the believers asked Janet about the church. She said, "It was all fake up in there." A series of jokes ensued, with the Christians trying to engage a little bit and the unbelievers just joking around. "What is God?" one of the boys kept asking, in a tone of mock seriousness. Janet shouted, "Jesus was from Africa! He wasn't white!" The rest of the class, which hadn't been paying much attention, was suddenly rapt. They laughed. One of the boy unbelievers, who was jumping up and down and practicing his basketball moves, said, "What's the point of God when you got basketball?" The other unbeliever girl, Shakira, said, "So God had sex with teenage girls, what kind of God is that?" Shakira was braiding another unbeliever's hair, a boy named William, who was sitting in the middle of the stage, not paying much attention to anything.

The teacher looked increasingly frustrated, hitting his first into his hand. Janet said, "He raped a teenage girl! I'm not feeling that." Students in the crowd laughed and said "Oooooh!"

"Okay, okay, let's stop here," said Mr. Lopez. "Those of us that believe in Jesus Christ, this is why it's important that we practice things like this. I'm not judging you based on this. I was itching to get in there to help you . . . you can't take it personally what people say to you. If I was going to take personal what people say to me, like when I'm on the train, when I'm witnessing, I would never do anything. I noticed some of you were taking it personal. Keep your eyes on the cross. Focus on Jesus Christ—this is so important."

Students asked Mr. Lopez if he would "show them how it's done." "You want to see me try it?" he asked. "Yeah," said some kids, though many weren't paying attention and were busy talking to each other. "Okay, okay," he responded, walking up on onto the stage. Mr. Lopez is a physically impressive guy, with the big body and confidence of a bouncer. He asked William about his life and William said, "I was raped by my father, my brother died . . . " The teacher said, "Okay, so you're in the closet." "No, I'm not gay!" responded William with vehemence. His audience laughed. "And my mother died too," said another of the unbeliever boys, Jacob. The teacher said, "Mother died, that's not something I can relate to. Why don't you pick something I can relate to . . . " "I'm a drug dealer, just trying to make some money. My girlfriend left me, and she's pregnant with twins," said Jacob. "Ooooh!" said a bunch of the students, though only about half were paying attention at this point.

When Mr. Lopez got onto the stage, his manner shifted dramatically. He became deferential, easily shifting into a language and bodily comportment he didn't use while teaching, saying things like "all right, all right," "no disrespect," and "I don't want no beef" when Janet was offended by random things he said, looking to get a laugh. He was mostly talking to William, however, whose hair was still being braided by Shakira. The "Christians" had all returned to their seats, and it was basically just William and Janet talking with Mr. Lopez. But then Shakira spoke up, still braiding William's hair. "What makes you different from Islam or Jehovah's Witnesses?"

Mr. Lopez, amidst interruptions, was telling his (real life) story of how he was a drug dealer. "I was out selling drugs—that cash comes fast, but with that cash comes consequences," he told them. He talked about how he eventually met someone that made him happy in a way that girls and selling drugs never could, asking "Don't you want to know the person that gave me happiness?"

The question was rebutted with more laugh lines, and eventually Mr. Lopez himself couldn't suppress giggles, calling the whole thing off. He told the students, "The nonbelievers, they allowed the enemy to put up this wall, they allowed the enemy to build that block between them and Jesus Christ."

For many students, participating in the scenario as Mr. Lopez intended was not nearly as important as getting a laugh, getting work done for another class, or just talking to a friend nearby. Mr. Lopez was frustrated because students did not take the role-play seriously, which, ironically, is precisely the reason he wanted the students to carry out the exercise. Yet all is not as it appears: many of the students who said offensive things as "nonbelievers" would later call themselves Christian in my interviews with them. They saw the role-play as a chance to let off some carnival-style energy. Studies of carnival—festivals in which, for a brief time, social norms are disregarded and the masses can freely mock their betters—have disagreed with each other about the politics of the process. Is carnival a radical challenging of social norms? Or is carnival a conservative maintenance of those norms through a few days of letting off steam?[3]

At least in the case of this role-play, the answer appears to be both, in that students were able to imagine themselves as not religious but were also held accountable by other students' gasps and shocked laughter and by the teacher's own corrections. This might well have been a glimmer of a radical critique of Christianity, but its placement within a religious class, supervised by a religious teacher and surrounded by religious students, meant it would never be much more than letting off steam, at least within the school. Yet, as with any carnival, there is a glimmer of another way of imagining the world, and that glimmer might well not disappear when the world goes back to normal.

Yet, the real concern for Mr. Lopez and others was not so much that people might reject Jesus with the ferocity of the played "unbelievers" but that they would behave as the audience did, that is, with relative inattention. For the purposes of this class's situatedness within an urban community, the most important reminder might be Mr. Lopez himself, in that he is able to exemplify a Christian narrative that goes all the way back to the Apostle Paul: he is the evangelist who was lost and then found, and he wants you to be found too. In other classes, Mr. Lopez and other faculty regularly discussed the possibility of "backsliding," of losing your Christian faith or of not taking it seriously in the first place.

As Mr. Lopez showed, it was personal charisma that did some of this work, and this was true for nearly all of the influential teachers I describe in this book. Yet each of these teachers depended on more than charisma for their authority. They all knew the chaos revealed in the skit I just described was not actually that far away. Their students were in danger, and they were in danger not only of sin but of the meaninglessness Peter Berger describes when he insists on the need for a sacred canopy.

Like Christian Smith, I suggest that Berger is not quite right that people need an entire canopy: a community-wide umbrella might well suffice. But that umbrella is maintained, I argue, less by beliefs in some abstract sense than by practices. It is true—indeed, it is sometimes even common—that those practices are themselves the speaking out and repetition, whether out loud on in the mind, of certain key beliefs. However, by emphasizing how beliefs are themselves *practiced,* I hope to show how even orthodoxy is itself a form of orthopraxy. The practices I have been describing in this book are first, and perhaps most importantly, the repeated and habituated en-actment of boundaries, especially in politics, gender, and sexuality. Those boundaries do their work through helping communities work out what is essential to their identity and what might well be accidental. Yet boundaries do some more work too: they combine with certain other practices to bring to life what I have been calling external authorities. And these external authorities—scripture, prayer, and science—do their work through acting and authorizing action in communities in a way that is relatively external from any one person. To the extent students' futures will not be the chaos played out in Mr. Lopez's skit, it will not be because of Mr. Lopez or any other teacher. It will be these external authorities, scripture and prayer es-pecially, guiding, instructing, acting out their mandates as agents of God.

Yet it would be too simple to end this study with a reference to God, essential as God was in these schools. In his study of public religion in the modern world, sociologist José Casanova has described contemporary re-ligious movements as "counterfactuals" to secular modernity, showing that these are ways to imagine a modern world that does not move to-ward the secular, godless endpoint many scholars already take for granted.[4] Relatedly, philosopher Charles Taylor has labeled as a "subtraction story" the assumption that if you subtract away all the religious beliefs and practices, then somehow you'll get to real social life.[5] As Casanova, Taylor, and many others argue, religion is actually not so special. All of us have cer-tain practices that help us to maintain our social world, driving our implicit beliefs and sensibilities. None of these practices are necessarily obvious in the way that gravity seems to be obvious. Democracy is as historically arbi-trary as fascism, and the felt reality of a religious service is as "natural" as the felt reality of an election night. Taylor calls these underlying sources of our constitutive practices "social imaginaries," and it is these imaginaries which form our ability to sense the difference between right and wrong, to feel when something does or doesn't seem important or injurious or insane. Essences and authorities are important in these religious sites, but neither the difference between essence and accident nor the concept of an external authority is uniquely religious. Instead, these are theoretical concepts that I hope can benefit broader conversations about culture and social life, in the old tradition of sociologists of religion using religious sites to answer cultural questions. Whether or not this book proves helpful in those questions is now outside of my authority.

Methodological Appendix

THE PLIGHT OF THE FIELDWORKER

One day near the end of my fieldwork, I was observing one of the boys' junior religion classes at one of the Muslim schools I studied, *Al Haqq*. It's a basement room, the chairs loosely arranged in a semi-circle, and the teacher, Brother Yaqub, was trying very hard to be patient as the boys joked and roughhoused. Brother Yaqub was a local sheikh who came in to teach just four Islamic Studies classes a week. He worked as a youth minister, and he was gifted with young people, though his theological and intellectual seriousness sometimes butted up against the boys' playfulness. He had just gotten the boys settled enough to begin class when two girls—I didn't know their ages, but they looked like junior high students or freshmen—came in to give a survey. The teacher looked annoyed at losing his class time, but the girls insisted it had to be that period, and he relented, sighing and saying to keep it quick. One of the girls read something that sounded like it was designed by an Institutional Review Board about benefits and risks and how the students didn't have to take the questionnaire. The boys continued joking and laughing, and the girl read the form in an increasingly annoyed tone.

As the girl was reading, the boys kept asking the teacher, "What are we doing?" making him more and more annoyed. When the girl finished reading her form, one of the boys asked the teacher, "What if we all just agree not to take it? What would you do then?" The girls looked at each other and the teacher, and weren't sure what to do. The teacher sighed and asked the students, "How many of you want to take the survey?" A few boys said they wanted to take it. Others laughed. Another boy asked, "Do we have to?" and then a few more nodded. The girls sensed they were losing the room and looked to the teacher for help. Brother Yaqub said, "You don't have to take it, but we have to get this started. We're just going to have to do this." The girl who had been reading immediately seized the opportunity: "We're just going to pass it out and you can do what you want." She gave it to the first five boys in the semi-circle of desks and then asked them to pass it around. They looked at the teacher, who repeated, "Pass it around" with urgency. The boys obeyed. Then they looked at the questions and joked among themselves, filling out the demographic information. Eventually, the girls asked the boys to do a memory test, reading a series of words, then asking them some questions, and then asking them to remember the original list. The boys laughed and joked throughout the process, with the girls and the teacher looking increasingly annoyed.

This group of students was always particularly difficult for all the teachers, and I do not mean this story to be an example of *Al Haqq*'s unruliness: I was often struck by how well students there paid attention and behaved in comparison to my experience at other schools. The moral of this story is instead that I kept thinking how easily an attempt to study a group could fall into utter chaos. Nobody has to let me study them, and even if someone does, nobody has to take that study seriously. I was constantly in fear of just this sort of chaos, and in hindsight, I'm quite grateful for how rarely I encountered it. Of course, even chaos is sociologically interesting, and, as thousands of ethnographic works have shown, chaos is never actually chaotic. In this scene, for example, there were certain boys dominating the opposition to the survey, and the opposition was interestingly proposed by a less popular boy. There were marked displays of power along lines of gender, age, and social position, and there was a use of humor to reinscribe social hierarchies (between male and female and older and younger students) and to challenge others (between teacher and students). There is obviously something to learn from chaos. Yet, when you have a specific questionnaire or set of interview questions, it is nice to have the opportunity to ask them and to have them taken seriously. I am extremely grateful that this seriousness was overwhelmingly the case.

WORK IN THE SCHOOLS

Over time, I became close with faculty members, students, and staff at each school, although in different ways. At Good Tree, it took me some time to develop a rapport with many of the faculty and even the principal, and I got the sense there was a widespread suspicion about my work. The fact that I am from a secular institution certainly made people feel uncomfortable, yet I think part of the problem was also simply my outsider status: this is a suburban school community in which many students, faculty, and staff had been involved for much of their lives. Parents regularly volunteered to serve as "lunch ladies," to do maintenance work on the school's large physical plant, and any of countless other tasks a K–12 school requires. People knew each other well, newcomers did not show up often, and I was a newcomer.

That doesn't mean I felt unwelcome. Evangelical Christians tend to take hospitality very seriously, and I always felt a kind reception. Yet, at least in the beginning, this welcome felt a little bit formal and, honestly, suspicious. Near the beginning of my work, I walked into the classroom of the Old Testament scripture teacher, Dr. Martin Hawthorne, to ask if I could observe his classes the next day. Dr. Hawthorne told me of course, but the teacher he was talking with, Tom Kiroff—whom I hadn't met yet—looked me up and down and said, "You're the guy from Yale who's snooping on us, huh?" I wasn't sure what to say, so I just smiled and paused, hoping he would say something else. He did: "You know, up in New Haven—I have a friend—she runs a bed and breakfast. She's an excellent woman, very godly. She keeps up on all the issues, she's very intelligent."

This was not an unusual response to me in any of my field sites, in two senses. The latter of these responses is to assume that "very intelligent" is a meaningful and important category for me, perhaps before all others. Observe the progression of adjectives describing this "excellent" woman: she, first, is godly, but then she is "very intelligent" because she keeps up on all the issues. This emphasis on piety as the forefront of virtue was repeated at all four schools. But I saw intelligence as the secondary virtue, generally, only in reference to me. It was often assumed that as a doctoral candidate at a place like Yale, I not only was intelligent but I cared about intelligence, often before everything else. A teacher at Al Amal asked me what I thought about opera, without really knowing me at all. When I responded that I prefer to go to movies rather than opera, he appeared relieved. "Yeah, I don't go to opera that often either," he said.

The other sense in which Tom Kiroff's concern was not unusual was that I was, in fact, "snooping." While I might use another word, I was watching what these communities did and writing it down. It was the writing that was nearly always noticed, and students, teachers, and staff would often come up to me and ask what I was writing. Every once in a while, students would ask if they could see my notes (I generally said no but would some-times turn to a page that I knew was particularly innocuous and flash it for a second). I often tried to explain to students (who were by far the most curious) that I was not writing about them per se but just about students in general, using their experience as data for larger arguments. They usually nodded, but I'm not sure how many of them ever stopped thinking of me as a journalist there to depict the scene.

Teachers would notice me writing, too, and they sometimes gently teased me about it. One day at Al Amal, there was a lot happening in the gym as the female students were taking down decorations from a play and setting up food for a party. I was trying to describe the scene as best I could in my notebook, and the biology teacher, Brother Ahmed, jokingly half-yelled, "Write, write Jeff, get all this down!" At a party at The Good Tree in my second year there, a few teachers introduced me to some new teachers, saying "This is Jeff, he's the guy who's sitting in the back row, writing down everything you say." Other teachers laughed and nodded and I realized what an impression I apparently made.

This constant observation obviously had an effect on people, particularly the teachers. On my first day at Al Amal, Brother Ahmed said the students were better behaved because I was there, but pretty soon they were acting as they always had. Yet, teachers remained somewhat more sensitive. Sheikh Khaled, the Islamic Studies teacher at Al Amal, once warned his students, "If you want to hang our dirty clothes for the visitor to see, go ahead." He would also compare the students' behavior "in front of our guest" to that of other students, telling a class that an earlier group had been well behaved while I was there, and he would see how they would do. All of which is to say that I may have affected the situation through my observing, but it was not necessarily to anyone's specific advantage or disadvantage. In one class at Al Amal, Shabir, a jolly student who was constantly in trouble, noticed me jotting down notes in an Islamic Studies class. He made eye contact with me and half-yelled, "Jeff, what are you writing?" He then looked at the teacher: "I insist that I not have to say anything until Jeff stops writing." "Okay," I said. "I can stop writing." I put down my pen for the rest of the class. After class, Shabir went to shake my hand as he was walking out of class—something many of the male students did. I held onto his hand and leaned forward so I could quietly ask, "Is it true you don't want me to observe you?" He smirked, as was his wont. "Nah," he said. "I was just saying that to get out of presenting." If students would sometimes try to take advantage of my presence, so too would teachers, principals, and staff members. I was often asked by adults at the schools what I thought about students or other adults, sometimes being invited into all sorts of politics—an invitation I always politely declined (even if I used the entrée to ask a few questions).

Generally, however, I became a fly-on-the-wall in the classroom, sitting in the back, writing down my observations, first on a notepad, then, in my last semester, on a laptop. There were a few teachers who wanted me to be more active, but that was fairly uncommon. I also participated in school events, and at these I was a bit more of a personality: telling jokes and talking about common life experiences, though usually just listening and paying attention. Mostly, I got to know people the same way anyone else does at schools: I chatted with students and teachers at lunch, between classes, and before and after school. As with any other settings, there were certain people I clicked with right away and others with whom I never seemed to get along. As my mother taught me, a self-deprecating joke tends to be a safe way to gain people's trust. In time, I was told by people at all four of the schools that I had come to fit in and be part of the family. The biology teacher at Good Tree, Ms. James, told me that my presence was awkward at first—something I definitely felt—but by the end of my work there, it felt weird to her when I was not there. This was my experience at all four of the schools: over time, I truly felt like I became a part of each community, and I was quite grateful for their hospitality, graciousness, and warmth. The experience, of course, varied. On a ride home from a school fair at Good Tree—where I had volunteered to have pies thrown at my face—the psychology and sophomore Doctrine teacher, Mr. Smith, told me, "You're loved! You're an outsider who might have been met with suspicion but has been universally welcomed." It was a kind thing for him to say, and he was already one of my best friends at the school; he invited me to his house, and we had long, wide-ranging conversations. Yet earlier, at the fair, one of the senior girls who was running my "station" asked an elementary school girl, "Do you want to hit Mr. G in the face with a pie?" (Mr. G is what I was called when I taught high school, and the principal at Good Tree didn't want me going my first name). The little girl looked at me and said, "I don't know who you are," turned her nose, and walked away. We all laughed.

THE ETHNOGRAPHER AS CAUSE OF DISCOMFORT

Besides just not knowing this strange man, there was sometimes a discomfort with me being in the schools. This discomfort was sensible enough, and it moved in two directions. The first was a simple question, said most simply in the words of a spritely sophomore boy at Al Amal who noticed me writing alone in a room after everyone else had left: "You gonna make us look bad?" "I'll be honest," I said in response. The boy, Seyyed, nodded, and perhaps felt uncomfortable because he thought I might be writing about how he and his classmates were making his teacher's life difficult (I was).

Before asking me any more about what I wrote, he said, "Well, we match the classroom." "What do you mean?" I asked. "You gonna have a classroom like this, you're gonna have students like this." He pointed around the room: "Look at this, the chair's broken, the desk is broken, the walls need paint." Seyyed was right about the room. The walls sorely needed paint and there were mismatched white patches from where holes were filled but hadn't been repainted. The front desk had broken drawers, the floor had papers all over it, and there were black kick stains at the bottom of the front wall. There was a broken broom in the front of the class.

There was, to be fair, a pretty amazing redecoration over the summer and the place looked a lot better in the fall. Nonetheless, the fact that I am writing this description now proves there was some merit to this concern, but I hope that this project shows I am much more interested in making an argument and telling a story than I am in digging up any dirt (or dirtiness). I was often asked, "What are you going to say about us?" in some form or another, and I usually shrugged and said I wasn't sure yet, which was true. At one of the Christian schools, I sat in the back of a religion class while the students had to do an in-class assignment that involved quiet readings. Two girls, Laura and Carolyn, were complaining that they were unable to be quiet long enough to do the assignment. As Carolyn said, "Turn a few pages so it looks like we read." I wrote that down and another girl said, "Did you see that? He wrote it down! He wrote it down! He's observing us." "I'm writing about Christians schools," I said, shrugging. "I'm not representing Christianity well!" said Laura, laughing. Other students laughed too.

Besides worrying that they were not living up to certain standards, there was the other fear that I would misrepresent what I observed or simply be too intrusive. One teacher at Al Haqq told me, "As a Muslim, I'm always under scrutiny, I'm not saying anything about you, you never know what will happen in the future, if you turn on us or—I'm not saying that's going to happen." She trailed off then, "but if it does . . . " Sometimes this concern expressed itself through not speaking: of the five principals I worked with, nearly all of them were quite talkative with me, yet after I found out from a certain teacher his side of a somewhat scandalous dispute with one of these principals, that principal and I had a relatively difficult and awkward five minutes together waiting for someone else. I could sense that this principal wanted to ask me about what the teacher and I had talked about, and yet also wanted to respect my privacy. I could not blame this person for wanting to know what I had heard, for wanting to control the narrative, for hoping I would not release the details to the world (I have not: they're just not relevant for my argument). I realized at that point the sort of power I have, and the trust I have been given. I hope to have used it wisely.

There were occasional scandals at the schools, and while I could have written a more salacious book, it would not have been as good of an argument. I was not afraid to make the schools look bad if it was necessary for what I wanted to say, but I did not want to weaken the book or harm the trust I had been given just to put in something juicy. I'm not interested in making the schools look bad (or good): I'm interested in making an argument. There were various embarrassing moments that happened for these schools and the individuals within them that I did not put into my field notes, or, even if I put them into my field notes I did not report here.

The other direction the communities' concerns about me could take was not what I would say afterward but what I might do while still in the school. As with most elements of my ethnography, the rules here were fairly unclear and not immediately obvious unless I broke them. My presence alone, for example, made certain teachers or students uncomfortable, and they asked me not to observe their classes. One female teacher at Al Haqq was always quite shy and aloof with me, something that I attributed to her personality until I saw her joking and laughing with other teachers and with both male and female students. I realized it was me and, I assumed, my maleness that made her so reticent. Another teacher at Al Haqq told me, "The students yesterday, in . . . . class, some of them were like why is he in the room, they feel like they're being scrutinized—so I said, I'll talk to him and tell him not to come [to that particular class] anymore, Islamic Studies [which she also teaches] is fine." I asked about why the students were uncomfortable and she said, "I remember you observed one time in a lab. The kids are obviously casual with each other in a lab, and I don't know, they were talking about sports or something, and one of them came up to me, and he said this guys' writing down every single thing we said . . . . It's something unknown to them. They don't know how a thesis works. I think that might be the reason why." I said, "I'm sorry I made them uncomfortable," and she laughed. "It's okay. It's kind of a joke I have. One of them walked into class and saw you and he said, *Man hatha* [who is this], and I said you know he speaks Arabic, and now they're always walking around when they see you and they say *man hatha.*"

I noticed this discomfort with my observing was even more pronounced when I used my laptop to write observations. On balance, the laptop was excellent for allowing me to get down virtually every word spoken to me, yet it was also much more obvious that I was writing. The handy thing about the laptop, though, was that I could maintain eye contact, even if my respondents sometimes found it unsettling to make eye contact with me while I was typing.

Perhaps most dramatically, I was asked to leave my work at Al Amal early by the board of trustees. I have written about this experience elsewhere, but suffice it to say here that I was asked to leave shortly after the beginning of my second semester at the school, and, when I met with the board of trustees, they said it was because they were concerned I was spending too much time with female students. I made a deliberate effort to spend more time with the male students, but I also recognize the school prized gender separation, and any time I spent with female students might be viewed with suspicion. Upon reflection, I think the main reasons I was asked to leave were a nervous and hyper-vigilant board of trustees as well as a new principal worried about an ethnographer the previous principal had allowed into the school. Yet, it is also the case that I was naïve about how my maleness would be read at the school. In some ways I forgot I was a male body and instead thought of myself simply as an ethnographer gathering data. That obliviousness to how I am read is an example of a certain kind of male privilege but also, as is often the case, a helpful opportunity to learn through messing up, a common theme in ethnographic research. As I write about elsewhere, I certainly did learn from the experience, and I was much more prepared to be a male researcher at a Muslim school at Al Haqq.

An awareness of how I might affect life at the schools forced me to change how I acted in each of the schools in sometimes subtle and sometimes more intense ways. At each of the schools, I worked on cursing a bit less, a sin not so severely punished at Yale and actually somewhat prized in my version of Jesuit-educated Catholicism. I was aware of other distinctions, too. I was mindful about how I ate in Muslim schools, trying to avoid eating with my left hand even though I'm left-handed. I dressed like the average male teacher, never wearing a tie at Apostles and always wearing one at Al Amal. The issue of dress is something other school ethnographers[1] worried about in terms of dressing like teachers or students and the relative access they would have accordingly. I never thought dressing like a teacher would prevent access to students, perhaps because, as a former high school teacher, I knew how much my students had shared with me once we had established trust.

At the Christian schools I was very careful about how I talked about evolution. In the SAT class I taught at Good Tree, we were going over an example test that happened to have a section on evolutionary biology. I asked the students to skip it, and a boy taking AP Biology at the time joked, "It'd be funny if we were just like oh my gosh and threw the test up." The other students laughed as he gestured what this would look like. "Yeah," said another boy. What if we just were like, forget this!" Later on, we ran into a section on evolutionary psychology that they asked me to explain, and

I didn't feel like I could do an adequate job without running into the same problems. I realized then how often evolution shows up and how difficult it is to escape.

This care in discussion—a tension between an ethical concern about being respectful to the local community, a sincere commitment to my own intellectual and spiritual integrity, and a pragmatic preoccupation about staying in the schools—was probably most pronounced in matters of religion. Various teachers and students at all four schools talked to me about my religious faith, though most did so simply as a matter of getting to know me rather than trying to convert me. The people who seemed most interested in converting me—perhaps because I knew them the longest—were a few teachers and students at Al Amal and Good Tree.

A group of junior boys I came to know from teaching them SAT prep at Al Amal were chatting with me during a free period. One of them, a student leader named Ra'ed, asked me why I didn't convert, and I told him that was a fair question, but I had to be honest that it was hard for me to talk about why I was not Muslim without saying what my criticisms of Islam are. They told me I could say what I want, and Ra'ed looked around saying, "Guys, keep this quiet, okay? This has to stay in this room." The conversation did remain private, yet I didn't actually share any criticisms. I told them instead that I was born into my religion and it made sense to me in a way that's hard to explain and impossible to prove. Being born Catholic, I said, is like being born into a certain language. Whether or not it's the most true didn't really matter to me. I don't even see how the question makes sense; it's like asking if Spanish is more true than French. Catholicism is simply how I understand the world, but perhaps because of that, it's hard for me to imagine another way of understanding the world. The boys nodded and said my argument made sense, even if Ra'ed still seemed convinced I would eventually see the errors of my ways.

FIELD NOTES, QUOTES, CONFIDENTIALITY, AND INDEX

At first I took field notes writing down everything on a legal pad. I switched to a laptop in my time at Al Haqq and Apostles. Unless I describe a quote as coming from a taped interview (all of which were transcribed), all quotes in this text are from my field notes. Readers should therefore be aware that these are most likely not *exact* quotes. In keeping with certain ethnographic conventions, I did put quotes around these words, but they are not necessarily word-for-word quotations in the sense that a transcribed interview would provide. I toyed with other ways to indicate quotes from field notes, but quotation marks make for less confusing text than dashes at the front (but not at the end) of quotes, which is the other common way to indicate quotations.

I did always get down as much as I could and then, when I knew it was a quote I wanted to keep, I wrote nearly all of it in the moment while it was still in my memory (sometimes excusing myself to go to another room to get everything down). I would then add it to field notes.

I changed everyone's name and the names of the schools as well. I sometimes changed some small descriptions of locations to keep the schools a bit more anonymous. For times when I was concerned that a teacher or student was saying something controversial and would be recognized by community members, I usually just said something like "a teacher," and I sometimes changed unimportant descriptive qualities (hair color, height) to protect students' anonymity.

It's also worth noting here that my spelling of Arabic terms is fairly idiosyncratic even if, *inshallah*, consistent. I started with the IJMES transliterations, but the formal structures felt too distinct from how my English-speaking respondents themselves spelled and used these words, so I attempted some middle way for each of the different terms. *Astaghfirullah*.

I am the primary author of this book's index. Amber Herrle was a great help in both organizing and referencing, though any errors are obviously my own. I have tried to be theologically and politically fair in how I organize the various topics, though some might take issue with what I place with what, and where. I have listed in the index those students and teachers who appear often in the book, organizing them by the name they regularly used in the schools. As such, the students are listed by their first names, the Muslim teachers are also listed by their first names, and the Christian teachers are listed by their last names.

INTERVIEWS AND SURVEY

In addition to my ethnographic observations, I also gave out a questionnaire at Good Tree and conducted tape-recorded interviews at all four schools.

I had intended to use the questionnaire at each of the schools but ended up only using it at Good Tree. I gave it to all students at the high school except one whose parents opted out, and two more who were absent the week it was given. The questionnaire was given over a week in December of 2011. I administered the exam to each class where it was given and gave each of them the same instructions. There was no need for a questionnaire for faculty, administration, staff, and parents because I interviewed as many of the relevant staff and faculty as I could. To protect their confidentiality, students were given the option of not signing the permission form on the first page. If they did sign the page, they indicated that they were willing to be interviewed about what they had written on the questionnaire.

The process through which I determined how to do the interviews was much more ornate. Through a dialectical process, I was able to develop interview questions after I had spent time in the schools, first testing the interviews with select students and staff.[2] The fact that I was doing a simultaneous, multi-site ethnography meant that I could figure out questions that applied to all schools, and other questions I would only ask at specific schools. At Good Tree, the one school where I was able to conduct a questionnaire with virtually all of the students, I asked students if they would be willing to be interviewed about their responses. Of the approximately half who said yes, I selected ten students at random from each grade and sent permission forms to their parents. While not all of these students agreed to be interviewed, I eventually found ten from each grade. At the other two schools where I conducted extensive student interviews (Apostles and Al Haqq), I consulted with teachers to identify a representative sample of students. I was given more freedom to engage students myself at Apostles; at Al Haqq, the teachers distributed parent permission forms, though some students approached me themselves and, with permission, I interviewed them as well.

The interviews included questions on relationship to the school (e.g., how long the person has been there, why s/he chose to be part of the school) as well as reflections on prayer, scripture, the Internet, and science. Interviews were generally tape recorded, although a few teachers (and no students) expressed discomfort with being recorded and I simply typed notes as they spoke. Nearly all interviews took place in the schools themselves, with a few taking place in a neutral location chosen with the interviewee. All interviews required the signature of the interviewee on a consent form created in consultation with the Yale Institutional Review Board. Interviews with minors required signed consent from a parent, also on a form written with the Yale IRB. Besides many informal interviews, I conducted formal, tape-recorded interviews with four students at Al Amal, 51 students at Good Tree (40 from the survey; 11 because they were student leaders or were selected for relevance to research themes), 27 students at Al Haqq, and 26 students at Apostles. I conducted 14 formal (tape recorded) interviews with Good Tree adults: ten faculty, three administrators, and one parent. I conducted three formal interviews with Al Amal teachers and seven with Al Haqq teachers. I conducted 11 interviews with adults at Apostles: three with administrators and eight with faculty.

POSITIONALITY

I have no way of knowing exactly how much my being a white, male, straight Christian at an Ivy League school helped me to gain access to these schools and to facilitate my research within them. Given what sociologists know about privilege and structural prejudice, it seems safe to claim my identities provided me with a great deal of privilege, even if sometimes they also created obstacles to connection. In a choice that some might consider politically problematic and some might consider politically necessary, I have decided not to make myself or my privilege a key part of this text, except inasmuch as my specific interactions had something to do with the argument at hand. However, simply because I am not explicit about my power and privilege throughout the work does not mean the issue is unimportant to me or my argument. For example, in my study of gender at these schools, I was aware that my maleness made me more interesting to some of the girls at the Muslim school precisely because of the gender separations there. I was similarly aware that my heterosexual maleness gave me a kind of authority at the Evangelical schools that I would have had to work harder for (or simply not have been given) as a female or queer ethnographer.

There is a politics to this inequality of privilege and access, a politics I believe I am morally bound to engage. However—rightly or wrongly—I do not believe this book is the avenue for that engagement, at least not explicitly. In the chapter on gender, I hope to have shown how my identities have affected my interactions and my interpretations of those interactions. But to delve deeper into these questions would make this a book about me, or at least a book about me in these communities, and that is not the book I want to write or which I feel would best honor the communities who invited me to share their stories. Of course, I am aware that this book is implicitly entirely a book about me, inasmuch as I am the one writing it about my experiences. But to acknowledge that we are the source of our ethnographies in all their insights, errors, obtuseness, and originality is still a world away from making the ethnography the story of me.

I was honored to be invited to share the stories of the communities described here. To do so was a privilege, one supported by other privileges. I have reached out to members of each of these communities for feedback on this text, and I have made some changes based on their comments. This book is a work of sociology very much written for a guild, and it is also a book about real people quite different from me, whom I hope will find the book meaningful, fair, and interesting. It was important to me from the beginning that my respondents understood my project's many purposes. I believe they did, and many were actually quite excited about helping me to get the communities right and to work out my arguments based on those communities. It was also quite important to me that nobody felt I was taking advantage of my invitation, a hope that was not always realized[3] but which I did my best to achieve. It is my wish that both my respondents and others with identities they share—American Muslims, American Evangelicals, and those involved in religious schools—will find something helpful in the observations this outsider was able to bring.

NOTES

CHAPTER 1

1. All names of individuals and organizations have been changed. To reflect how names worked at the schools, I usually identify teachers at the Christian schools by their title and then their last name, and I identify teachers at the Muslim schools by Brother or Sister (and sometimes Sheikh) and then their last name. I identify students by their first names. I include students' last names and teachers' first names when I first introduce them in the text, but only if they appear often in the book. I have also indexed those individuals who appear often, with parentheses after each name in the index that indicate the person's role in the school.
2. Genesis is the first book of both the Christian and Hebrew Bible. I will describe Young Earth creationism more extensively in Chapter 7.
3. Of course, the United States is actually far from equal, and outright coercion happens all the time, often along lines of racial and sexual difference. Yet there is nonetheless an ongoing thread in American life—even preceding De Tocqueville—that understands equality as perhaps the central social good (Kloppenberg 2016).
4. Guhin 2014.
5. The old sociological model of socialization tended to draw from the mid-century sociologist Talcott Parsons (1937, 1959, 1964, 1970, Parsons and Platt 1970), whose work emphasizes a process of internalization through which people's values and orienting commitments tend to resemble those around them, with these values themselves then driving further action. Among other important critiques, Wrong's classic 1961 study of the "oversocialized conception of man in modern sociology" led to a gradual movement away from this focus on internalization toward a more careful analysis of power, agency, and heterogeneity. A few decades later, DiMaggio's (1997) and Swidler's (1986, 2001) work helped to show that action is much less driven by internalized teleologies than some might claim. However, there is a middle ground here, as articulated by Vaisey 2009, Lizardo 2017, and Luft 2015, showing how people's cultural expressions and experiences are actually multifaceted, with some more embodied and baked in, and others more declarative and contingently held. Using work from Chapter 6, my coauthor Daniel Winchester and I (2019) show how a Deweyan (2002) understanding of practices can help us to understand and explain how socialization works via pragmatic habituation. This is just as true for religious socialization: a "tradition" is never blindly passed down from one generation to another. Even the most conservative form of "traditionalism" necessarily makes adaptations to the environment at hand (Gorski 2017, Roy 2004, 2005). In this way, my study of habituation

via engagement has much in common with Asad's (1993, 2003, 2009) fusion of Foucault and MacIntyre, though more via Bourdieu and other sociologists in the practice tradition. I am also grateful for, though less able to engage, recent leaders in the sociology of religion who have centered the importance of practice, especially Nancy Ammerman 2020 and Roberth Wuthnow 2000.

6. The study of peer and neighborhood effects as opposed to family and school effects is a long-standing and particularly challenging problem for scholars of youth and education. Van Ham, Mankley, Bailey, Simpson, and Maclennan (2012) have an excellent edited volume disentangling neighborhood effects from other causes (though see also Sampson, Morenoff, and Gannon-Rowley 2002). The study of peer cultures and children's own capacity for agency (Corsaro 2017, Calarco 2018, Pugh 2014) is especially important in showing how socialization, as described above, is always an agentic and mediated process.

7. The classic study of schools as organizations remains Bidwell's 2001 programmatic statement. The organizational study of schools has been important for both education and organization scholars (Corwin 1975, Hallett 2010, Meyer and Rowan 1977, Meyer, Heinz-Dieter, and Rowan 2006, Sergiovanni 1994, Weick 1976).

8. Durkheim 1961 and Durkheim 1995, Meyer and Rowan 1977, Meyer 1977.

9. The study of boundaries in the sociology of science (Gieryn 1983, 1999, Star and Griesemer 1989), the sociology of culture (Lamont and Molnár 2002), the sociology of ethnicity (Barth 1998, Wimmer 2013), and the sociology of religion (Lichterman 2005, Tavory 2010, 2016, Yukich 2010) have all been extremely helpful in developing this book. Following Lamont and Molnár, my use of boundaries is more along the lines of their distinction of "symbolic boundaries" (as opposed to "social boundaries"), but I will describe how that does not exactly fit in Chapter 2.

10. This paragraph is taken from Guhin 2016: 154. See Schatzki 1996, Turner 1994, and MacIntyre 1984 for other definitions of practice and especially Camic (1986) for the overlap with the study of habit.

11. Weber's (1978: 215) study of authority and legitimacy remains classic, even if somewhat vague (Cohen, Hazelrigg, Pope 1975, Matheson 1987).

12. Weber 1978: 244.

13. Meyer 2009.

14. Meyer 1977: 75–76.

15. Meyer and Rowan 1977.

16. Hallett and Ventresca 2006: 214; Hallett 2010. While Hallett and his coauthors' study of "inhabited institutions" gets quite close to what I'm describing in terms of how various institutions are habituated and practiced in day-to-day interactions, they do not focus, as I do here, on how these institutions become understood as autonomous "external authorities" with agency to make demands and declarations.

17. Meyer and Jepperson 2000 describe how power in the world has shifted from religious and natural sources into individuals themselves. Intriguingly, the argument does not describe how such agency is felt to inhere within institutions like, for example, science, even though the argument appears implicit in some of Meyer et al.'s earlier work. This is perhaps best analyzed in their book, *Science in the Modern World Polity* (2002). See Chapter 7, note 4.

18. For more on the Constitution and DSM as, respectively, powerful semi-autonomous entities, see Fallon 2004 and Fried 2005 alongside Strand 2011, as

well as a "formal theory of scripture" I outline as one example of religion "as a site" (Guhin 2014).

19. Meyer and Jepperson 2000.

20. See especially Taylor's *Sources of the Self* (1989) and *A Secular Age* (2007), though also note Seigel 2005, Siedentop 2014, and Trilling 2009.

21. For a historical view on how American Evangelicals go much further than Luther might have intended, see Hatch 1989 and Noll 2002. For a contemporary view on how many modern Americans, including and especially Evangelicals, tend to center the individual experience as the ultimate barometer of God's presence, see, among many others, Bellah et al. 2007, Ammerman 1997, 2013, and McGuire 2008.

22. Khaled Abou El Fadl emphasizes an "Islamic ethic of noncoercion and the principle of nonaggression" rooted in, among other Quranic citations, al-Baqara 256 (2014: 399–405). Crone 2016 and 1977 argues such readings of the line can be anachronistic; see also Schirrmacher 2016.

23. See especially Grewal 2013, Mahmood 2011, and Zaman 2010 and 2012. Jonathan Brown 2015 argues that the Salafi insistence on the democratic access to the meanings of texts is a rhetorical tactic against mainstream Sunnis rather than a general practice.

24. Reed 2017 and Meyer and Jepperson 2000 make similar though distinct arguments about the role of agents.

25. There are interesting philosophical questions about whether such external authorities are then really real, that is, whether we can talk about an ontological emergence to social forces as Margaret Archer (2000, 2003) and critical realists describe, or in an opposite though interestingly parallel approach, whether non-humans and non-individuals can be understood as actors (and actants) via the "flat ontology" of Bruno Latour (2005) and other proponents of actor-network-theory. For the purposes of this book, I mostly bracket these questions, though obviously my approach gives external authorities an emergent quality that has more in common with Meyer's institutionalism than Latour's theory.

26. For a similar social paradox on the role of authority in schools, see Swidler 1979.

27. Reed's recent work (2013, 2017, 2019) shows how power takes on a necessarily relational quality, drawing especially from Adams 1996 and 2011. In different ways, both Foucault (1990, 1994, 1995) and Berger and Luckmann (1967) describe institutions in this semi-autonomous quality, even if Berger and Luckmann are clearer about them. It seems nonetheless to be the case that semi-autonomous institutions exist for Foucault between the level of the individual and the level of society itself: power-knowledge might well be exerting a kind of autonomy, but so are things like "the prison" or "the clinic." My project here uses the term *external authority* to emphasize the reified, agentic quality of these authorities in the communities I studied.

28. Whether the power of external authorities proves they are "real in their effects" or whether the only real reality is individual actors making individual decisions, I leave to the philosophers (at least for now). While I will mostly be leaning on Dewey as the pragmatist underpinning of this book's argument, James's model of empiricism (1975: 31–32) is helpful here: the important point is that a kind of extra-personal agency has "cash value" in these communities and might well not elsewhere. My hunch, of course, is that my description holds in other contexts, and what I am describing here is a much more broadly generalizable argument, something I will describe more in the book's conclusion.

29. Though to be fair to Parsons, his work can often be quite caricatured and presented as a straw man. For example, in *The Social System* (1964), Parsons is quite insistent that all socialization is relational and necessarily interactive, even if he does not pay much attention to practices.

30. Dewey 1925, 1935, 1997, and 2002.

31. I am indebted to a variety of writings on emotions for this project, especially Katz 2001, Nussbaum 2003, Sharp 2010, Stets and Turner 2014, and Turner and Stets 2005. I have also benefited from Hitlin and Piliavin's 2004 study of values, particularly the distinctions between values, traits, and emotions. The emphasis on "feeling" is especially indebted to Damasio 1999. I agree with Stets (2010: 265) that work remains to be done "beyond the general idea that culture sets up expectations regarding what feelings should be experienced and expressed in situations."

32. Asad 2009.

33. Lichterman 2005, Tavory 2010 and 2016, Lamont 1992 and 2009, Gieryn 1983 and 1999.

34. The classic work on distinction is, of course, Bourdieu's (1984), but Lamont (1992, 2009) provides an excellent example of showing how boundary-making as a practice of distinction need not be considered a zero-sum game of field competition.

35. C. Smith 1998.

36. Much of the work on American Islam written in the past 40 years—even before September 11, 2001—described prejudice experienced by Muslims, albeit different kinds of prejudice experienced by immigrant Muslims and Black Muslims. See especially Braunstein 2017, GhaneaBassiri 2010, Grewal 2013, Khabeer 2016, and Rouse 2004. See also Norris and Inglehart 2012. For more on Christian nationalism and Trump's "unexpected orothodoxy", see Whitehead and Perry 2020 and Martí 2019.

37. Aristotle 1963 and 1994. See also Gill 1991. Alexander's 2006 study of how the civil sphere changes its requirements for membership over time does not engage Aristotle's metaphysics directly, but its argument is more or less about how something once considered essential (race, gender, religion) can come to be accidental. While Brubaker's "Ethnicity without groups" (2004) also does not directly engage Aristotlian essentialism, his concept of "common sense groupism" as a folk category captures much of what I am intending here, though I am more interested in how community-level processes drive distinctions about what is necessary for a group's identity versus what is optional. Like Brubaker and his coauthors, I am interested in how, as a sociological question, such group definitions are shifted via both cognitive and broader social processes (see also Luft 2020).

38. See Mahalingam's work (especially 2007) for how actors "essentialize" social categories. The study of social essentialism is a growing research site within psychology and anthropology (Gil-White 2001), though not really in sociology. However, much of the work in psychology tends to emphasize ethnicity or gender as the category of essentialization. My work here is obviously more expansive.

39. Different psychologists who study essentialism are more or less explicitly indebted to Aristotle's essence/accident distinction, but some of the most cited works make the influence quite clear: see Gelman 2004 and Medin and Ortony 1989.

40. This book pulls from growing literature in both the study of American Evangelicalism and American Islam, the vast majority of which will be cited in later endnotes. However, most influential have been Ali 2018, Bielo 2009b, Bilici 2012, Elisha 2011, Grewal 2013, Howe 2018, and Worthen 2013. Also, it

is important to acknowledge that many sociologists of religion would call the Christians with whom I worked "conservative Protestants" (Woodberry and Smith 1998) rather than Evangelicals. I continue with the word *Evangelical* because many in the schools called themselves Evangelicals. The more common terms respondents used to describe themselves were actually Christian or Bible-Believing Christian (Smith with Denton 2009), but this causes some conceptual confusion because I often distinguish these Evangelicals from other Christians. I also call both schools Evangelical because they fit the broad understanding of the term in both theological and sociological literatures: these were conservative Protestants committed to the literal truth of the Bible and eager to be a part of broader American culture, even as they also sought to differentiate themselves from it. I refer to the Muslim (rather than, for example, Sunni) schools as Muslim because that is how they referred to themselves. Also, as Muslims are such a pronounced minority in this country, there is considerably less conceptual confusion in referring to the people with whom I worked as Muslims.

41. See especially Bartkowksi and Read 2003 and Ali et al.'s 2008 comparison of Muslim and Evangelical women. While not in sociology, there is a very old tradition of theological comparison of Christianity and Islam.

42. See note 62, this chapter.

43. The most immediate objection to this comparison might be a lack of symmetry: Evangelicals are commonly understood to be a subcategory of Protestants, themselves a subcategory of Christians, while Sunnis are the largest 'denomination' within Islam. However, the Protestant–Catholic division does not map at all neatly onto the Sunni–Shia divide (let alone the various other groups in both Christianity and Islam, such as the Orthodox and Sufi respectively), and Sunni Muslims, unlike, for example, Catholic Christians, rarely refer to themselves as Sunnis except when explicitly contrasting their ideas to those of other Muslim groups. When I talked to Sunnis at the schools I studied about the difference between them and Shia Muslims, the majority insisted they were all simply Muslims. And, again, the point is not a global comparison of Sunnis and Evangelicals but a comparison of Muslim Americans and Evangelical Americans, who are broadly comparable as religious subcultures in the United States.

44. Pew Research Center, https://www.pewforum.org/2017/07/26/political-and-social-views/. Accessed October 31, 2019. For both Evangelicals and Muslims, however, these attitudes have become much more open in the past 10 years.

45. Pew, https://www.pewforum.org/2015/11/03/chapter-4-social-and-political-attitudes/. Accessed October 31, 2019.

46. Ali 2018, Howe 2018.

47. Guhin and Wyrzten 2013.

48. This is not a new argument in the anthropology of Christianity. See especially Coleman 1996, Maffly-Kipp, Schmidt, and Valeri 2006, and Bielo 2009a and 2009b. For more on the difficulty of these terms, especially considering Asad's 2009 study of Muslim "orthodoxy," see Wilson 2009. For the closest thing to a parallel argument in sociology (one to which I am indebted), see Brophy's 2016 study of how certain conservative Protestants turn orthodoxy into a "project."

49. Asad 2009: 21–22, italics his.

50. Wilson 2009: 179–185; quote from page 185. While Asad might reject the comparison (2003: 2–5), I understand his use of orthodoxy as similar to Taylor's conception of social imaginaries or Bourdieu's concept of a field, albeit more centrally

built upon the role of key texts than the other authors' understanding, and much more sensitive to power than Taylor is generally understood to be.

51. Strand and Lizardo 2015, Calder 2001: 67.

52. Allen 2013, Adams 1996 and 2011, Bourdieu 1990 and 1991, Butler 1997, Foucault 1995, Lukes 2004.

53. The phrase is Riceour's (1970, 1981). Jeffrey Alexander's discussion of *The Civil Sphere* is a powerful rejoinder to what he calls "the tradition of Thrasymachus" (2006: 39) a similar rejection of a study of culture that boils all meaning down to powers and interests. Whether or not such critiques are universally true of Foucault, Bourdieu, and others inspired by Nietzsche's genealogical method and "hermeneutics of suspicion" is material for another book, though, to put my cards on the table, I think that reading of Foucault is too reductive and that reading of Bourdieu is not entirely fair, though it does have merit (Alexander, 1995, Guhin and Klett 2019). And of course, the necessary role of power in instituting a sense of what is true goes all the way back through Rousseau to Augustine and Plato, though these earlier authors (and even, to some degree, Nietzsche) often understand such power as guiding toward the Truth rather than toward an arbitrary configuration of power.

54. Mahmood's (2005) *Politics of Piety* draws especially from Asad's work (1993, 2003), particularly Asad's synthesis of Foucault's study of power and MacIntyre's concept of tradition (1984, 1988, 1999).

55. See note 2, this chapter.

56. The new sociology of morality can be seen most clearly in Hitlin and Vaisey's 2010 and 2013 work, though see also Abend 2014, Bargheer 2018, Brophy 2014 and 2016, Luft 2015 and 2020, and Tavory 2011, among many others. While this point is already acknowledged at various points in Hitlin and Vaisey's edited collection, it is worth repeating that Weber, Durkheim 1995, 1961, and Du Bois 2007 were all deeply concerned about the sociology of morality, as were many important mid-century thinkers, among others Parsons, Berger, and Luckmann; Goffman 1959, Bellah 1991, and, including anthropologists who read and were read by sociologists, Douglas 2003 and Geertz 1973. Studies of religion—especially qualitative work—were almost always about moral life, most famously seen in Bellah and Berger but in many others as well.

57. Abend 2014 is influenced by Taylor (see 2007, though much else) in his description of the moral background. My understanding of morality is neo-Aristotelean as articulated by Taylor 1989 and MacIntyre 1984 and 1988, both influenced by Anscombe 1958. This is also a very Deweyan book, which I do not see as a contradiction. I am not the first to argue that Dewey can be understood as a kind of virtue ethicist (Carden 2006, Teehan 1995).

58. There is a massive literature on the role of emotions in moral philosophy. For a good review, see Bagnoli's 2011 edited volume.

59. Durkheim 1961.

60. Lukes 2010: 549–560; see Strawson 1962 for citation. See also Tavory 2011 for how any sociology of morality must be sensitive to emotions.

61. See especially Collins 2014, Summers-Effler 2010, Xu 2017.

62. While religious schools are significantly understudied in the sociology of education, there have been more important works in religious studies and the anthropology of religion. For Muslim schools, see Khan and Siddiqui 2017, Hefner and Zaman 2007, and Zine 2008. For Evangelical schools, see Rose 2017, Wagner 1990, and Peshkin 1988. For a more general study that includes studies of Evangelical and Muslim schools, see Hunter and Olson 2018.

63. See especially Brint 2013, Guhin and Klett 2018, Mehta and Davies 2018, and Stevens 2008.

64. Two of the classic articles on schools as loosely coupled are Weick 1976 (though see also Orton and Weick 1990) and Meyer and Rowan 1977. For more on Du Bois on citizenship, see Westbrook's 2013 edited collection. In forthcoming work (Guhin 2021), I explore the counterfactual of a sociology of education more rooted in questions of culture, politics, and moral life, drawing from the educational writings of Durkheim, Dewey, and Du Bois.

65. The study of gender and sexuality as they intersect with religion forms many broad and important conversations, certainly in religious studies and the anthropology of religion, but increasingly in the sociology of religion as well. While I will cite more work in Chapters 3 and 4, key influences for this book are Ahmed 1992, Avishai 2008, Burke 2016, Gallagher 2003, 2004a, and 2004b, Griffth 1997 and 2017, Irby 2014a and 2014b, Mahmood 2011, and Perry 2019. It is worth pointing out here that words like gender, sex, and sexuality are complicated and much debated within sociology, in other academic disciplines, and in the world at large. Throughout this book, I use the word gender rather than sex, especially in reference to the Muslim schools' focus on gender separation, for two reasons. First, this is the word the schools themselves used. Second, as I understand the terms, neither sex nor gender are inherent or biological, but gender is generally the more obviously interpretable self-presentation, and it was the means by which community members sorted each other. Within these communities (and society at large), gender is largely binary (man/woman, boy/girl). I heard no reference to transgender and genderqueer identities at these schools, but clearly that does not mean nobody at the schools had such identities. I use the language of gender without intending to erase people who do not identify with either gender, or with the gender to which their community assigned them. I am especially grateful to Kelsy Burke for help in making and articulating these choices, and even the wording of this very footnote!

66. Scripture and prayer are generally understudied in the sociology of religion. However, there is significantly more work in the anthropology of religion and religious studies, as will be described in Chapters 4 through 7. This book is especially influenced by Bielo 2009a and 2009b, Luhrmann 2012, Smith 1993, and Sharp 2010, 2012a, 2012b, 2013a, and 2013b.

67. See especially Ecklund 2010, Evans 2011, 2013, and 2016, Hameed 2015, Harrison 2015, Guhin 2016, Numbers 2006, and Roos 2014.

68. For more on science as a social category relatively autonomous from scientists themselves (even if they have a role in it), see Epstein 1996, Jasanoff 2012, Moore 1996, and Shapin 1994 and 2008, among others. See especially Drori et al. 2003.

69. https://nces.ed.gov/programs/digest/d16/tables/dt16_208.20.asp?current=yes. Accessed January 15, 2019.

70. https://nces.ed.gov/surveys/pss/tables/table_2011_02.asp. Accessed January 15, 2019.

71. See Pew's (2015) "America's Changing Religious Landscape."

72. See Keyworth 2009 and Khan and Siddiqui 2017. See also Pew's ongoing work on Muslims Americans, especially the contemporaneous http://www.people-press.org/2011/08/30/muslim-americans-no-signs-of-growth-in-alienation-or-support-for-extremism/ (accessed January 2019) and Pew 2015.

73. Nordin and Turker 1980, Carper 1983, Laats 2010.

74. For more on color-blind ideology (Bonilla-Silva 2017) in white Evangelicalism, see Emerson and Smith 2000.

75. Rashid and Mohammad 1992.
76. Bilici 2012. See also Hammer and Safi 2013 and Marzouki 2017.
77. Ahmad and Szpara 2003, El-Haj 2015.
78. See my working paper, "On Being Kicked Out of a Fieldsite" http://jeffguhin.com/wp-content/uploads/2019/08/On-Being-Kicked-Out-of-a-Fieldsite.pdf.

CHAPTER 2

1. There is a growing literature on the Islamophobia that colors media descriptions of Islam. See, among many others, Bail 2014, Beydoun 2018, Braunstein 2017, Cainkar 2009, and Marzouki 2017. For initial references to the massive literature on American Evangelicals and politics, see Schwadel 2017, FitzGerald 2017, and Gorski 2019.
2. For example, in Peshkin's 1988 classic study of the "total world of a fundamentalist Christian school," politics and right-wing mobilization is just about everywhere. In contrast, while the Christians with whom I worked were largely politically conservative (Brint and Abrutyn 2010, Steensland and Wright 2014), they often distinguished themselves from those who aggressively politicized their religion (Hunter 1983).
3. Chowdhury 2014.
4. The term *politics* usually refers in some sense to the State (this is true for Aristotle as well), though often (as also for Aristotle) with a broader sense of how people relate to each other and organize their common lives. Many political theorists share this more expansive sense: see, among countless others, W. Brown 2015 and Wolin 2016.
5. See Aristotle's *Politics* (2013) and Plato's *Republic* (2016). See also Dewey's *Democracy and Education* (1997) and an excellent collection of DuBois's educational writings edited by Randall Westbrook (2013).
6. Lamont and Molnár 2002: 168. The literature on boundaries is far too large to engage here. See especially Barth 1998, Tilly 2004, Gieryn 1999, and Wimmer 2013, and Wang, Piazza, and Soule 2018.
7. Avishai 2008, Burke 2012, and Rinaldo 2013 have all done impressive work to show how complicated gender boundaries are in conservative religion. See also Kate Manne's work on patriarchy, discussed more extensively in chapter 3, footnote 12.
8. Bourdieu's study of symbolic power is an important theme throughout his work; see especially *Language and Symbolic Power* (1991).
9. Luker 1985 describes a similar tension.
10. These debates are controversial in philosophy, and, again, for my purposes whether or not essences are really real is actually not important. For a grounding in the philosophical work, see Cohen 1978 and Nussbaum 1992.
11. There is a massive literature on the critique of religion as a category. See especially J.Z. Smith 1998, Guhin 2014, and Masuzawa 2005.
12. Durkheim 1961.
13. The question of "what is a nation" is an ongoing and still difficult-to-answer question in political science and sociology, though see Hobsbawn 2012, Gellner 1983.
14. Love 2017.
15. Roy 2014: 23–56.
16. See especially Bilici 2012, Grewal 2013, Marzouki 2017, Ahmed 2010.
17. Mamdani 2005.
18. Cainkar 2009, Maghbouleh 2017, Selod 2013, 2015.

19. Byng 2010, Furseth 2011, Williams 2007
20. It's important to recognize that although Jews and ethnic Catholics (e.g., the Italians, Irish, and Polish) were often severely mistreated in their nineteenth-century and early twentieth century immigration to the United States, they were almost always granted the privilege of being categorized as white, often explicitly and nearly always implicitly. As such, whiteness was a "teleology" (Seamster and Ray 2018) available for them that was never available for Black Americans (Goldstein 2006, Jacobson 1999). For a discussion of racial categories within American Islam, see Guhin 2018, Jackson 2005, Khabeer 2016, Maghbouleh 2017.
21. A not uncommon problem within immigrant Islam: see Jackson 2005 and 2009, Husain 2017, and Guhin 2018; See also Kashani 2014 and Khabeer 2016.
22. For an overview of the color-blind ideology, see Manning, Hartmann, and Gerteis 2016 and Bonilla-Silva 2017.
23. Jackson 2005, Hussain 2017.
24. See Seamster and Ray's 2018 critique of "teleology in the study of race."
25. This is not dissimilar from Alexander's account of the social performance of marginalized groups in *The Civil Sphere* (2006), which shows how Black people, women, and Jews can be included in the American self-conception. See also Hooker's 2016 critique of Allen 2004 for how such "democratic sacrifice" makes unjust demands on marginalized communities.
26. Of course, American politics were not the only things that mattered at the Muslim schools. The Arab Spring occurred while I was at Al Amal, and the students lifted teachers into the air when Mubarak was deposed. There were many Egyptian-American students and faculty at Al Amal, and while the students occasionally talked about Egypt (quite a few asked me what I thought about Mubarak in our conversations), it was a topic of nonstop conversation in the faculty lounge, with the computers often logged onto Arabic-language television stations covering Egyptian politics. Quite a few students at Al Amal left school early to go to protests in support of the Arab Spring. Palestine came up often in *khutbahs* [the Friday sermons during required Friday afternoon prayer] and was occasionally a topic of conversation, especially for the Palestinian-American children at both schools.
27. Bilici 2012: 104.
28. Martin and Desmond 2010.
29. Ahmed 2007: 157.
30. Cobb, Perry, and Dougherty 2015.
31. For more on the power of rumors and concerns about the Illuminati and other grand conspiracies within Pentecostal Evangelicalism, see Thompson 2005.
32. Brophy 2016. There is an entire sociological literature on how people think about their futures. See Mische 2014, Tavory and Eliasoph 2013, Frye 2012, and Simko 2018.
33. Thuesen 2009.
34. Zakaria 2015.

CHAPTER 3

1. Abu-Lughod 2013, Irby 2014b, Lester 2005, Ong 1990, Rinaldo 2013. As described in chapter one (see note 65), I tend to emphasize the word "gender" rather than "sex" in this book, especially in reference to the separation of students. I do so both because that was the word community members themselves tended to use

and also because gender was the more immediately intellible means by which community members sorted each other (Risman and Davis 2013). In emphasizing gender over sex, I do not intend to imply that either gender or sex are in fact biologically given or immutable, and neither do I intend to erase community members or readers who identity with neither gender or with a gender different from the one to which their community has assigned them.

2. Bartkowski 2001, Lee-Barnewall 2016.

3. See Gallagher and Smith 1999 and Gallagher 2003. See Irby 2014a for changes in later generations.

4. Gallagher 2004a, 2004b, Rinaldo 2013.

5. The obvious reference here is to Austin's "performative" theory of speech (1975), which has been broadly influential in philosophy and social scientific theory, paralleling similar insights via Nietzsche in phenomenology and "poststructuralist" accounts of gender, sex, and sexuality (see especially Butler 1997, 2011). For a sociological account of how beliefs are enacted, see Strand and Lizardo 2015.

6. Keane 2002, Winchester and Guhin 2019.

7. Read and Bartkowski 2000.

8. Ammerman 1997, Verba, Schlozman, and Brady 1995.

9. Griffiths 2017; for data on conservative Protestant and divorce, see Glass and Levchak 2014. For data on conservative Protestants and first sex, see Uecker 2008 and Landor and Simons 2014.

10. Cadge and Ecklund 2007, Voas and Fleischmann 2012, Yang and Ebaugh 2001.

11. Byng 2010, Furseth 2011, Williams and Vashi 2007.

12. Whether or not the hijab is in fact patriarchal is a subject of massive debate. As revealed in this chapter, many Muslims—male and female—believe it is not (I did not interview any Muslims who identified themselves to me as non-binary). There is evidence for a majority *global* support for patriarchy among Muslims (Alexander and Welzel 2011), but again, how such patriarchy is understood is often complex and contested (see especially Abu-Lughod 2013 and Hammer 2012). In her important book on the "logic of misogyny," Kate Manne describes how misogyny is fundamentally a social and political problem, as it is "metaphysically dependent on there being norms and expectations of a patriarchal nature" (2017: 67). Manne's work has been quite helpful for me, especially her deeply sociological insight into the way patriarchy at once rewards good women and girls while policing and punishing those who fall out of line. However, for the purpose of this study, I bracket my own judgements or deductions on whether or not these communities are misogynistic or patriarchal, though I recognize the importance of these judgements for other scholars and for community members themselves. I also recognize how it might be hard for some to see how what I describe here is *not* patriarchal. However, I am, at least for the purpose of this project, a sociological ethnographer rather than a moral philosopher, and it is important for me to present my respondents' opposition to descriptions of their communities as misogynistic or patriarchal, even if some of their practices might meet with Manne's criteria. In addition to depicting the power of these communities' authorities, it is also important for me to show how the "norms" Manne describes in her work are contested and given opposing meanings, sometimes even within the same social location. As such, I present my data with my own interpretations through which others, and community members themselves, can reach their own conclusions.

13. one of the great Muslim scholars, especially well known for his hadith collection.

14. There is a substantial scholarly literature on why "boys generally underperform relative to girls in schools throughout the industrialized world" (Legewie and DiPrete 2012: 463; see also Meece, Glienke, and Burg 2006).

15. Feminism is obviously diverse and multi-faceted, though it was interesting how monolithic the concept seemed to be in these schools. Few if any were aware of the various "waves" for example.

16. Griffith 1997. See also Manne's (2017) discussion of how patriarchy rewards certain women for exactly this kind of speech.

17. Ammerman 1987, Balswick and Balswick 2006.

18. See Gallagher 2004a for negative views of feminism. For educational attainment, see Darnell and Sherkat 1997, Sherkat and Darnell 1999, and Sherkat 2000; for life outcomes, see Gallagher and Smith 1999 and Gallagher 2003; for marital decision making, see Denton 2004. For more on marriage age and gaps in education, see Fitzgerald and Glass 2008.

19. Gonsoulin 2010: 239.

20. Payne 2015, Kwilecki 1987.

21. For a classic though still quite helpful overview of Islam, sex, and gender, including rules about clothing and gender separation, see Ahmed 1992.

22. Karim 2008, Mishra and Shirazi 2010, Williams and Vashi 2007.

23. Avishai 2008, Irby 2014b, Mahmood 2005, Rinaldo 2013.

24. Fernando 2010, Mahmood 2005, Rinaldo 2013, van Doorn-Harder 2006.

25. See Tavory 2010 and 2016 for a similar study of the power of the yarmulke to "summon" particular kinds of interactions, and Jerolmack and Tavory 2014 for a study of interaction with non-humans.

26. Ortner 1996.

27. Ajrouch 2004, Mir 2014.

28. O'Brien 2017: 7.

29. These tensions reflect the complicated identity work Muslim immigrants must do as they resolve their ethnicity, race, adopted nation, and religion (Fine and Sirin 2008, Naber 2005, Sirin et al. 2008). While broader studies of Muslim immigration find an eventual accommodation with the host countries (Leonard 2003, van Doorn-Harder 2006, Voas and Fleischmann 2012), this is often done on Muslims' own terms (Ali 2018, Bilici 2012, GhaneaBassiri 1997).

30. One of the schools of Sunni jurisprudence.

31. Naber 2006.

32. To be clear, despite Islamophobic rhetoric to the contrary, there is nothing uniquely Muslim about a desire to control young women's sexuality, and a fear that the "outside world" is too sexually permissive and might ruin young women's virtue is a fairly consistent concern in much of the world, whether secular or religious (Ortner 1978, 1997), including American culture (Luker 2006) and American Evangelicals more specifically (DeRogatis 2014, Moslener 2015). See also L'Espiritu 2001 for a parallel study of Filipina Americans. For more on how gender and religion intersect with immigration, see Cadge and Ecklund (2007).

33. Many Muslims believe that gender separation is draconian. The Qur'an passage is "Tell the believing men to lower their eyes and guard their private parts. That is purer for them. Surely God is Aware of whatsoever they do. And tell the believing women to lower their eyes and to guard their private parts, and to not display their adornment except that which is visible thereof. And let them draw their kerchiefs over their breasts, and not display their adornment except to their husbands, or their fathers, or their husbands' fathers, or their sons, or their husbands' sons, or

their brothers, or their brothers' sons, or their sisters' sons, or their women, or those whom their right hands possess, or male attendants free of desire, or children who are innocent of the private areas of women. Nor let them stamp their feet such that the ornaments they conceal become known. And repent unto God all together, O believers, that haply you may prosper" (24:30–31, *The Study Quran*, edited by Seyyed Hossein Nasr).

34. My account of being asked to leave Al Amal is available at my website, www.jeffguhin.com, and more precisely at http://jeffguhin.com/wp-content/uploads/2019/08/On-Being-Kicked-Out-of-a-Fieldsite.pdf.
35. For a critical review of single-sex education, see Williams 2016.
36. Abdelhadi 2017.
37. Abdelhadi 2019.
38. Abu-Lughod 2013, Rinaldo 2013.

CHAPTER 4

1. Evangelical sexuality, especially as it intersects with the Internet, has been increasingly studied lately: see especially Perry 2019 and Burke 2016.
2. See Carpenter 2005 for a broader cultural study of virginity and Reid, Elliott, and Webber 2011 for a study of how the "double standard" is changing, even as "gendered sexual scripts" that emphasize female chastity remain. Also, as I describe in the chapter, I encountered almost no references to LGBTQ Muslims in the school I studied, yet obviously that does not mean nobody in the schools was LGBTQ. For more on queer Muslims, see El-Tayed 2012, Abraham 2009, Rahman 2010, Shah 2017.
3. See Bersamin, Fisher, Walker, Hill, and Grube 2007 for the complicated nature of these definitions. See Brückner and Bearman 2005 for how virginity pledges can lead to other kinds of sexual behavior.
4. Bean and Martinez 2014. See Moon, Tobin, and Sumerau 2019 and Coley 2018 for how some conservative Christians are adapting how they think about sexuality specifically in reference to LBGTQ identities and practices.
5. Jakobsen and Pellegrini 2004, Vines 2014; see also Thumma 1991, Fuist 2018, and Moon, Tobin, and Sumerau 2019.
6. Whether or not sexual attraction is genetic remains a complicated question (O'Riordan 2012, Whisman 2012), and there are much thornier questions about the politics and "performativity" of sex and gender (see especially Butler 1997, 2011).
7. Perry and Hayward 2017: 1775–1776; the authors also find that the negative relationships between pornography viewing and religious service attendance are "statistically strong but modest in size," though the effects are strongest for those aged 13–17 (1774–1775). It is difficult to determine exactly how many adolescents are using pornography (Peter and Valkenburg 2016), though it seems clear that even conservative religious young people both have access to and often consume pornography (Perry 2019).
8. This is not a DSM-classified disorder, but as Perry 2019 describes, it is a common description of pornography usage, especially among conservative Christians, and, as my data shows, certain conservative Muslims.
9. See Wimmer 2013: 31 and Riesch 2010: 460.
10. Grubbs, Kraus, and Perry 2019 show that the language of addiction to pornography tends to correlate with religiosity and a sense of moral incongruence.

11. Perry 2019: 55 interprets this greater focus on pornography over masturbation as the result of what he calls "the interpretive prisms of biblicism and pietistic idealism," which fits well with my argument here.

12. Of course, it is not only religious schools with concerns about their students' online behavior.

CHAPTER 5

1. My conception of reification is especially influenced by Berger and Luckman 1967, though see also Honneth 2008.

2. This focus on how local practices and the broader social world in which they exist co-constitute each other is a key element of sociological theory, seen all the way back in Weber and Durkheim and through Parsons, Giddens (1979), Bourdieu, Archer, Sewell (1992), Swidler, and many other theorists.

3. Hoenes del Pinal 2009, Smith 1993. "Interpretive community" is a term from Fish 1980.

4. Asad 1993, Bielo 2009a, 2009b, Engelke 2007, Rutherford 2000, Smith 1993.

5. See Scott 2014 for an overview of sociological definitions of institutions.

6. Bourdieu 1998.

7. Kutchins and Kirk 2003, Strand 2011.

8. Fish 1980. For an earlier articulation of this argument, see Guhin 2014 on religion as a "site."

9. Austin 1975.

10. This understanding of agency is connected to the theories (Adams 1996 and 2011, Reed 2017, and Reed and Weinman 2019) that I described in the introduction, though I recognize they might not agree that something like scripture could actually be an agent.

11. MacCulloch 2005, Ryrie 2017.

12. Shantz 2013, Stoeffler 1965.

13. Brenneman 2013, Kintz 1997.

14. Smith 1959, 1993, Renard 2011.

15. Smith 1993. Yet, these are still Christian categories. That's forgivable enough as a source for analogies to explain the Qur'an to an audience more familiar with Christianity, yet it runs into the same problems Said 1979 describes. Categories don't just help us understand; they also form our understanding. In this chapter, I try to show how scripture functioned as an external authority in the schools less through either religion's theological categories and more through the sociological conception of *external authority* I am developing here. This, of course, runs another risk of turning people's *religious* experiences into *sociological* stories, but, as I describe in the methodological appendix, I hope that this book's treatment of religion in a sociological way is fair and interesting to religious readers, rather than a form of imposition and erasure.

16. Bartkowski 1996, Longfield 1993, Marsden 2006, Noll 2002.

17. Crone and Cook 1977, Sadeghi and Goudarzi 2012.

18. Duderija 2016, 2017, Safi 2013. See also Kurzman 1998.

19. Ohlander 2009, Ahmed 2013, Moosa 2005.

20. Mattson 2013.

21. Bielo 2009a: 1. For more on how Bible translations reveal politics and subcultural identity, especially within Evangelicalism, see Perry and Grubbs 2020.

22. Though the status of hadith as scripture is itself subject to debate. See especially Musa 2008, and for a good overview of hadith and their controversies, see Brown 2017.

23. Hallaq 2009, El Shamsy 2013, Zaman 2010, 2012.

24. This group—loosely called "Salafi" in its insistence on returning to the Muslim first generations (or *salaf*), is quite diverse (Brown 2015, Salomon 2016, Knysh 2007, Duderija 2010). Some want simply to demote the importance of, rather than ignore, previous generations of scholarship, and others acknowledge that any reading of a text is an interpretive paradigm, thus creating a certain "Salafi" tradition as potentially problematic as those it critiqued.

25. Grewal 2013.

26. Malley 2004. Some Pentecostals do have a more reverent relationship with the physical Bible, which they sometimes use for healing. Certain Pentecostals use passages of the Bible to enact miracles in a manner similar to what I describe Muslims doing in this chapter. However, in the schools I studied, I only encountered this use of scripture in Muslims and not in Christians.

27. See Ham and Beemer 2009 for an example of a panicked genre telling parents "why your kids will quit church."

CHAPTER 6

1. I'm methodologically atheist (Berger 1969) as to whether prayer actually "works" in the sense that there is, in fact, an omnipotent God or any other kind of supernatural entity(ies) who answers people's prayers and acts in the world. Note that methodological atheism does not mean personal atheism as my actual religious beliefs are both more complicated and less interesting. Neither does it mean the prayers of my respondents were unimportant or unworthy of respect, as I hope this chapter demonstrates.

2. Prayer is increasingly a field of study within the social sciences, and generally following these two senses. First, social scientists have examined prayer's ability to "do something" in the world (Bender 2008, Cerulo 2011, Cerulo and Barra 2008, Wuthnow 2008a, 2008b). Second, another group of studies has examined prayer's relationship to social structures and projects of self-cultivation (Baker 2008, Bowen 1989, Winchester 2008, Luhrmann and Morgain 2012, Mahmood 2005, Sharp 2010, Winchester and Guhin 2019). Sharp (2010, 2012a, 2012b, 2013a, 2013b) is one of the few sociologists who provides more general studies of prayer.

3. Foucault's concept of the technology of the self (1988) has been applied to prayer in various anthropological studies, including Mahmood's (2005). See Mellor and Shilling's 2010 review.

4. Luhrmann 2012.

5. The English word *prayer* is imperfect in the Muslim context, both because it is loaded with Christian baggage and because there simply is no one word that matches it within Islam. Other scholars have studied Muslim prayer and make different categorizations (Padwick 1996, Katz 2013).

6. There is no God but God; Glory to be to God; and Praise be to God.

7. See my 2019 article in the *Journal of Education in Muslim Societies* on *du'a*.

8. To follow the pattern of many of the American Muslims with whom I worked, I use English plurals here for the Arabic words throughout. The Arabic plural of *rakat* is *raka'at* and the Arabic plural of *du'a* is *ad'iyah*.

9. The word *sunna*—or *sunnah*—is a broader term denoting the corpus of the Prophet Muhammad's behaviors, sayings, and example. The word can also refer to those actions and sayings of the Prophet's companions. It is a sunna practice to say additional prayers before and/or after the *fard*, or required, ritual prayers. Muslims often refer to these additional prayers as sunna prayers.

10. Katz 2013: 28–29.

11. See especially Hammer 2012, Katz 2013: 177–214, Wadud 2007: 158–186.

12. See especially Coleman's influential 1996 study of "words as things" in Evangelical Protestant worship.

13. Within the Sufi tradition of Islam, there can be an ambivalence about form that can even lead to a sense in which practitioners have superseded form completely (Katz 2013: 168–169). However, I did not run into these sorts of commitments at the schools I studied.

14. Winchester and Guhin 2019.

15. Coleman 1996. Unfortunately, both historians of Islam and historians of Christianity generally pay much less attention to changing forms of prayer than they do to changing forms of theology and church leadership. These lacunae have as much to do with historians' general interest in politics, economics, and intellectual life as with Western scholars' own insistence that their beliefs matter more than their deeds. Yet see the influential 2006 edited volume, *Practicing Protestants*, edited by Laurie F. Maffly-Kipp, Leigh Schmidt, and Mark Valeri.

16. Synan 1997: 84–106; Luhrmann 2012: 15.

17. Miller 1997: 1.

18. Shantz 2013.

19. Hatch 1989.

20. De Tocqueville 2000.

21. Brenneman 2013.

22. Prothero 2003: 53.

23. To be clear, prayer at the Muslim schools I studied was in many ways just as democratic: nobody needed a "priest" for them to connect to God. Yet if the access was spontaneous, the form itself was not. Of course, as I have described elsewhere (Winchester and Guhin 2019), Evangelical prayer was not actually as democratic and spontaneous as it was believed to be.

24. Jami` at-Tirmidhi, Book of Salat, Hadith 413, https://muflihun.com/tirmidhi/2/413. Accessed July 22, 2019.

25. Best translated as "the catastrophe," *al-nakba* refers to the day after the declaration of the independence of Israel and the beginning of the Palestinian diaspora.

26. Bilici 2012: 103.

27. For example, see Hunter's tragic sensibility (2010) in contrast to Good Tree's senior textbook, *How Now Shall We Live?* (2004), with its more optimistic, culture-war sensibility.

28. http://syatp.com. Accessed August 25, 2017.

29. Of course, it's an empirical question to what degree the United States actually has a Christian heritage, and secular scholars of American history generally describe a much less Christian past than the one on display in history books for religious markets. However inaccurate, this idea that America is abandoning its Christian heritage is incredibly common at both Evangelical schools and in the Evangelical world more broadly. For a sensible acknowledgment that religion has had a role in

American government but never really the way conservative Protestants describe it, see Gorski 2017.

30. See Nussbaum 2003 for a similar study of emotions' intelligence, or see the large literature on "affective expectations" (Lisle, Kraft, and Wetzel 1989). See also Winchester and Guhin 2019 on the "normative frames" of Evangelical prayer.

31. Nederhof 1985, Presser and Stinson 1998.

32. Reed 2017.

33. Daniel Winchester (2008) has shown how Muslim converts sought a certain kind of Bourdieusian habitus through which their prayer could become unconscious and habituated. Simon (2009), Katz (2013), and Powers (2004) focus on the bodily practices and intention of Muslims. There have also been important studies of Evangelical prayer's physicality (Luhrmann and Morgain 2012, Coleman 1996), particularly Pentecostal Christians (Shoaps 2002), and of the physical nature of prayer more generally (Mellor and Shilling 2010, Haynes 2013).

34. Like many Arabic words, the spelling of du'a in English varies.

35. My coauthor and I call these assemblages *normative frames* (2019).

36. Foucault 1988.

37. For example, https://islamqa.info/en/36881. Accessed August 25, 2017.

38. Katz 2013: 56–58; Mahmood 2005.

39. Katz 2013: 62–74.

40. For a social-scientific perspective on an old theological problem see Sharp 2013, "When Prayers Go Unanswered." For a perspective engaging this question within Islamic theology see, among many others, Khalil 2011. The broader problem of theodicy is also well covered in Simko 2012, who provides a useful overview of the importance of the concept to early sociologists.

41. See for example Kelsay's 1989 study of Calvin's reconciling of prayer and predestination, as well as Katz 2013: 42–43 for the tension between du'a and the sovereignty of Allah.

42. See note 35 above.

43. Hamdy 2009, Edgar and Henig 2010.

CHAPTER 7

1. Guhin 2016.

2. Pinkton 1997: 28.

3. Harun Yahya (1999) is the pseudonym of Adnan Oktar, a controversial Turkish public figure perhaps most famous outside of Turkey for his publications against evolution (Riexinger 2008, 2010).

4. There are important parallels here with Drori et al.'s 2003 study of the mythic power of science around the world. As described in the introduction, this chapter develops these institutionalist insights by showing how the category of science is "peopled" (to use Timothy Hallett's term) via embodied practices and boundaries, as well as how science is experienced as an external authority with agency.

5. Marsden 2006, Noll 1985, 1994, Toumey 1991, 1994, 1996.

6. Dallal 2010, Guessoum 2011.

7. Dewey 2002. Of course, it is ironic that Dewey, ever the fan of science and evolution, is cited to explain creationism. My description of science as a diffuse network is indebted to Thomas Gieryn's focus on cultural boundaries in science (1999), as well as Fujimura's study of how "the definition of the situation constructed by molecular biologists became the accepted definition" (1996: 205). Any study of a "network" in science calls to mind Latour's Actor Network Theory (2005), and

I am quite indebted to Latour's many studies of science. However, this study of "external authorities" is different enough from Latour that I felt any highlighting of the common use of the word network would be both distracting and a disservice to the ongoing theoretical work developed by ANT practitioners. This project is obviously most indebted to other studies of creationism, especially Binder 2009, Bielo 2018, Kaden 2018, Moran 2011, Locke 2014, and Toumey 1991, 1996.

8. Merton 1973: 267; see also Merton 1996.

9. Shapin 2008: 21–91; see Merton 1973: 21–23.

10. Cartwright 1999, Knorr-Cetina 1999.

11. Morning 2011.

12. Irwin and Wynne 2003, Wynne 1992.

13. See philosopher of science Susan Haack (2003: 23) for a not altogether different definition of science (though obviously not from a creationist perspective).

14. Hacking 1999: 163—165, though see the entire book.

15. Latour 1987.

16. The classic study on this is Collins's 1992 study of the "experimenter's regress." I am grateful to Dan Hirschman for many points in this chapter, especially this one.

17. To be clear, the concept of speciation within biology is quite complicated and debated (Hey 2006, Leaché et al. 2014, Mayr 1996). For more on contemporary microevolution, see Hendry and Kinnison 1999.

18. Ham 2012.

19. Morris 1994.

20. Scott 1997, Numbers 2006.

21. There is impressive, now almost 40-year-old work from Richard Lenski at Michigan State University on the macroevolution of *E. coli* (Barrick et al 2009). However, the majority of evidence in support of macroevolution does not come out of falsifiable, synchronic lab experiments, though, within the philosophy of science, science studies, and scientific practice, the meanings of "lab" and "expirements"—not to mention science—can vary pretty widely.

22. Mitchell and White 2008: 210.

23. Denton 1986: 75.

24. Yet, Denton (1986) then goes on, in the same page, to cite a thinker, Paul Feyerabend who some might describe as relativist on the cultural arbitrariness of scientific knowledge. While Popper and Feyerabend might take a bit more work to synthesize than Denton pulls off (Feyerabend 1974; see also 1965, 1993), his linking of the two is emblematic of how creationists (or simply the evolution-suspicious) engage the philosophy of science. There is an overall emphasis on creativity and finding an argument that works at the moment, which is not what most would argue is in the spirt of Karl Popper 2005.

25. Rudge 1999, Hagen 1999, Kettlewell 1961.

26. Behe 1996, 2008.

27. More famous intelligent design arguments—like the irreducible complexity of an eye or a unicellular animal's flagellum—are much less controversial in evolutionary theory, provoking, at most, polite ignorance. Yet there is still a lot of confusion about the biochemical mechanisms that go into cellular processes, as well as the mechanisms through which proteins and amino acids reproduced themselves before the first cell. The disconnect is that few mainstream scientists and others who believe in evolution see these challenges in themselves as convincing evidence that the theory of evolution is flawed. By pointing out real challenges in

the data—what historian of science Thomas Kuhn (1962) would call "normal science"—they claim what Kuhn would call a paradigm shift, or a total reorienting of how we think about the world.

28. See, for example, Denton 1986, whose entire argument is basically that evolution is a paradigm in crisis. The textbook is Colson and Pearcey 2004.

29. Woodward 2003, 2006.

30. In a 2016 article I describe why the Muslim schools are less concerned about evolution despite also being creationist. In brief, it is because evolution does not challenge key boundaries and practices as it does for the Evangelical schools I studied. Whereas the theory of evolution is deeply dissonant with key practices and boundaries of reading the Bible literally, it is much less dissonant with the Muslim practice of salah and the boundary of gender performance. However, the purpose of this chapter is less a recapitulation of that earlier article than it is a study of science as an external authority.

31. Asghar, Hameed, and Farahani 2014, Clément 2015, Elshakry 2011, 2014.

32. Masci 2017.

33. Muslim opposition to evolution is based on a literal reading of the various accounts of creation in the Qur'an. Because references to creation are generally used as proof of Allah's power and compassion rather than as an outright historical account, references are spread throughout the text. Key passages are 6:2, 7:11–25; 7:54, 14:19, 15:26, 21:30, 22:47, 24:45, 32:7–8, 35:11, 41:11, 49:13, 50:15, 50:38, 51:47, 55:14, 71:13–17, and 82:8.

34. Hameed 2010: 135.

35. Hoenes del Pinal 2009.

36. Numbers 2006.

37. Hatch 1989.

38. I heard similar jokes about hitting children at the Christian schools. While they made me uncomfortable and clearly reflect some comfort with corporeal punishment, I found absolutely no indication of corporeal punishment at any of the schools.

39. Hoffer 2009: 8; see also Luft, Bell, and Gess-Newsome 2008.

40. Of course, whether or not there really is a consistent reality, and then whether or not there's a thing called science with an authority to study that reality form a whole series of big questions in metaphysics, epistemology, the philosophy of science, and science studies. "Science" could be said to reveal a fallibilist sense of not-yet falsified theories that continue to work (Popper 2005), a pragmatist (or anti-realist) conception of how to manipulate the world in consistent ways (Van Fraassen 1980), or a realist claim to know what the world is and how it works (Psillos 1999). For my arguments here, it is actually not important which I fall upon, though I am especially influenced by Ian Hacking 1999 and 2002.

41. Kuhn 1996: 138, Slater 2008.

42. Pickering 1992: 7.

43. Morning 2011, Toumey 1996.

44. Evans and Evans 2008.

45. Blancke et al. 2013, Edis 1999, Riexinger 2008, Toumey 1991, Riexinger 2010.

46. This distinction gets at ongoing studies of "motivated reasoning," all of which argue that more or better information does not affect—and can even act against—people changing their minds on issues salient to their identity. See especially Kahan 2013, Kraft et al. 2015, and Kunda 1990.

47. See note 47 above on motivated reasoning.

48. Haught 2018 is one of the standard accounts of theistic evolution, though the attempt at a synthesis even precedes Darwin.
49. Gieryn 1999: 27.
50. See Locke 2014, especially his fourth chapter on "Why God made evolutionists."
51. Lisle 2009, 2010.
52. Elsdon-Baker 2009.
53. Gould 1999, Gould and Eldredge 1993.
54. Meyer 2009.
55. Bourdieu 1996.
56. Evans 2011: 711; see also Evans and Evans 2008 and Evans 2013. As Joshua Tom (2018) describes, "scientific deviance" can have a social origin and can connect other forms of scientific denial, but it need not be a totalizing rejection of science.
57. See also Zigerell 2012; see also Gauchat 2012.
58. Roos 2007, 2014.
59. Rughiniş 2011.
60. Kunda 1990, Kahan 2013.

CHAPTER 8

1. Berger 1969. His later reconsiderations of his theory can be found in an edited volume titled *The Descecularization of the World* (1999).
2. Christian Smith 1998: 106.
3. Stallybrass and White 1986.
4. Casanova 2011.
5. See Taylor 2007: 22 for his account of subtraction stories. Nearly the entire book is about the role of social imaginaries in one way or another.

METHODOLOGICAL APPENDIX

1. Pascoe 2007.
2. Rinaldo and Guhin 2019.
3. See my working paper, "On Being Kicked Out of a Fieldsite" http://jeffguhin.com/wp-content/uploads/2019/08/On-Being-Kicked-Out-of-a-Fieldsite.pdf.

BIBLIOGRAPHY

Abraham, Ibrahim. 2009. "'Out to get us': queer Muslims and the clash of sexual civilisations in Australia." *Contemporary Islam* 3 (1):79–97.

Abdelhadi, Eman. 2017. "Religiosity and Muslim women's employment in the United States." *Socius* 3:1–17.

Abdelhadi, Eman. 2019. "The Hijab and Muslim women's employment in the United States." *Research in Social Stratification and Mobility* 61:26–37.

Abend, Gabriel. 2014. *The Moral Background: An Inquiry into the History of Business Ethics.* Princeton: Princeton University Press.

Abu-Lughod, Lila. 2013. *Do Muslim Women Need Saving?* Cambridge, MA: Harvard University Press.

Adams, Julia. 1996. "Principals and agents, colonialists and company men: The decay of colonial control in the Dutch East Indies." *American Sociological Review* 61 (1):12–28.

Adams, Julia. 2011. "1-800-How-Am-I-Driving?: Agency in social science history." *Social Science History* 35 (1):1–17.

Ahmad, Iftikhar, and Michelle Y. Szpara. 2003. "Muslim children in urban America: The New York City schools experience." *Journal of Muslim Minority Affairs* 23 (2):295–301.

Ahmed, Akbar. 2010. *Journey into America: The Challenge of Islam.* Washington DC: Brookings Institution Press.

Ahmed, Leila. 1992. *Women and Gender in Islam: Historical Roots of a Modern Debate.* New Haven: Yale University Press.

Ahmed, Safdar. 2013. "Progressive Islam and Quranic Hermeneutics." In *Muslim Secular Democracy: Voices from Within*, edited by Lily Zubaidah Rahim, 77–92. New York: Palgrave Macmillan.

Ahmed, Sara. 2007. "A phenomenology of whiteness." *Feminist Theory* 8 (2):149–168.

Ajrouch, Kristine J. 2004. "Gender, race, and symbolic boundaries: Contested spaces of identity among Arab American adolescents." *Sociological Perspectives* 47 (4):371–391.

Alexander, Amy C., and Christian Welzel. 2011. "Islam and patriarchy: How robust is Muslim support for patriarchal values?" *International Review of Sociology* 21 (2):249–276.

Alexander, Jeffrey C. 1995. *Fin de siècle Social Theory: Relativism, Reduction, and the Problem of Reason.* New York: Verso.

Alexander, Jeffrey C. 2006. *The Civil Sphere*: Oxford University Press.

Ali, Muna. 2018. *Young Muslim America: Faith, Community, and Belonging.* New York: Oxford University Press.

Ali, Saba Rasheed, Amina Mahmood, Joy Moel, Carolyn Hudson, and Leslie Leathers. 2008. "A qualitative investigation of Muslim and Christian women's views of religion and feminism in their lives." *Cultural Diversity and Ethnic Minority Psychology* 14 (1):38–46.

Allen, Amy. 2013. *The Politics of Our Selves: Power, Autonomy, and Gender in Contemporary Critical Theory*. New York: Columbia University Press.

Allen, Danielle S. 2004. *Talking to Strangers. Anxieties of Citizenship since Brown v. Board of Education*. Chicago: University of Chicago Press.

Ammerman, Nancy T. 1987. *Bible Believers: Fundamentalists in the Modern World*. New Brunswick: Rutgers University Press.

Ammerman, Nancy T. 1997. "Organized religion in a voluntaristic society." *Sociology of Religion* 58 (3):203–215.

Ammerman, Nancy T. 2013. *Sacred Stories, Spiritual Tribes: Finding Religion in Everyday Life*. New York: Oxford University Press.

Ammerman, Nancy T. 2020. "Rethinking religion: Toward a practice approach." *American Journal of Sociology* 126 (1):6–51.

Anscombe, Gertrude Elizabeth Margaret. 1958. "Modern moral philosophy." *Philosophy* 33 (124):1–19.

Archer, Margaret. 2000. *Being Human: The Problem of Agency*. Cambridge: Cambridge University Press.

Archer, Margaret. 2003. *Structure, Agency and the Internal Conversation*. Cambridge: Cambridge University Press.

Aristotle. 1963. *Categories and De Interpretatione*. Translated by J. Ackrill, *Clarendon Aristotle Series*. Oxford: Clarendon Press.

Aristotle. 1994. *Metaphysics, Books Z and H, Clarendon Press*. Translated by David Bostock, *Clarendon Aristotle Series*. Oxford: Clarendon Press.

Aristotle. 2013. *Politics*. Translated by Carnes Lord. Chicago: University of Chicago Press.

Asad, Talal. 1993. *Genealogies of Religion*. Baltimore: Johns Hopkins University Press.

Asad, Talal. 2003. *Formations of the Secular: Christianity, Islam, Modernity*. Stanford: Stanford University Press.

Asad, Talal. 2009. "The idea of an anthropology of Islam." *Qui Parle* 17 (2):1–30.

Asghar, Anila, Salman Hameed, and Najme Kishani Farahani. 2014. "Evolution in biology textbooks: A comparative analysis of 5 Muslim countries." *Religion & Education* 41 (1):1–15.

Austin, John Langshaw. 1975. *How to Do Things with Words*. 2nd ed. New York: Oxford University Press. Original edition, 1962.

Avishai, Orit. 2008. "'Doing religion' in a secular world: Women in conservative religions and the question of agency." *Gender & Society* 22 (4):409–433.

Bagnoli, Carla. (Ed.). 2011. *Morality and the Emotions*. New York: Oxford University Press.

Bail, Christopher A. 2014. *Terrified: How Anti-Muslim Fringe Organizations Became Mainstream*. Princeton: Princeton University Press.

Baker, Joseph O. 2008. "An investigation of the sociological patterns of prayer frequency and content." *Sociology of Religion* 69 (2):169–185.

Balswick, Jack O., and Judith K. Balswick. 2006. *A Model for Marriage: Covenant, Grace, Empowerment and Intimacy*. Downers Grove, IL: InterVarsity Press.

Bargheer, Stefan. 2018. *Moral Entanglements: Conserving Birds in Britain and Germany*. Chicago: University of Chicago Press.

Barrick, Jeffrey E., Dong Su Yu, Sung Ho Yoon, Haeyoung Jeong, Tae Kwang Oh, Dominique Schneider, Richard E. Lenski, and Jihyun F. Kim. 2009. "Genome evolution and adaptation in a long-term experiment with *Escherichia coli*." *Nature* 461 (7268):1243–1247.

Barth, Fredrik. 1998. *Ethnic Groups and Boundaries: The Social Organization of Culture Difference*. Long Grove, IL: Waveland Press.

Bartkowski, John. 1996. "Beyond biblical literalism and inerrancy: Conservative Protestants and the hermeneutic interpretation of scripture." *Sociology of Religion* 57 (3):259–272.

Bartkowski, John P. 2001. *Remaking the Godly Marriage: Gender Negotiation in Evangelical Families*. New Brunswick: Rutgers University Press.

Bartkowski, John P., and Jen'nan Ghazal Read. 2003. "Veiled submission: Gender, power, and identity among evangelical and Muslim women in the United States." *Qualitative sociology* 26 (1):71–92.

Behe, Michael J. 1996. *Darwin's Black Box: The Biochemical Challenge to Evolution*. New York: Free Press.

Behe, Michael J. 2008. *The Edge of Evolution: The Search for the Limits of Darwinism*. New York: Free Press.

Bellah, Robert N. 1991. *Beyond Belief: Essays on Religion in a Post-Traditionalist World*. Berkeley: University of California Press. Original edition, 1970.

Bellah, Robert N., Richard Madsen, William M. Sullivan, Ann Swidler, and Steven M. Tipton. 2007. *Habits of the Heart: Individualism and Commitment in American Life*. Berkeley: University of California Press. Original edition, 1985.

Bean, Lydia, and Brandon C. Martinez. 2014. "Evangelical ambivalence toward gays and lesbians." *Sociology of Religion* 75 (3):395–417.

Bender, Courtney. 2008. "How does God answer back?" *Poetics* 36 (5–6):476–492.

Berger, Peter L. 1969. *The Sacred Canopy: Elements of a Sociological Theory of Religion*. New York: Anchor Books.

Berger, Peter L. 1999. *The Desecularization of the World*. Washington, DC: Ethics and Public Policy Center.

Berger, Peter, and Thomas Luckmann. 1967. *The Social Construction of Reality: A Treatise in the Sociology of Knowledge*. New York: Anchor.

Bersamin, Melina M., Deborah A. Fisher, Samantha Walker, Douglas L. Hill, and Joel W. Grube. 2007. "Defining virginity and abstinence: Adolescents' interpretations of sexual behaviors." *Journal of Adolescent Health* 41 (2):182–188.

Beydoun, Khaled A. 2018. *American Islamophobia: Understanding the Roots and Rise of Fear*. Oakland: University of California Press.

Bidwell, Charles E. 2001. "Analyzing schools as organizations: Long-term permanence and short-term change." *Sociology of Education* 74 (Extra Issue):100–114.

Bielo, James S. 2009a. "Introduction: Encountering Biblicism." In *The Social Life of Scriptures: Cross-Cultural Perspectives on Biblicism*, edited by James Bielo, 1–9. New Brunswick, NJ: Rutgers University Press.

Bielo, James S. 2009b. *Words Upon the Word: An Ethnography of Evangelical Group Bible Study*. New York: NYU Press.

Bielo, James S. 2018. *Ark Encounter: The Making of a Creationist Theme Park*. New York: New York University Press.

Bilici, Mucahit. 2012. *Finding Mecca in America: How Islam is Becoming an American Religion*. Chicago: University of Chicago Press.

Binder, Amy J. 2009. *Contentious Curricula: Afrocentrism and Creationism in American Public Schools*. Princeton, NJ: Princeton University Press.

Blancke, Stefaan, Hans Henrik Hjermitslev, Johan Braeckman, and Peter C. Kjærgaard. 2013. "Creationism in Europe: Facts, gaps, and prospects." *Journal of the American Academy of Religion* 81 (4):996–1028.

Bonilla-Silva, Eduardo. 2017. *Racism Without Racists: Color-blind Racism and the Persistence of Racial Inequality in America*. 5th ed. Lanham, MD: Rowman & Littlefield. Original edition, 2003.

Bourdieu, Pierre. 1984. *Distinction: A Social Critique of the Judgement of Taste*. Translated by Richard Nice. Cambridge, MA: Harvard University Press. Original edition, 1979.

Bourdieu, Pierre. 1990. *The Logic of Practice*. Translated by Richard Nice. Stanford: Stanford University Press. Original edition, 1980.

Bourdieu, Pierre. 1991. *Language and Symbolic Power*. Translated by Gino Raymond and Matthew Adadmson. Malden, MA: Polity Press.

Bourdieu, Pierre. 1996. *The Rules of Art: Genesis and Structure of the Literary Field*. Translated by Susan Emanuel. Stanford: Stanford University Press. Original education, 1992.

Bourdieu, Pierre. 1998. *The State Nobility: Elite Schools in the Field of Power*. Translated by Lauretta C. Clough. Stanford: Stanford University Press. Original edition, 1989.

Bowen, John R. 1989. "Salat in Indonesia: The social meanings of an Islamic ritual." *Man*:600–619.

Braunstein, Ruth. 2017. "Muslims as outsiders, enemies, and others: The 2016 presidential election and the politics of religious exclusion." *American Journal of Cultural Sociology* 5 (3):355–372.

Brenneman, Todd M. 2013. *Homespun Gospel: The Triumph of Sentimentality in Contemporary American Evangelicalism*. New York: Oxford University Press.

Brint, Steven. 2013. "The 'collective mind' at work: A decade in the life of US sociology of education." *Sociology of Education* 86 (4):273–279.

Brint, Steven, and Seth Abrutyn. 2010. "Who's right about the right? Comparing competing explanations of the link between white evangelicals and conservative politics in the United States." *Journal for the Scientific Study of Religion* 49 (2):328–350.

Brophy, Sorcha A. 2014. "Making morals: Standard-setting in organizations." In *The Palgrave Handbook of Altruism, Morality, and Social Solidarity*, edited by Vincent Jeffries, 353–366. New York: Springer.

Brophy, Sorcha A. 2016. "Orthodoxy as project: Temporality and action in an American Protestant denomination." *Sociology of Religion* 77 (2):123–143.

Brown, Jonathan A.C. 2015. "Is Islam easy to understand or not?: Salafis, the democratization of interpretation and the need for the Ulema." *Journal of Islamic Studies* 26 (2):117–144.

Brown, Jonathan A.C. 2017. *Hadith: Muhammad's Legacy in the Medieval and Modern World*. New York: Simon and Schuster.

Brown, Wendy. 2015. *Undoing the Demos: Neoliberalism's Stealth Revolution*. Cambridge, MA: MIT Press.

Brubaker, Rogers. 2004. *Ethnicity without Groups*. Cambridge, MA: Harvard University Press.

Brückner, Hannah, and Peter Bearman. 2005. "After the promise: The STD consequences of adolescent virginity pledges." *Journal of Adolescent Health* 36 (4):271–278.

Burke, Kelsy. 2016. *Christians Under Covers: Evangelicals and Sexual Pleasure on the Internet*. Oakland, CA: University of California Press.

Burke, Kelsy C. 2012. "Women's agency in gender-traditional religions: A review of four approaches." *Sociology Compass* 6 (2):122–133.

Butler, Judith. 1997. *The Psychic Life of Power: Theories in Subjection*. Stanford: Stanford University Press.

Butler, Judith. 2011. *Gender Trouble: Feminism and the Subversion of Identity*. New York: Routledge. Original edition, 1990.

Byng, Michelle D. 2010. "Symbolically Muslim: Media, hijab, and the West." *Critical Sociology* 36 (1):109–129.

Cadge, Wendy, and Elaine Howard Ecklund. 2007. "Immigration and religion." *Annual Review of Sociology* 33:359–379.

Cainkar, Louis A. 2009. *Homeland Insecurity: The Arab American and Muslim American Experience after 9/11*. New York: Russell Sage Foundation.

Calarco, Jessica McCrory. 2018. *Negotiating Opportunities: How the Middle Class Secures Advantages in School*. New York: Oxford University Press.

Calder, Norman. 2001. "The limits of Islamic orthodoxy." In *Intellectual Traditions in Islam*, edited by Farhad Daftary, 66–86. New York: IB Tauris.

Camic, Charles. 1986. "The matter of habit." *American Journal of Sociology* 91 (5):1039–1087.

Carden, Stephen. 2006. *Virtue Ethics: Dewey and MacIntyre*. London: Continuum.

Carpenter, Laura. 2005. *Virginity Lost: An Intimate Portrait of First Sexual Experiences*. New York: NYU Press.

Carper, J.C. 1983. "The Christian day school movement." *The Educational Forum*. 47 (2):135–149.

Cartwright, Nancy. 1999. *The Dappled World: A Study of the Boundaries of Science*. New York: Cambridge University Press.

Casanova, José. 2011. *Public Religions in the Modern World*. Chicago: University of Chicago Press. Original edition, 1994.

Cerulo, Karen A. 2011. "Social interaction: Do non-humans count?" *Sociology Compass* 5 (9):775–791.

Cerulo, Karen A., and Andrea Barra. 2008. "In the name of . . . : Legitimate interactants in the dialogue of prayer." *Poetics* 36 (5–6):374–388.

Chowdhury, Nuzhat. 2014. "I, spy (but only on you): Raza v. City of New York, the civil rights disaster of religious & ethnic-based surveillance, and the national security excuse." *Columbia Human Rights Law Review* 46 (2):278–331.

Clément, Pierre. 2015. "Muslim teachers' conceptions of evolution in several countries." *Public Understanding of Science* 24 (4):400–421.

Cobb, Ryon J., Samuel L. Perry, and Kevin D. Dougherty. 2015. "United by faith? Race/ethnicity, congregational diversity, and explanations of racial inequality." *Sociology of Religion* 76 (2):177–198.

Cohen, Jere, Lawrence E. Hazelrigg, and Whitney Pope. 1975. "De-Parsonizing Weber: A critique of Parsons' interpretation of Weber's sociology." *American Sociological Review* 40 (2):229–241.

Cohen, S. Marc. 1978. "Essentialism in Aristotle." *The Review of Metaphysics* 31 (3):387–405.

Coleman, Simon. 1996. "Words as things: Language, aesthetics and the objectification of Protestant evangelicalism." *Journal of Material Culture* 1 (1):107–128.

Coley, Jonathan S. 2018. *Gay on God's Campus: Mobilizing for LGBT Equality at Christian Colleges and Universities*. Chapel Hill, North Carolina: University of North Carolina Press.

Collins, Harry. 1992. *Changing Order: Replication and Induction in Scientific Practice*. Chicago: University of Chicago Press.

Collins, Randall. 2014. *Interaction Ritual Chains*. Princeton: Princeton University Press. Original edition, 2004.

Colson, Charles, and Nancy Pearcey. 2004. *How Now Shall We Live?* Carol Stream, IL: Tyndale House Publishers. Original edition, 1999.

Corsaro, William A. 2018. *The Sociology of Childhood*. 5th ed. Los Angeles: Sage.

Corwin, Ronald G. 1975. "Innovation in organizations: The case of schools." *Sociology of Education* 48 (1):1–37.

Crone, Patricia. 2016. "'No compulsion in religion' Q. 2: 256 in mediaeval and modern interpretation." In *The Qur'ānic Pagans and Related Matters*, edited by Hanna Siurua, 351–409. Leiden: Brill.

Crone, Patricia, and Michael Cook. 1977. *Hagarism: The Making of the Islamic World*. Cambridge: Cambridge University Press.

Dallal, Ahmad S. 2010. *Islam, Science, and the Challenge of History*. New Haven: Yale University Press.

Damasio, Antonio R. 1999. *The Feeling of What Happens: Body and Emotion in the Making of Consciousness*. San Diego: Harcourt.

Darnell, Alfred, and Darren E. Sherkat. 1997. "The impact of Protestant fundamentalism on educational attainment." *American Sociological Review*:306–315.

De Tocqueville, Alexis. 2000. *Democracy in America*. Translated by Harvey C. Mansfield and Delba Winthrop. Chicago: University of Chicago Press. Original edition, 1835, 1840.

Denton, Melinda Lundquist. 2004. "Gender and marital decision making: Negotiating religious ideology and practice." *Social Forces* 82 (3):1151–1180.

Denton, Michael. 1986. *Evolution: A Theory in Crisis*. Chevy Chase, MD: Adler & Adler.

DeRogatis, Amy. 2014. *Saving Sex: Sexuality and Salvation in American Evangelicalism*. New York: Oxford University Press.

Dewey, John. 1925. *Experience and Nature*. Peru, IL: Open Court Publishing.

Dewey, John. 1935. "The future of liberalism." *The Journal of Philosophy* 32 (9):225–230.

Dewey, John. 1997. *Democracy and Education*. New York: The Free Press. Original edition, 1916.

Dewey, John. 2002. *Human Nature and Conduct*. Mineola, NY: Dover. Original edition, 1922.

DiMaggio, Paul. 1997. "Culture and cognition." *Annual Review of Sociology* 23 (1):263–287.

Douglas, Mary. 2003. *Purity and Danger: An Analysis of Concepts of Pollution and Taboo*. London: Routledge. Original edition, 1966.

Du Bois, W.E.B. 2007. *Souls of Black Folk*. New York: Oxford. Original edition, 1903.

Du Bois, W.E.B. 2013. *Education and Empowerment: The Essential Writings of W.E.B. DuBois*, edited by Randall Westbrook. East Brunswick, NJ: Hansen Publishing Group.

Duderija, Adis. 2010. "Constructing the religious self and the other: Neo-traditional Salafi manhaj." *Islam and Christian–Muslim Relations* 21 (1):75–93.

Duderija, Adis. 2016. *Constructing a Religiously Ideal 'Believer' and 'Woman' in Islam: Neo-traditional Salafi and Progressive Muslims' Methods of Interpretation*. New York: Palgrave Macmillan.

Duderija, Adis. 2017. *The Imperatives of Progressive Islam*. London: Routledge.

Durkheim, Emile. 1961. *Moral Education*. Translated by Everett K. Wilson and Herman Schnurer. New York: Free Press. Original edition, 1925.

Durkheim, Emile. 1995. *The Elementary Forms of Religious Life*. Translated by Karen E. Fields. New York: The Free Press. Original edition, 1912.

Durkheim, Emile. 1961. *Moral Education: A Study in the Theory and Application of the Sociology of Education*. Translated by Everett K. Wilson and Herman Schnurer. Edited by Everett K. Wilson. New York: The Free Press. Original edition, 1925.

Drori, Gili S., and John W. Meyer, Francisco O. Ramirez, and Evan Schofer. 2003. *Science in the Modern World Polity: Institutionalization and Globalization*. Stanford: Stanford University Press.

Ecklund, Elaine Howard. 2010. *Science vs. Religion: What Scientists Really Think*. New York: Oxford University Press.

Edgar, Iain, and David Henig. 2010. "Istikhara: The guidance and practice of Islamic dream incubation through ethnographic comparison." *History and Anthropology* 21 (3):251–262.

Edis, Taner. 1999. "Cloning creationism in Turkey." *Reports of the National Center for Science Education* 19 (6):30–35.

Effler, Erika Summers. 2010. *Laughing Saints and Righteous Heroes: Emotional Rhythms in Social Movement Groups*. Chicago: University of Chicago Press.

El Fadl, Khaled Abou. 2014. *Reasoning with God: Reclaiming Shari'ah in the Modern Age*. Lanham, MD: Rowman & Littlefield.

El-Haj, Thea Renda Abu. 2015. *Unsettled Belonging: Educating Palestinian American Youth after 9/11*. Chicago: University of Chicago Press.

El Shamsy, Ahmed. 2013. *The Canonization of Islamic Law: A Social and Intellectual History*. New York: Cambridge University Press.

Elisha, Omri. 2011. *Moral Ambition: Mobilization and Social Outreach in Evangelical Megachurches*. Berkeley: University of California Press.

Elsdon-Baker, Fern. 2009. *The Selfish Genius: How Richard Dawkins Rewrote Darwin's Legacy*. London: Faber & Faber.

Elshakry, Marwa. 2011. "Muslim hermeneutics and Arabic views of evolution." *Zygon* 46 (2):330–344.

Elshakry, Marwa. 2014. *Reading Darwin in Arabic, 1860–1950*. Chicago: University of Chicago Press.

El-Tayeb, Fatima. 2012. " 'Gays who cannot properly be gay': Queer Muslims in the neoliberal European city." *European Journal of Women's Studies* 19 (1):79–95.

Emerson, Michael O., and Christian Smith. 2000. *Divided by Faith: Evangelical Religion and the Problem of Race in America*. New York: Oxford University Press.

Engelke, Matthew. 2007. *A Problem of Presence: Beyond Scripture in an African Church*. Berkeley: University of California Press.

Epstein, Steven. 1996. *Impure Science: AIDS, Activism, and the Politics of Knowledge*. Berkeley: University of California Press.

Evans, John H. 2011. "Epistemological and moral conflict between religion and science." *Journal for the Scientific Study of Religion* 50 (4):707–727.

Evans, John H. 2013. "The growing social and moral conflict between conservative Protestantism and science." *Journal for the Scientific Study of Religion* 52 (2):368–385.

Evans, John H. 2016. *What Is a Human?: What the Answers Mean for Human Rights*. New York: Oxford University Press.

Evans, John H., and Michael S. Evans. 2008. "Religion and science: Beyond the epistemological conflict narrative." *Annual Review of Sociology* 34:87–105.

Fallon Jr., Richard H. 2005. "Legitimacy and the constitution." *Harvard Law Review* 118 (6):1787.

Fernando, Mayanthi L. 2010. "Reconfiguring freedom: Muslim piety and the limits of secular law and public discourse in France." *American Ethnologist* 37 (1): 19–35.

Feyerabend, Paul. 1965. "Problems of empiricism." In *Beyond the Edge of Certainty*, edited by Robert Colodny, 145–260. Englewood Cliffs, NJ: Prentice-Hall.

Feyerabend, Paul. 1974. "Popper's objective knowledge." *Inquiry* 17 (1–4):475–507.

Feyerabend, Paul. 1993. *Against Method*. 3rd ed. London: Verso. Original edition, 1975.

Fine, Michelle, and Selcuk R. Sirin. 2008. *Muslim American Youth: Understanding Hyphenated Identities through Multiple Methods*. New York: NYU Press.

Fish, Stanley Eugene. 1980. *Is There a Text in This Class?: The Authority of Interpretive Communities*. Cambridge, MA: Harvard University Press.

FitzGerald, Frances. 2017. *The Evangelicals: The Struggle to Shape America*. New York: Simon and Schuster. ·

Fitzgerald, Scott T., and Jennifer Glass. 2008. "Can early family formation explain the lower educational attainment of US conservative Protestants?." *Sociological Spectrum* 28 (5):556–577.

Foucault, Michel. 1988. "Technologies of the Self." In *Technologies of the Self: A Seminar with Michel Foucault*, edited by Luther H. Martin, Huck Gutman, and Patrick H. Hutton, 16–49. Amherst, MA: University of Massachusetts Press.

Foucault, Michel. 1994. *The Birth of the Clinic*. Translated by Alan Sheridan. New York: Vintage. Original edition, 1963.

Foucault, Michel. 1995. *Discipline & Punish: The Birth of the Prison*. 2nd ed. Translated by Alan Sheridan. New York: Vintage. Original edition, 1975.

Foucault, Michel. 1990. *The History of Sexuality: Volume 1*. Translated by Robert Hurley. New York: Vintage Books. Original edition, 1976.

Fried, Charles. 2005. *Saying What the Law Is: the Constitution in the Supreme Court*. Cambridge, MA: Harvard University Press.

Fuist, Todd Nicholas. 2016. "'It just always seemed like it wasn't a big deal, yet I know for some people they really struggle with it': LGBT religious identities in context." *Journal for the Scientific Study of Religion* 55 (4):770–786.

Fujimura, Joan. 1996. *Crafting Science: A Sociohistory of the Quest for the Genetics of Cancer*. Cambridge, MA: Harvard University Press.

Furseth, Inger. 2011. "The hijab: Boundary work and identity negotiations among immigrant Muslim women in the Los Angeles area." *Review of Religious Research* 52 (4):365–385.

Gallagher, Sally K. 2003. *Evangelical Identity and Gendered Family Life*. New Brunswick, NJ: Rutgers University Press.

Gallagher, Sally K. 2004a. "The marginalization of evangelical feminism." *Sociology of Religion* 65 (3):215–237.

Gallagher, Sally K. 2004b. "Where are the antifeminist evangelicals? Evangelical identity, subcultural location, and attitudes toward feminism." *Gender & Society* 18 (4):451–472.

Gallagher, Sally K., and Christian Smith. 1999. "Symbolic traditionalism and pragmatic egalitarianism: Contemporary evangelicals, families, and gender." *Gender & Society* 13 (2):211–233.

Gauchat, Gordon. 2012. "Politicization of science in the public sphere: A study of public trust in the United States, 1974 to 2010." *American Sociological Review* 77 (2):167–187.

Geertz, Clifford. 1973. *The Interpretation of Cultures*. New York: Basic Books.

Gellner, Ernest. 1983. *Nations and Nationalism*. Ithaca: Cornell University Press.

Gelman, Susan A. 2004. "Psychological essentialism in children." *Trends in Cognitive Sciences* 8 (9):404–409.

GhaneaBassiri, Kambiz. 1997. *Competing Visions of Islam in the United States: A Study of Los Angeles*. Westport, CT: Greenwood Publishing Group.

GhaneaBassiri, Kambiz. 2010. *A History of Islam in America: From the New World to the New World Order*. New York: Cambridge University Press.

Giddens, Anthony. 1979. *Central Problems in Social Theory: Action, Structure, and Contradiction in Social Analysis*. Berkeley, CA: University of California Press.

Gieryn, Thomas F. 1983. "Boundary-work and the demarcation of science from non-science: Strains and interests in professional ideologies of scientists." *American Sociological Review* 48 (6):781–795.

Gieryn, Thomas F. 1999. *Cultural Boundaries of Science: Credibility on the Line*. Chicago: University of Chicago Press.

Gil-White, Francisco J. 2001. "Are ethnic groups biological 'species' to the human brain? Essentialism in our cognition of some social categories." *Current Anthropology* 42 (4):515–553.

Gill, Mary Louise. 1991. *Aristotle on Substance: The Paradox of Unity*. Princeton: Princeton University Press.

Glass, Jennifer, and Philip Levchak. 2014. "Red states, blue states, and divorce: Understanding the impact of conservative Protestantism on regional variation in divorce rates." *American Journal of Sociology* 119 (4):1002–1046.

Goffman, Erving. 1959. *The Presentation of Self in Everyday Life*. New York: Doubleday.

Goldstein, Eric L. 2006. *The Price of Whiteness: Jews, Race, and American Identity*. Princeton: Princeton University Press.

Gonsoulin, Margaret E. 2010. "Gender ideology and status attainment of conservative Christian women in the 21st century." *Sociological Spectrum* 30 (2):220–240.

Gorski, Philip. 2017. *American Covenant: A History of Civil Religion from the Puritans to the Present*. Princeton: Princeton University Press.

Gorski, Philip. 2019. "Why evangelicals voted for Trump: A critical cultural sociology." In *Politics of Meaning/Meaning of Politics: Cultural Sociology of the 2016 U.S. Presidential Election*, edited by Jason L. Mast and Jeffrey C. Alexander, 165–183. New York: Palgrave Macmillan.

Gould, Stephen Jay. 1999. *Rocks of Ages: Science and Religion in the Fullness of Life*. New York: Random House.

Gould, Stephen Jay, and Niles Eldredge. 1993. "Punctuated equilibrium comes of age." *Nature* 366 (6452):223–227.

Grewal, Zareena. 2013. *Islam is a Foreign Country: American Muslims and the Global Crisis of Authority*. New York: NYU Press.

Griffith, R. Marie. 1997. *God's Daughters: Evangelical Women and the Power of Submission*. Berkeley: University of California Press.

Griffith, R Marie. 2017. *Moral Combat: How Sex Divided American Christians and Fractured American Politics*. New York: Basic Books.

Grubbs, Joshua B., Shane W. Kraus, and Samuel L. Perry 2019. "Self-reported addiction to pornography in a nationally representative sample: The roles of use habits, religiousness, and moral incongruence." *Journal of Behavioral Addictions* 8 (1):88–93.

Guessoum, Nidhal. 2011. *Islam's Quantum Question: Reconciling Muslim Tradition and Modern Science*. London: IB Tauris.

Guhin, Jeffrey. 2014. "Religion as Site Rather than Religion as Category: on the Sociology of Religion's Export Problem." *Sociology of Religion* 75 (4):579–593.

Guhin, Jeffrey. 2016. "Why worry about evolution? Boundaries, practices, and moral salience in Sunni and Evangelical high schools." *Sociological Theory* 34 (2):151–17.

Guhin, Jeffrey. 2018. "Colorblind Islam: The racial hinges of immigrant Muslims in the United States." *Social Inclusion* 6 (2):87–97.

Guhin, Jeffrey. 2019. "Defining du'a: A study of contested meanings in immigrant Muslim schools in the New York City area." *Journal of Education in Muslim Societies* 1 (1):26–43.

Guhin, Jeffrey. 2021. "Why Study Schools?" In *Handbook of Classical Sociological Theory*, edited by Seth Abrutyn and Omar Lizardo. New York: Springer.

Guhin, Jeffrey, and Joseph Klett. 2018. "Internal goods in the sociology of education: Skills, habits, virtues, and the problem of power." Last Modified April 20, 2020. https://osf.io/preprints/socarxiv/sv23y/.

Guhin, Jeffrey, and Jonathan Wyrtzen. 2013. "The violences of knowledge: Edward Said, sociology, and post-orientalist reflexivity." In *Postcolonial Sociology*, edited by Julian Go, 231–262. Emerald Group Publishing Limited.

Haack, Susan. 2003. *Defending Science-Within Reason: Between Scientism and Cynicism*. New York: Prometheus Books.

Hacking, Ian. 1999. *The Social Construction of What?* Cambridge, MA: Harvard University Press.

Hacking, Ian. 2002. *Historical Ontology*. Cambridge, MA: Harvard University Press.

Hagen, Joel B. 1999. "Retelling experiments: HBD Kettlewell's studies of industrial melanism in peppered moths." *Biology and Philosophy* 14 (1):39–54.

Hallaq, Wael B. 2009. *Shari'a: Theory, Practice, Transformations*. New York: Cambridge University Press.

Hallett, Timothy and Marc J. Ventresca. 2006. "Inhabited Institutions: Social interactions and organizational forms in Gouldner's *Patterns of Industrial Bureaucracy*." *Theory and Society* 35:213–236.

Hallett, Timothy. 2010. "The myth incarnate: Recoupling processes, turmoil, and inhabited institutions in an urban elementary school." *American Sociological Review* 75 (1):52–74.

Ham, Ken. 2012. *The Lie: Evolution*. Green Forest, AR: Master Books.

Ham, Ken, and Britt Beemer. 2009. *Already Gone: Why Your Kids Will Quit Church and What You Can Do to Stop It*. Green Forest, AR: New Leaf Publishing Group.

Hamdy, Sherine F. 2009. "Islam, fatalism, and medical intervention: lessons from Egypt on the cultivation of forbearance (sabr) and reliance on God (tawakkul)." *Anthropological Quarterly* 82 (1):173–196.

Hameed, Salman. 2010. "Evolution and creationism in the Islamic world." In *Science and Religion: New Historical Perspectives*, edited by T DIxon, G. Cantor and S. Pumfrey, 133–152. New York: Cambridge University Press.

Hameed, Salman. 2015. "Making sense of Islamic creationism in Europe." *Public Understanding of Science* 24 (4):388–399.

Hammer, Juliane. 2012. *American Muslim Women, Religious Authority, and Activism: More Than a Prayer*. Austin: University of Texas Press.

Hammer, Juliane, and Omid Safi. 2013. (eds.) *The Cambridge Companion to American Islam*. New York: Cambridge University Press.

Harrison, Peter. 2015. *The Territories of Science and Religion*. Chicago: University of Chicago Press.

Hatch, Nathan O. 1989. *The Democratization of American Christianity*. New Haven: Yale University Press.

Haught, John F. 2018. *God After Darwin: A Theology of Evolution*. New York: Routledge.

Haynes, Naomi. 2013. "On the potential and problems of Pentecostal exchange." *American Anthropologist* 115 (1):85–95.

Hefner, Robert W., and Muhammad Qasim Zaman. 2007. *Schooling Islam: The Culture and Politics of Modern Muslim Education*. Princeton: Princeton University Press.

Hendry, Andrew P., and Michael T. Kinnison. 1999. "Perspective: the pace of modern life: measuring rates of contemporary microevolution." *Evolution* 53 (6):1637–1653.

Hey, Jody. 2006. "On the failure of modern species concepts." *Trends in Ecology & Evolution* 21 (8):447–450.

Hitlin, Steven, and Jane Allyn Piliavin. 2004. "Values: Reviving a dormant concept." *Annual Review of Sociology* 30:359–393.

Hitlin, Steven, and Stephen Vaisey. 2010. *Handbook of the Sociology of Morality*. New York: Springer.

Hitlin, Steven, and Stephen Vaisey. 2013. "The new sociology of morality." *Annual Review of Sociology* 39:51–68.

Hobsbawm, Eric J. 2012. *Nations and Nationalism Since 1780: Programme, Myth, Reality*. 2nd ed. New York: Cambridge University Press. Original edition, 1990.

Hoenes del Pinal, Eric. 2009. "How Q'eqchi'-Maya Catholics become legitimate interpreters of the Bible: Two models of religious authority in sermons." In *The Social Life of Scriptures: Cross-Cultural Perspectives on Biblicism*, edited by James S. Bielo, 80–99. New Brunswick, NJ: Rutgers University Press.

Hoffer, Wendy Ward. 2009. *Science as Thinking: The Constants and Variables of Inquiry Teaching, Grades 5-10*. Portsmouth, NH: Heinemann Educational Books.

Honneth, Axel. 2008. *Reification: A New Look at an Old Idea*. New York: Oxford University Press.

Hooker, Juliet. 2016. "Black Lives Matter and the paradoxes of US Black politics: From democratic sacrifice to democratic repair." *Political Theory* 44 (4):448–469.

Howe, Justine. 2018. *Suburban Islam*. New York: Oxford University Press.

Hunter, James Davison. 1983. *American Evangelicalism: Conservative Religion and the Quandary of Modernity, Journal for the Scientific Study of Religion*. New Brunswick, NJ: Rutgers University Press.

Hunter, James Davison. 1984. "Religion and political civility: The coming generation of American evangelicals." *Journal for the Scientific Study of Religion* 23 (4):364–380.

Hunter, James Davison. 2010. *To change the World: The Irony, Tragedy, and Possibility of Christianity in the Late Modern World*. New York: Oxford University Press.

Hunter, James Davison, and Ryan S. Olson. (eds.) 2018. *The Content of Their Character: Inquiries into the Varieties of Moral Formation*. New York: Finstock & Tew Publishers.

Husain, Atiya. 2017. "Moving beyond (and back to) the black–white binary: a study of black and white Muslims' racial positioning in the United States." *Ethnic and Racial Studies* 42 (4):589–606.

Irby, Courtney Ann. 2014a. "Dating in light of Christ: Young evangelicals negotiating gender in the context of religious and secular American culture." *Sociology of Religion* 75 (2):260–283.

Irby, Courtney Ann. 2014b. "Moving beyond agency: A review of gender and intimate relationships in conservative religions." *Sociology Compass* 8 (11):1269–1280.

Irwin, Alan, and Brian Wynne. 2003. *Misunderstanding Science?: The Public Reconstruction of Science and Technology*. New York: Cambridge University Press.

Jackson, Sherman A. 2005. *Islam and the Black American: Looking Toward the Third Resurrection*. New York: Oxford University Press.

Jackson, Sherman A. 2009. *Islam and the Problem of Black Suffering*. New York: Oxford University Press.

Jacobson, Matthew Frye. 1999. *Whiteness of a Different Color*. Cambridge, MA: Harvard University Press.

James, William. 1975. *Pragmatism*. Cambridge, MA: Harvard University Press. Original edition, 1907.

Jasanoff, Sheila. 2012. *Science and Public Reason*. New York: Routledge.

Jerolmack, Colin, and Iddo Tavory. 2014. "Molds and totems: Nonhumans and the constitution of the social self." *Sociological Theory* 32 (1):64–77.

Kaden, Tom. 2018. *Creationism and Anti-Creationism in the United States: A Sociology of Conflict*. Leiden: Springer. Original edition, 2015.

Kahan, Dan M. 2013. "Ideology, motivated reasoning, and cognitive reflection." *Judgment and Decision Making* 8 (4):407–424.

Karim, Jamillah. 2008. *American Muslim Women: Negotiating Race, Class, and Gender within the Ummah*. New York: NYU Press.

Kashani, Maryam. 2014. "Seekers of sacred knowledge: Zaytuna College and the education of American Muslims." Dissertation. Anthropology, The University of Texas at Austin.

Katz, Jack. 2001. *How Emotions Work*. Chicago: University of Chicago Press.

Katz, Marion Holmes. 2013. *Prayer in Islamic Thought and Practice*. New York: Cambridge University Press.

Keane, Webb. 2002. "Sincerity, 'modernity,' and the Protestants." *Cultural Anthropology* 17 (1):65–92.

Kelsay, John. 1989. "Prayer and ethics: Reflections on Calvin and Barth." *Harvard Theological Review* 82 (2):169–184.

Kettlewell, H.B.D. 1961. "The phenomenon of industrial melanism in Lepidoptera." *Annual Review of Entomology* 6 (1):245–262.

Keyworth, Karen. 2009. "Islamic schools of America: Data-based profiles." In *Educating the Muslims of America*, edited by Yvonne Y. Haddad, Farid Senzai, and Jane I. Smith, 21–38. New York: Oxford University Press.

Khabeer, Su'ad Abdul. 2016. *Muslim Cool: Race, Religion, and Hip Hop in the United States*. New York: New York University Press.

Khalil, Atif. 2011. "Is God obliged to answer prayers of petition (du'a)? The response of classical Sufis and Qur'anic exegetes." *Journal of Medieval Religious Cultures* 37 (2):93–109.

Khan, Sabith, and Shariq Siddiqui. 2017. *Islamic Education in the United States and the Evolution of Muslim Nonprofit Institutions*. Northampton, MA: Edward Elgar.

Kintz, Linda. 1997. *Between Jesus and the Market: The Emotions that Matter in Right-wing America*. Durham, NC: Duke University Press.

Kloppenberg, James T. 2016. *Toward Democracy: The Struggle for Self-Rule in European and American Thought*. New York: Oxford University Press.

Knorr-Cetina, Karin. 1999. *Epistemic Cultures: How the Sciences Make Knowledge*. Cambridge, MA: Harvard University Press.

Knysh, Alexander. 2007. "Contextualizing the Salafi–Sufi conflict (from the Northern Caucasus to Hadramawt)." *Middle Eastern Studies* 43 (4):503–530.

Kraft, Patrick W., Milton Lodge, and Charles S Taber. 2015. "Why people 'don't trust the evidence': Motivated reasoning and scientific beliefs." *The Annals of the American Academy of Political and Social Science* 658 (1):121–133.

Kuhn, Thomas. 1962. *The Structure of Scientific Revolutions*. Chicago: University of Chicago Press.

Kunda, Ziva. 1990. "The case for motivated reasoning." *Psychological Bulletin* 108 (3):480.

Kurzman, Charles. (ed.) 1998. *Liberal Islam: A Source Book*. New York: Oxford University Press.

Kutchins, Herb, and Stuart A Kirk. 1997. *Making Us Crazy*. New York: The Free Press.

Kwilecki, Susan. 1987. "Contemporary Pentecostal clergywomen: Female Christian leadership, old style." *Journal of Feminist Studies in Religion* 3 (2):57–75.

Laats, Adam. 2010. "Forging a fundamentalist 'One Best System': Struggles over curriculum and educational philosophy for Christian day schools, 1970–1989." *History of Education Quarterly* 50 (1):55–83.

Lamont, Michèle. 1992. *Money, Morals, and Manners: The Culture of the French and the American Upper-Middle Class*. Chicago: University of Chicago Press.

Lamont, Michèle. 2000. *The Dignity of Working Men: Morality and the Boundaries of Race, Class, and Immigration*. Cambridge, MA: Harvard University Press.

Lamont, Michèle, and Virág Molnár. 2002. "The study of boundaries in the social sciences." *Annual Review of Sociology* 28 (1):167–195.

Landor, Antoinette M., and Leslie Gordon Simons. 2014. "Why virginity pledges succeed or fail: The moderating effect of religious commitment versus religious participation." *Journal of Child and Family Studies* 23 (6):1102–1113.

Latour, Bruno. 1987. *Science in Action: How to Follow Scientists and Engineers through Society*. Cambridge, MA: Harvard University Press.

Latour, Bruno. 2005. *Reassembling the Social: An Introduction to Actor-Network-Theory*. New York: Oxford University Press.

Le Espiritu, Yen. 2001. "'We don't sleep around like white girls do': Family, culture, and gender in Filipina American lives." *Signs: Journal of Women in Culture and Society* 26 (2):415–440.

Leaché, Adam D., Matthew K. Fujita, Vladimir N. Minin, and Remco R. Bouckaert. 2014. "Species delimitation using genome-wide SNP data." *Systematic Biology* 63 (4):534–542.

Lee-Barnewall, Michelle. 2016. *Neither Complementarian nor Egalitarian: A Kingdom Corrective to the Evangelical Gender Debate*. Grand Rapids, MI: Baker Academic.

Legewie, Joscha, and Thomas A DiPrete. 2012. "School context and the gender gap in educational achievement." *American Sociological Review* 77 (3):463–485.

Leonard, Karen. 2003. "American Muslim politics: Discourses and practices." *Ethnicities* 3 (2):147–181.

Lester, Rebecca J. 2005. *Jesus in Our Wombs: Embodying Modernity in a Mexican Convent*. Berkeley: University of California Press.

Lichterman, Paul. 2005. *Elusive Togetherness: Church Groups Trying to Bridge America's Divisions*. Princeton: Princeton University Press.

Lisle, Jason. 2009. *The Ultimate Proof of Creation: Resolving the Origins Debate*. Green Forest, AR: New Leaf Publishing Group.

Lisle, Jason. 2010. "Anisotropic synchrony convention—A solution to the distant starlight problem." *Answers Research Journal* 3 (1):191–207.

Lizardo, Omar. 2017. "Improving cultural analysis: Considering personal culture in its declarative and nondeclarative modes." *American Sociological Review* 82 (1):88–115.

Locke, Simon. 2014. *Constructing the Beginning: Discourses of Creation Science*. New York: Routledge.

Longfield, Bradley J. 1993. *The Presbyterian Controversy: Fundamentalists, Modernists, and Moderates*. New York: Oxford University Press.

Love, Erik. 2017. *Islamophobia and Racism in America*. New York: NYU Press.

Luft, Aliza. 2015. "Toward a dynamic theory of action at the micro level of geno-cide: Killing, desistance, and saving in 1994 Rwanda." *Sociological Theory* 33 (2):148–172.

Luft, Aliza. 2020. "Theorizing Moral Cognition: Culture in Action, Situations, and Relationships. *Socius* 6:1–15.

Luft, Julie, Randy L. Bell, and Julie Gess-Newsome. 2008. *Science as Inquiry in the Secondary Setting*. Arlington, VA: NSTA Press.

Luhrmann, Tanya M. 2012. *When God Talks Back: Understanding the American Evangelical Relationship with God*. New York: Vintage.

Luhrmann, Tanya M., and Rachel Morgain. 2012. "Prayer as inner sense cultivation: An attentional learning theory of spiritual experience." *Ethos* 40 (4):359–389.

Luker, Kristin. 1985. *Abortion and the Politics of Motherhood*. Berkeley: University of California Press.

Luker, Kristin. 2006. *When Sex Goes to School: Warring Views on Sex—and Sex Education—Since the Sixties*. New York: W.W. Norton.

Lukes, Steven. 2004. *Power: A Radical View*. 2nd ed. New York: Palgrave Macmillan.

Lukes, Steven. 2010. "The social construction of morality?." In *Handbook of the Sociology of Morality*, edited by Steven Hitlin and Stephen Vaisey, 549–560. New York: Springer.

MacCulloch, Diarmaid. 2005. *The Reformation*. New York: Penguin.

MacIntyre, Alasdair. 1984. *After Virtue*. Notre Dame: Notre Dame University Press.

MacIntyre, Alasdair. 1988. *Whose Justice? Which Rationality?* Notre Dame: University of Notre Dame Press.

MacIntyre, Alasdair. 1999. *Dependent Rational Animals: Why Human Beings Need the Virtues*. Peru, Illinois: Open Court.

Maffly-Kipp, Laurie F., Leigh E. Schmidt, and Mark Valeri. 2006. *Practicing Protestants: Histories of Christian Life in America, 1630–1965*. Baltimore: Johns Hopkins University Press.

Maghbouleh, Neda. 2017. *The Limits of Whiteness: Iranian Americans and the Everyday Politics of Race*. Stanford: Stanford University Press.

Mahalingam, Ramaswami. 2007. "Essentialism, power, and the representation of social categories: A folk sociology perspective." *Human Development* 50 (6):300–319.

Mahmood, Saba. 2005. *Politics of Piety: The Islamic Revival and the Feminist Subject*. Princeton: Princeton University Press.

Malley, Brian. 2004. *How the Bible Works: An Anthropological Study of Evangelical Biblicism*. Walnut Creek, CA: AltaMira Press.

Mamdani, Mahmood. 2005. *Good Muslim, Bad Muslim: America, the Cold War, and the Roots of Terror*. New York: Harmony.

Manne, Kate. 2017. *Down Girl: The Logic of Misogyny*. New York: Oxford University Press.

Manning, Alex, Douglas Hartmann, and Joseph Gerteis. 2015. "Colorblindness in black and white: An analysis of core tenets, configurations, and complexities." *Sociology of Race and Ethnicity* 1 (4):532–546.

Marsden, George M. 2006. *Fundamentalism and American Culture*. New York: Oxford University Press.

Martí, Gerardo. 2019. "The Unexpected Orthodoxy of Donald J. Trump: White Evangelical Support for the 45th President of the United States." 80 (1):1–8.

Martin, John Levi, and Matthew Desmond. 2010. "Political position and social know-ledge." *Sociological Forum* 25 (1):1–26.

Marzouki, Nadia. 2017. *Islam: An American Religion*. New York: Columbia University Press.

Masci, David. 2017. "For Darwin Day, 6 facts about the evolution debate." Pew Research Center, http://www.pewresearch.org/fact-tank/2017/02/10/darwin-day/#.

Masuzawa, Tomoko. 2005. *The Invention of World Religions: Or, How European Universalism was Preserved in the Language of Pluralism*. Chicago: University of Chicago Press.

Matheson, Craig. 1987. "Weber and the Classification of Forms of Legitimacy." *British Journal of Sociology* 38 (2):199–215.

Mattson, Ingrid. 2013. *The Story of the Qur'an: Its History and Place in Muslim Life*. 2nd ed. Malden, MA: John Wiley & Sons. Original edition, 2008.

Mayr, Ernst. 1996. "What is a species, and what is not?" *Philosophy of Science* 63 (2):262–277.

McGuire, Meredith B. 2008. *Lived Religion: Faith and Practice in Everyday Life*. New York: Oxford University Press.

Medin, Douglas, and Andrew Ortony. 1989. "Psychological essentialism." In *Similarity and Analogical Reasoning*, edited by Stella Vosniadou and Andrew Ortony, 179–195. New York: Cambridge University Press.

Meece, Judith L., Beverly Bower Glienke, and Samantha Burg. 2006. "Gender and motivation." *Journal of School Psychology* 44 (5):351–373.

Mehta, Jal, and Scott Davies. (eds.) 2018. *Education in a New Society: Renewing the Sociology of Education*. Chicago: University of Chicago Press.

Mellor, Philip A., and Chris Shilling. 2010. "Body pedagogics and the religious habitus: A new direction for the sociological study of religion." *Religion* 40 (1):27–38.

Merton, Robert K. 1973. *The Sociology of Science: Theoretical and Empirical Investigations*. Chicago: University of Chicago Press.

Merton, Robert K. 1996. *On Social Structure and Science*. Edited by Pioter Sztompka. Chicago: University of Chicago Press.

Meyer, Heinz-Dieter, and Brian Rowan. 2006. "Institutional analysis and the study of education." In *The New Institutionalism in Education*, edited by Heinz-Dieter Meyer and Brian Rowan, 1–13. Albany: State University of New York Press.

Meyer, John W. 1977. "The effects of education as an institution." *American Journal of Sociology* 83 (1):55–77.

Meyer, John W. 2009. *World Society: The Writings of John W. Meyer*. Edited by John Meyer, Georg Krücken, and Gili S. Drori. New York: Oxford University Press.

Meyer, John W., and Brian Rowan. 1977. "Institutionalized organizations: Formal structure as myth and ceremony." *American Journal of Sociology* 83 (2):340–363.

Meyer, John W., and Ronald L. Jepperson. 2000. "The 'actors' of modern society: The cultural construction of social agency." *Sociological Theory* 18.1:100–120.

Meyer, Stephen C. 2009. *Signature in the Cell: DNA and the Evidence for Intelligent Design*. New York: HarperOne.

Miller, Donald E. 1997. *Reinventing American Protestantism: Christianity in the New Millennium*. Berkeley: University of California Press.

Mir, Shabana. 2014. *Muslim American Women on Campus: Undergraduate Social Life and Identity*. Chapel Hill, NC: University of North Carolina Press.

Mische, Ann. 2014. "Measuring futures in action: Projective grammars in the Rio+20 debates." *Theory and Society* 43 (3–4):437–464.

Mishra, Smeeta, and Faegheh Shirazi. 2010. "Hybrid identities: American Muslim women speak." *Gender, Place & Culture* 17 (2):191–209.

Mitchell, Tommy, and A.J. Monty White. 2008. "Is evolution a religion?" In *The New Answers Book 2*, edited by Ken Ham, 207–218. Green Forest, AR: Master Books.

Moon, Dawne, Theresa W. Tobin, and J.E. Sumerau. 2019. "Alpha, omega, and the letters in between: LGBTQI conservative Christians undoing gender." *Gender & Society* 33 (4):583–606.

Moore, Kelly. 1996. "Organizing integrity: American science and the creation of public interest organizations, 1955–1975." *American Journal of Sociology* 101 (6):1592–1627.

Moosa, Ebrahim. 2005. *Ghazali and the Poetics of Imagination*. Chapel Hill: University of North Carolina Press.

Moran, Jeffrey P. 2011. *American Genesis: The Evolution Controversies from Scopes to Creation Science*. New York: Oxford University Press.

Morning, Ann. 2011. *The Nature of Race: How Scientists Think and Teach about Human Difference*. Berkeley: University of California Press.

Morris, John D. 1994. *The Young Earth: The Real History of the Earth - Past, Present, and Future*. Green Forest, AR: Master Books.

Moslener, Sara. 2015. *Virgin Nation: Sexual Purity and American Adolescence*. New York: Oxford University Press.

Musa, Aisha. 2008. *Hadith as Scripture*. New York: Palgrave.

Naber, Nadine. 2005. "Muslim first, Arab second: A strategic politics of race and gender." *The Muslim World* 95 (4):479–495.

Naber, Nadine. 2006. "Arab American femininities: Beyond Arab virgin/American (ized) whore." *Feminist Studies* 32 (1):87–111.

Nederhof, Anton J. 1985. "Methods of coping with social desirability bias: A review." *European Journal of Social Psychology* 15 (3):263–280.

Noll, Mark A. 1985. "Common sense traditions and American evangelical thought." *American Quarterly* 37 (2):216–238.

Noll, Mark A. 1994. *The Scandal of the Evangelical Mind*. Grand Rapids, MI: William B. Eerdmans.

Noll, Mark A. 2002. *America's God: From Jonathan Edwards to Abraham Lincoln*. New York: Oxford University Press.

Nordin, Virginia Davis, and William Lloyd Turner. 1980. "More than segregation academies: The growing Protestant fundamentalist schools." *The Phi Delta Kappan* 61 (6):391–394.

Norris, Pippa, and Ronald F. Inglehart. 2012. "Muslim integration into western cultures: Between origins and destinations." *Political Studies* 60 (2):228–251.

Numbers, Ronald L. 2006. *The Creationists: From Scientific Creationism to Intelligent Design*. Cambridge, MA: Harvard University Press.

Nussbaum, Martha C. 1992. "Human functioning and social justice: In defense of Aristotelian essentialism." *Political Theory* 20 (2):202–246.

Nussbaum, Martha C. 2003. *Upheavals of Thought: The Intelligence of Emotions*. New York: Cambridge University Press.

O'Brien, John. 2017. *Keeping It Halal: The Everyday Lives of Muslim American Teenage Boys*. Princeton: Princeton University Press.

Ohlander, Erik. 2009. "Modern Qur'anic hermeneutics." *Religion Compass* 3 (4):620–636.

Ong, Aihwa. 1990. "State versus Islam: Malay families, women's bodies, and the body politic in Malaysia." *American Ethnologist* 17 (2):258–276.

O'Riordan, Kate. 2012. "The life of the gay gene: From hypothetical genetic marker to social reality." *Journal of Sex Research* 49 (4):362–368.

Ortner, Sherry B. 1978. "The virgin and the state." *Feminist Studies* 4 (3):19–35.

Ortner, Sherry B. 1996. *Making Gender: The Politics and Erotics of Culture.* Boston: Beacon Press.

Orton, J. Douglas, and Karl E Weick. 1990. "Loosely coupled systems: A reconceptualization." *Academy of Management Review* 15 (2):203–223.

Padwick, Constance Evelyn. 1961. *Muslim Devotions: A Study of Prayer-Manuals in Common Use.* Oxford: Oneworld.

Parsons, Talcott. 1937. *The Structure of Social Action, Volume 1.* New York: Free Press.

Parsons, Talcott. 1959. "The school class as a social system: Some of its functions in American society." *Harvard Educational Review* 29 (4):297–318.

Parsons, Talcott. 1970. *Social Structure and Personality.* New York: The Free Press. Original edition, 1964.

Parsons, Talcott. 1964. *The Social System.* New York: Free Press. Original edition, 1951.

Parsons, Talcott, and Gerald M. Platt. 1970. "Age, social structure, and socialization in higher education." *Sociology of Education* 43 (1):1–37.

Payne, Leah. 2015. *Gender and Pentecostal revivalism: Making a female ministry in the early twentieth century.* New York: Palgrave Macmillan.

Pascal, Blaise. 2013. *Pensées.* Translated by W.F. Trotter. Mineola, NY: Dover. Original edition, 1670.

Pascoe, C. J. 2011. *Dude, You're a Fag: Masculinity and Sexuality in High School.* Berkeley: University of California Press.

Perry, Samuel L. 2019. *Addicted to lust: Pornography in the lives of conservative Protestants.* New York: Oxford University Press.

Perry, Samuel L., and George M. Hayward. 2017. "Seeing is (not) believing: How viewing pornography shapes the religious lives of young Americans." *Social Forces* 95 (4):1757–1788.

Perry, Samuel L., and Joshua B. Grubbs. 2020. "Formal or functional? Traditional or inclusive? Bible translations as Markers of religious subcultures." *Sociology of Religion* 81 (3):319–342.

Peshkin, Alan. 1988. *God's Choice: The Total World of a Fundamentalist Christian School.* Chicago: University of Chicago Press.

Peter, Jochen, and Patti M. Valkenburg. 2016. "Adolescents and pornography: A review of 20 years of research." *The Journal of Sex Research* 53 (4–5):509–531.

Pickering, Andrew. 1992. "From science as knowledge to science as practice." In *Science as Practice and Culture*, edited by Andrew Pickering, 1–26. Chicago: University of Chicago Press.

Pinkton, William S. 1997. *Biology for Christian Schools: Teacher's Edition.* Greenville, SC: Bob Jones University Press.

Plato. 2016. *The Republic.* 2nd ed. Translated by Allan Bloom. New York: Basic Books.

Popper, Karl. 2005. *The Logic of Scientific Discovery.* New York: Routledge. Original edition, 1935.

Powers, Paul R. 2004. "Interiors, intentions, and the 'spirituality' of Islamic ritual practice." *Journal of the American Academy of Religion* 72 (2):425–459.

Presser, Stanley, and Linda Stinson. 1998. "Data collection mode and social desirability bias in self-reported religious attendance." *American Sociological Review* 63 (1):137–145.

Prothero, Stephen. 2003. *American Jesus: How the Son of God Became a National Icon.* New York: Farrar, Straus, and Giroux.

Psillos, Stathis. 1999. *Scientific Realism: How Science Tracks Truth.* London: Routledge.

Pugh, Allison J. 2014. "The theoretical costs of ignoring childhood: Rethinking independence, insecurity, and inequality." *Theory and Society* 43 (1):71–89.

Rahman, Momin. 2010. "Queer as intersectionality: Theorizing gay Muslim identities." *Sociology* 44 (5):944–961.

Rashid, Hakim M., and Zakiyyah Muhammad. 1992. "The Sister Clara Muhammad schools: Pioneers in the development of Islamic education in America." *The Journal of Negro Education* 61 (2):178–185.

Read, Jen'nan Ghazal, and John P. Bartkowski. 2000. "To veil or not to veil? A case study of identity negotiation among Muslim women in Austin, Texas." *Gender & Society* 14 (3):395–417.

Reed, Isaac Ariail. 2013. "Power: Relational, discursive, and performative dimensions." *Sociological Theory* 31 (3):193–218.

Reed, Isaac Ariail. 2017. "Chains of power and their representation." *Sociological Theory* 35 (2):87–117.

Reed, Isaac Ariail, and Michael Weinman. 2019. "Agency, power, modernity: A manifesto for social theory." *European Journal of Cultural and Political Sociology* 6 (1):6–50.

Reid, Julie A., Sinikka Elliott, and Gretchen R. Webber. 2011. "Casual hookups to formal dates: Refining the boundaries of the sexual double standard." *Gender & Society* 25 (5):545–568.

Renard, John. 2011. *Islam and Christianity: Theological themes in comparative perspective*. Berkeley: University of California Press.

Ricoeur, Paul. 1970. *Freud and Philosophy: An Essay on Interpretation*. Translated by Dennis Savage. New Haven: Yale University Press. Original edition, 1965.

Ricoeur, Paul. 1981. *Hermeneutics and the Human Sciences: Essays on Language, Action and Interpretation*. Edited and translated by John B. Thompson. New York: Cambridge University Press.

Riesch, Hauke. 2010. "Theorizing boundary work as representation and identity." *Journal for the Theory of Social Behaviour* 40 (4):452–473.

Riexinger, Martin. 2008. "Propagating Islamic creationism on the internet." *Masaryk University Journal of Law and Technology* 2 (2):99–112.

Riexinger, Martin. 2010. "Islamic opposition to the Darwinian theory of evolution." In *Handbook of Religion and the Authority of Science*, edited by James R. Lewis and Olav Hammer, 483–510. Leiden: Brill.

Rinaldo, Rachel. 2013. *Mobilizing Piety: Islam and Feminism in Indonesia*. New York: Oxford University Press.

Rinaldo, Rachel, and Jeffrey Guhin. 2019. "How and Why Interviews Work: Ethnographic Interviews and Meso-level Public Culture." *Sociological Methods & Research*: 1–34. https://doi.org/10.1177/0049124119882471

Risman, Barbara J., and Georgiann Davis. 2013. "From sex roles to gender structure." *Current Sociology* 61 (5–6):733–755.

Roos, J. Micah. 2014. "Measuring science or religion? A measurement analysis of the National Science Foundation sponsored science literacy scale 2006–2010." *Public Understanding of Science* 23 (7):797–813.

Rose, Susan D. 2017. *Keeping Them Out of the Hands of Satan: Evangelical Schooling in America*. New York: Routledge. Original edition, 1988.

Rouse, Carolyn. 2004. *Engaged Surrender: African American Women and Islam*. Berkeley: University of California Press.

Roy, Olivier. 2004. *Globalized Islam: The Search for a New Ummah*. New York: Columbia University Press.

Roy, Olivier. 2005. *Secularism Confronts Islam*. Translated by George Holoch. New York: Columbia University Press.

Roy, Olivier. 2014. *Holy Ignorance: When Religion and Culture Part Ways*. Translated by Ros Schwartz. London: Oxford University Press.

Rudge, David Wyss. 1999. "Taking the peppered moth with a grain of salt." *Biology and Philosophy* 14 (1):9–37.

Rughiniş, Cosima. 2011. "A lucky answer to a fair question: Conceptual, methodological, and moral implications of including items on human evolution in scientific literacy surveys." *Science Communication* 33 (4):501–532.

Rutherford, Danilyn. 2000. "The white edge of the margin: textuality and authority in Biak, Irian Jaya, Indonesia." *American Ethnologist* 27 (2):312–339.

Ryrie, Alec. 2017. *Protestants: The Faith That Made the Modern World*. New York: Penguin.

Sadeghi, Behnam, and Mohsen Goudarzi. 2012. "Ṣanʿāʾ and the Origins of the Qurʾān." *Der Islam* 87 (1–2):1–129.

Said, Edward. 1979. *Orientalism*. New York: Vintage Books. Original edition, 1978.

Salomon, Noah. 2016. *For Love of the Prophet: An Ethnography of Sudan's Islamic State*. Princeton: Princeton University Press.

Sampson, Robert J., Jeffrey D. Morenoff, and Thomas Gannon-Rowley. 2002. "Assessing 'neighborhood effects': Social processes and new directions in research." *Annual Review of Sociology* 28 (1):443–478.

Schatzki, Theodore R. 1996. *Social Practices: A Wittgensteinian Approach to Human Activity and the Social*. New York: Cambridge University Press.

Schirrmacher, Christine. 2016. *Let There Be No Compulsion in Religion (Sura 2: 256): Apostasy from Islam as Judged by Contemporary Islamic Theologians: Discourses on Apostasy, Religious Freedom, and Human Rights*. Eugene, OR: Wipf and Stock Publishers.

Schwadel, Philip. 2017. "The Republicanization of evangelical Protestants in the United States: An examination of the sources of political realignment." *Social Science Research* 62:238–254.

Scott, Eugenie C. 1997. "Antievolution and creationism in the United States." *Annual Review of Anthropology* 26 (1):263–289.

Scott, W Richard. 2014. *Institutions and organizations: Ideas, interests, and identities*. 4th ed. Los Angeles: Sage Publications. Original edition, 1994.

Seamster, Louise, and Victor Ray. 2018. "Against teleology in the study of race: Toward the abolition of the progress paradigm." *Sociological Theory* 36 (4):315–342.

Seigel, Jerrold. 2005. *The Idea of the Self: Thought and Experience in Western Europe Since the Seventeenth Century*. New York: Cambridge University Press.

Selod, Saher. 2015. "Citizenship denied: The racialization of Muslim American men and women post-9/11." *Critical Sociology* 41 (1):77–95.

Selod, Saher, and David G. Embrick. 2013. "Racialization and Muslims: Situating the Muslim experience in race scholarship." *Sociology Compass* 7 (8):644–655.

Sergiovanni, Thomas J. 1994. "Organizations or communities? Changing the metaphor changes the theory." *Educational Administration Quarterly* 30 (2):214–226.

Sewell Jr, William H. 1992. "A theory of structure: Duality, agency, and transformation." *American Journal of Sociology* 98 (1):1–29.

Shah, Shanon. 2017. *The Making of a Gay Muslim: Religion, sexuality and identity in Malaysia and Britain*. Cham, Switzerland: Springer.

Shantz, Douglas H. 2013. *An Introduction to German Pietism: Protestant Renewal at the Dawn of Modern Europe*. Baltimore: Johns Hopkins University Press.

Shapin, Steven. 1994. *A Social History of Truth: Civility and Science in Seventeenth-Century England.* Chicago: University of Chicago Press.

Shapin, Steven. 2008. *The Scientific Life: A Moral History of a Late Modern Vocation.* Chicago: University of Chicago Press.

Sharp, Shane. 2010. "How does prayer help manage emotions?" *Social Psychology Quarterly* 73 (4):417–437.

Sharp, Shane. 2012a. "For a social psychology of prayer." *Sociology Compass* 6 (7):570–580.

Sharp, Shane. 2012b. "Prayer utterances as aligning actions." *Journal for the Scientific Study of Religion* 51 (2):257–265.

Sharp, Shane. 2013a. "How to do things with prayer utterances." *Symbolic Interaction* 36 (2):159–176.

Sharp, Shane. 2013b. "When prayers go unanswered." *Journal for the Scientific Study of Religion* 52 (1):1–16.

Sherkat, Darren E. 2000. "'That they be keepers of the home': The effect of conservative religion on early and late transitions into housewifery." *Review of Religious Research* 41 (3):344–358.

Sherkat, Darren E., and Alfred Darnell. 1999. "The effect of parents' fundamentalism on children's educational attainment: Examining differences by gender and children's fundamentalism." *Journal for the Scientific Study of Religion* 38 (1):23–35.

Shoaps, Robin A. 2002. "'Pray earnestly': The textual construction of personal Involvement in Pentecostal prayer and song." *Journal of Linguistic Anthropology* 12 (1):34–71.

Siedentop, Larry. 2014. *Inventing the Individual: The Origins of Western Liberalism.* Cambridge, MA: Harvard University Press.

Simko, Christina. 2015. *The Politics of Consolation: Memory and the Meaning of September 11.* New York: Oxford University Press.

Simko, Christina. 2018. "From difficult past to imagined future: Projective reversal and the transformation of ground zero." *Poetics* 67:39–52.

Simon, Gregory M. 2009. "The soul freed of cares? Islamic prayer, subjectivity, and the contradictions of moral selfhood in Minangkabau, Indonesia." *American Ethnologist* 36 (2):258–275.

Sirin, Selcuk R., Nida Bikmen, Madeeha Mir, Michelle Fine, Mayida Zaal, and Dalal Katsiaficas. 2008. "Exploring dual identification among Muslim-American emerging adults: A mixed methods study." *Journal of Adolescence* 31 (2):259–279.

Slater, Matthew H. 2008. "How to justify teaching false science." *Science Education* 92 (3):526–542.

Smith, Christian. 1998. *American Evangelicalism: Embattled and Thriving.* Chicago: University of Chicago Press.

Smith, Christian, and Melina Lundquist Denton. 2009. *Soul Searching: The Religious and Spiritual Lives of American Teenagers.* New York: Oxford University Press.

Smith, Jonathan Z. 1998. "Religion, religions, religious." In *Critical Terms for Religious Studies,* edited by Mark C. Taylor, 269–284. Chicago: University of Chicago Press.

Smith, Wilfred Cantwell. 1959. "Some similarities and differences between Christianity and Islam." *The World of Islam*:47–59.

Smith, Wilfred Cantwell. 1993. *What is Scripture?: A Comparative Approach.* Minneapolis: Fortress Press.

Stallybrass, Peter, and Allon White. 1986. *The Politics and Poetics of Transgression.* Ithaca, NY: Cornell University Press.

Star, Susan Leigh, and James R. Griesemer. 1989. "Institutional ecology, translations' and boundary objects: Amateurs and professionals in Berkeley's Museum of Vertebrate Zoology, 1907–39." *Social Studies of Science* 19 (3):387–420.

Steensland, Brian, and Eric L. Wright. 2014. "American Evangelicals and conservative politics: Past, present, and future." *Sociology Compass* 8 (6):705–717.

Stets, Jan E. 2010. "Future directions in the sociology of emotions." *Emotion Review* 2 (3):265–268.

Stets, Jan E., and Jonathan H. Turner. (eds.) 2014. *Handbook of the Sociology of Emotions, Volume II*. New York: Springer.

Stevens, Mitchell L. 2008. "Culture and education." *The Annals of the American academy of Political and Social Science* 619 (1):97–113.

Stoeffler, F. Ernest. 1965. *The Rise of Evangelical Pietism*. Leiden: E.J. Brill.

Strand, Michael. 2011. "Where do classifications come from? The DSM-III, the transformation of American psychiatry, and the problem of origins in the sociology of knowledge." *Theory and Society* 40 (3):273–313.

Strand, Michael, and Omar Lizardo. 2015. "Beyond World Images: Belief as embodied action in the world." *Sociological Theory* 33 (1):44–70.

Strawson, Peter F. 1962. "Freedom and Resentment." *Proceedings of the British Academy* 48:187–211.

Swidler, Ann. 1979. *Organization Without Authority: Dilemmas of Social Control in Free Schools*. Cambridge, MA: Harvard University Press.

Swidler, Ann. 1986. "Culture in action: Symbols and strategies." *American Sociological Review* 51 (2):273–286.

Swidler, Ann. 2001. *Talk of Love: How Culture Matters*. Chicago: University of Chicago Press.

Synan, Vinson. 1997. *The Holiness-Pentecostal Tradition: Charismatic Movements in the Twentieth Century*. 2nd ed. Grand Rapids, MI: William B. Eerdmans. Reprint, 1971.

Tavory, Iddo. 2010. "Of yarmulkes and categories: Delegating boundaries and the phenomenology of interactional expectation." *Theory and Society* 39 (1):49–68.

Tavory, Iddo. 2011. "The question of moral action: A formalist position." *Sociological Theory* 29 (4):272–293.

Tavory, Iddo. 2016. *Summoned: Identification and Religious Life in a Jewish Neighborhood*. Chicago: University of Chicago Press.

Tavory, Iddo, and Nina Eliasoph. 2013. "Coordinating futures: Toward a theory of anticipation." *American Journal of Sociology* 118 (4):908–942.

Taylor, Charles. 1989. *Sources of the Self: The Making of the Modern Identity*. Cambridge, MA: Harvard University Press.

Taylor, Charles. 2007. *A Secular Age*. Cambridge, MA: Harvard University Press.

Teehan, John. 1995. "Character, integrity and Dewey's virtue ethics." *Transactions of the Charles S. Peirce Society* 31 (4):841–863.

Thompson, Damian. 2005. *Waiting for Antichrist: Charisma and Apocalypse in a Pentecostal Church*. New York: Oxford University Press.

Thuesen, Peter J. 2009. *Predestination: The American Career of a Contentious Doctrine*. New York: Oxford University Press.

Thumma, Scott. 1991. "Negotiating a religious identity: The case of the gay evangelical." *Sociological Analysis* 52 (4):333–347.

Tilly, Charles. 2004. "Social boundary mechanisms." *Philosophy of the Social Sciences* 34 (2):211–236.

Tom, Joshua C. 2018. "Social origins of scientific deviance: examining creationism and global warming skepticism." *Sociological Perspectives* 61 (3):341–360.

Toumey, Christopher P. 1991. "Modern creationism and scientific authority." *Social Studies of Science* 21 (4):681–699.

Toumey, Christopher P. 1996. *Conjuring Science: Scientific Symbols and Cultural Meanings in American Life*. New Brunswick, NJ: Rutgers University Press.

Trilling, Lionel. 2009. *Sincerity and Authenticity*. Cambridge, MA: Harvard University Press. Original edition, 1971.

Turner, Jonathan H., and Jan E. Stets. 2005. *The Sociology of Emotions*. New York: Cambridge University Press.

Turner, Stephen P. 1994. *The Social Theory of Practices: Tradition, Tacit Knowledge and Presuppositions*. Chicago: University of Chicago Press.

Uecker, Jeremy E. 2008. "Religion, pledging, and the premarital sexual behavior of married young adults." *Journal of Marriage and Family* 70 (3):728–744.

Vaisey, Stephen. 2009. "Motivation and justification: A dual-process model of culture in action." *American Journal of Sociology* 114 (6):1675–1715.

van Doorn-Harder, Pieternella. 2006. *Women Shaping Islam: Reading the Qu'ran in Indonesia*. Urbana, IL: University of Illinois Press.

Van Fraassen, Bas C. 1980. *The Scientific Image*. Oxford: Clarendon Press.

Van Ham, Maarten, David Manley, Nick Bailey, Ludi Simpson, and Duncan Maclennan. 2012. "Neighbourhood effects research: New perspectives." In *Neighbourhood Effects Research: New Perspectives*, edited by Maarten Van Ham, David Maney, and Nick Baiely, 1–21. New York: Springer.

Verba, Sidney, Kay Lehman Schlozman, and Henry E. Brady. 1995. *Voice and Equality: Civic Voluntarism in American Politics*. Cambridge, MA: Harvard University Press.

Voas, David, and Fenella Fleischmann. 2012. "Islam moves west: Religious change in the first and second generations." *Annual Review of Sociology* 38:525–545.

Wadud, Amina. 2007. *Inside the Gender Jihad: Women's Reform in Islam*. London: Oneworld.

Wagner, Melinda Bollar. 1990. *God's Schools: Choice and Compromise in American Society*. New Brunswick, NJ: Rutgers University Press.

Wang, Dan, Alessandro Piazza, and Sarah A. Soule. 2018. "Boundary-spanning in social movements: Antecedents and outcomes." *Annual Review of Sociology* 44:167–187.

Weber, Max. 1978. *Economy and Society: An Outline of Interpretive Sociology*. Translated by Guenther Ross and Claus Wittich. Berkeley: University of California Press. Original edition, 1922.

Weick, Karl E. 1976. "Educational organizations as loosely coupled systems." *Administrative Science Quarterly* 21 (1):1–19.

Whitehead, Andrew L., and Samuel L. Perry. 2020. *Taking America Back for God: Christian Nationalism in the United States*. New York: Oxford University Press.

Whisman, Vera. 2012. *Queer by Choice: Lesbians, Gay Men, and the Politics of Identity*. New York: Routledge.

Williams, Juliet. 2016. *The Separation Solution?: Single-Sex Education and the New Politics of Gender Equality*. Oakland: University of California Press.

Williams, Rhys H., and Gira Vashi. 2007. "Hijab and American Muslim women: Creating the space for autonomous selves." *Sociology of Religion* 68 (3):269–287.

Wilson, M. Brett. 2009. "The failure of nomenclature: The concept of 'orthodoxy' in the study of Islam." *Comparative Islamic Studies* 3 (2):169–194.

Wilson, Timothy D., Douglas J. Lisle, Dolores Kraft, and Christopher G. Wetzel. 1989. "Preferences as expectation-driven inferences: Effects of affective expectations on affective experience." *Journal of Personality and Social Psychology* 56 (4):519.

Wimmer, Andreas. 2013. *Ethnic Boundary Making: Institutions, Power, Networks*. New York: Oxford University Press.

Winchester, Daniel. 2008. "Embodying the faith: Religious practice and the making of a Muslim moral habitus." *Social Forces* 86 (4):1753–1780.

Winchester, Daniel, and Jeffrey Guhin. 2019. "Praying 'Straight from the Heart': Evangelical sincerity and the normative frames of culture in action." *Poetics* 72:32–42.

Woodward, Thomas. 2003. *Doubts about Darwin: A History of Intelligent Design*. Grand Rapids, MI: Baker Books.

Woodward, Thomas. 2006. *Darwin Strikes Back: Defending the Science of Intelligent Design*. Grand Rapids, MI: Baker Books.

Wolin, Sheldon S. 2016. *Politics and Vision: Continuity and Innovation in Western Political Thought-Expanded Edition*. Princeton, NJ: Princeton University Press. Originally published 1960.

Woodberry, Robert D., and Christian Smith. 1998. "Fundamentalism et al: Conservative protestants in America." *Annual Review of Sociology* 24 (1):25–56.

Worthen, Molly. 2013. *Apostles of Reason: The Crisis of Authority in American Evangelicalism*. New York: Oxford University Press.

Wrong, Dennis H. 1961. "The oversocialized conception of man in modern sociology." *American Sociological Review* 26 (2):183–193.

Wuthnow, Robert. 2008a. "Prayer, cognition, and culture." *Poetics* 36 (5–6):333–337.

Wuthnow, Robert. 2008b. "Teach us to pray: The cognitive power of domain violations." *Poetics* 36 (5–6):493–506.

Wuthnow, Robert. 2020. *What Happens When We Practice Religion?: Textures of Devotion in Everyday Life*. Princeton, NJ: Princeton University Press.

Wynne, B. 1992. "Misunderstood misunderstanding: The social basis of expert credibility." *Public Understanding of Science* 1 (3):271–294.

Xu, Bin. 2017. *The Politics of Compassion: The Sichuan Earthquake and Civic Engagement in China*. Stanford: Stanford University Press.

Yahya, Harun. 1999. *The Evolution Deceit*. London: Ta-Ha Publishers.

Yang, Fenggang, and Helen Rose Ebaugh. 2001. "Transformations in new immigrant religions and their global implications." *American Sociological Review* 66 (2):269–288.

Yukich, Grace. 2010. "Boundary work in inclusive religious groups: Constructing identity at the New York Catholic Worker." *Sociology of Religion* 71 (2):172–196.

Zakaria, Wan Fariza Alyati Wan. 2015. "Qadar in classical and modern Islamic discourses: Commending a futuristic perspective." *International Journal of Islamic Thought* 7:39–48.

Zaman, Muhammad Qasim. 2010. *The Ulama in Contemporary Islam: Custodians of Change*. Princeton: Princeton University Press.

Zaman, Muhammad Qasim. 2012. *Modern Islamic Thought in a Radical Age: Religious Authority and Internal Criticism*. New York: Cambridge University Press.

Zigerell, L.J. 2012. "Science knowledge and biblical literalism." *Public Understanding of Science* 21 (3):314–322.

Zine, Jasmin. 2008. *Canadian Islamic Schools: Unravelling the Politics of Faith, Gender, Knowledge, and Identity*. Toronto: University of Toronto Press.

INDEX

For the benefit of digital users, indexed terms that span two pages (e.g., 52–53) may, on occasion, appear on only one of those pages.